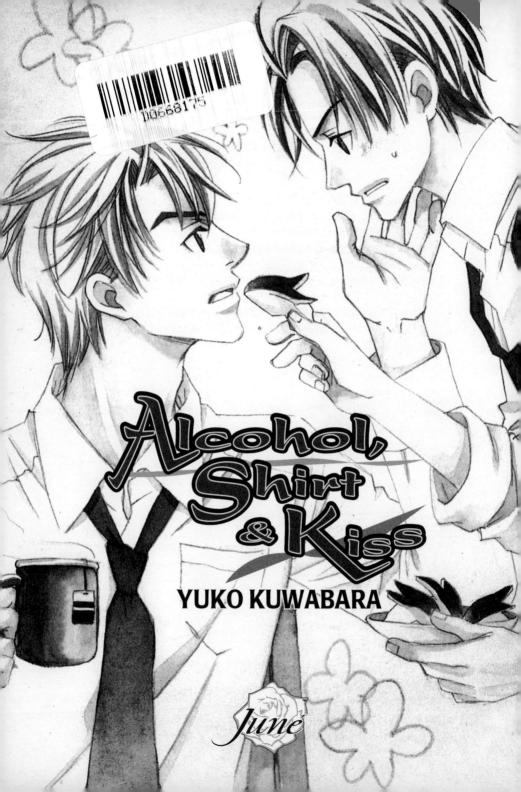

Alcohol, Shirt & Kiss

YUKO KUWABARA

June

Alcohol, Shirt & Kiss

Translation	Issei Shimizu
Editing	Daryl Kuxhouse
Lettering	Elise Knowles
Graphic Design/Layout	Daryl Kuxhouse/Fred Lui
Editor in Chief	Fred Lui
Publisher	Hikaru Sasahara

English Edition Published by
DIGITAL MANGA PUBLISHING
A division of DIGITAL MANGA, Inc.
1487 W 178th Street, Suite 300
Gardena, CA 90248

www.dmpbooks.com

First Edition: March 2007
ISBN-10: 1-56970-840-1
ISBN-13: 978-1-56970-840-8

1 3 5 7 9 10 8 6 4 2

Printed in China

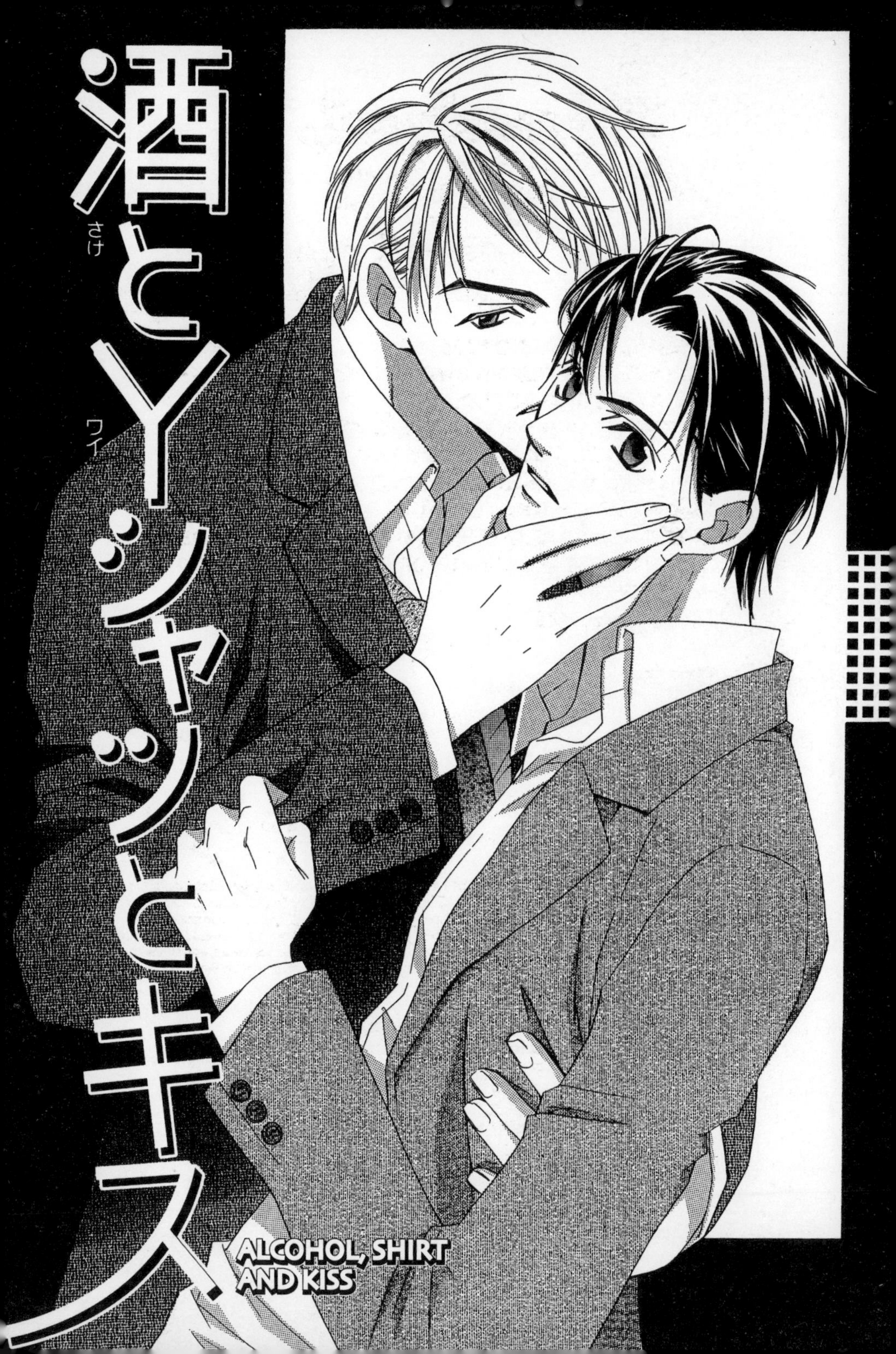
酒(さけ)とY(ワイ)シャツとキス
ALCOHOL, SHIRT AND KISS

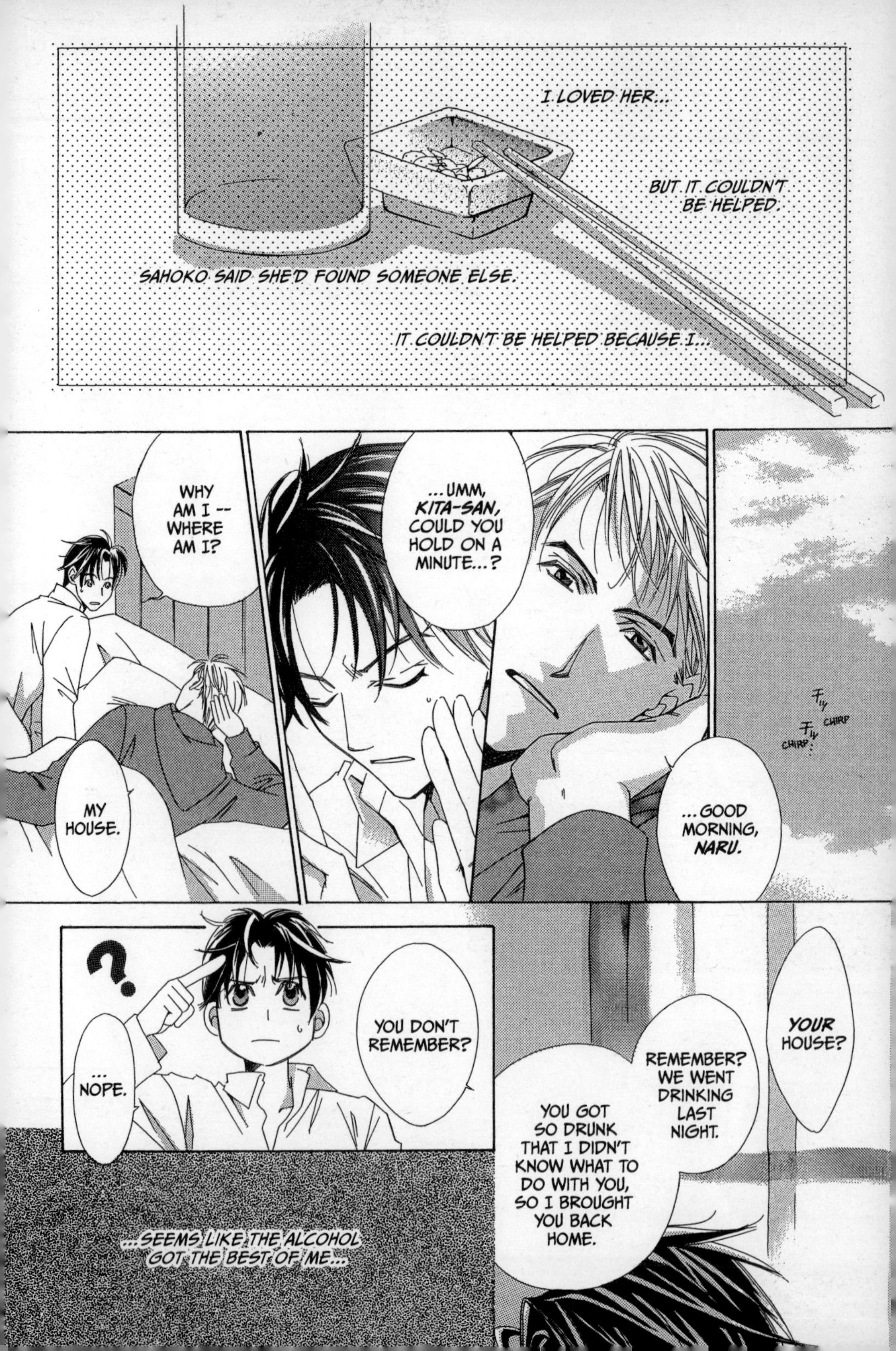

I LOVED HER...
BUT IT COULDN'T BE HELPED.
SAHOKO SAID SHE'D FOUND SOMEONE ELSE.
IT COULDN'T BE HELPED BECAUSE I...
CHIRP
CHIRP
...GOOD MORNING, NARU.
...UMM, KITA-SAN, COULD YOU HOLD ON A MINUTE...?
WHY AM I -- WHERE AM I?
MY HOUSE.
YOUR HOUSE?
REMEMBER? WE WENT DRINKING LAST NIGHT.
YOU GOT SO DRUNK THAT I DIDN'T KNOW WHAT TO DO WITH YOU, SO I BROUGHT YOU BACK HOME.
YOU DON'T REMEMBER?
... NOPE.
...SEEMS LIKE THE ALCOHOL GOT THE BEST OF ME...

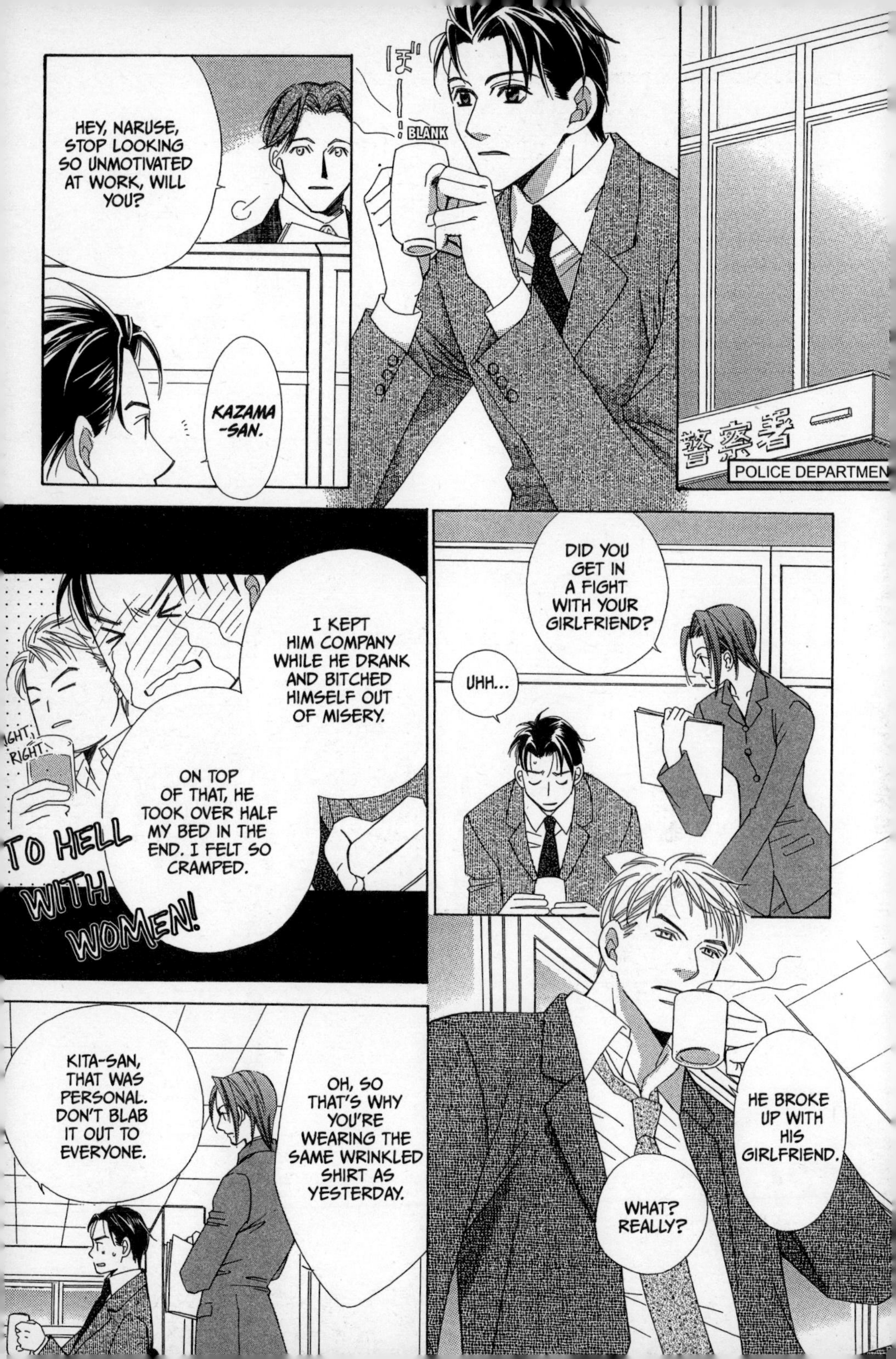
警察署
POLICE DEPARTMEN
ぼー
BLANK
HEY, NARUSE, STOP LOOKING SO UNMOTIVATED AT WORK, WILL YOU?
KAZAMA -SAN.
DID YOU GET IN A FIGHT WITH YOUR GIRLFRIEND?
UHH...
HE BROKE UP WITH HIS GIRLFRIEND.
WHAT? REALLY?
I KEPT HIM COMPANY WHILE HE DRANK AND BITCHED HIMSELF OUT OF MISERY.
IGHT, RIGHT
TO HELL WITH WOMEN!
ON TOP OF THAT, HE TOOK OVER HALF MY BED IN THE END. I FELT SO CRAMPED.
OH, SO THAT'S WHY YOU'RE WEARING THE SAME WRINKLED SHIRT AS YESTERDAY.
KITA-SAN, THAT WAS PERSONAL. DON'T BLAB IT OUT TO EVERYONE.

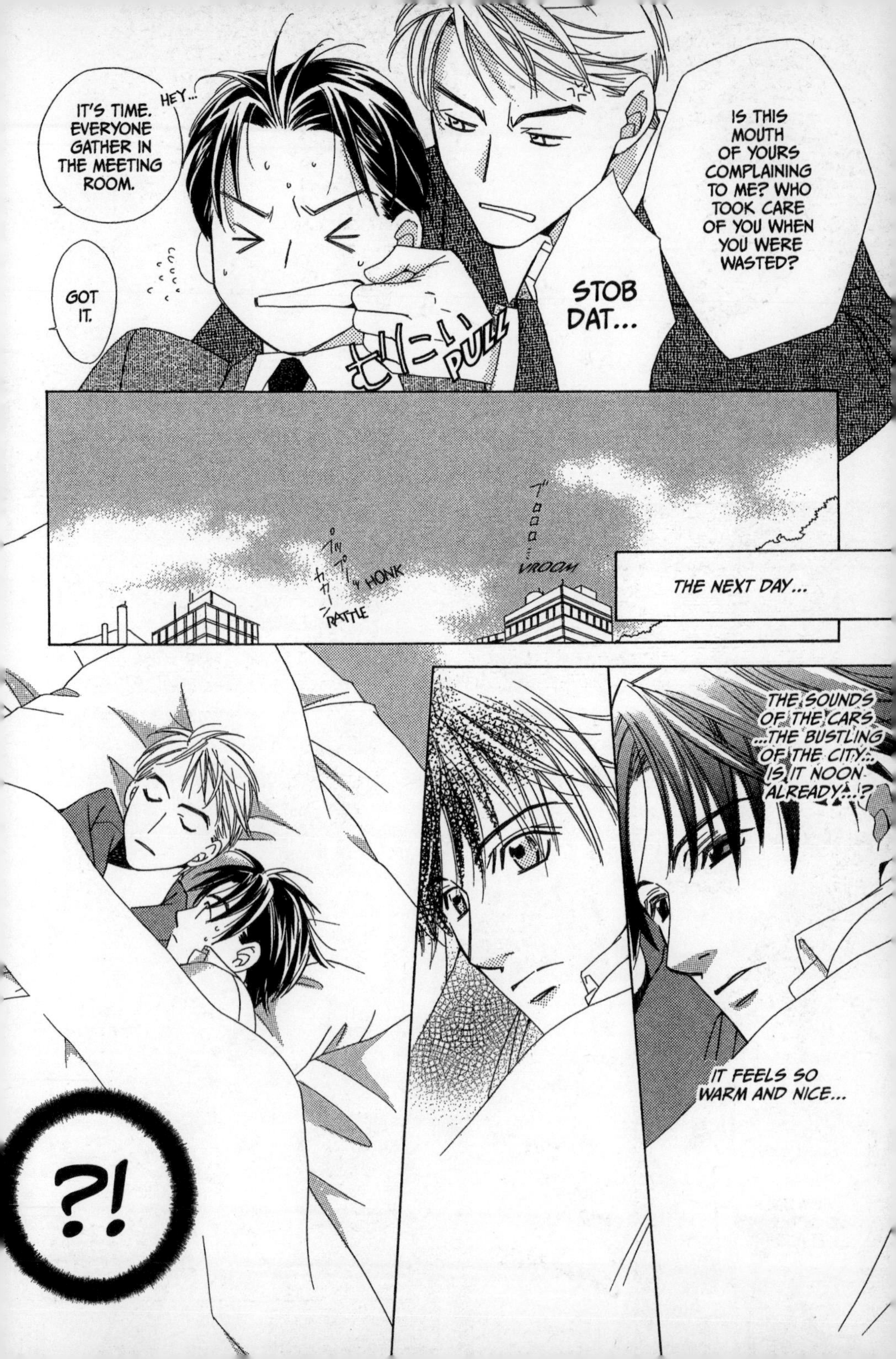
IS THIS MOUTH OF YOURS COMPLAINING TO ME? WHO TOOK CARE OF YOU WHEN YOU WERE WASTED?
STOB DAT...
PULL
HEY...
IT'S TIME. EVERYONE GATHER IN THE MEETING ROOM.
GOT IT.
THE NEXT DAY...
VROOM
HONK
RATTLE
THE SOUNDS OF THE CARS ...THE BUSTLING OF THE CITY... IS IT NOON ALREADY...?
IT FEELS SO WARM AND NICE...
?!

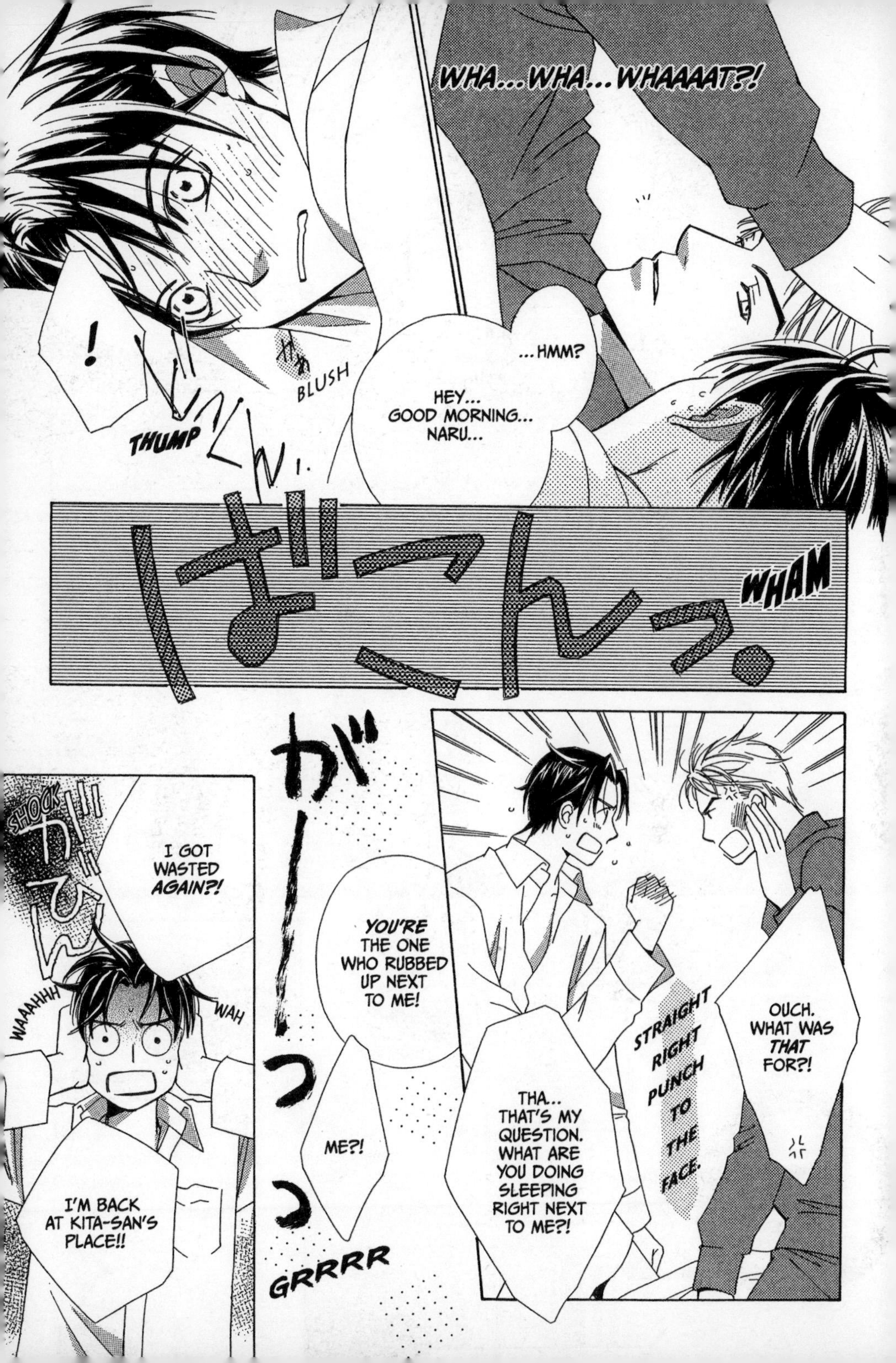
WHA...WHA...WHAAAAT?!
...HMM?
HEY... GOOD MORNING... NARU...
BLUSH
THUMP
!
ばこんっ
WHAM
OUCH. WHAT WAS THAT FOR?!
STRAIGHT RIGHT PUNCH TO THE FACE.
THA.. THAT'S MY QUESTION. WHAT ARE YOU DOING SLEEPING RIGHT NEXT TO ME?!
YOU'RE THE ONE WHO RUBBED UP NEXT TO ME!
ME?!
がーっっ
GRRRR
SHOCK
がびーん
I GOT WASTED AGAIN?!
WAAAHHH
WAH
I'M BACK AT KITA-SAN'S PLACE!!

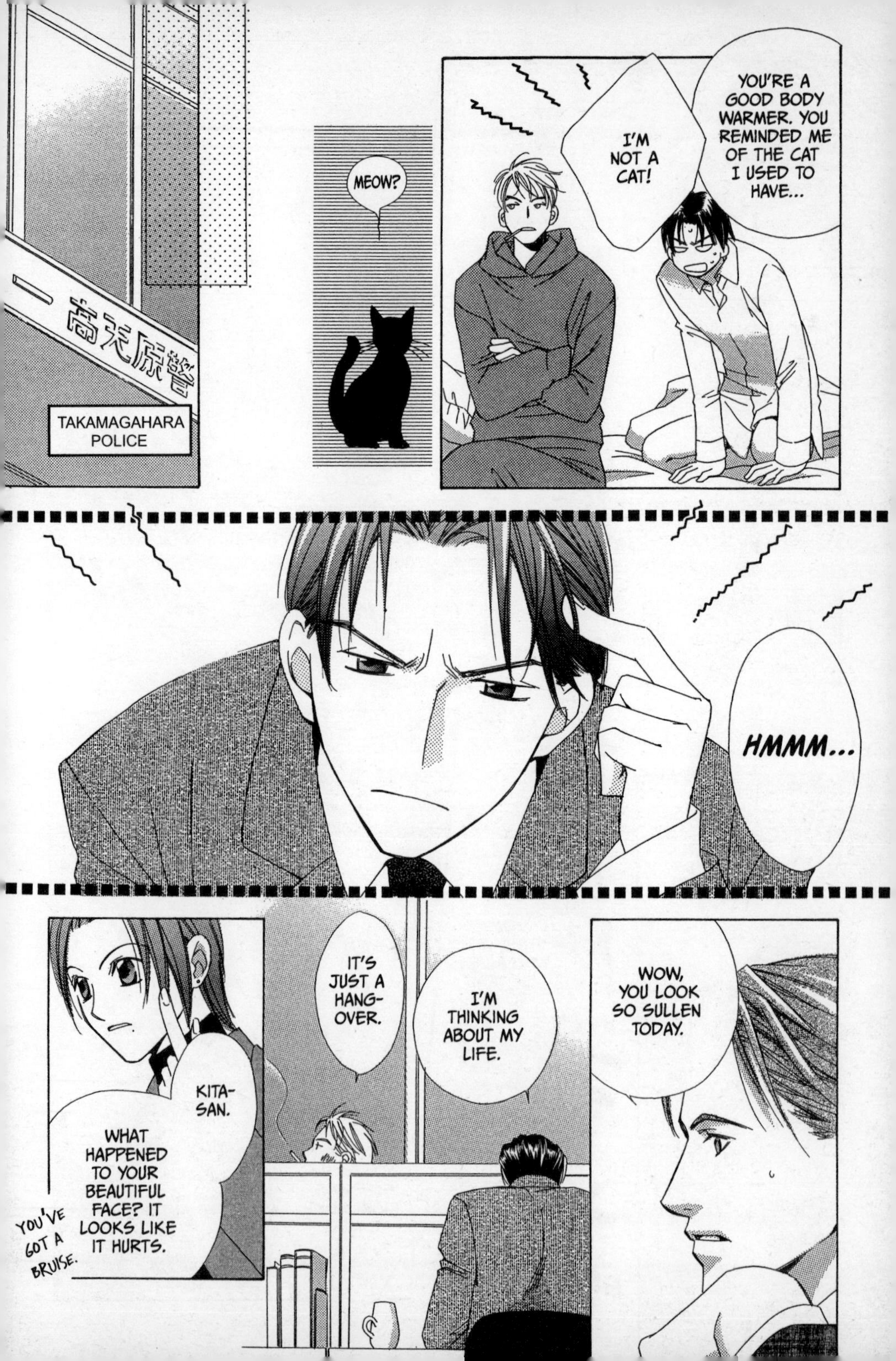
YOU'RE A GOOD BODY WARMER. YOU REMINDED ME OF THE CAT I USED TO HAVE...
I'M NOT A CAT!
MEOW?
TAKAMAGAHARA POLICE
HMMM...
WOW, YOU LOOK SO SULLEN TODAY.
I'M THINKING ABOUT MY LIFE.
IT'S JUST A HANG-OVER.
KITA-SAN.
WHAT HAPPENED TO YOUR BEAUTIFUL FACE? IT LOOKS LIKE IT HURTS.
YOU'VE GOT A BRUISE.

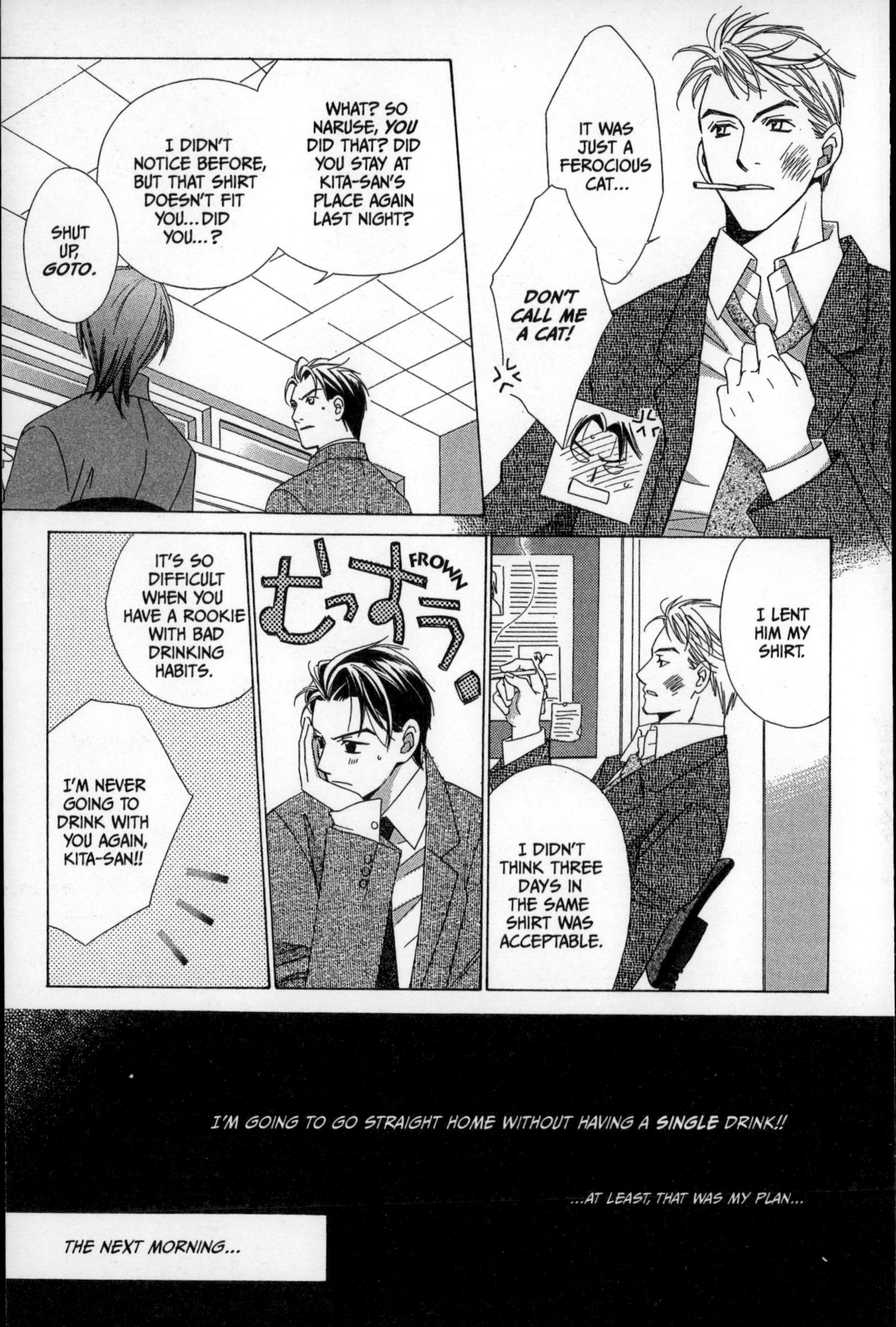
IT WAS JUST A FEROCIOUS CAT...
DON'T CALL ME A CAT!
WHAT? SO NARUSE, *YOU* DID THAT? DID YOU STAY AT KITA-SAN'S PLACE AGAIN LAST NIGHT?
I DIDN'T NOTICE BEFORE, BUT THAT SHIRT DOESN'T FIT YOU...DID YOU...?
SHUT UP, GOTO.
I LENT HIM MY SHIRT.
I DIDN'T THINK THREE DAYS IN THE SAME SHIRT WAS ACCEPTABLE.
むっすう
FROWN
IT'S SO DIFFICULT WHEN YOU HAVE A ROOKIE WITH BAD DRINKING HABITS.
I'M NEVER GOING TO DRINK WITH YOU AGAIN, KITA-SAN!!
I'M GOING TO GO STRAIGHT HOME WITHOUT HAVING A SINGLE DRINK!!
...AT LEAST, THAT WAS MY PLAN...
THE NEXT MORNING...

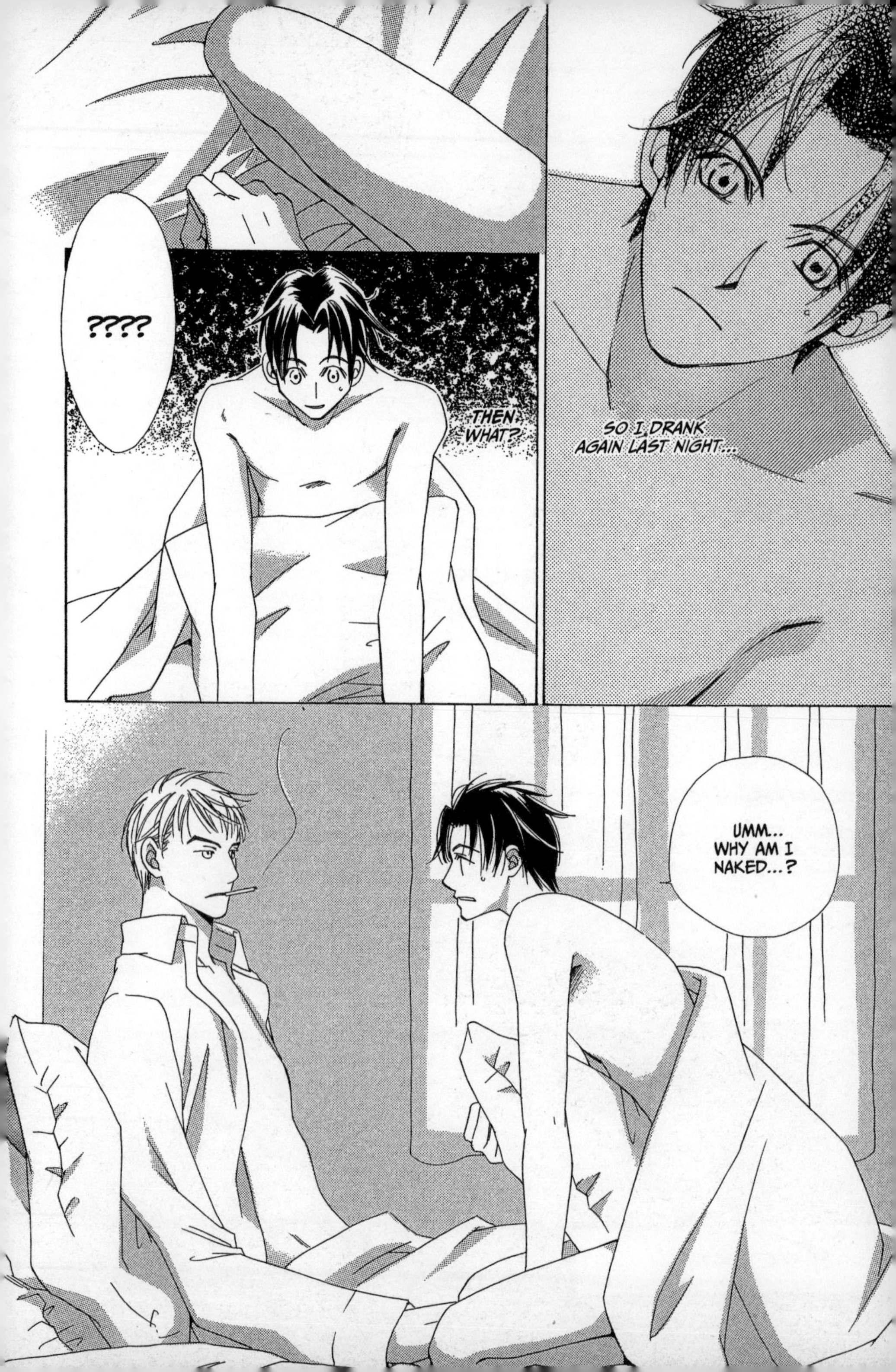
SO I DRANK AGAIN LAST NIGHT...
????
THEN WHAT?
UMM... WHY AM I NAKED...?

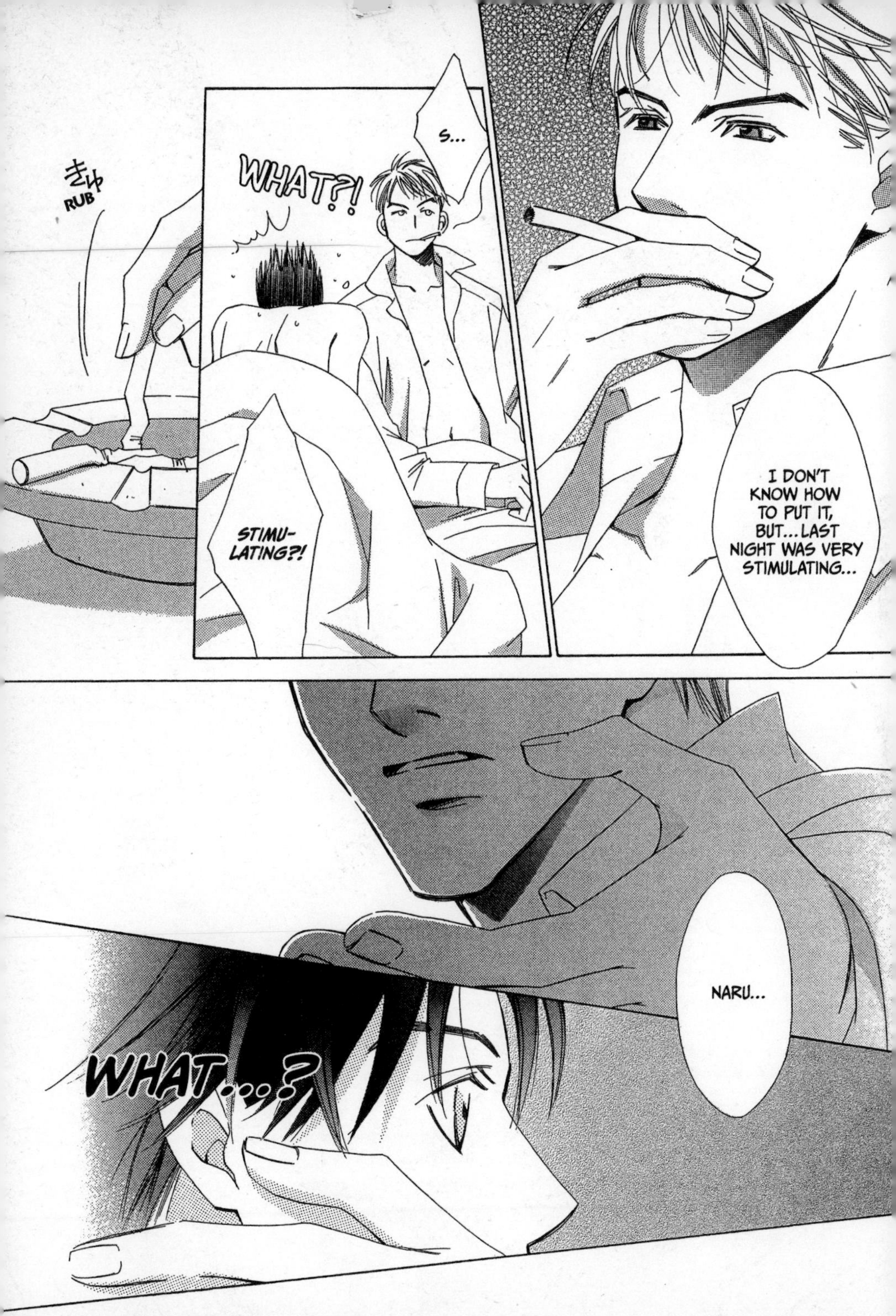
I DON'T KNOW HOW TO PUT IT, BUT...LAST NIGHT WAS VERY STIMULATING...
S...
WHAT?!
STIMU-LATING?!
きゅ
RUB
NARU...
WHAT...?

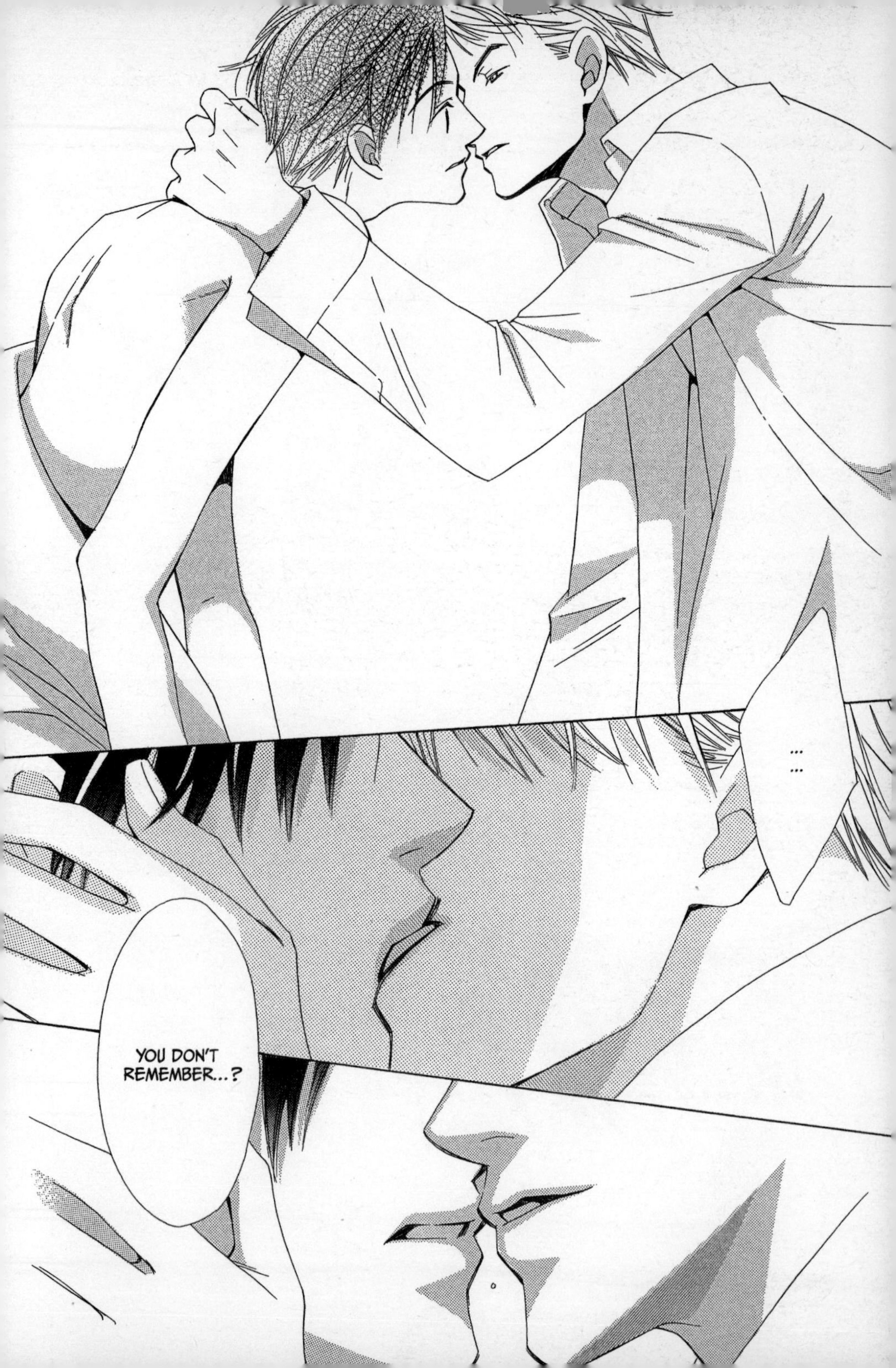
……
YOU DON'T REMEMBER...?

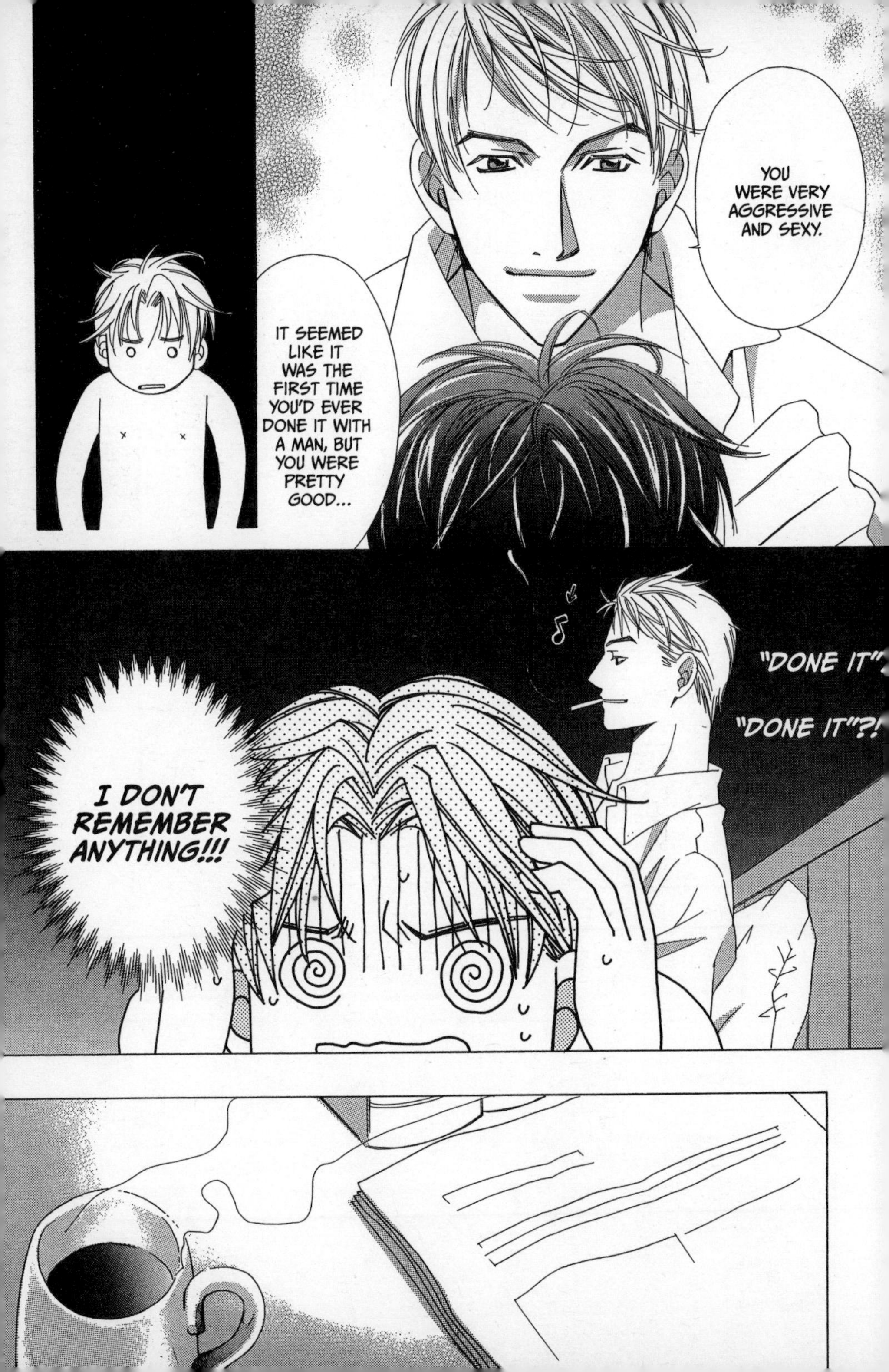

YOU WERE VERY AGGRESSIVE AND SEXY.
IT SEEMED LIKE IT WAS THE FIRST TIME YOU'D EVER DONE IT WITH A MAN, BUT YOU WERE PRETTY GOOD...
"DONE IT"
"DONE IT"?!
I DON'T REMEMBER ANYTHING!!!

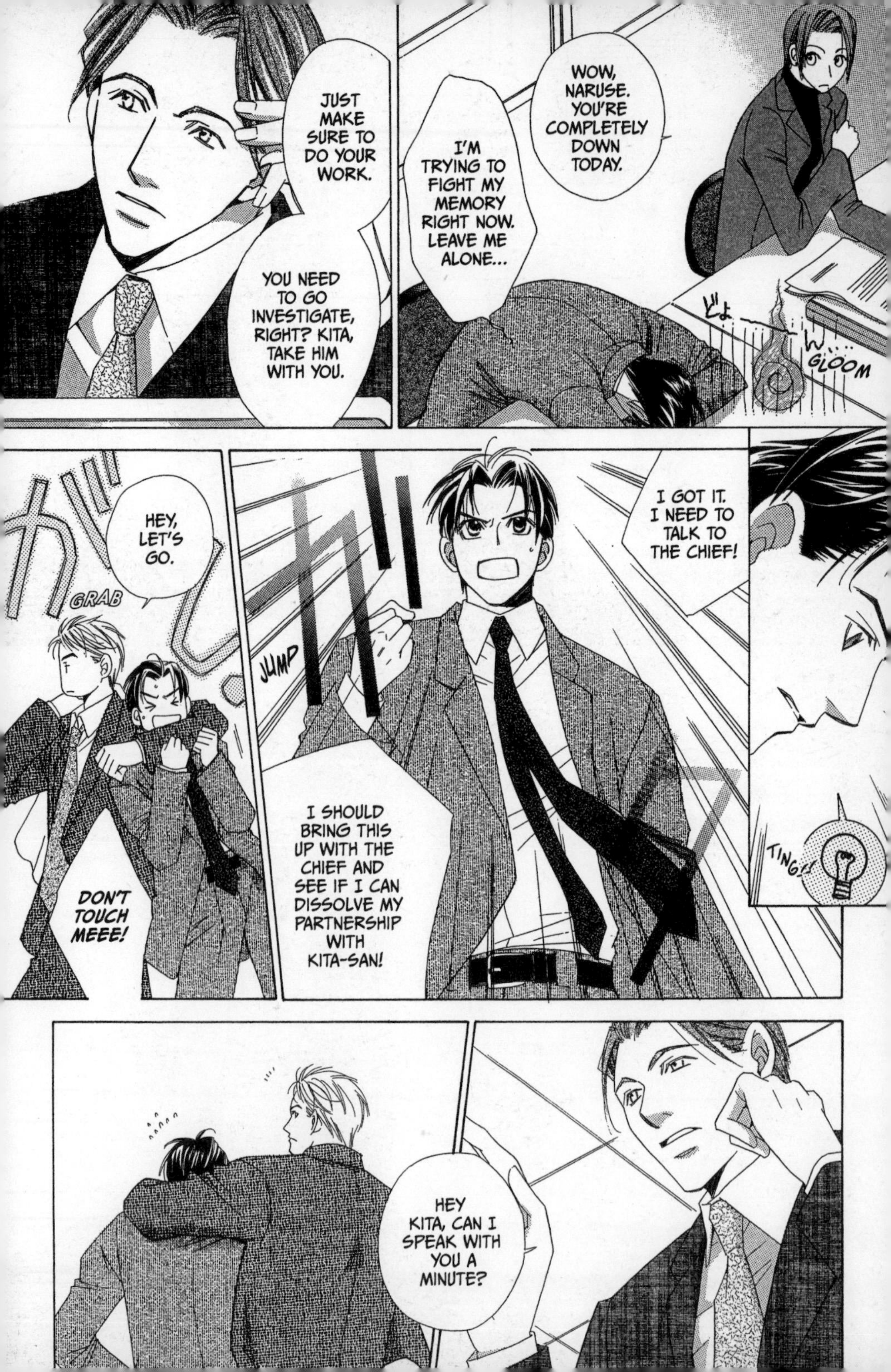
WOW, NARUSE. YOU'RE COMPLETELY DOWN TODAY.
I'M TRYING TO FIGHT MY MEMORY RIGHT NOW. LEAVE ME ALONE...
どよ
GLOOM
JUST MAKE SURE TO DO YOUR WORK.
YOU NEED TO GO INVESTIGATE, RIGHT? KITA, TAKE HIM WITH YOU.
I GOT IT. I NEED TO TALK TO THE CHIEF!
TING!!
JUMP
I SHOULD BRING THIS UP WITH THE CHIEF AND SEE IF I CAN DISSOLVE MY PARTNERSHIP WITH KITA-SAN!
GRAB
HEY, LET'S GO.
DON'T TOUCH MEEE!
HEY KITA, CAN I SPEAK WITH YOU A MINUTE?

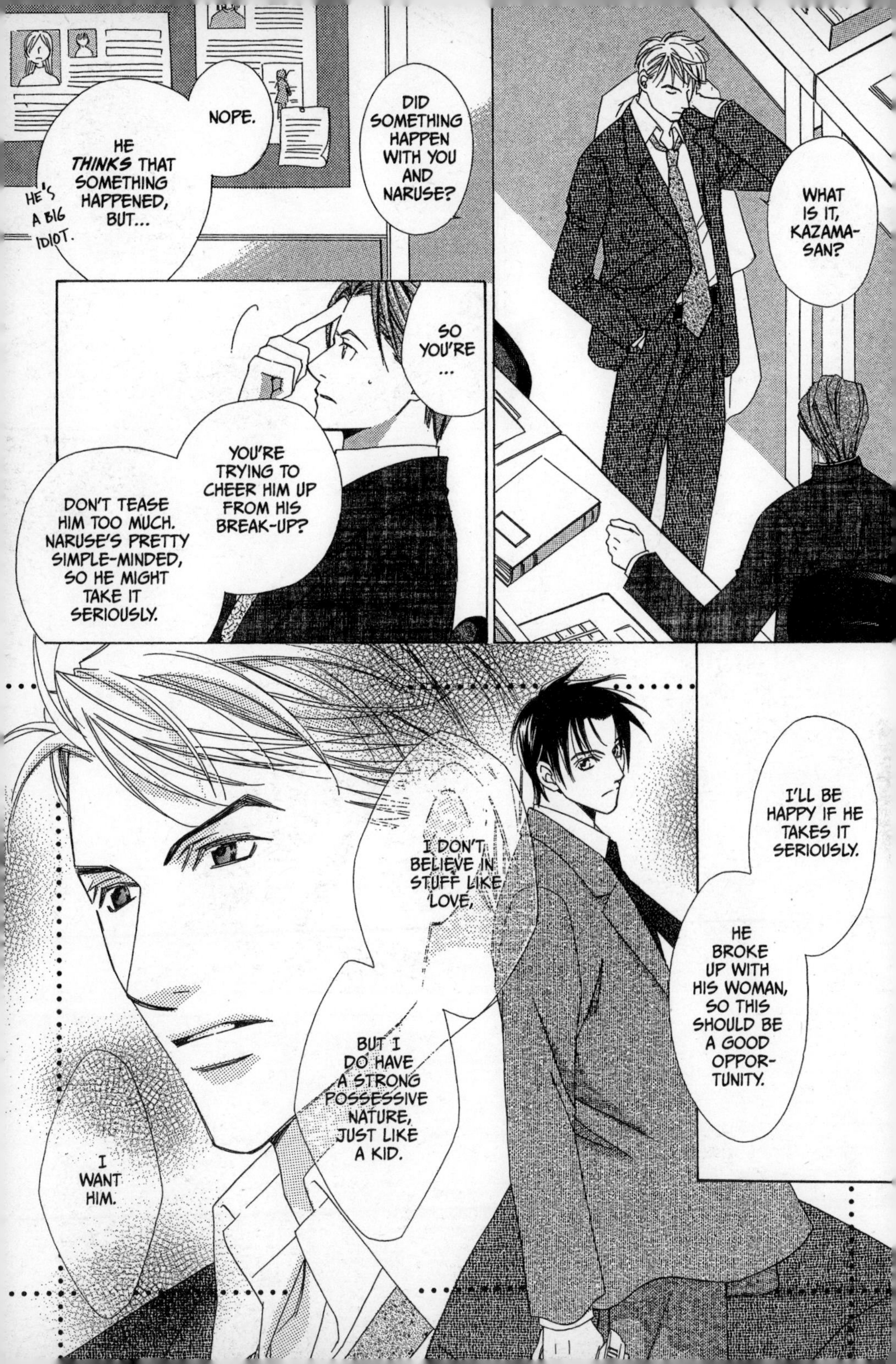

WHAT IS IT, KAZAMA-SAN?
DID SOMETHING HAPPEN WITH YOU AND NARUSE?
NOPE.
HE *THINKS* THAT SOMETHING HAPPENED, BUT...
HE'S A BIG IDIOT.
SO YOU'RE ...
YOU'RE TRYING TO CHEER HIM UP FROM HIS BREAK-UP?
DON'T TEASE HIM TOO MUCH. NARUSE'S PRETTY SIMPLE-MINDED, SO HE MIGHT TAKE IT SERIOUSLY.
I'LL BE HAPPY IF HE TAKES IT SERIOUSLY.
HE BROKE UP WITH HIS WOMAN, SO THIS SHOULD BE A GOOD OPPOR-TUNITY.
I DON'T BELIEVE IN STUFF LIKE LOVE,
BUT I DO HAVE A STRONG POSSESSIVE NATURE, JUST LIKE A KID.
I WANT HIM.

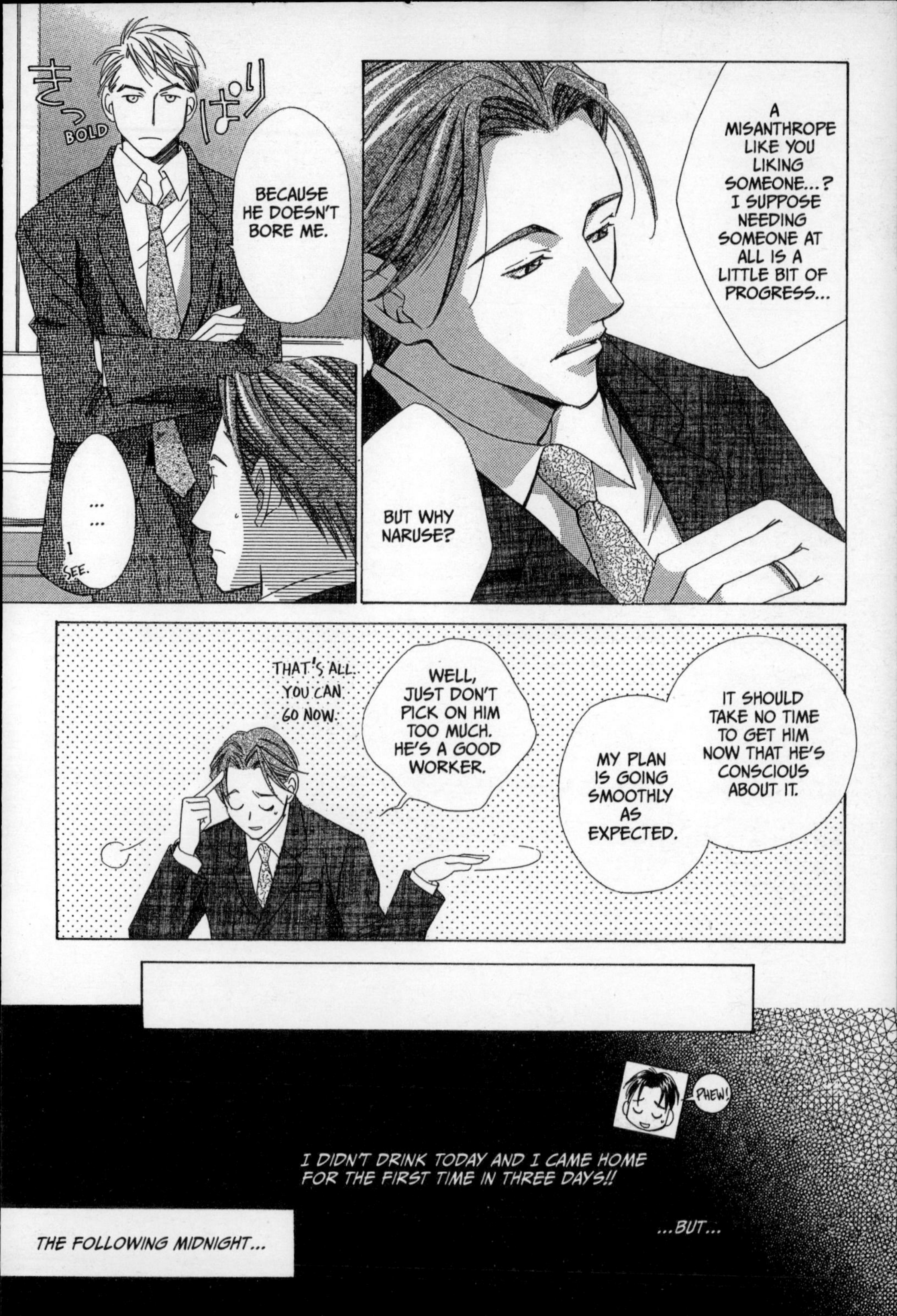
A MISANTHROPE LIKE YOU LIKING SOMEONE...? I SUPPOSE NEEDING SOMEONE AT ALL IS A LITTLE BIT OF PROGRESS...
BUT WHY NARUSE?
きっぱり
BOLD
BECAUSE HE DOESN'T BORE ME.
... ... I SEE.
IT SHOULD TAKE NO TIME TO GET HIM NOW THAT HE'S CONSCIOUS ABOUT IT.
MY PLAN IS GOING SMOOTHLY AS EXPECTED.
WELL, JUST DON'T PICK ON HIM TOO MUCH. HE'S A GOOD WORKER.
THAT'S ALL. YOU CAN GO NOW.
PHEW!
I DIDN'T DRINK TODAY AND I CAME HOME FOR THE FIRST TIME IN THREE DAYS!!
...BUT...
THE FOLLOWING MIDNIGHT...

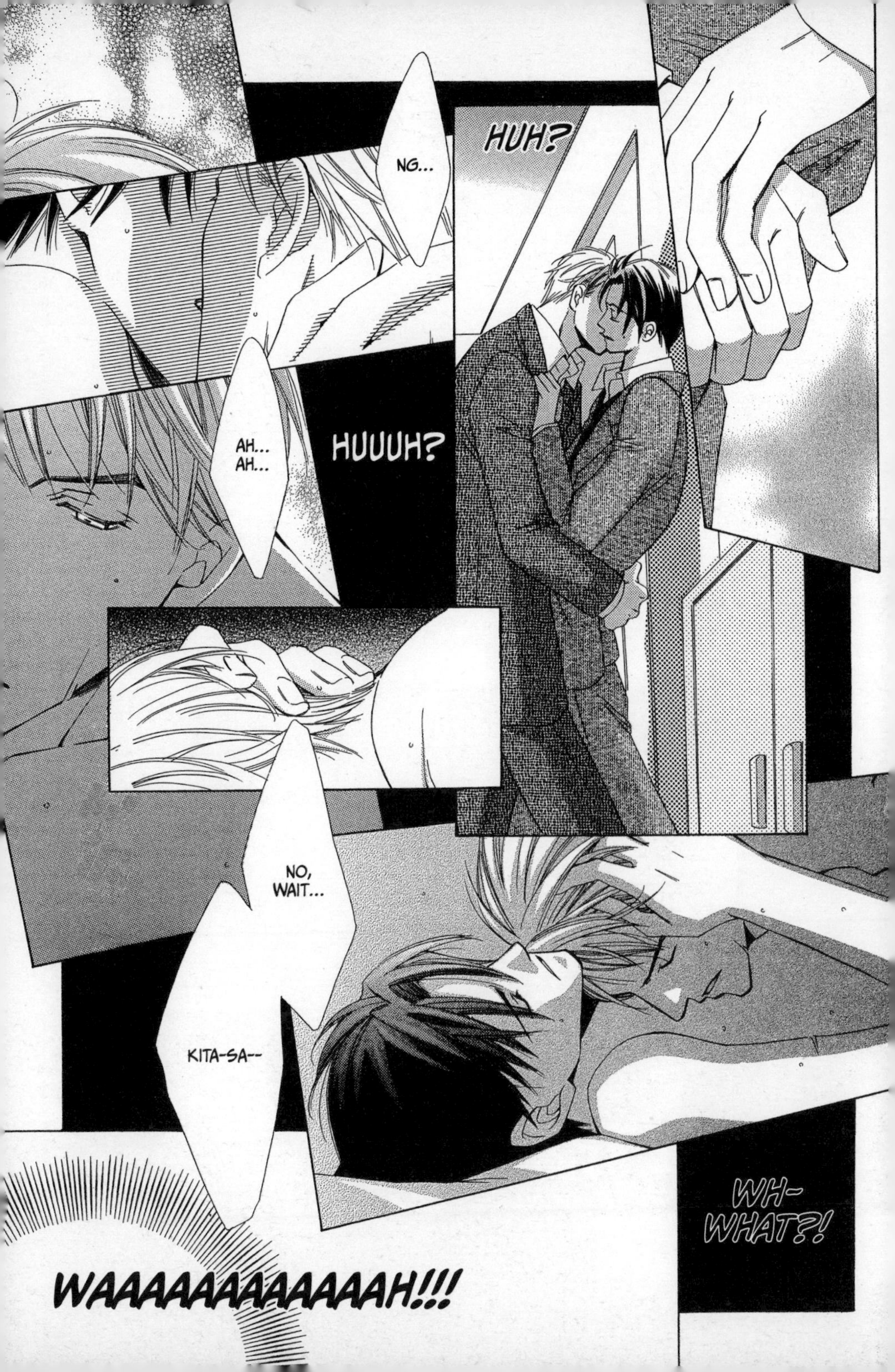
HUH?
HUUUH?
NG...
AH...
AH...
NO, WAIT...
KITA-SA--
WH-
WHAT?!
WAAAAAAAAAAAAAH!!!

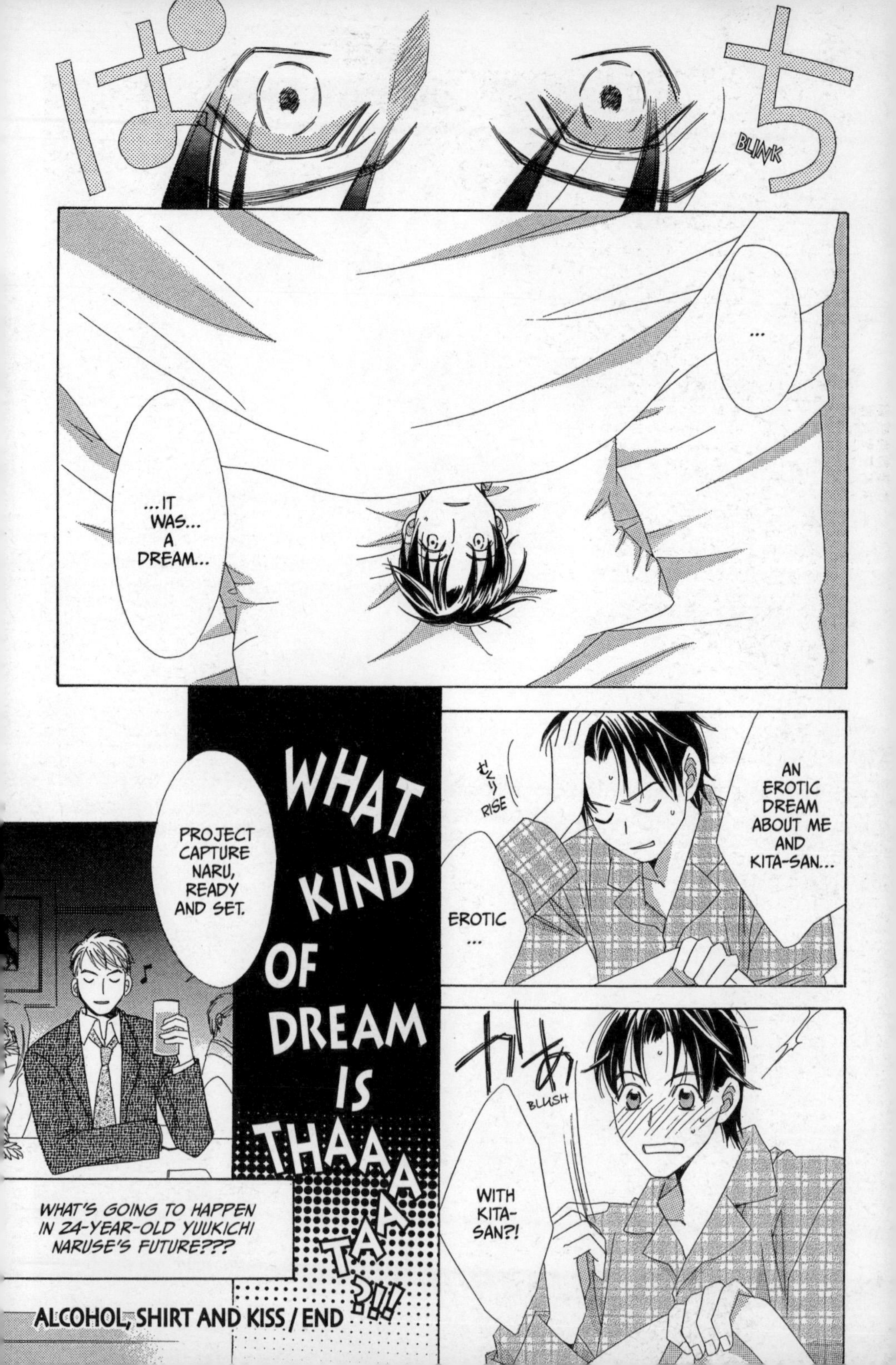
ぱち
BLINK
...
...IT WAS... A DREAM...
むくり
RISE
AN EROTIC DREAM ABOUT ME AND KITA-SAN...
EROTIC ...
かあ
BLUSH
WITH KITA-SAN?!
WHAT KIND OF DREAM IS THAAAAATA?!!
PROJECT CAPTURE NARU, READY AND SET.
WHAT'S GOING TO HAPPEN IN 24-YEAR-OLD YUUKICHI NARUSE'S FUTURE???
ALCOHOL, SHIRT AND KISS / END

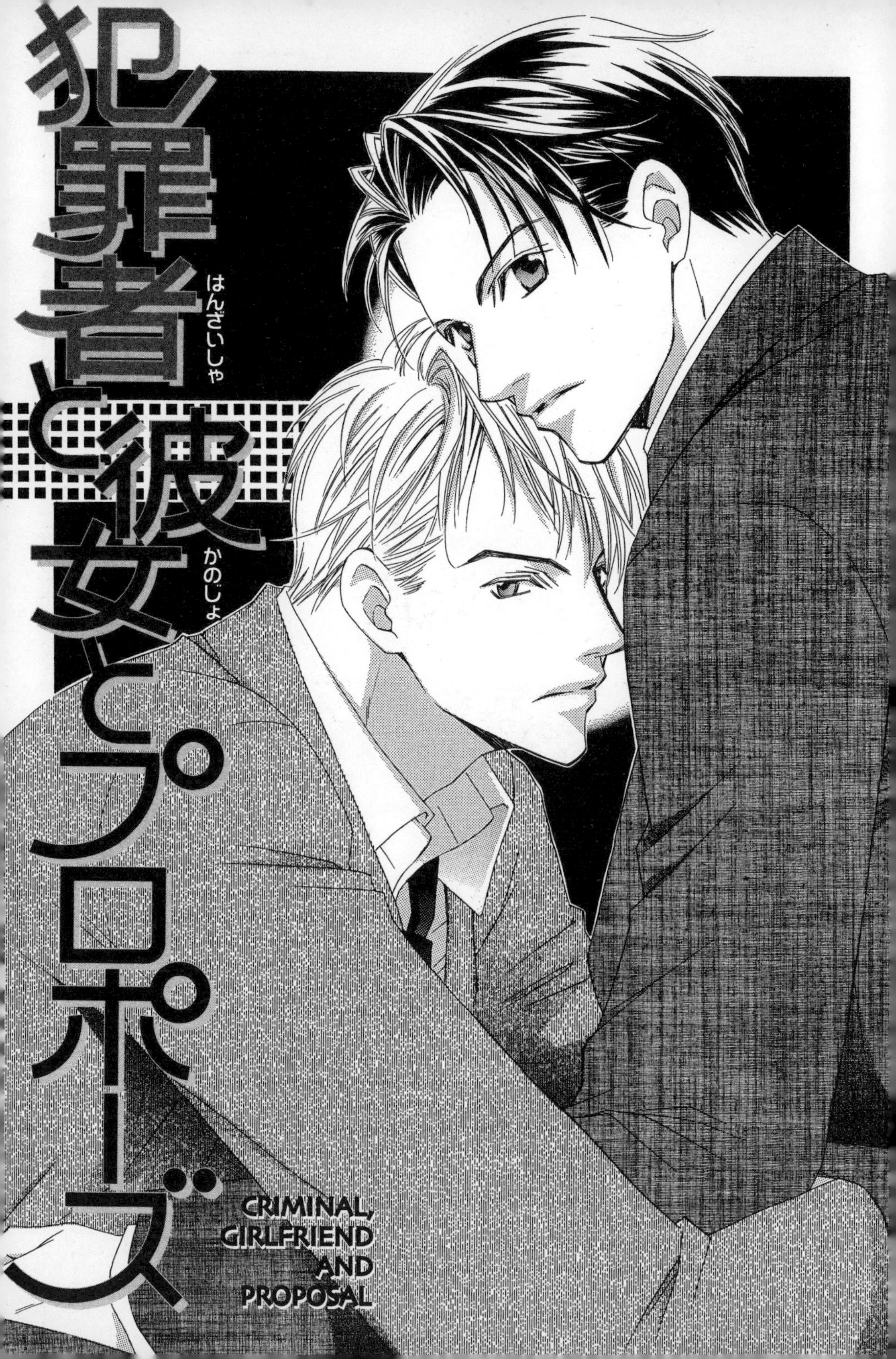
犯罪者(はんざいしゃ)と彼女(かのじょ)とプロポーズ
CRIMINAL, GIRLFRIEND AND PROPOSAL

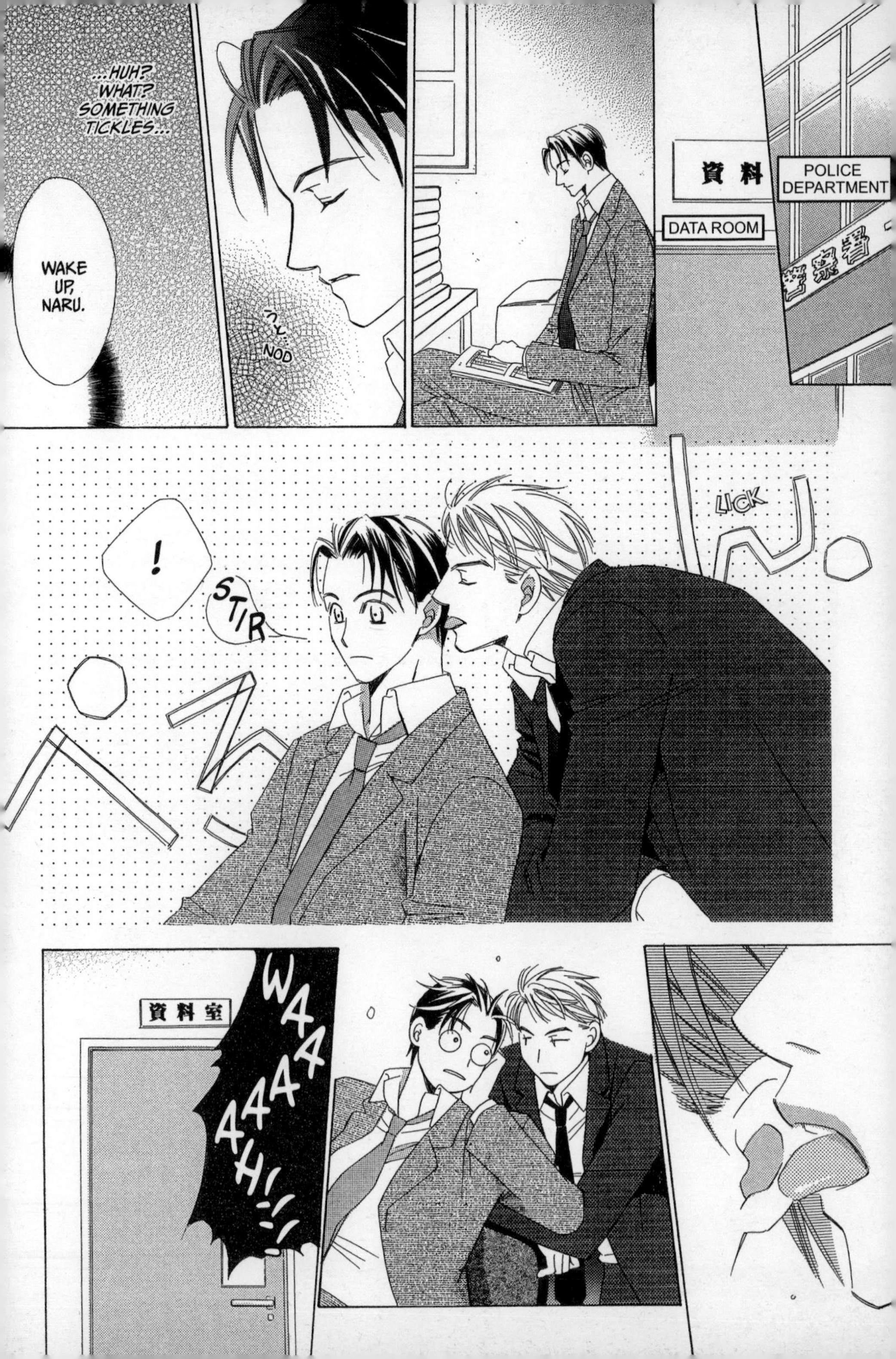
POLICE DEPARTMENT
資料
DATA ROOM
NOD
...HUH? WHAT? SOMETHING TICKLES...
WAKE UP, NARU.
LICK
!
STIR
WAAAAAAAH!!!
資料室

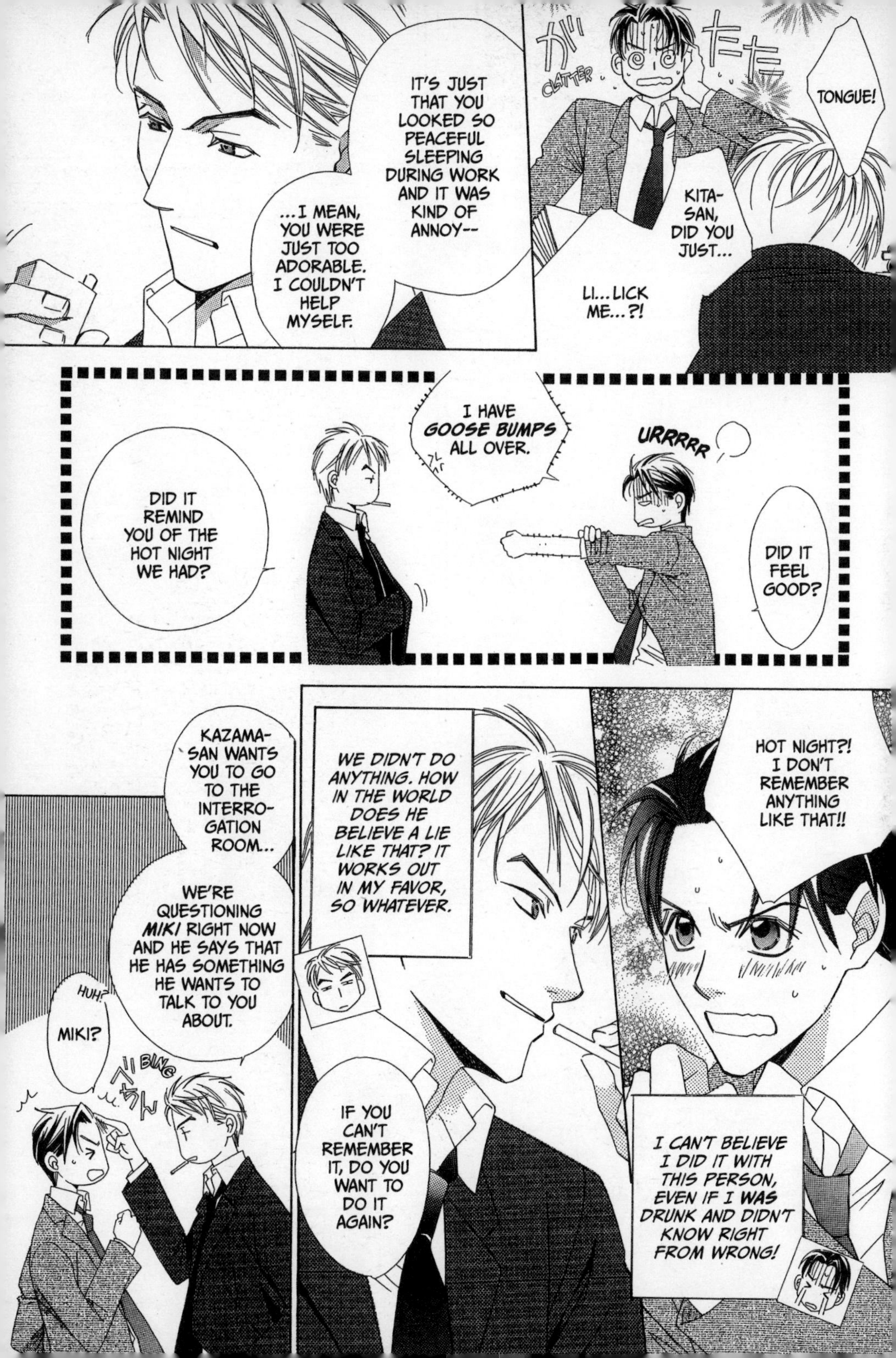

TONGUE!
CLATTER
KITA-SAN, DID YOU JUST...
LI...LICK ME...?!
IT'S JUST THAT YOU LOOKED SO PEACEFUL SLEEPING DURING WORK AND IT WAS KIND OF ANNOY--
...I MEAN, YOU WERE JUST TOO ADORABLE. I COULDN'T HELP MYSELF.
DID IT FEEL GOOD?
URRRRR
I HAVE GOOSE BUMPS ALL OVER.
DID IT REMIND YOU OF THE HOT NIGHT WE HAD?
HOT NIGHT?! I DON'T REMEMBER ANYTHING LIKE THAT!!
I CAN'T BELIEVE I DID IT WITH THIS PERSON, EVEN IF I WAS DRUNK AND DIDN'T KNOW RIGHT FROM WRONG!
WE DIDN'T DO ANYTHING. HOW IN THE WORLD DOES HE BELIEVE A LIE LIKE THAT? IT WORKS OUT IN MY FAVOR, SO WHATEVER.
IF YOU CAN'T REMEMBER IT, DO YOU WANT TO DO IT AGAIN?
KAZAMA-SAN WANTS YOU TO GO TO THE INTERROGATION ROOM...
WE'RE QUESTIONING MIKI RIGHT NOW AND HE SAYS THAT HE HAS SOMETHING HE WANTS TO TALK TO YOU ABOUT.
HUH?
MIKI?
BING

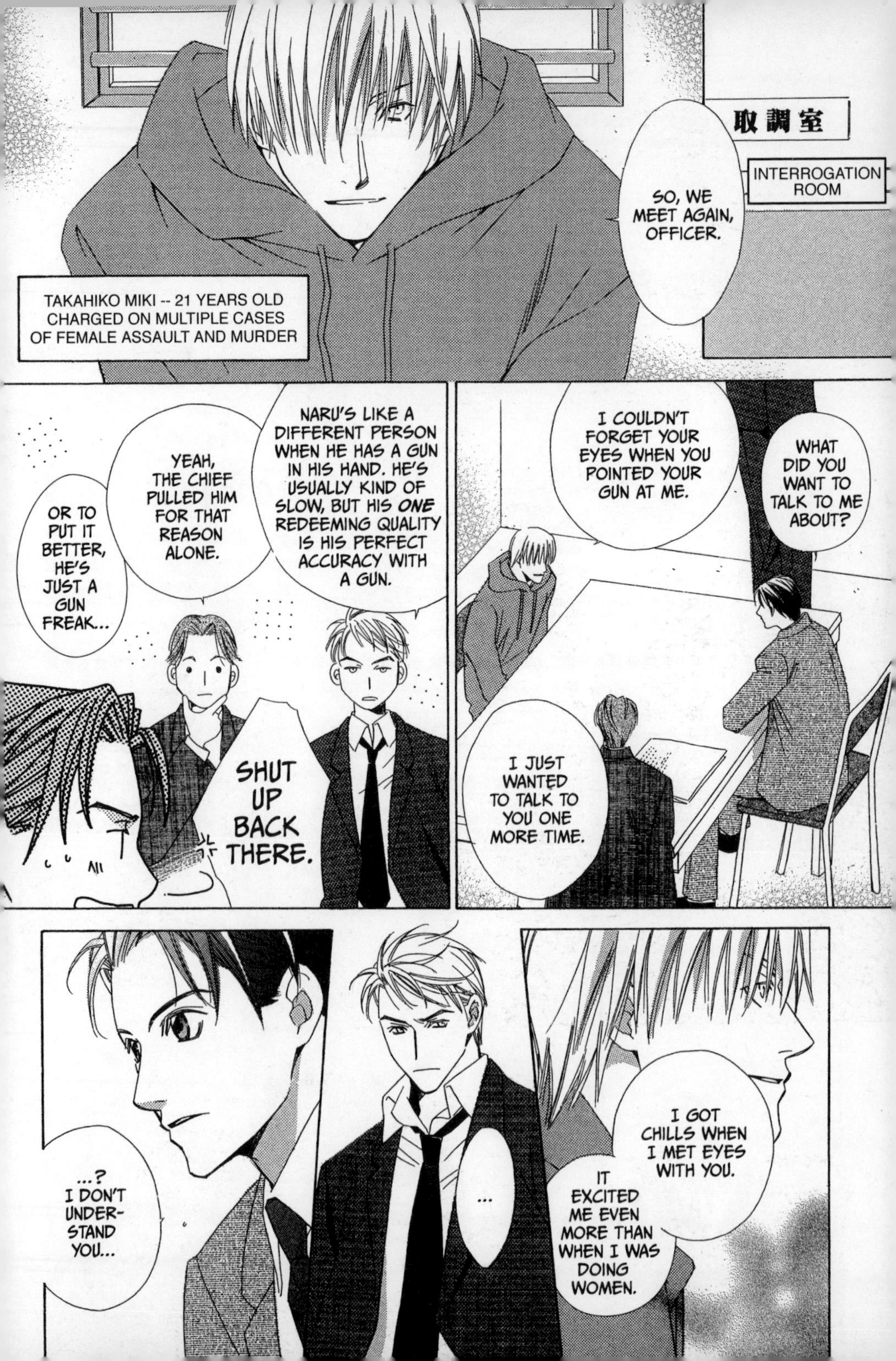
取調室
INTERROGATION ROOM
SO, WE MEET AGAIN, OFFICER.
TAKAHIKO MIKI -- 21 YEARS OLD CHARGED ON MULTIPLE CASES OF FEMALE ASSAULT AND MURDER
WHAT DID YOU WANT TO TALK TO ME ABOUT?
I COULDN'T FORGET YOUR EYES WHEN YOU POINTED YOUR GUN AT ME.
I JUST WANTED TO TALK TO YOU ONE MORE TIME.
NARU'S LIKE A DIFFERENT PERSON WHEN HE HAS A GUN IN HIS HAND. HE'S USUALLY KIND OF SLOW, BUT HIS *ONE* REDEEMING QUALITY IS HIS PERFECT ACCURACY WITH A GUN.
YEAH, THE CHIEF PULLED HIM FOR THAT REASON ALONE.
OR TO PUT IT BETTER, HE'S JUST A GUN FREAK...
SHUT UP BACK THERE.
I GOT CHILLS WHEN I MET EYES WITH YOU.
IT EXCITED ME EVEN MORE THAN WHEN I WAS DOING WOMEN.
...
...? I DON'T UNDER-STAND YOU...

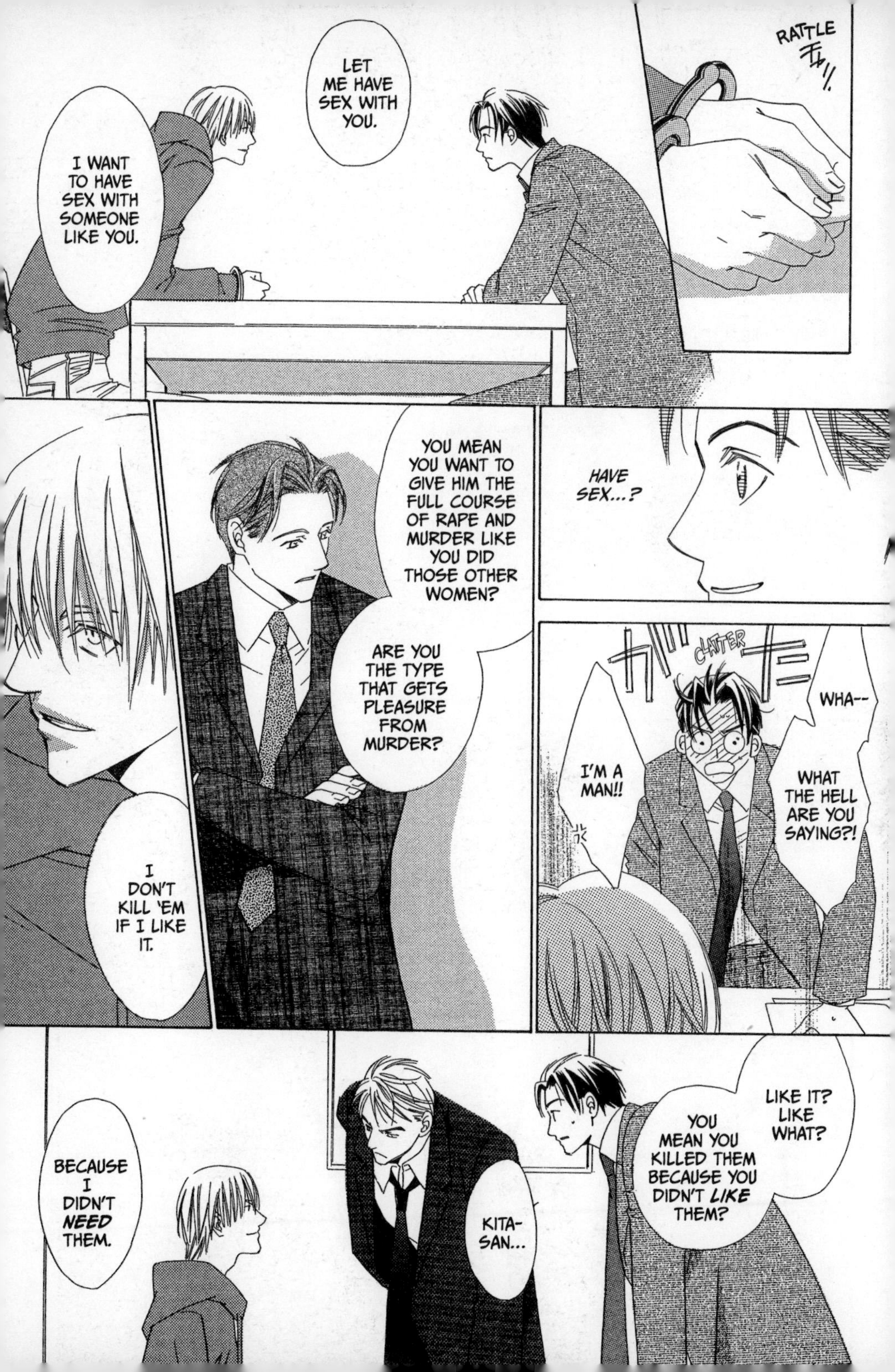
RATTLE
LET ME HAVE SEX WITH YOU.
I WANT TO HAVE SEX WITH SOMEONE LIKE YOU.
HAVE SEX...?
CHATTER
WHA--
WHAT THE HELL ARE YOU SAYING?!
I'M A MAN!!
YOU MEAN YOU WANT TO GIVE HIM THE FULL COURSE OF RAPE AND MURDER LIKE YOU DID THOSE OTHER WOMEN?
ARE YOU THE TYPE THAT GETS PLEASURE FROM MURDER?
I DON'T KILL 'EM IF I LIKE IT.
LIKE IT? LIKE WHAT?
YOU MEAN YOU KILLED THEM BECAUSE YOU DIDN'T *LIKE* THEM?
KITA-SAN...
BECAUSE I DIDN'T *NEED* THEM.

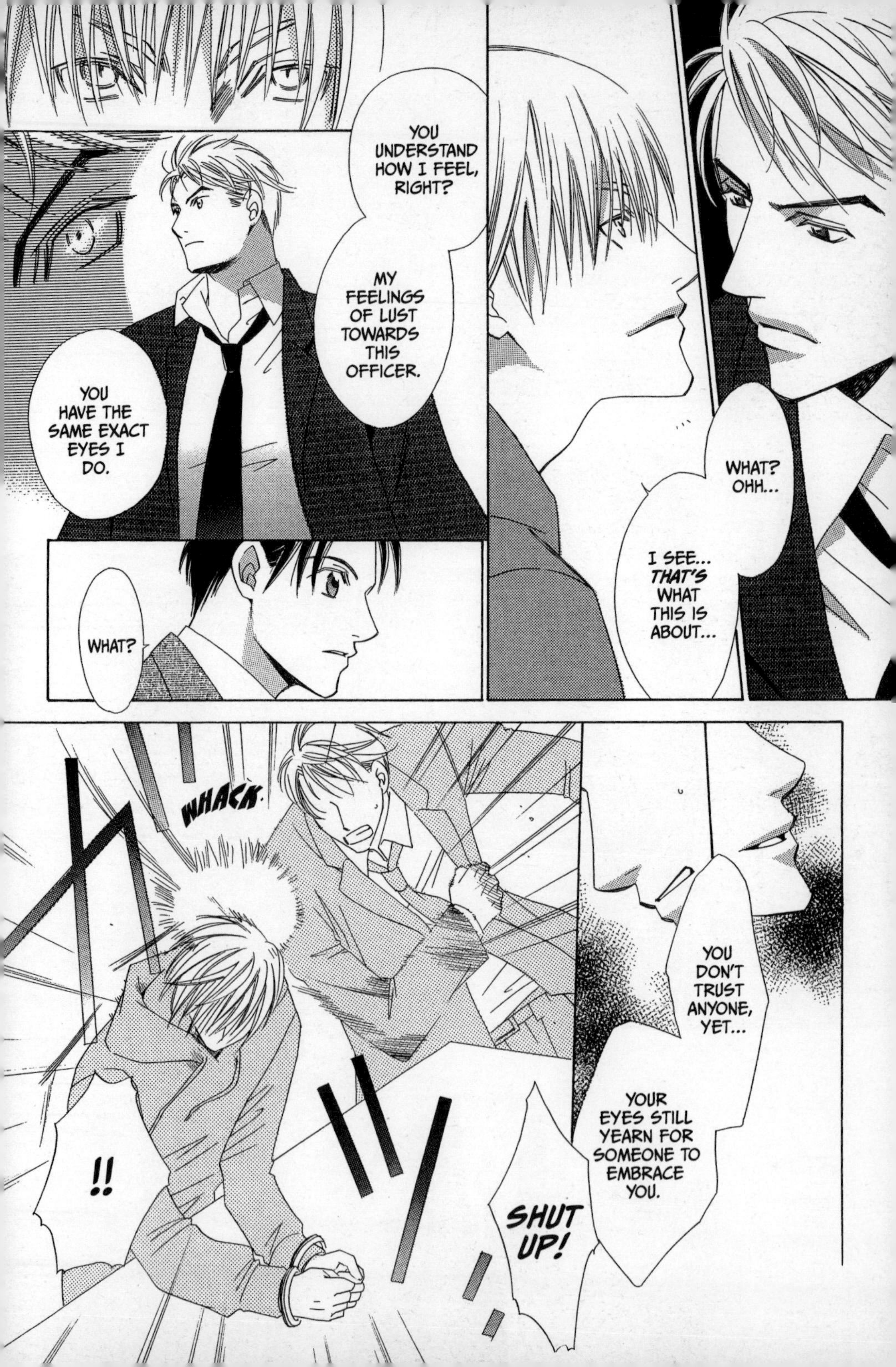
WHAT? OHH...
I SEE... *THAT'S* WHAT THIS IS ABOUT...
YOU UNDERSTAND HOW I FEEL, RIGHT?
MY FEELINGS OF LUST TOWARDS THIS OFFICER.
YOU HAVE THE SAME EXACT EYES I DO.
WHAT?
YOU DON'T TRUST ANYONE, YET...
YOUR EYES STILL YEARN FOR SOMEONE TO EMBRACE YOU.
SHUT UP!
WHACK
!!

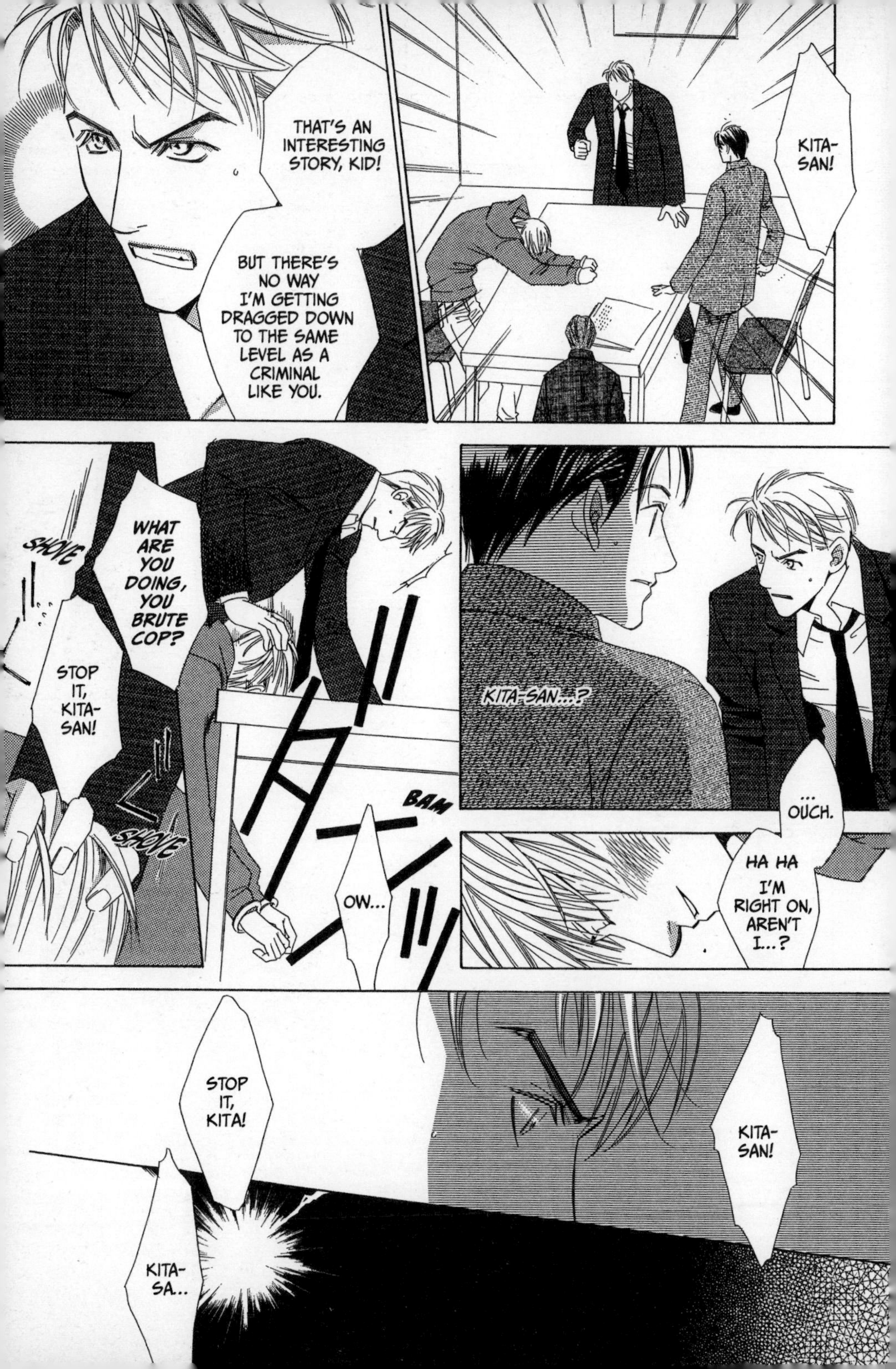
KITA-SAN!
THAT'S AN INTERESTING STORY, KID!
BUT THERE'S NO WAY I'M GETTING DRAGGED DOWN TO THE SAME LEVEL AS A CRIMINAL LIKE YOU.
KITA-SAN...?
...OUCH.
HA HA I'M RIGHT ON, AREN'T I...?
WHAT ARE YOU DOING, YOU BRUTE COP?
SHOVE
STOP IT, KITA-SAN!
SHOVE
BAM
OW...
KITA-SAN!
STOP IT, KITA!
KITA-SA...

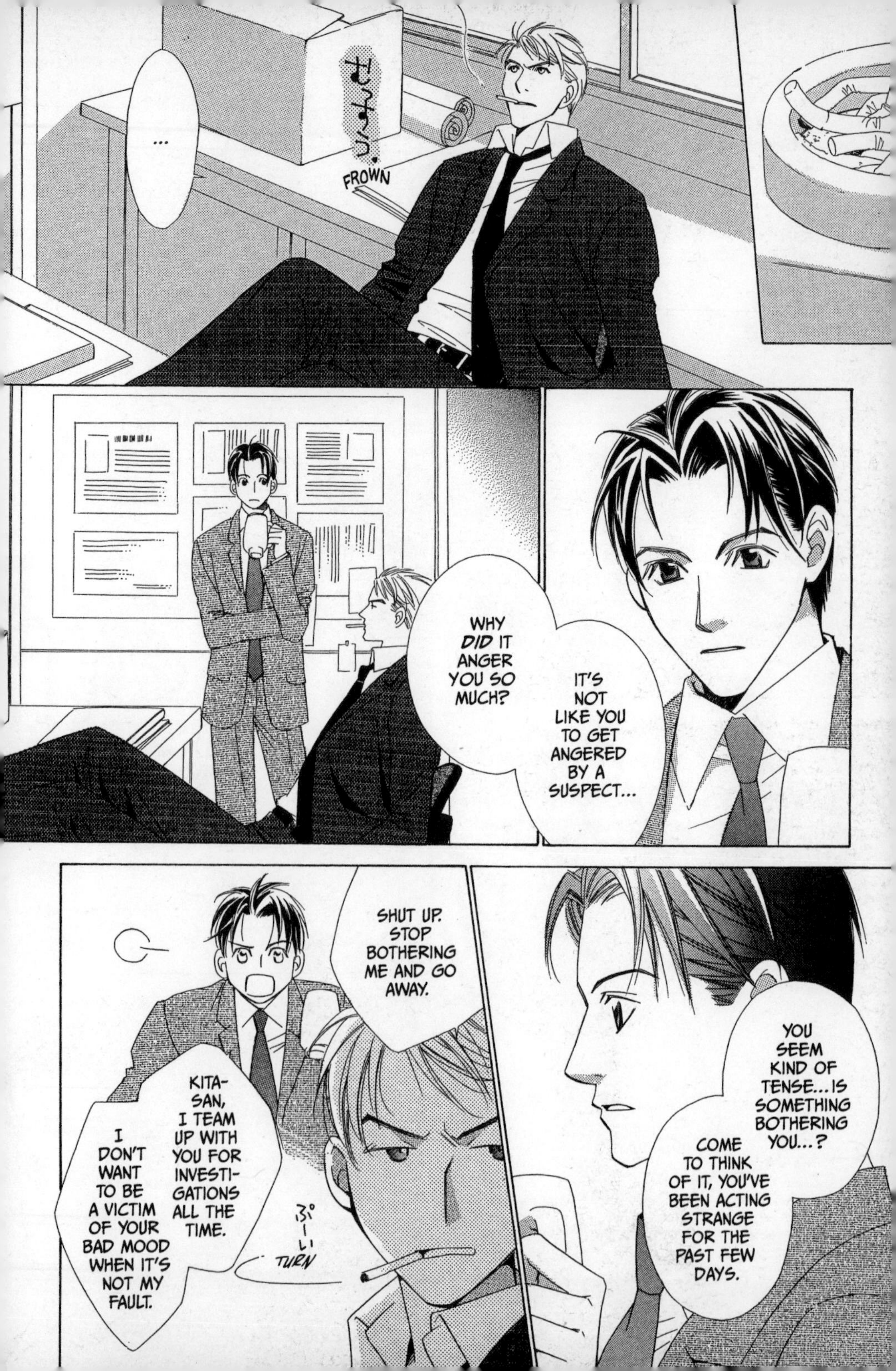
FROWN
...
IT'S NOT LIKE YOU TO GET ANGERED BY A SUSPECT...
WHY DID IT ANGER YOU SO MUCH?
YOU SEEM KIND OF TENSE...IS SOMETHING BOTHERING YOU...?
COME TO THINK OF IT, YOU'VE BEEN ACTING STRANGE FOR THE PAST FEW DAYS.
SHUT UP. STOP BOTHERING ME AND GO AWAY.
KITA-SAN, I TEAM UP WITH YOU FOR INVESTIGATIONS ALL THE TIME.
TURN
I DON'T WANT TO BE A VICTIM OF YOUR BAD MOOD WHEN IT'S NOT MY FAULT.

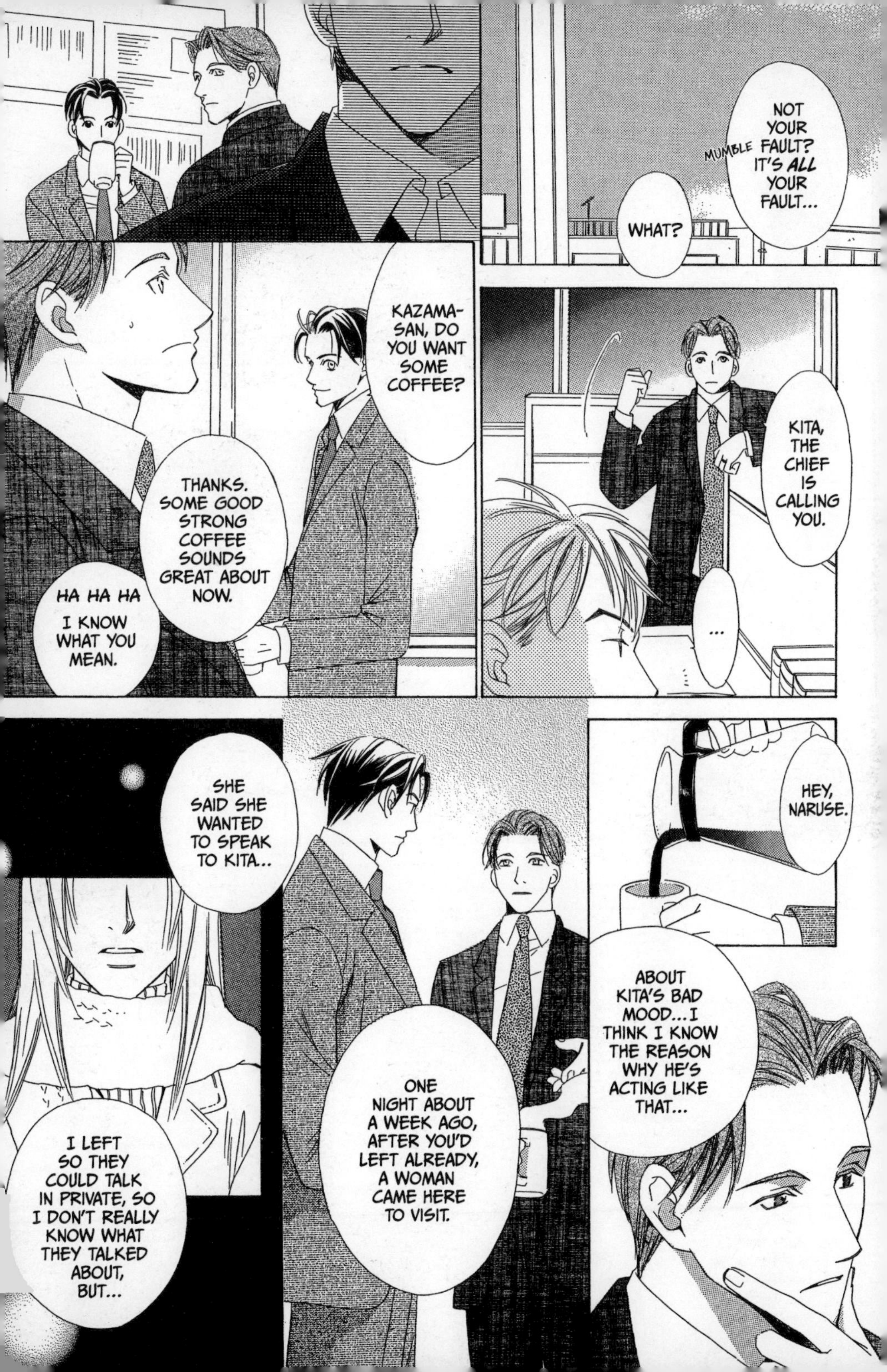
MUMBLE
NOT YOUR FAULT? IT'S ALL YOUR FAULT...
WHAT?
KITA, THE CHIEF IS CALLING YOU.
...
KAZAMA-SAN, DO YOU WANT SOME COFFEE?
THANKS. SOME GOOD STRONG COFFEE SOUNDS GREAT ABOUT NOW.
HA HA HA
I KNOW WHAT YOU MEAN.
HEY, NARUSE.
ABOUT KITA'S BAD MOOD...I THINK I KNOW THE REASON WHY HE'S ACTING LIKE THAT...
ONE NIGHT ABOUT A WEEK AGO, AFTER YOU'D LEFT ALREADY, A WOMAN CAME HERE TO VISIT.
SHE SAID SHE WANTED TO SPEAK TO KITA...
I LEFT SO THEY COULD TALK IN PRIVATE, SO I DON'T REALLY KNOW WHAT THEY TALKED ABOUT, BUT...

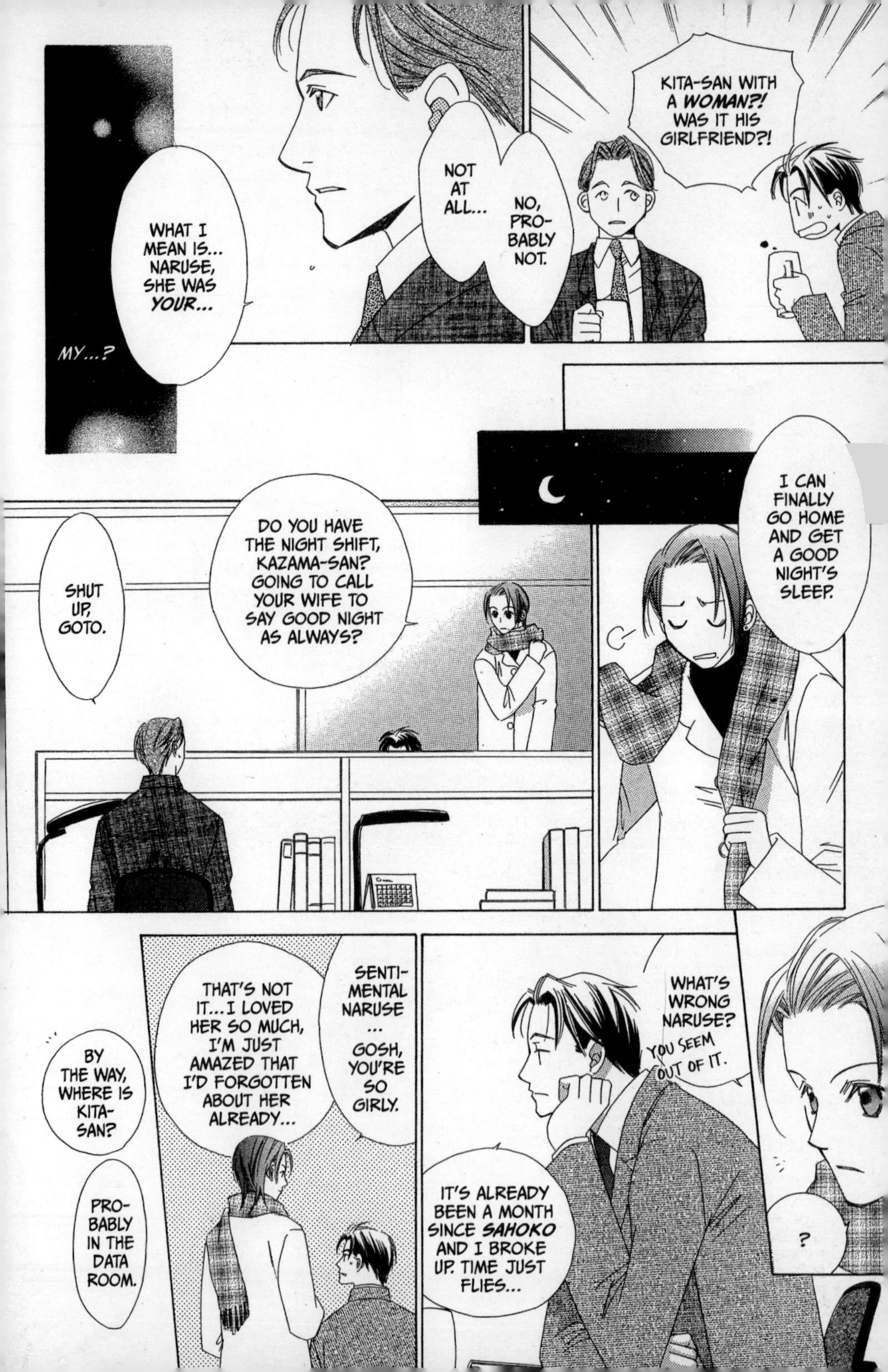
KITA-SAN WITH A *WOMAN?!* WAS IT HIS GIRLFRIEND?!
NOT AT ALL...
NO, PRO-BABLY NOT.
WHAT I MEAN IS... NARUSE, SHE WAS *YOUR...*
MY...?
I CAN FINALLY GO HOME AND GET A GOOD NIGHT'S SLEEP.
DO YOU HAVE THE NIGHT SHIFT, KAZAMA-SAN? GOING TO CALL YOUR WIFE TO SAY GOOD NIGHT AS ALWAYS?
SHUT UP, GOTO.
WHAT'S WRONG NARUSE?
YOU SEEM OUT OF IT.
?
IT'S ALREADY BEEN A MONTH SINCE *SAHOKO* AND I BROKE UP. TIME JUST FLIES...
SENTI-MENTAL NARUSE ... GOSH, YOU'RE SO GIRLY.
THAT'S NOT IT... I LOVED HER SO MUCH, I'M JUST AMAZED THAT I'D FORGOTTEN ABOUT HER ALREADY...
BY THE WAY, WHERE IS KITA-SAN?
PRO-BABLY IN THE DATA ROOM.

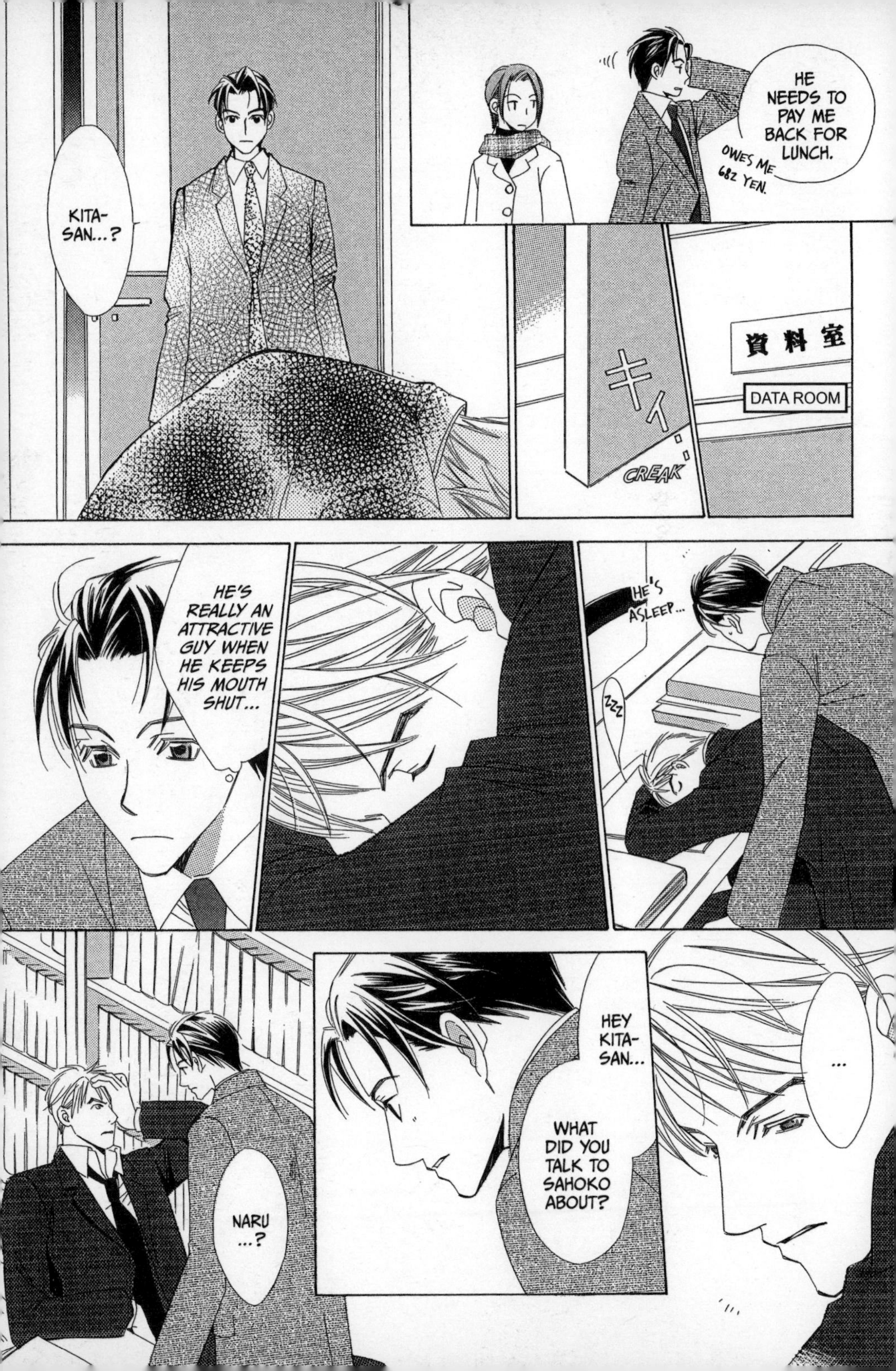
HE NEEDS TO PAY ME BACK FOR LUNCH.
OWES ME 682 YEN.
資料室
DATA ROOM
キイ
CREAK
KITA-SAN...?
HE'S ASLEEP...
ZZZ
HE'S REALLY AN ATTRACTIVE GUY WHEN HE KEEPS HIS MOUTH SHUT...
...
HEY KITA-SAN...
WHAT DID YOU TALK TO SAHOKO ABOUT?
NARU ...?

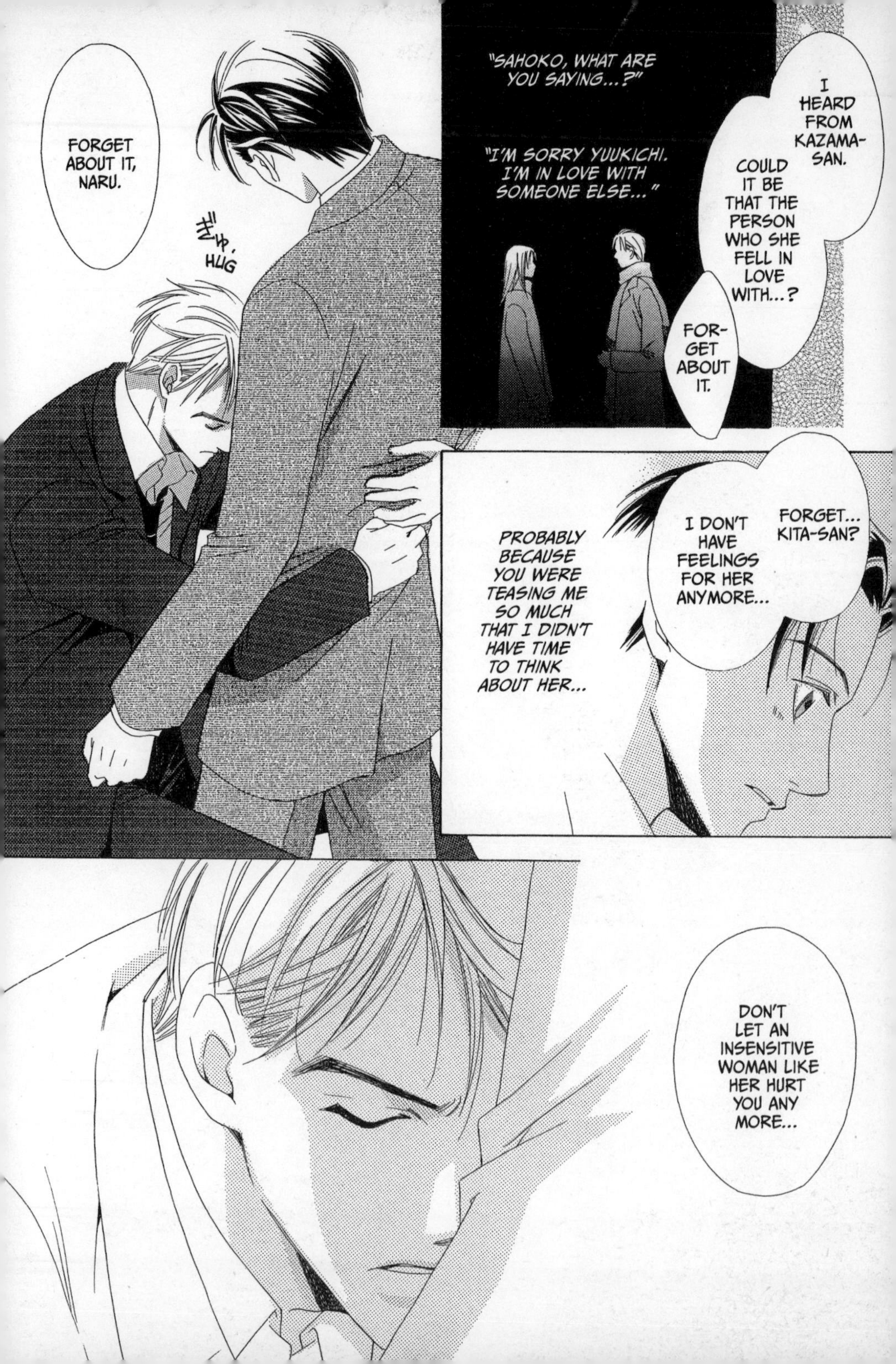
I HEARD FROM KAZAMA-SAN.
COULD IT BE THAT THE PERSON WHO SHE FELL IN LOVE WITH...?
"SAHOKO, WHAT ARE YOU SAYING...?"
"I'M SORRY YUUKICHI. I'M IN LOVE WITH SOMEONE ELSE..."
FOR-GET ABOUT IT.
FORGET... KITA-SAN?
I DON'T HAVE FEELINGS FOR HER ANYMORE...
PROBABLY BECAUSE YOU WERE TEASING ME SO MUCH THAT I DIDN'T HAVE TIME TO THINK ABOUT HER...
FORGET ABOUT IT, NARU.
ぎゅ, HUG
DON'T LET AN INSENSITIVE WOMAN LIKE HER HURT YOU ANY MORE...

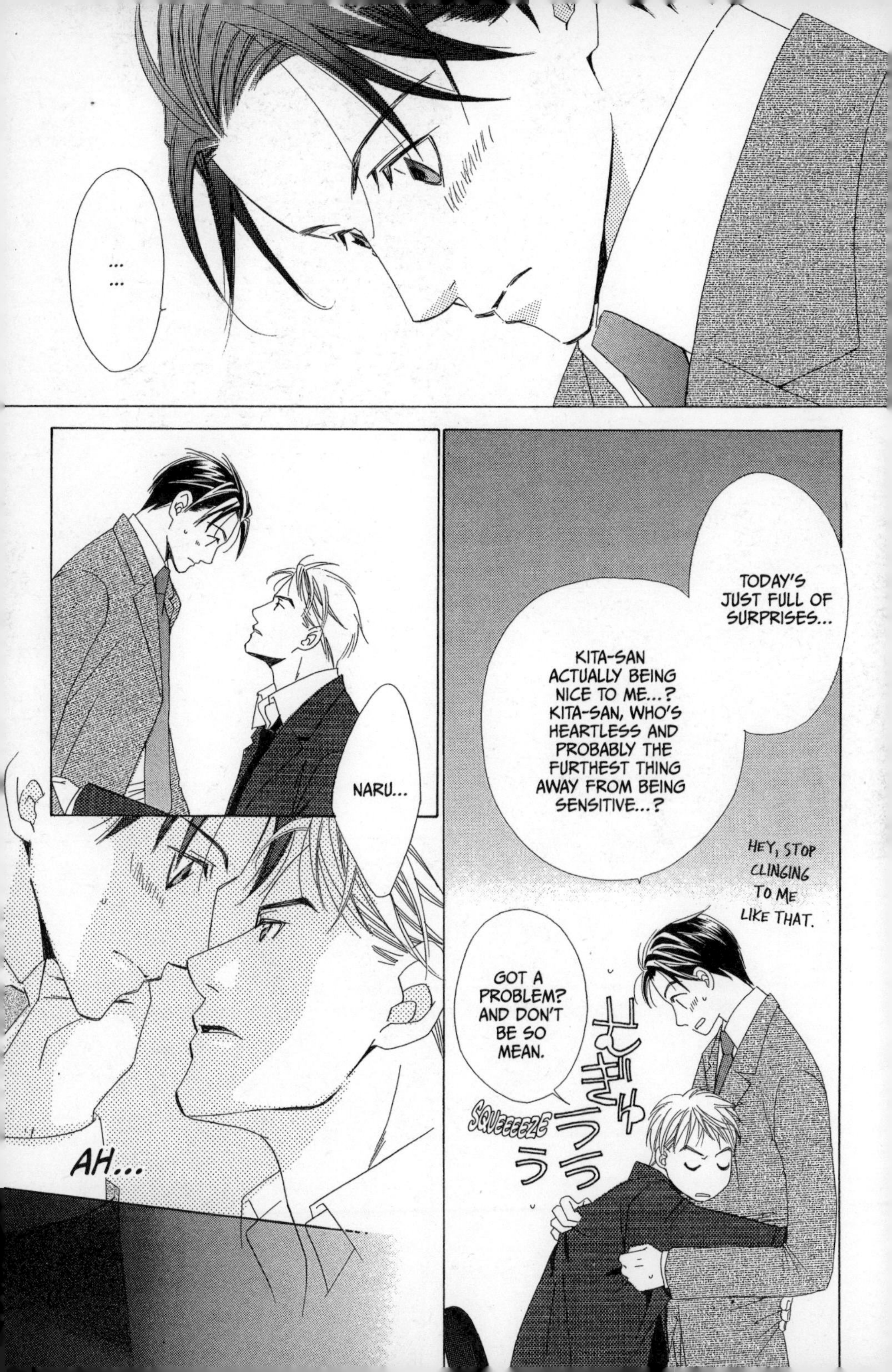
......
TODAY'S JUST FULL OF SURPRISES...
KITA-SAN ACTUALLY BEING NICE TO ME...? KITA-SAN, WHO'S HEARTLESS AND PROBABLY THE FURTHEST THING AWAY FROM BEING SENSITIVE...?
HEY, STOP CLINGING TO ME LIKE THAT.
GOT A PROBLEM? AND DON'T BE SO MEAN.
むぎゅううう
SQUEEEEEZE
NARU...
AH...

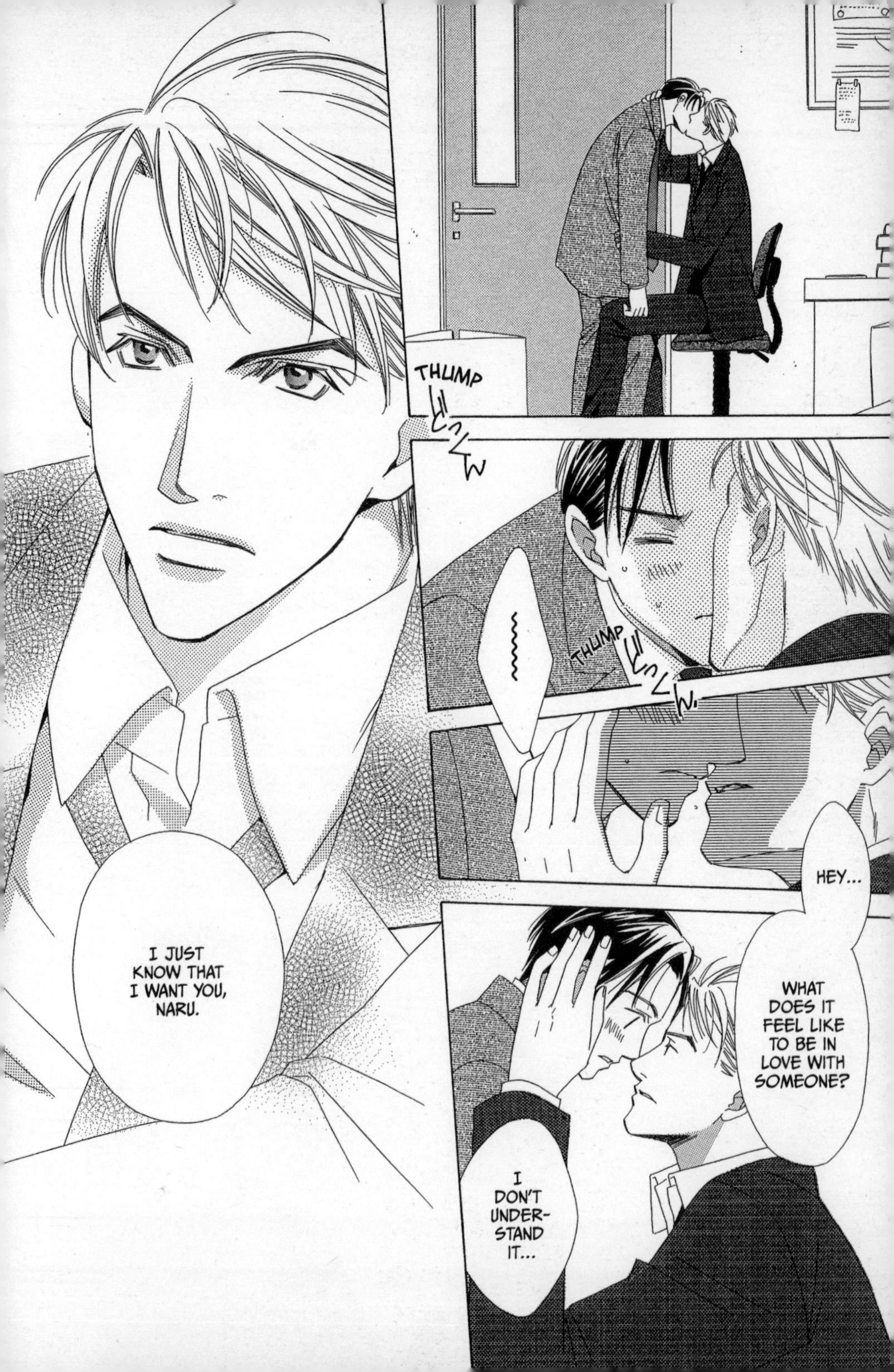
THUMP
THUMP
HEY...
WHAT DOES IT FEEL LIKE TO BE IN LOVE WITH SOMEONE?
I DON'T UNDER-STAND IT...
I JUST KNOW THAT I WANT YOU, NARU.

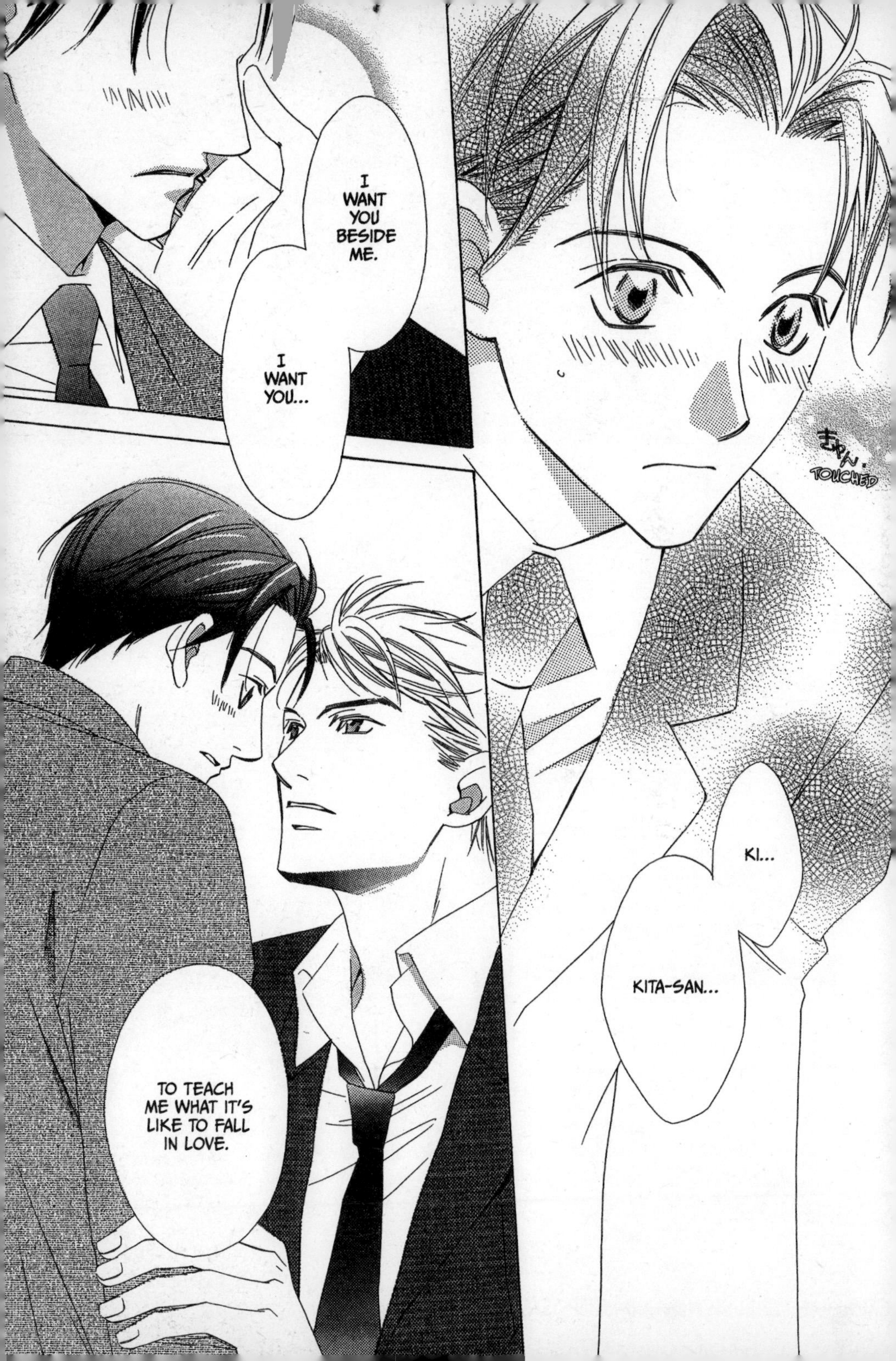
TOUCHED
KI...
KITA-SAN...
I WANT YOU BESIDE ME.
I WANT YOU...
TO TEACH ME WHAT IT'S LIKE TO FALL IN LOVE.

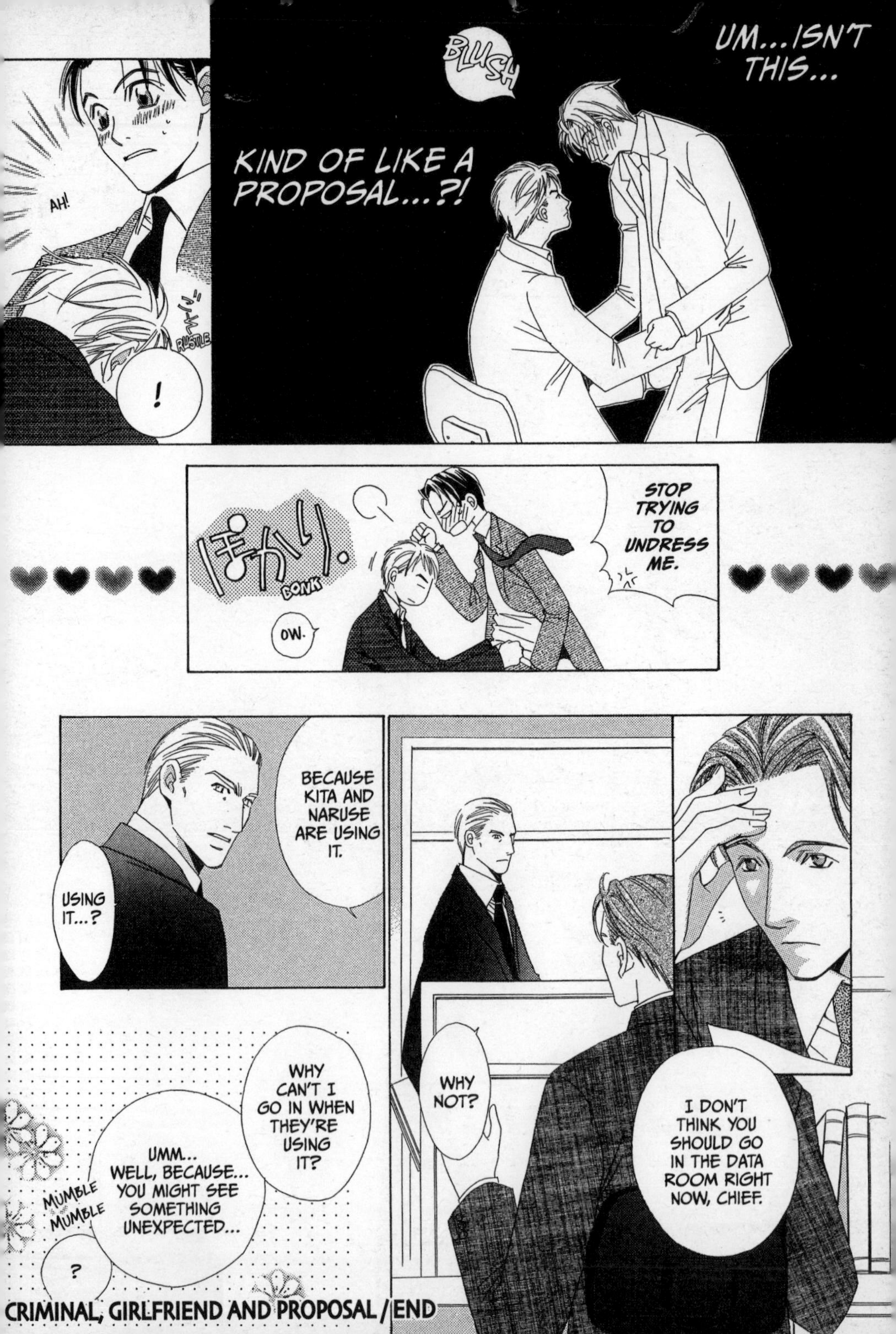
UM...ISN'T THIS...
BLUSH
KIND OF LIKE A PROPOSAL...?!
AH!
RUSTLE
!
STOP TRYING TO UNDRESS ME.
ぽかり
BONK
OW.
I DON'T THINK YOU SHOULD GO IN THE DATA ROOM RIGHT NOW, CHIEF.
WHY NOT?
BECAUSE KITA AND NARUSE ARE USING IT.
USING IT...?
WHY CAN'T I GO IN WHEN THEY'RE USING IT?
UMM.. WELL, BECAUSE... YOU MIGHT SEE SOMETHING UNEXPECTED...
MUMBLE MUMBLE
?

CRIMINAL, GIRLFRIEND AND PROPOSAL / END

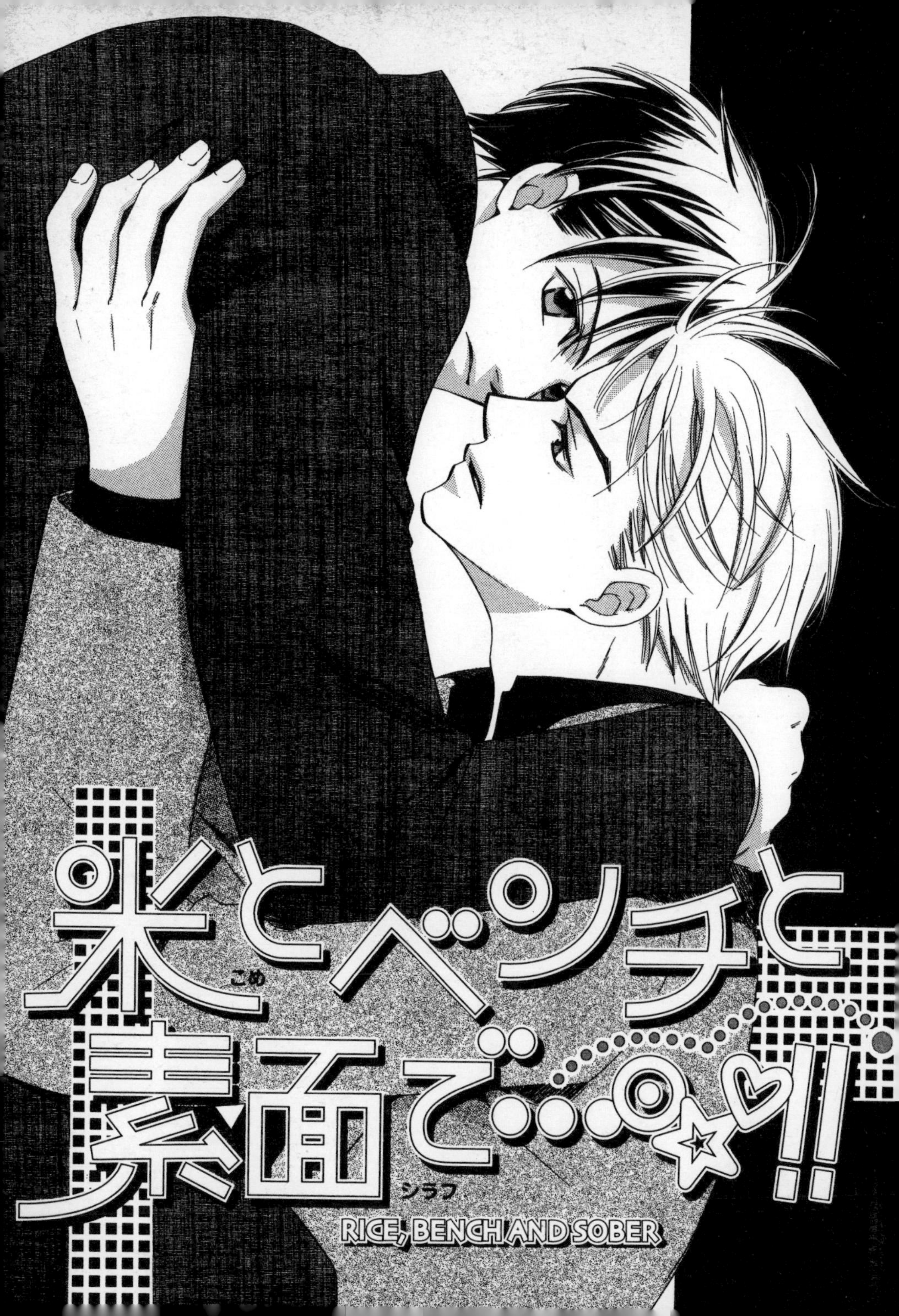
米(こめ)とベンチと素面(シラフ)で…♥!!
RICE, BENCH AND SOBER

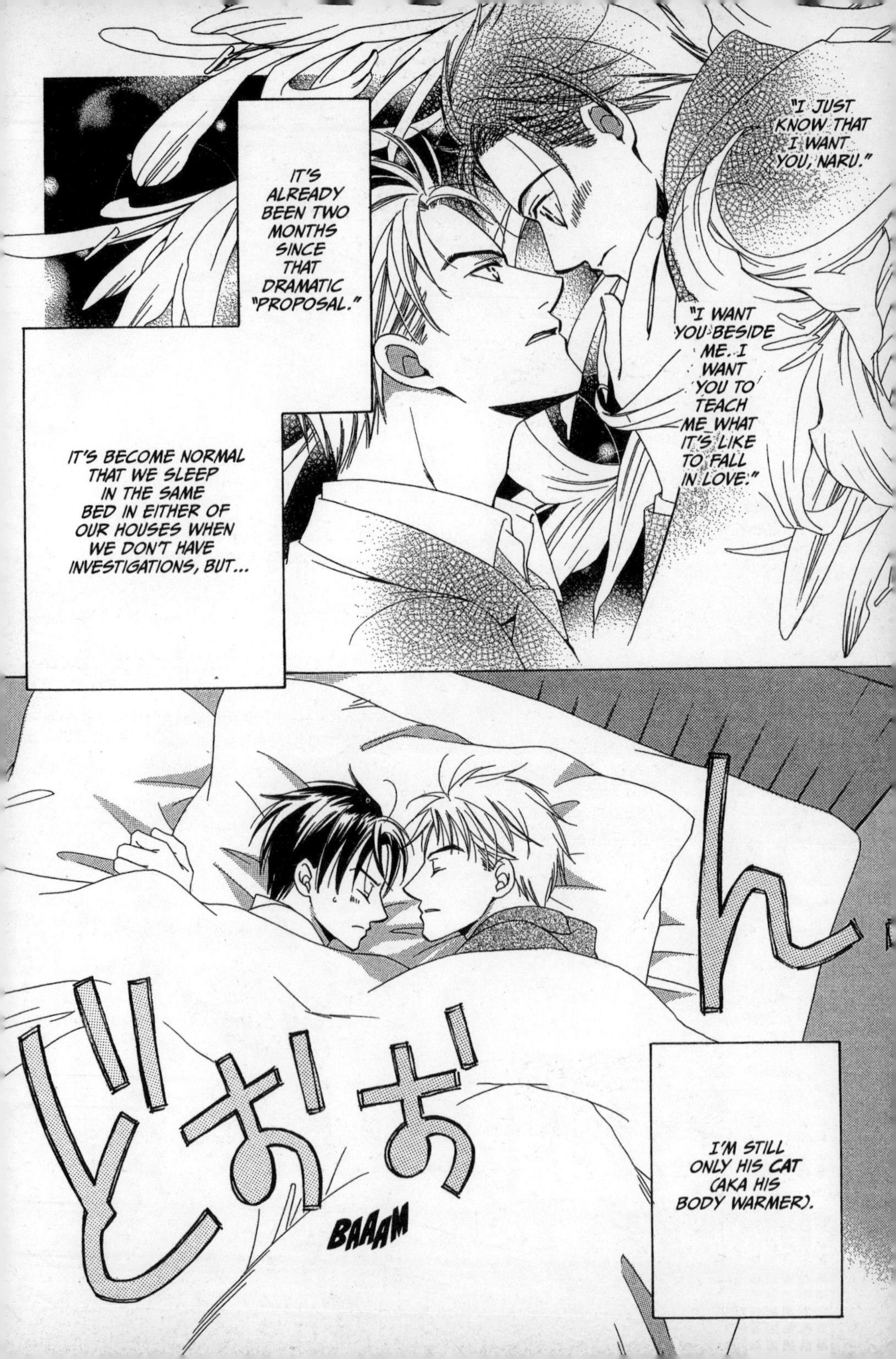
"I JUST KNOW THAT I WANT YOU, NARU."
"I WANT YOU BESIDE ME. I WANT YOU TO TEACH ME WHAT IT'S LIKE TO FALL IN LOVE."
IT'S ALREADY BEEN TWO MONTHS SINCE THAT DRAMATIC "PROPOSAL."
IT'S BECOME NORMAL THAT WE SLEEP IN THE SAME BED IN EITHER OF OUR HOUSES WHEN WE DON'T HAVE INVESTIGATIONS, BUT...
I'M STILL ONLY HIS CAT (AKA HIS BODY WARMER).
BAAAM

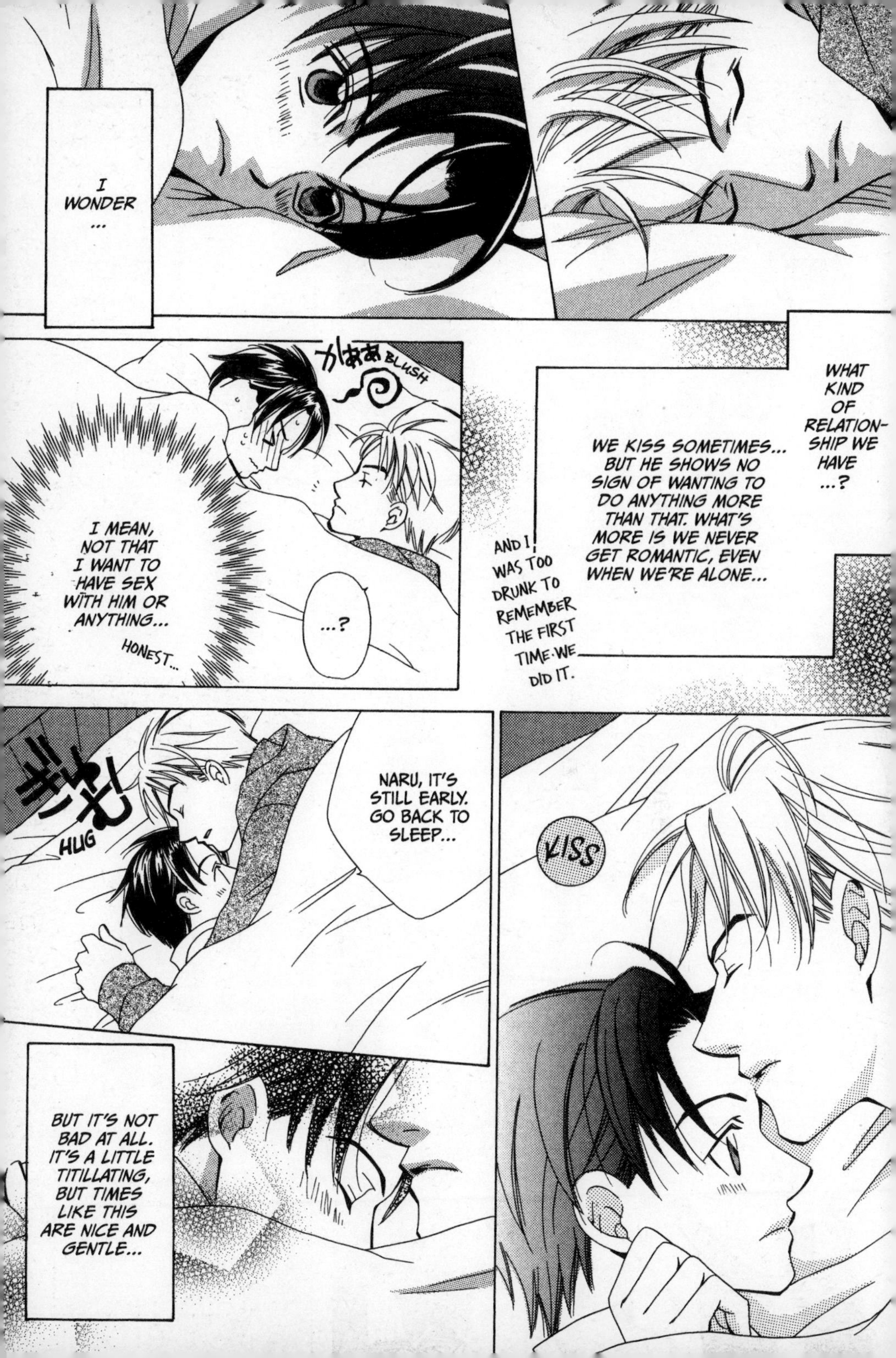
I WONDER ...
WHAT KIND OF RELATION-SHIP WE HAVE ...?
WE KISS SOMETIMES... BUT HE SHOWS NO SIGN OF WANTING TO DO ANYTHING MORE THAN THAT. WHAT'S MORE IS WE NEVER GET ROMANTIC, EVEN WHEN WE'RE ALONE...
AND I WAS TOO DRUNK TO REMEMBER THE FIRST TIME WE DID IT.
かああ BLUSH
I MEAN, NOT THAT I WANT TO HAVE SEX WITH HIM OR ANYTHING...
HONEST...
...?
KISS
HUG
NARU, IT'S STILL EARLY. GO BACK TO SLEEP...
BUT IT'S NOT BAD AT ALL. IT'S A LITTLE TITILLATING, BUT TIMES LIKE THIS ARE NICE AND GENTLE...

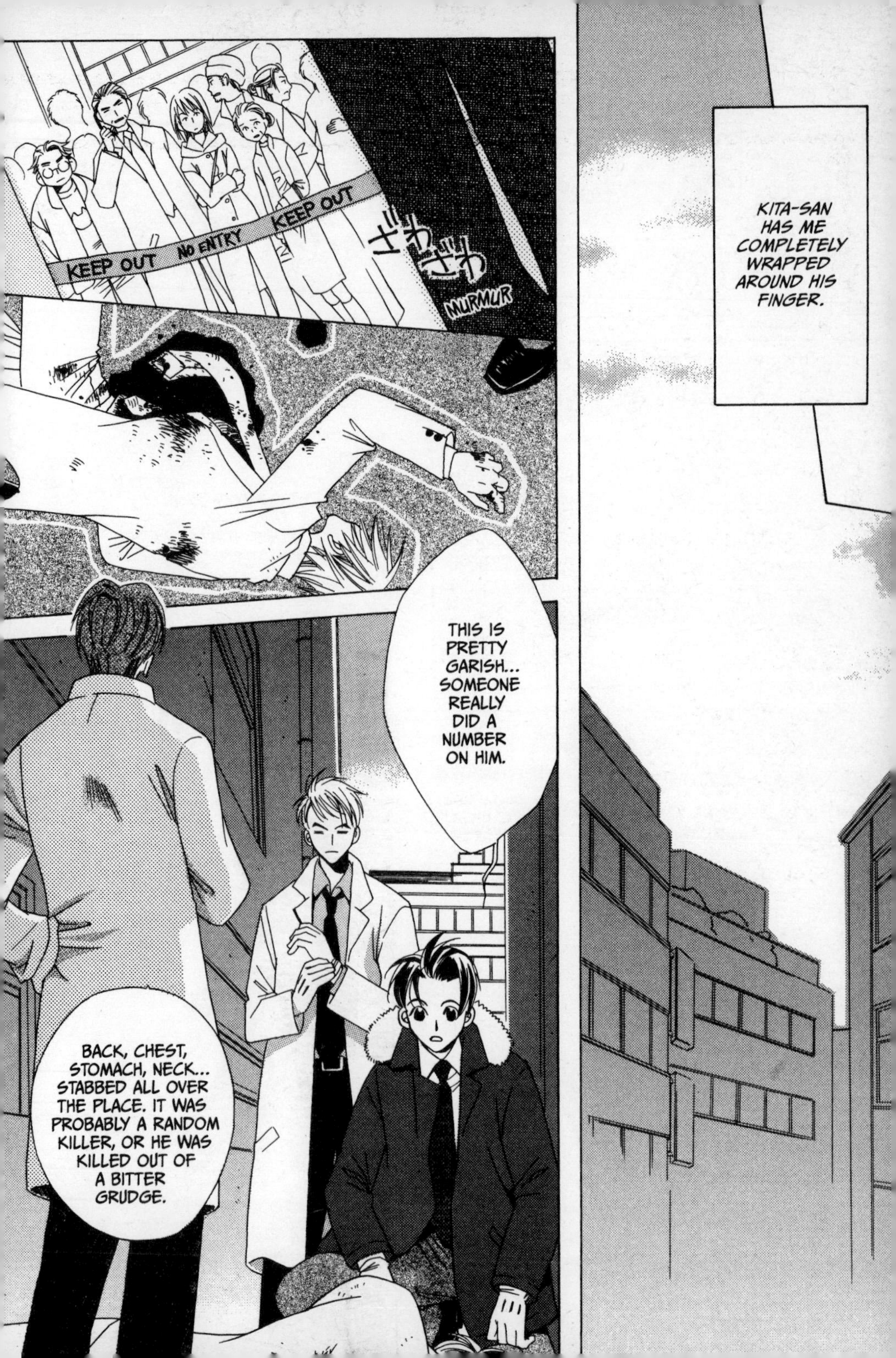
KITA-SAN HAS ME COMPLETELY WRAPPED AROUND HIS FINGER.
ざわざわ
MURMUR
KEEP OUT
NO ENTRY
KEEP OUT
THIS IS PRETTY GARISH... SOMEONE REALLY DID A NUMBER ON HIM.
BACK, CHEST, STOMACH, NECK... STABBED ALL OVER THE PLACE. IT WAS PROBABLY A RANDOM KILLER, OR HE WAS KILLED OUT OF A BITTER GRUDGE.

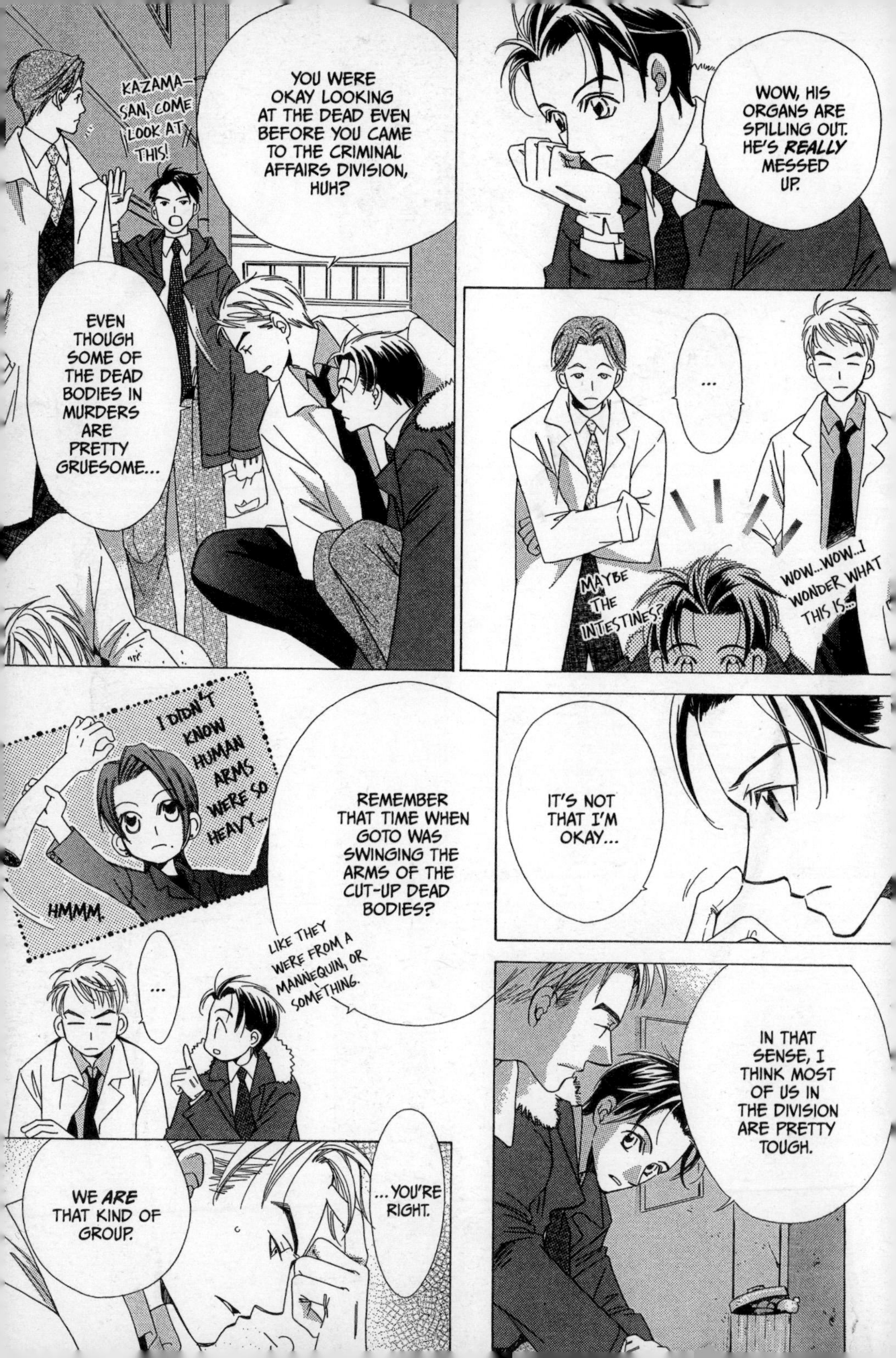
WOW, HIS ORGANS ARE SPILLING OUT. HE'S *REALLY* MESSED UP.
...
WOW...WOW...I WONDER WHAT THIS IS...
MAYBE THE INTESTINES?
YOU WERE OKAY LOOKING AT THE DEAD EVEN BEFORE YOU CAME TO THE CRIMINAL AFFAIRS DIVISION, HUH?
KAZAMA-SAN, COME LOOK AT THIS!
EVEN THOUGH SOME OF THE DEAD BODIES IN MURDERS ARE PRETTY GRUESOME...
IT'S NOT THAT I'M OKAY...
REMEMBER THAT TIME WHEN GOTO WAS SWINGING THE ARMS OF THE CUT-UP DEAD BODIES?
I DIDN'T KNOW HUMAN ARMS WERE SO HEAVY...
HMMM.
IN THAT SENSE, I THINK MOST OF US IN THE DIVISION ARE PRETTY TOUGH.
LIKE THEY WERE FROM A MANNEQUIN, OR SOMETHING.
...
...YOU'RE RIGHT.
WE *ARE* THAT KIND OF GROUP.

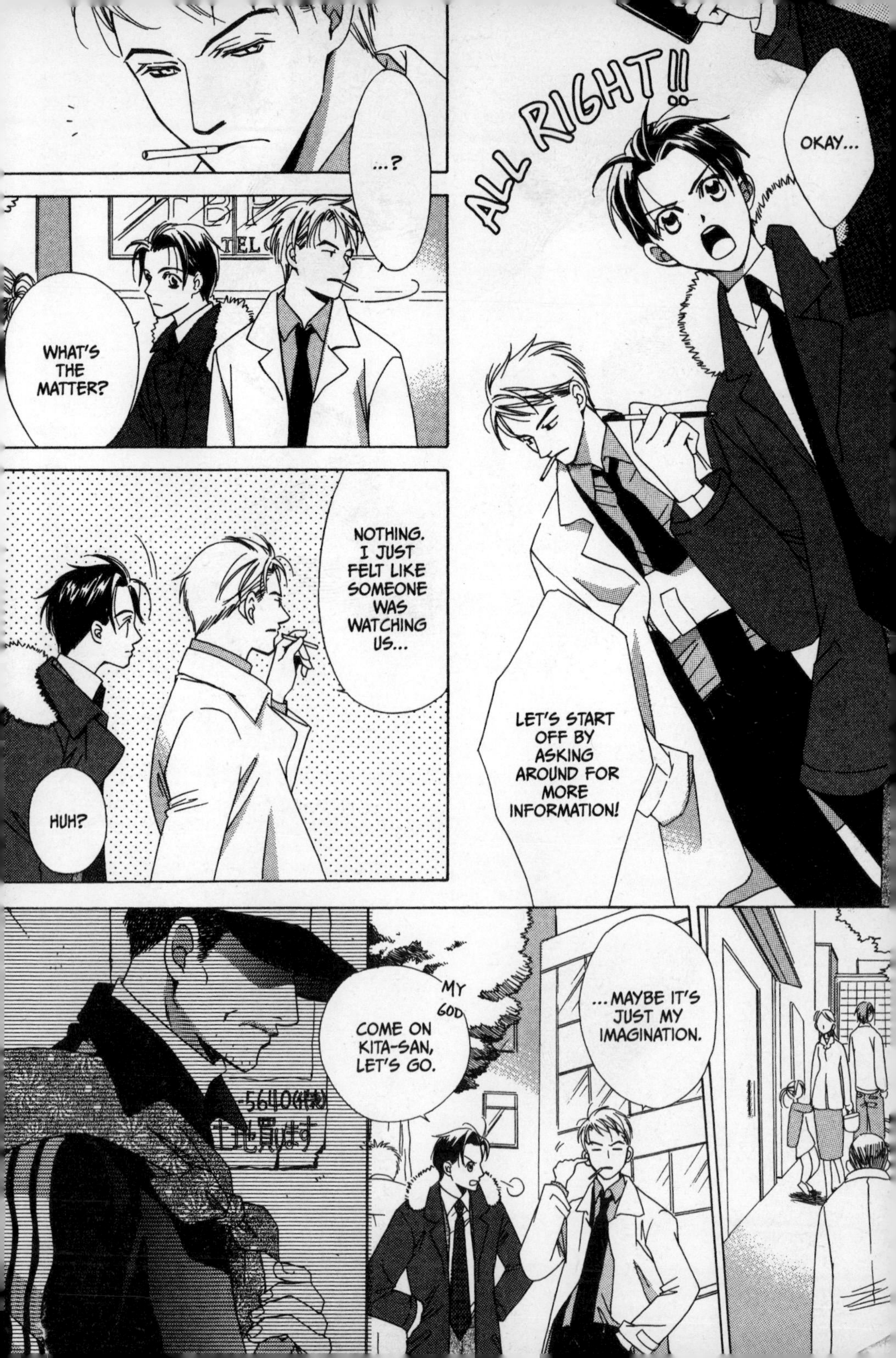
OKAY...
ALL RIGHT!!
LET'S START OFF BY ASKING AROUND FOR MORE INFORMATION!
...?
WHAT'S THE MATTER?
NOTHING. I JUST FELT LIKE SOMEONE WAS WATCHING US...
HUH?
...MAYBE IT'S JUST MY IMAGINATION.
COME ON KITA-SAN, LET'S GO.
MY GOD
-5640(代表)
土地買います

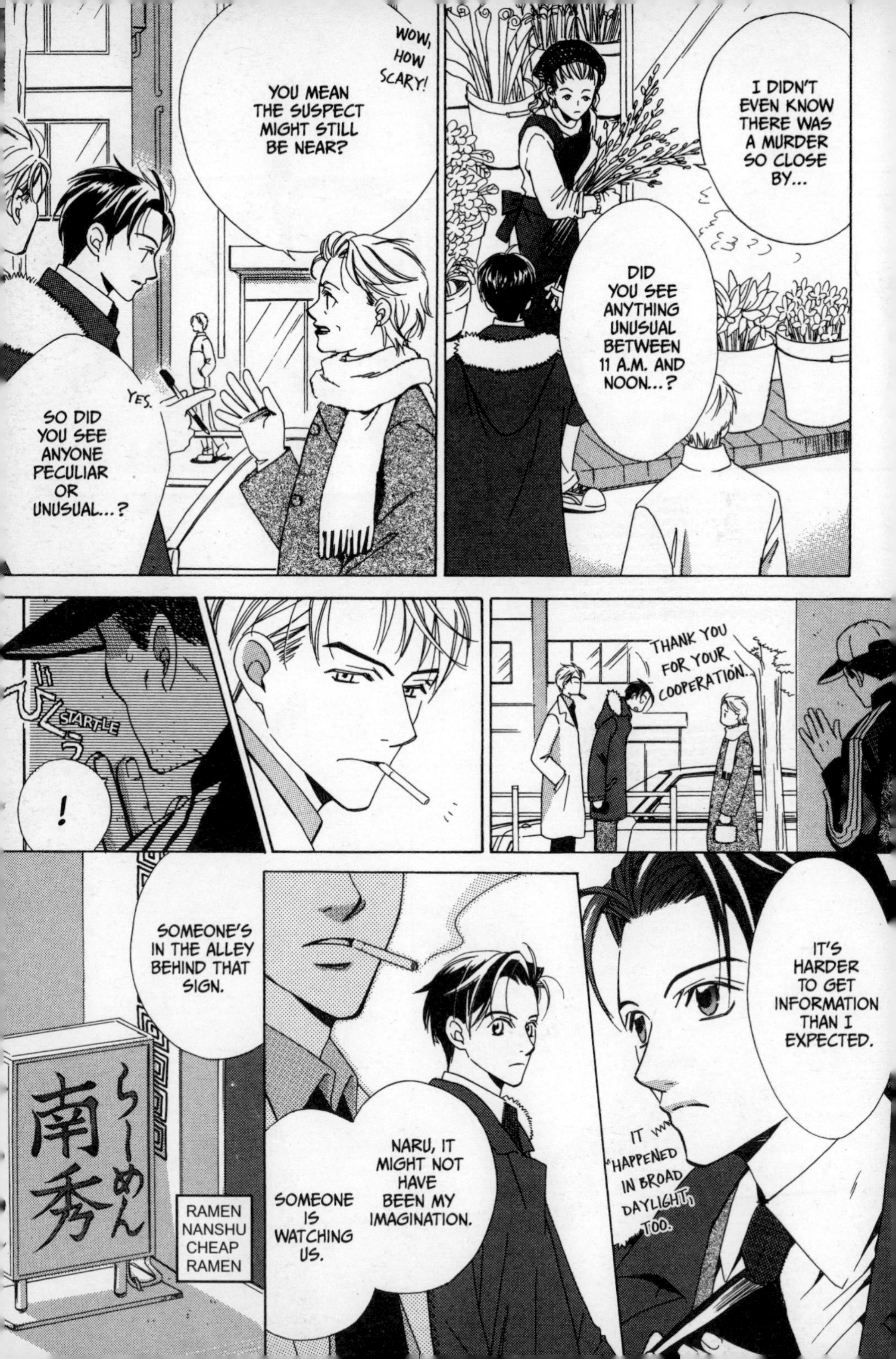

I DIDN'T EVEN KNOW THERE WAS A MURDER SO CLOSE BY...
DID YOU SEE ANYTHING UNUSUAL BETWEEN 11 A.M. AND NOON...?
WOW, HOW SCARY!
YOU MEAN THE SUSPECT MIGHT STILL BE NEAR?
YES.
SO DID YOU SEE ANYONE PECULIAR OR UNUSUAL...?
THANK YOU FOR YOUR COOPERATION.
STARTLE
!
IT'S HARDER TO GET INFORMATION THAN I EXPECTED.
IT HAPPENED IN BROAD DAYLIGHT, TOO.
NARU, IT MIGHT NOT HAVE BEEN MY IMAGINATION.
SOMEONE IS WATCHING US.
SOMEONE'S IN THE ALLEY BEHIND THAT SIGN.
らーめん 南秀
RAMEN NANSHU CHEAP RAMEN

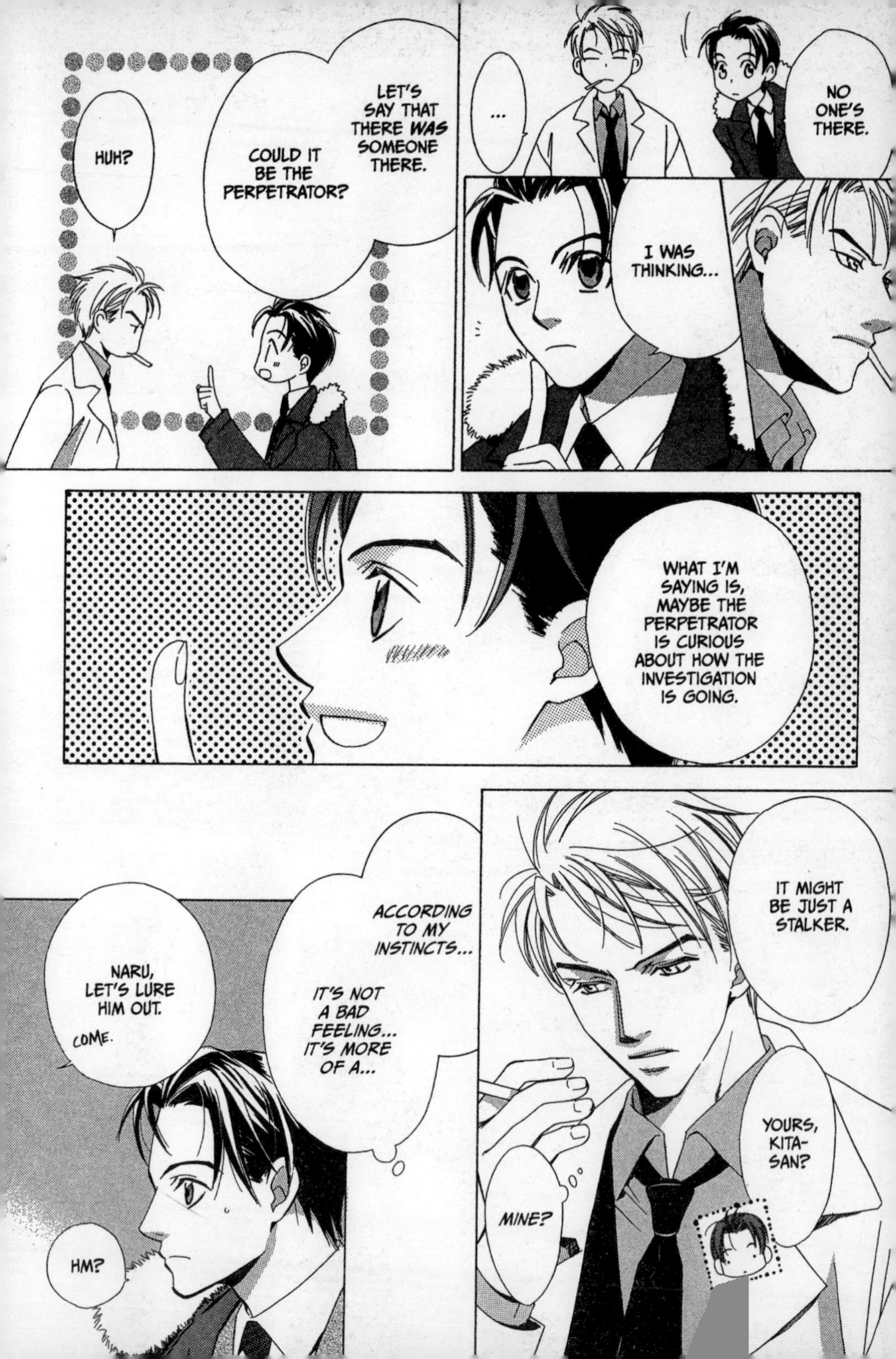
NO ONE'S THERE.
...
I WAS THINKING...
LET'S SAY THAT THERE *WAS* SOMEONE THERE.
COULD IT BE THE PERPETRATOR?
HUH?
WHAT I'M SAYING IS, MAYBE THE PERPETRATOR IS CURIOUS ABOUT HOW THE INVESTIGATION IS GOING.
IT MIGHT BE JUST A STALKER.
YOURS, KITA-SAN?
MINE?
ACCORDING TO MY INSTINCTS...
IT'S NOT A BAD FEELING... IT'S MORE OF A...
NARU, LET'S LURE HIM OUT.
COME.
HM?

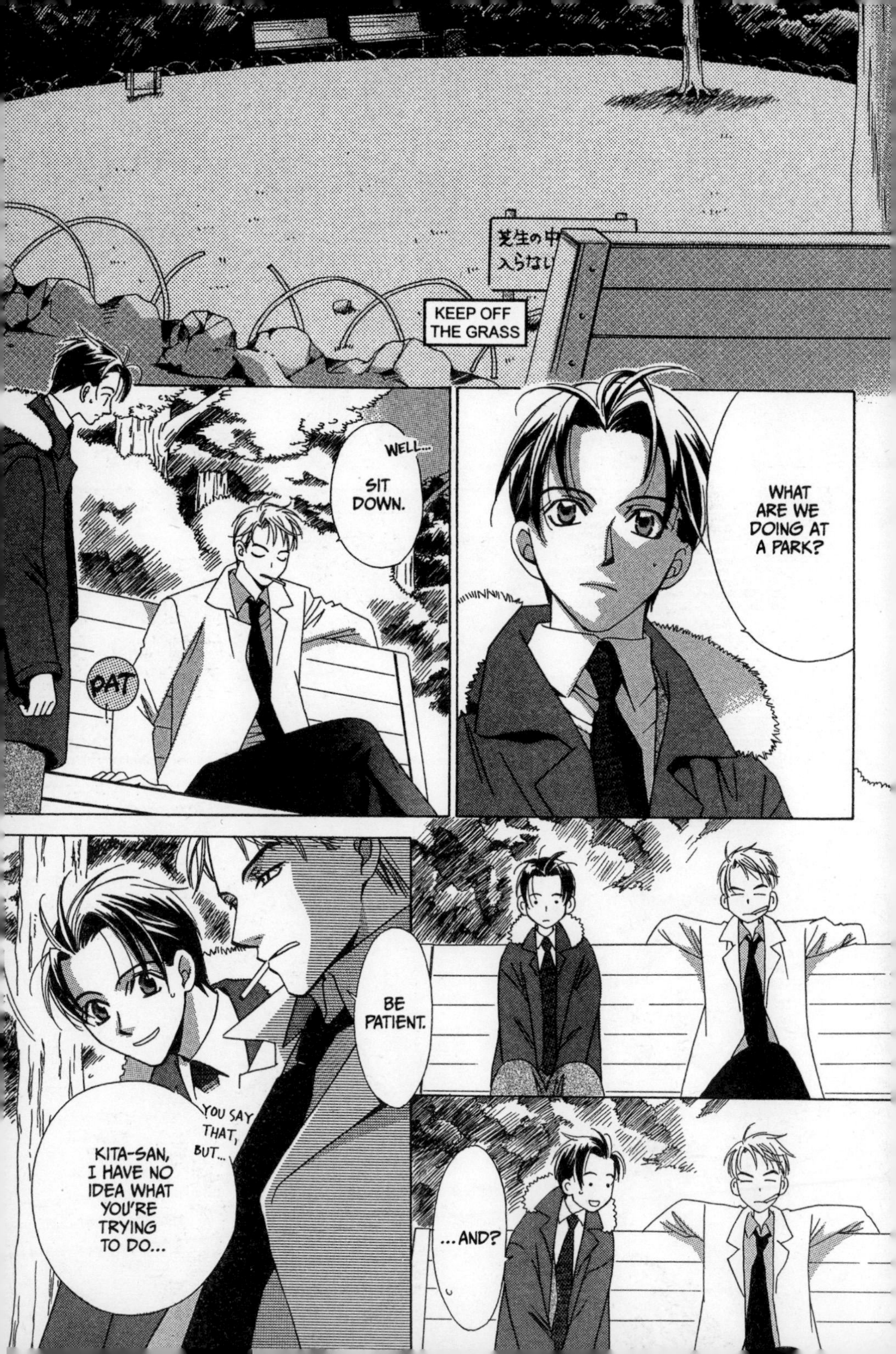
芝生の中
入らな
KEEP OFF THE GRASS
WHAT ARE WE DOING AT A PARK?
WELL...
SIT DOWN.
PAT
BE PATIENT.
...AND?
YOU SAY THAT, BUT...
KITA-SAN, I HAVE NO IDEA WHAT YOU'RE TRYING TO DO...

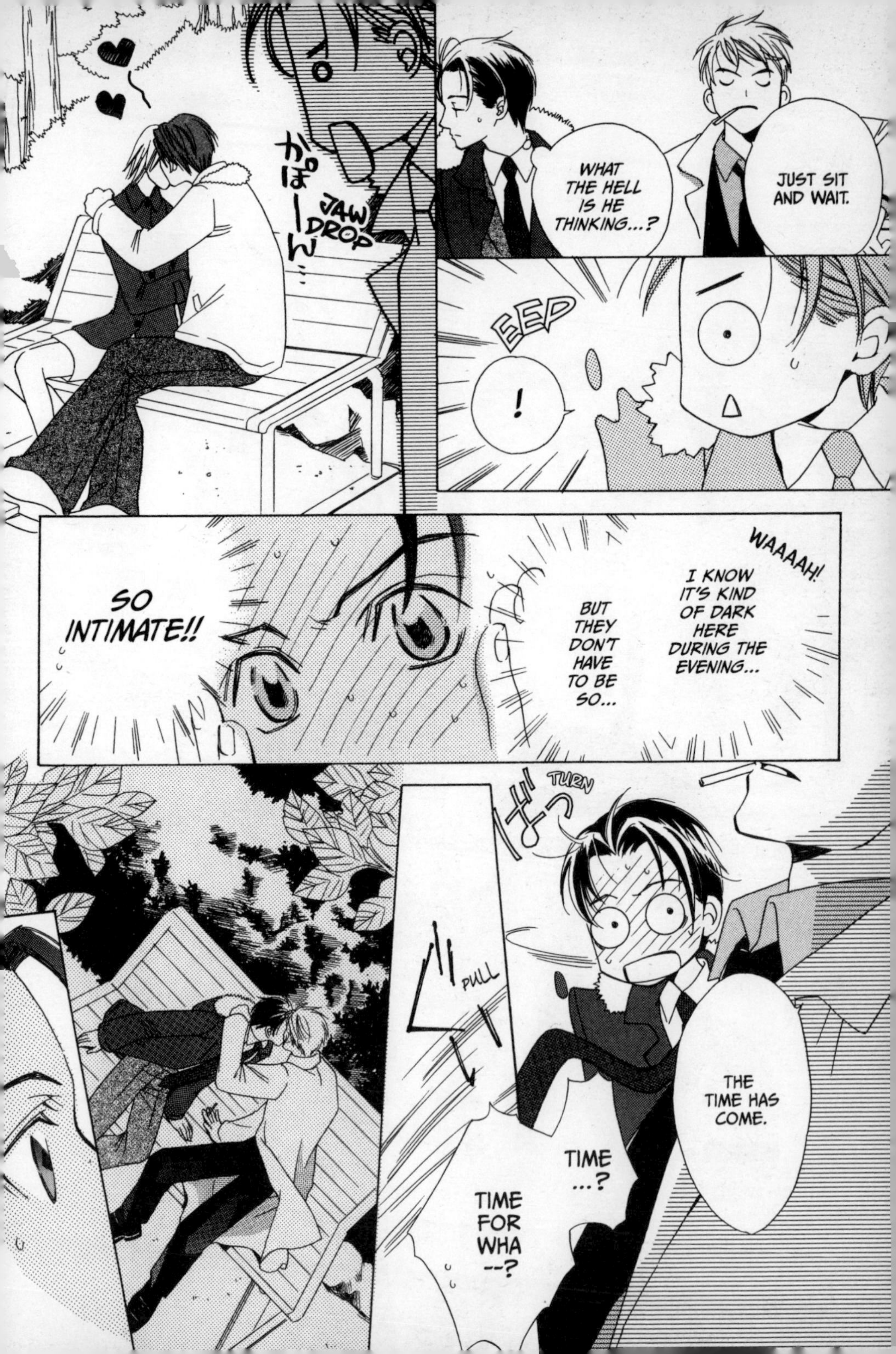
JUST SIT AND WAIT.
WHAT THE HELL IS HE THINKING...?
EEP
!
がぽーん…
JAW DROP
WAAAAH!
I KNOW IT'S KIND OF DARK HERE DURING THE EVENING...
BUT THEY DON'T HAVE TO BE SO...
SO INTIMATE!!
はっ
TURN
THE TIME HAS COME.
TIME ...?
TIME FOR WHA --?
PULL

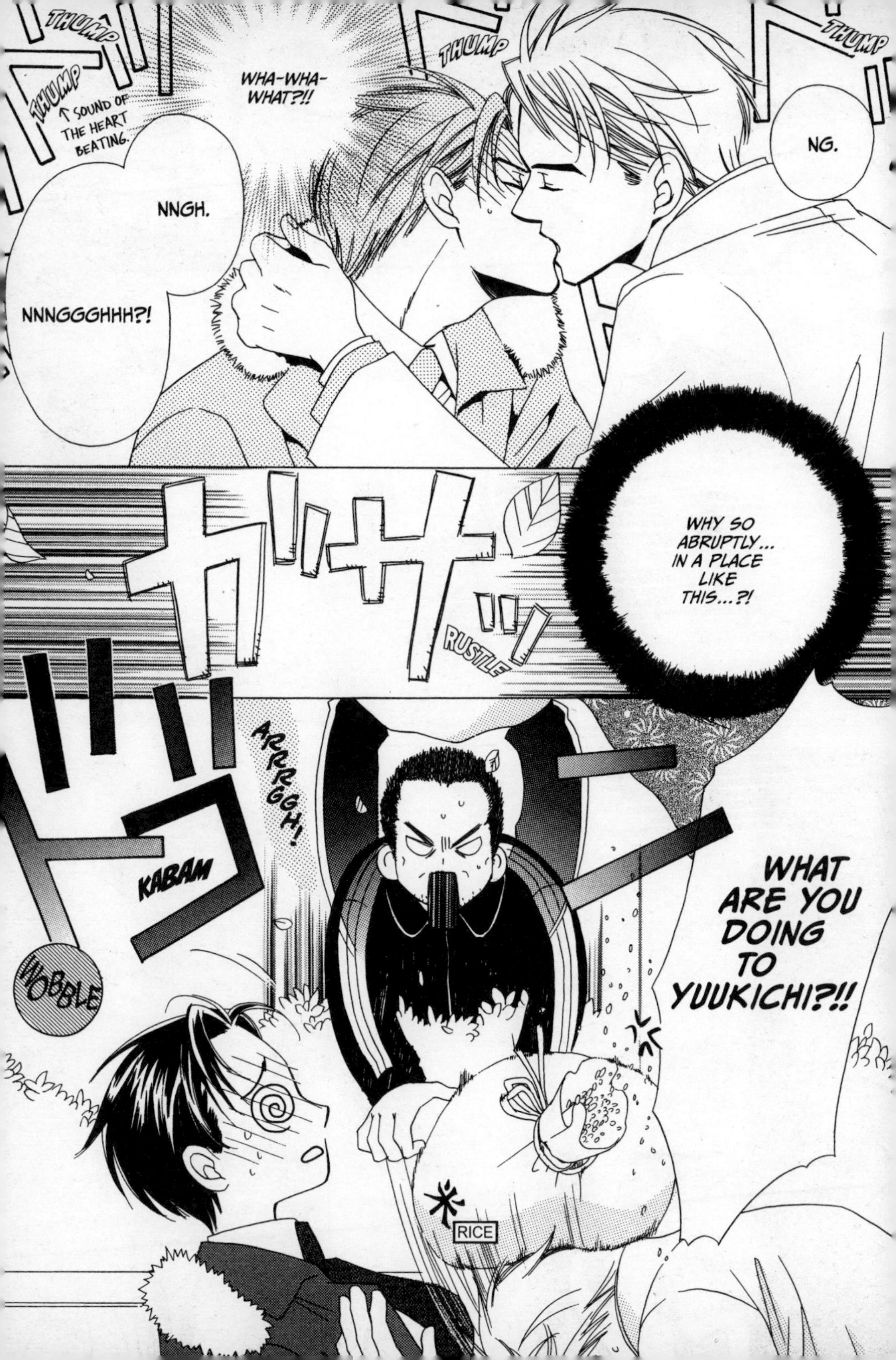
THUMP
NG.
THUMP
WHA-WHA-WHAT?!!
THUMP
THUMP
↑ SOUND OF THE HEART BEATING.
NNGH.
NNNGGGHHH?!
WHY SO ABRUPTLY... IN A PLACE LIKE THIS...?!
RUSTLE
WHAT ARE YOU DOING TO YUUKICHI?!!
ARRRGGH!
KABAM
WOBBLE
RICE

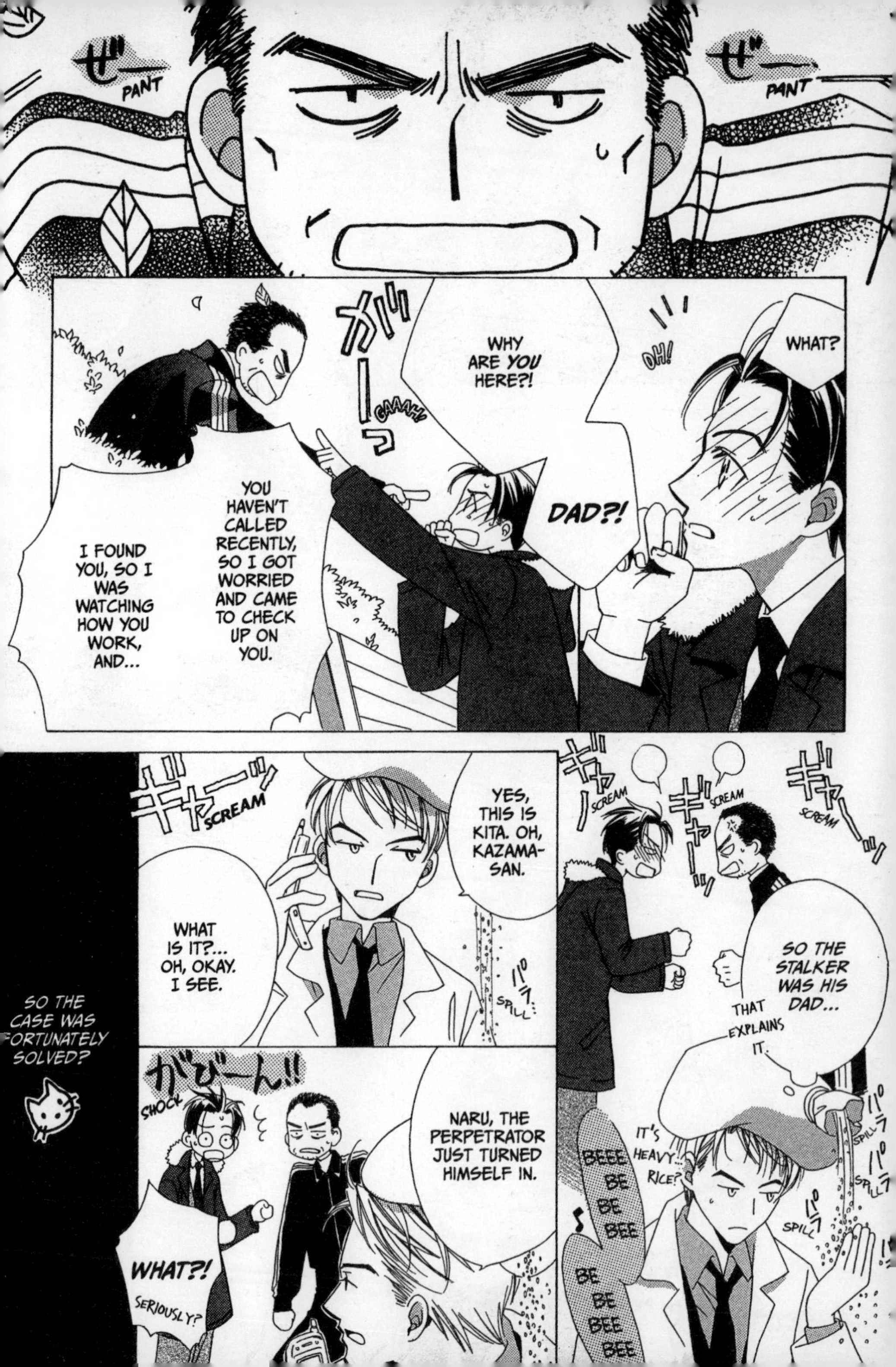
ゼー
PANT
ゼー
PANT
WHAT?
OH!
WHY ARE YOU HERE?!
DAD?!
がーっ
GAAAH!
YOU HAVEN'T CALLED RECENTLY, SO I GOT WORRIED AND CAME TO CHECK UP ON YOU.
I FOUND YOU, SO I WAS WATCHING HOW YOU WORK, AND...
ギャー
SCREAM
ギャー
SCREAM
ギャー
SCREAM
SO THE STALKER WAS HIS DAD...
THAT EXPLAINS IT.
パラ
SPILL
YES, THIS IS KITA. OH, KAZAMA-SAN.
WHAT IS IT?... OH, OKAY. I SEE.
ギャーッ
SCREAM
パラ
SPILL
パラ
SPILL
パラ
SPILL
IT'S HEAVY... RICE?
BEEE BE BE BEE
BE BE BEE BEE
NARU, THE PERPETRATOR JUST TURNED HIMSELF IN.
がびーん!!
SHOCK
WHAT?!
SERIOUSLY?
SO THE CASE WAS FORTUNATELY SOLVED?

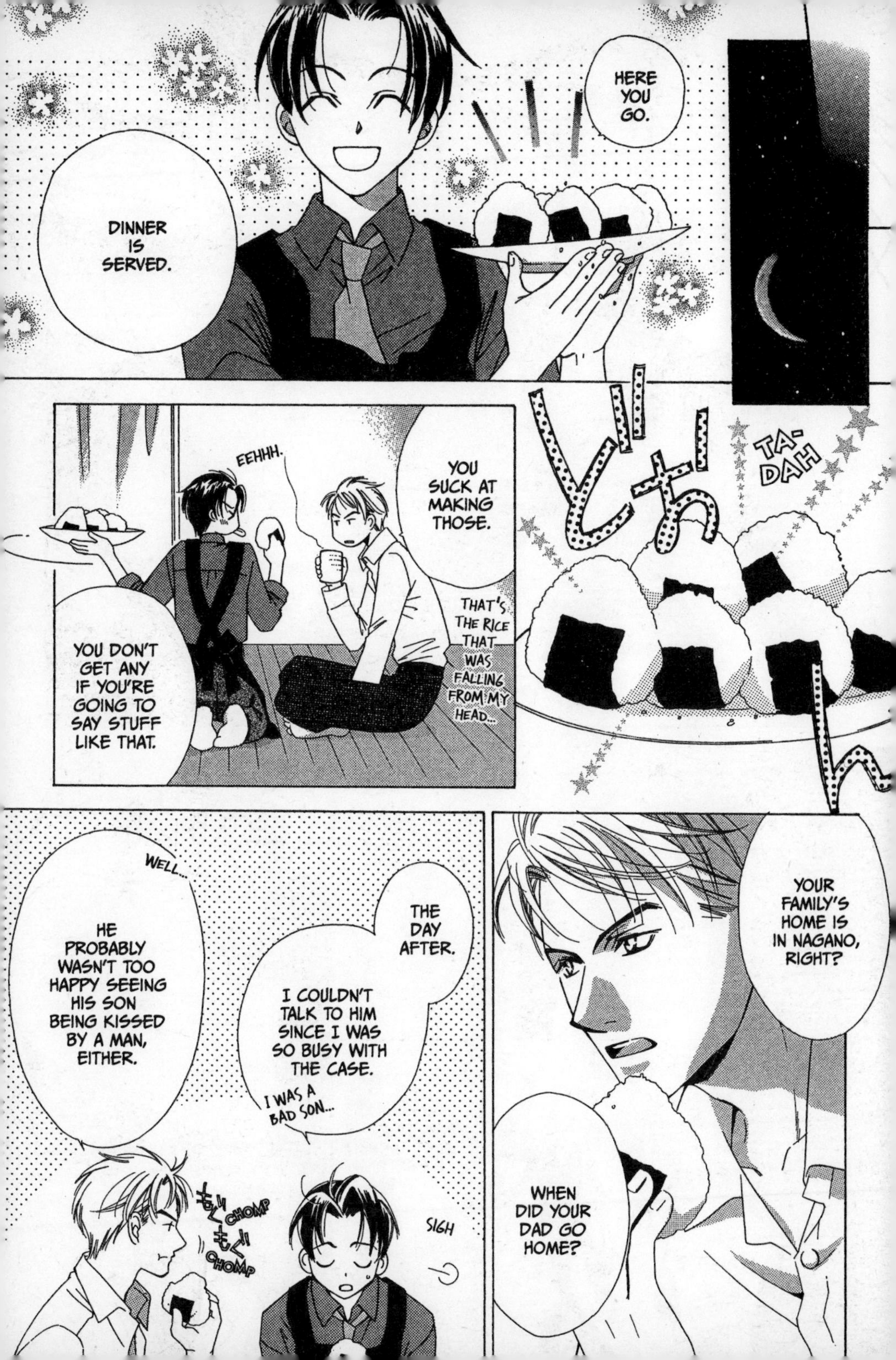
HERE YOU GO.
DINNER IS SERVED.
TA-DAH
YOU SUCK AT MAKING THOSE.
EEHHH.
THAT'S THE RICE THAT WAS FALLING FROM MY HEAD...
YOU DON'T GET ANY IF YOU'RE GOING TO SAY STUFF LIKE THAT.
YOUR FAMILY'S HOME IS IN NAGANO, RIGHT?
WHEN DID YOUR DAD GO HOME?
THE DAY AFTER.
I COULDN'T TALK TO HIM SINCE I WAS SO BUSY WITH THE CASE.
I WAS A BAD SON...
SIGH
WELL...
HE PROBABLY WASN'T TOO HAPPY SEEING HIS SON BEING KISSED BY A MAN, EITHER.
もぐ CHOMP
もぐ CHOMP

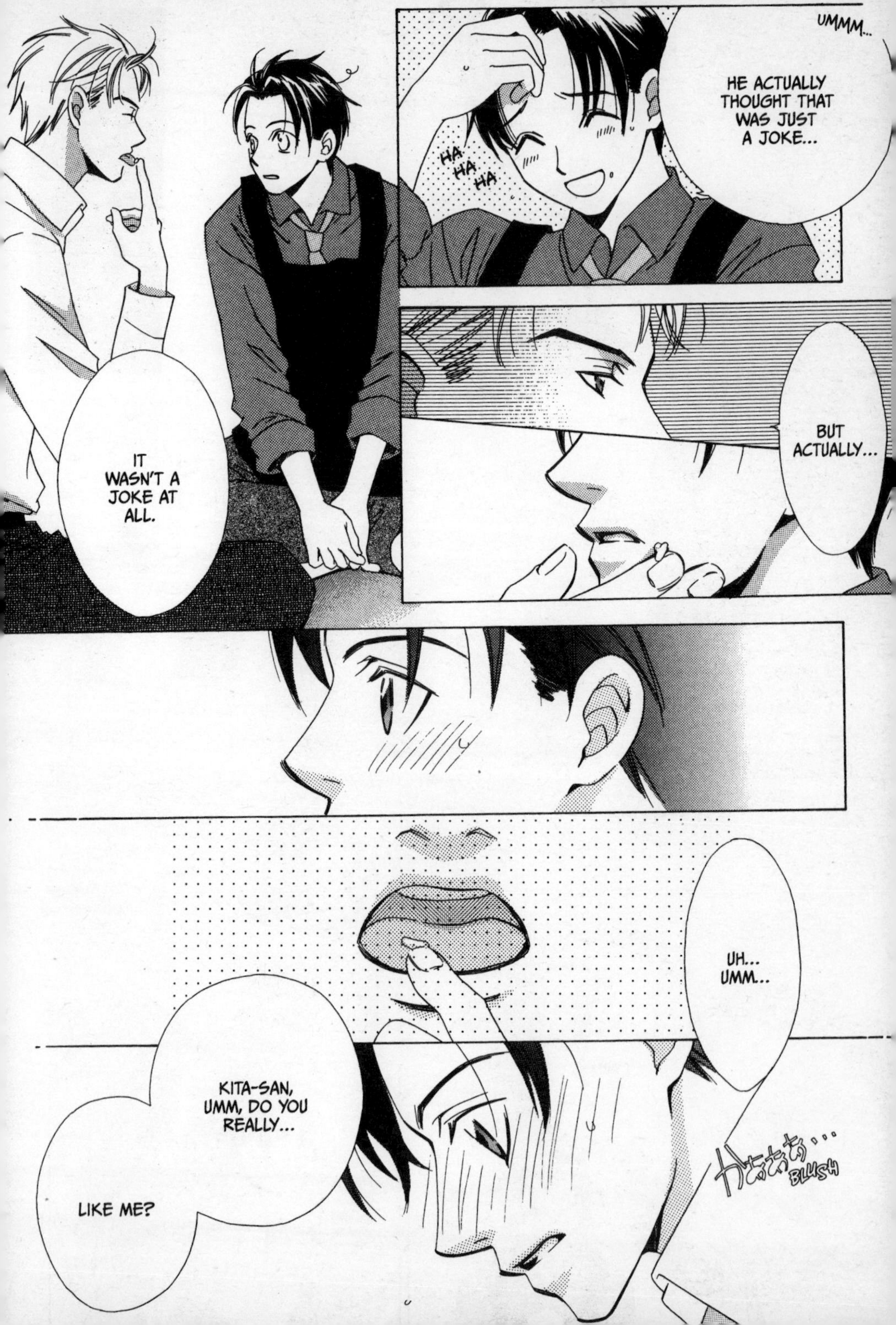
UMMM...
HE ACTUALLY THOUGHT THAT WAS JUST A JOKE...
HA HA HA
BUT ACTUALLY...
IT WASN'T A JOKE AT ALL.
UH... UMM...
BLUSH
KITA-SAN, UMM, DO YOU REALLY...
LIKE ME?

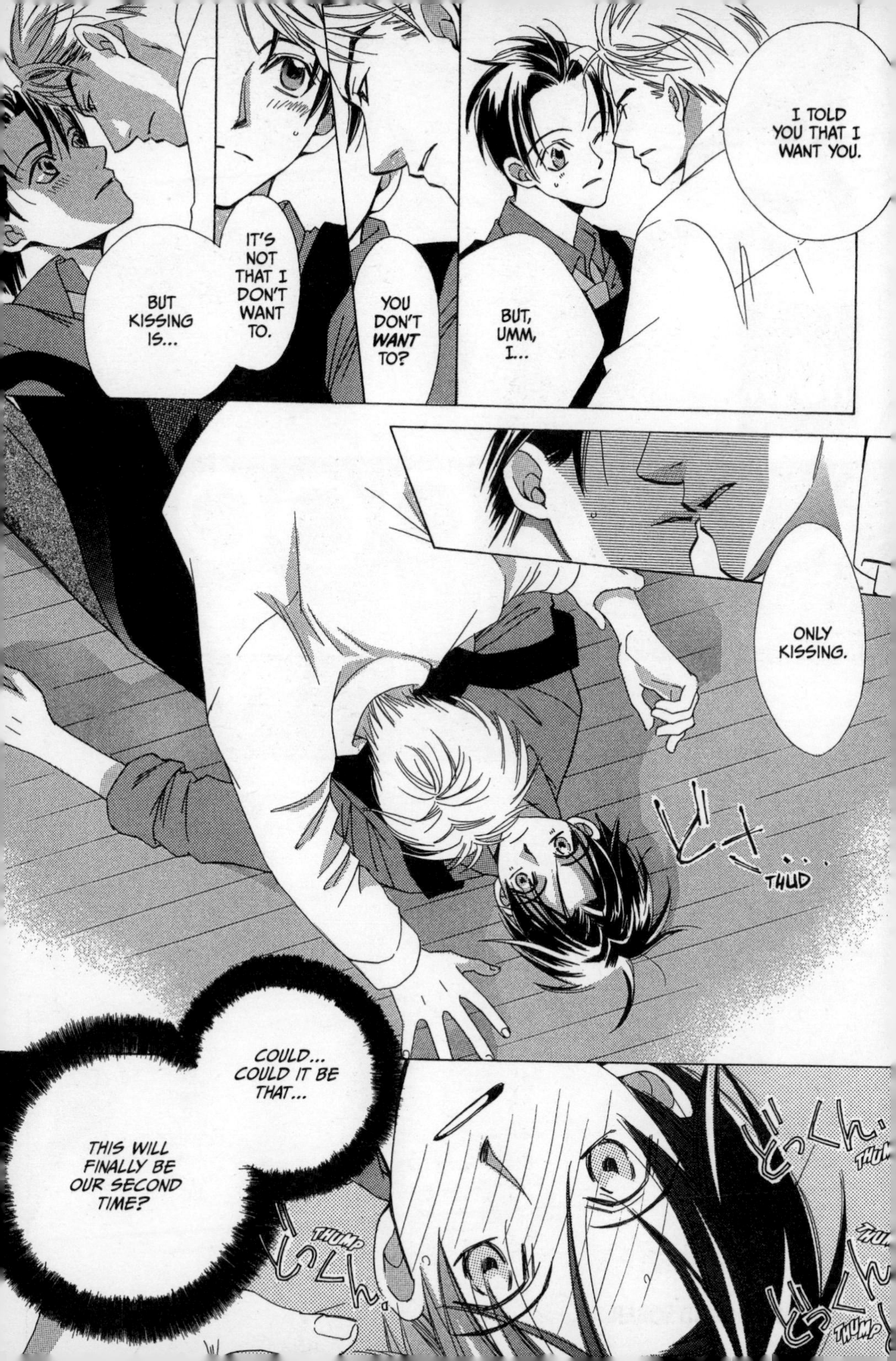
I TOLD YOU THAT I WANT YOU.
BUT, UMM, I...
YOU DON'T *WANT* TO?
IT'S NOT THAT I DON'T WANT TO.
BUT KISSING IS...
ONLY KISSING.
どさ…
THUD
どっくん
THUMP
どっくん
THUMP
COULD... COULD IT BE THAT...
THIS WILL FINALLY BE OUR SECOND TIME?
どっくん
THUMP

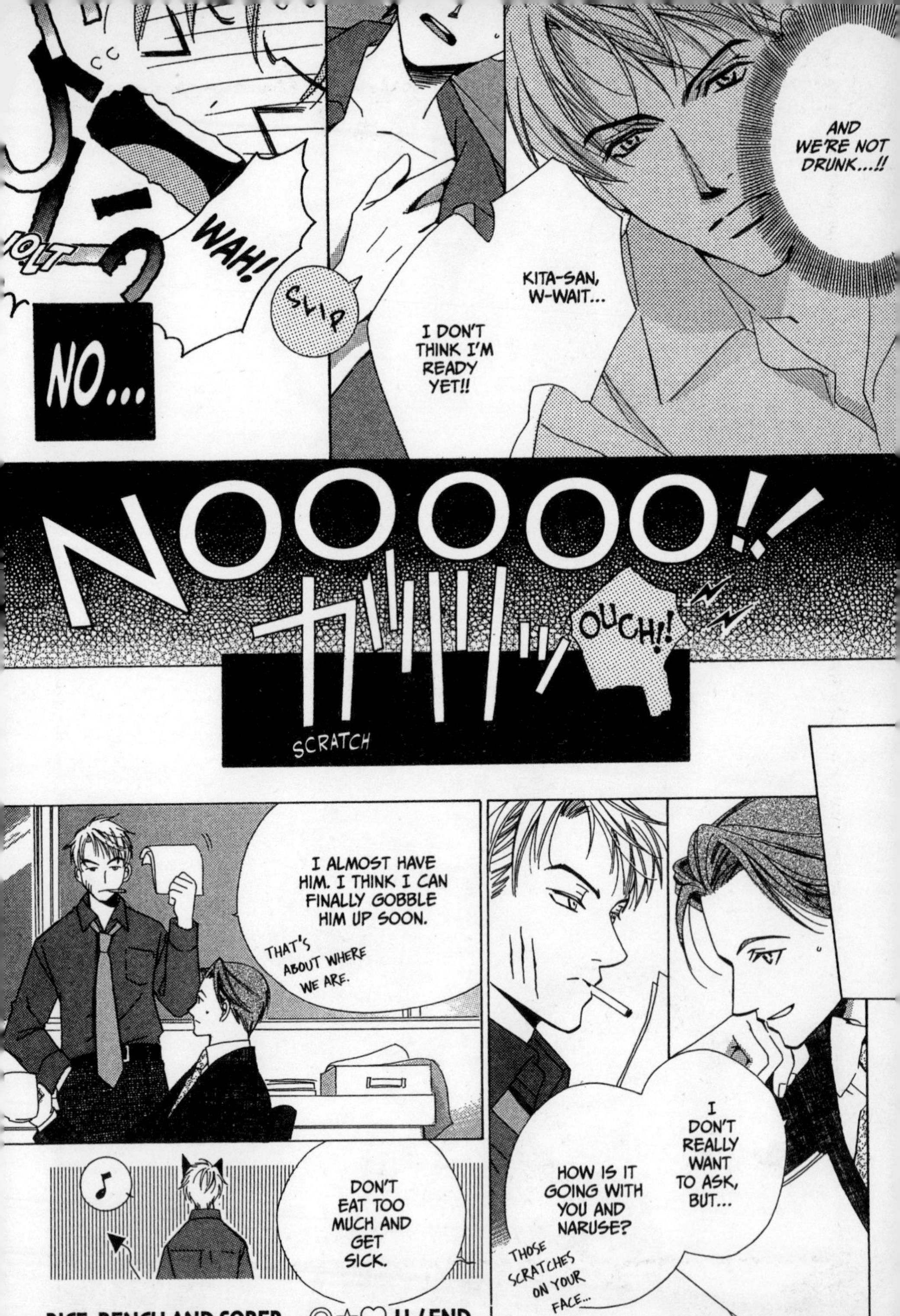
AND WE'RE NOT DRUNK...!!
KITA-SAN, W-WAIT...
I DON'T THINK I'M READY YET!!
SLIP
WAH!
JOLT
NO...
NOOOOO!!
OUCH!!
SCRATCH
I DON'T REALLY WANT TO ASK, BUT...
HOW IS IT GOING WITH YOU AND NARUSE?
THOSE SCRATCHES ON YOUR FACE...
I ALMOST HAVE HIM. I THINK I CAN FINALLY GOBBLE HIM UP SOON.
THAT'S ABOUT WHERE WE ARE.
DON'T EAT TOO MUCH AND GET SICK.

RICE, BENCH AND SOBER... ◎☆♡ !! / END

Kita & Naru series

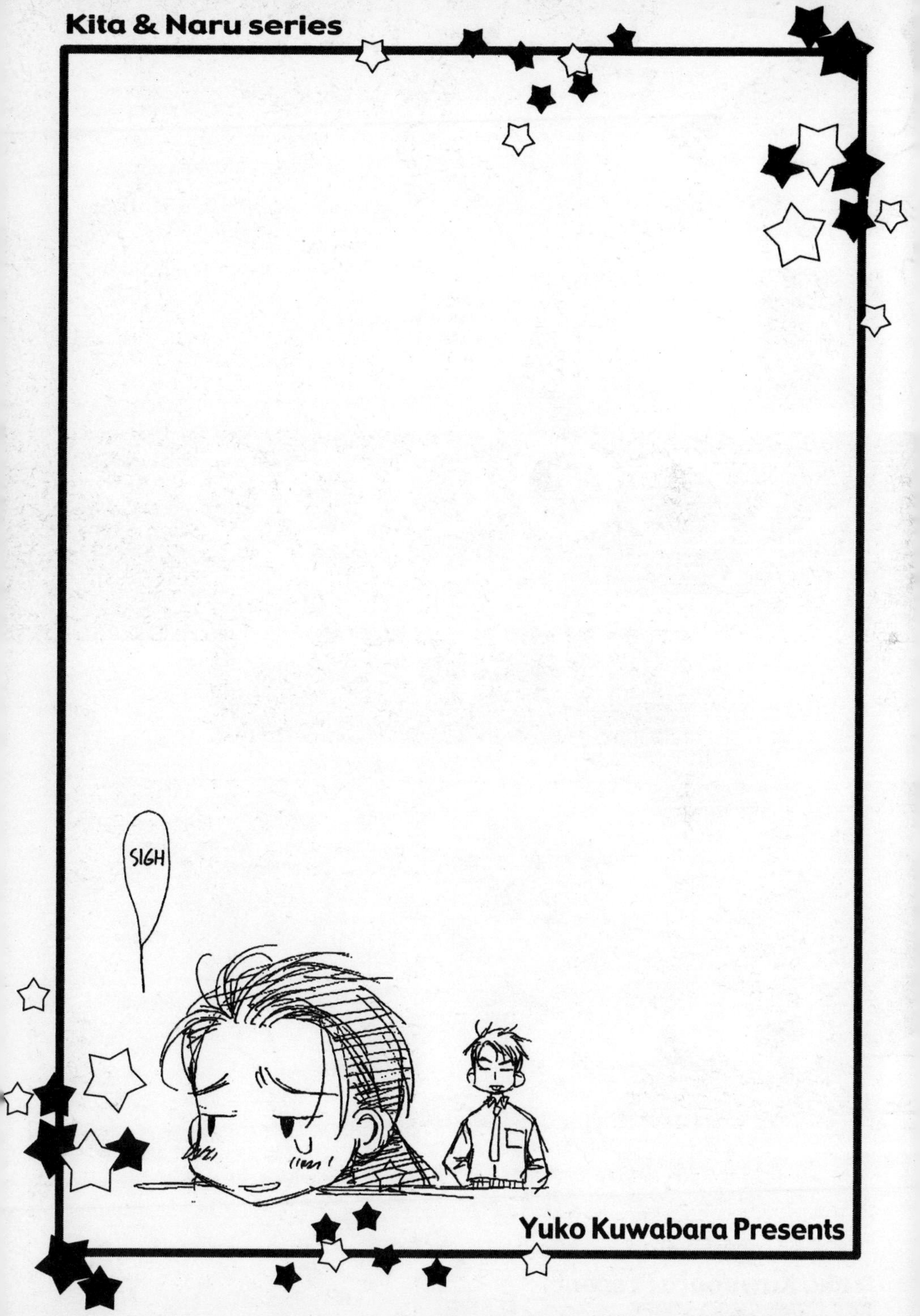
SIGH

Yuko Kuwabara Presents

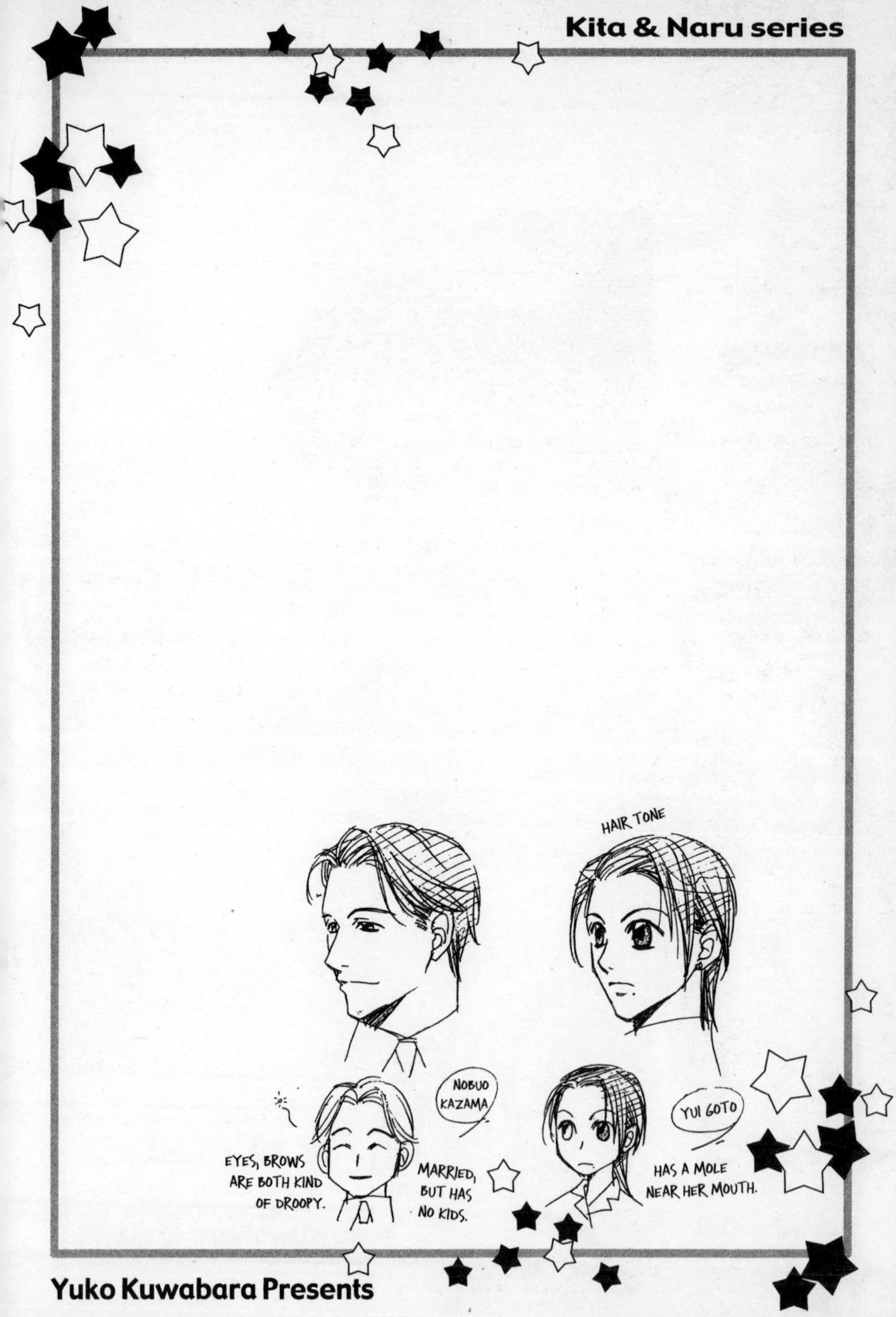
HAIR TONE
YUI GOTO
HAS A MOLE NEAR HER MOUTH.
NOBUO KAZAMA
MARRIED, BUT HAS NO KIDS.
EYES, BROWS ARE BOTH KIND OF DROOPY.

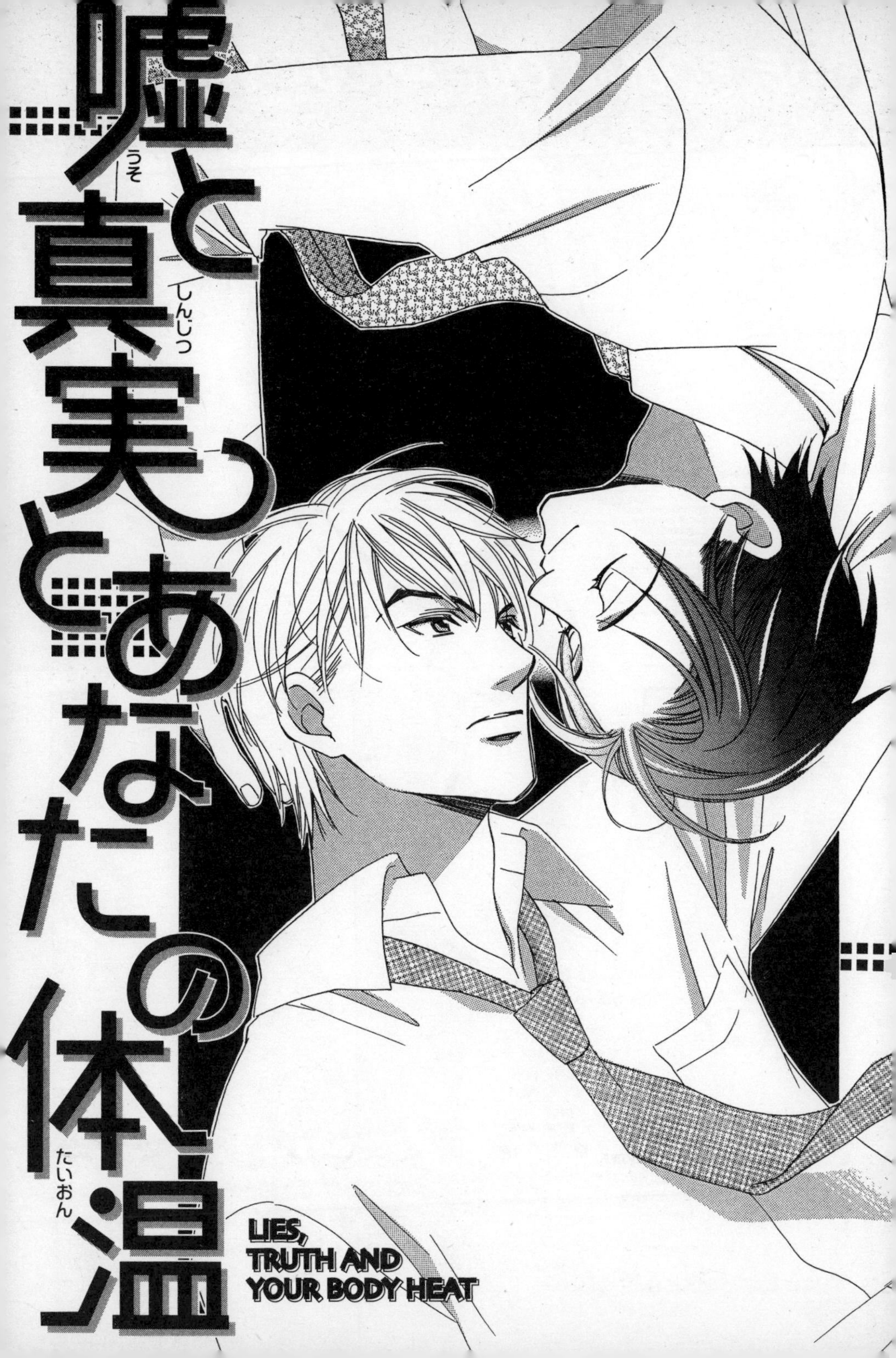
嘘と真実とあなたの体温
LIES, TRUTH AND YOUR BODY HEAT

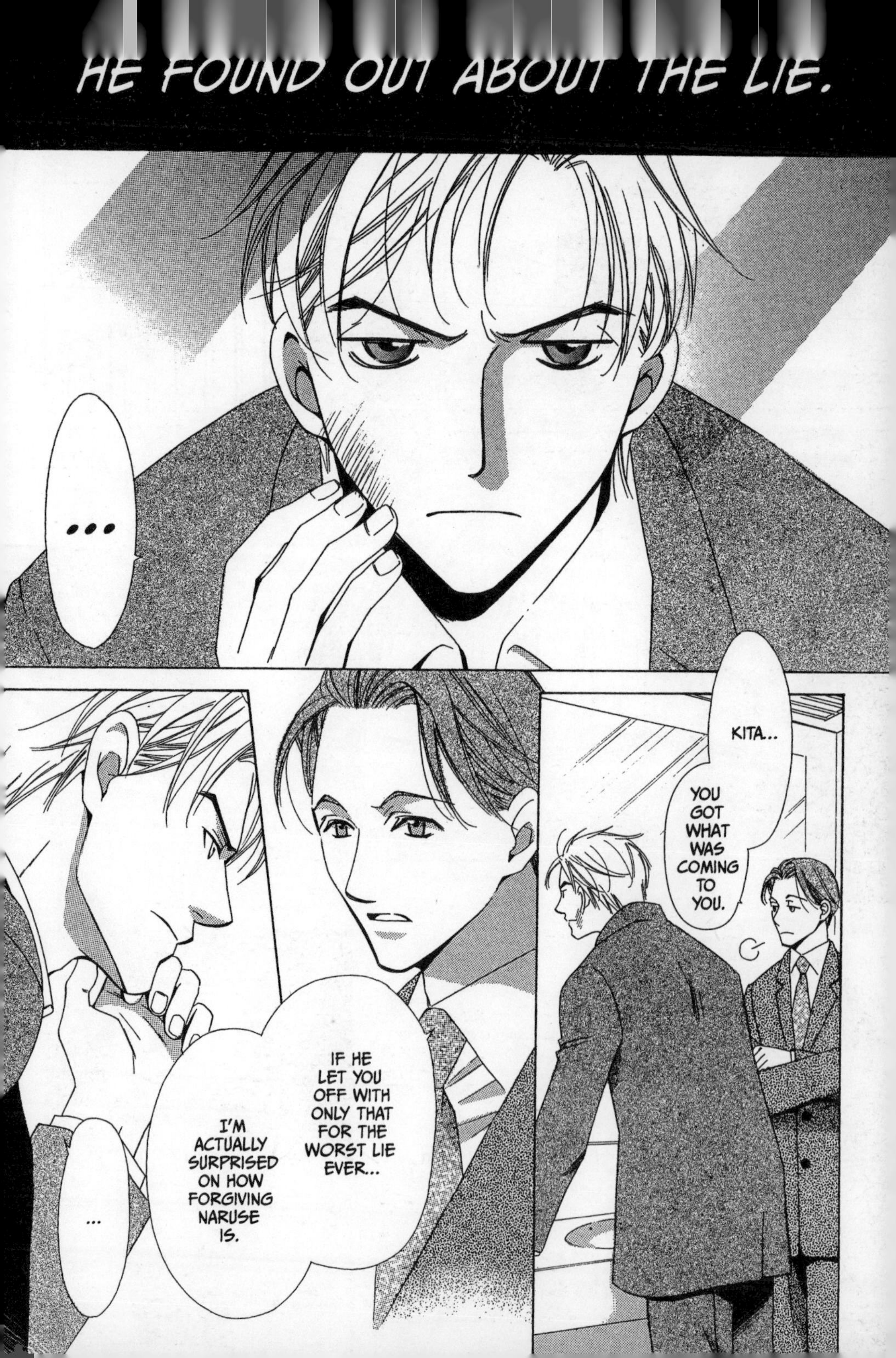
HE FOUND OUT ABOUT THE LIE.
...
KITA...
YOU GOT WHAT WAS COMING TO YOU.
IF HE LET YOU OFF WITH ONLY THAT FOR THE WORST LIE EVER...
I'M ACTUALLY SURPRISED ON HOW FORGIVING NARUSE IS.
...

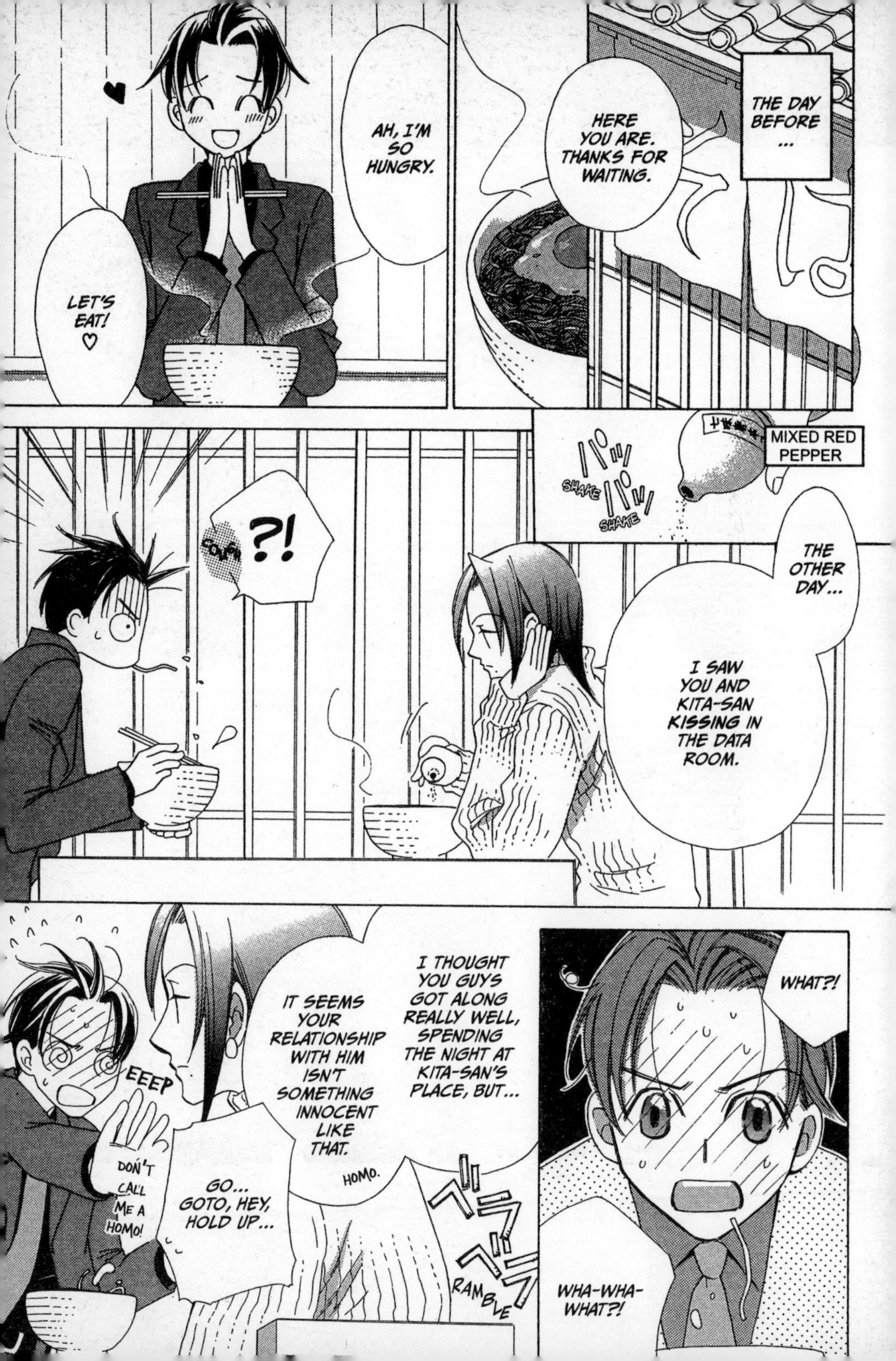
THE DAY BEFORE ...
HERE YOU ARE. THANKS FOR WAITING.
AH, I'M SO HUNGRY.
LET'S EAT! ♡
MIXED RED PEPPER
SHAKE
SHAKE
THE OTHER DAY...
I SAW YOU AND KITA-SAN KISSING IN THE DATA ROOM.
?!
WHAT?!
WHA-WHA-WHAT?!
I THOUGHT YOU GUYS GOT ALONG REALLY WELL, SPENDING THE NIGHT AT KITA-SAN'S PLACE, BUT...
IT SEEMS YOUR RELATIONSHIP WITH HIM ISN'T SOMETHING INNOCENT LIKE THAT.
HOMO.
RAMBLE
GO... GOTO, HEY, HOLD UP...
EEEP
DON'T CALL ME A HOMO!

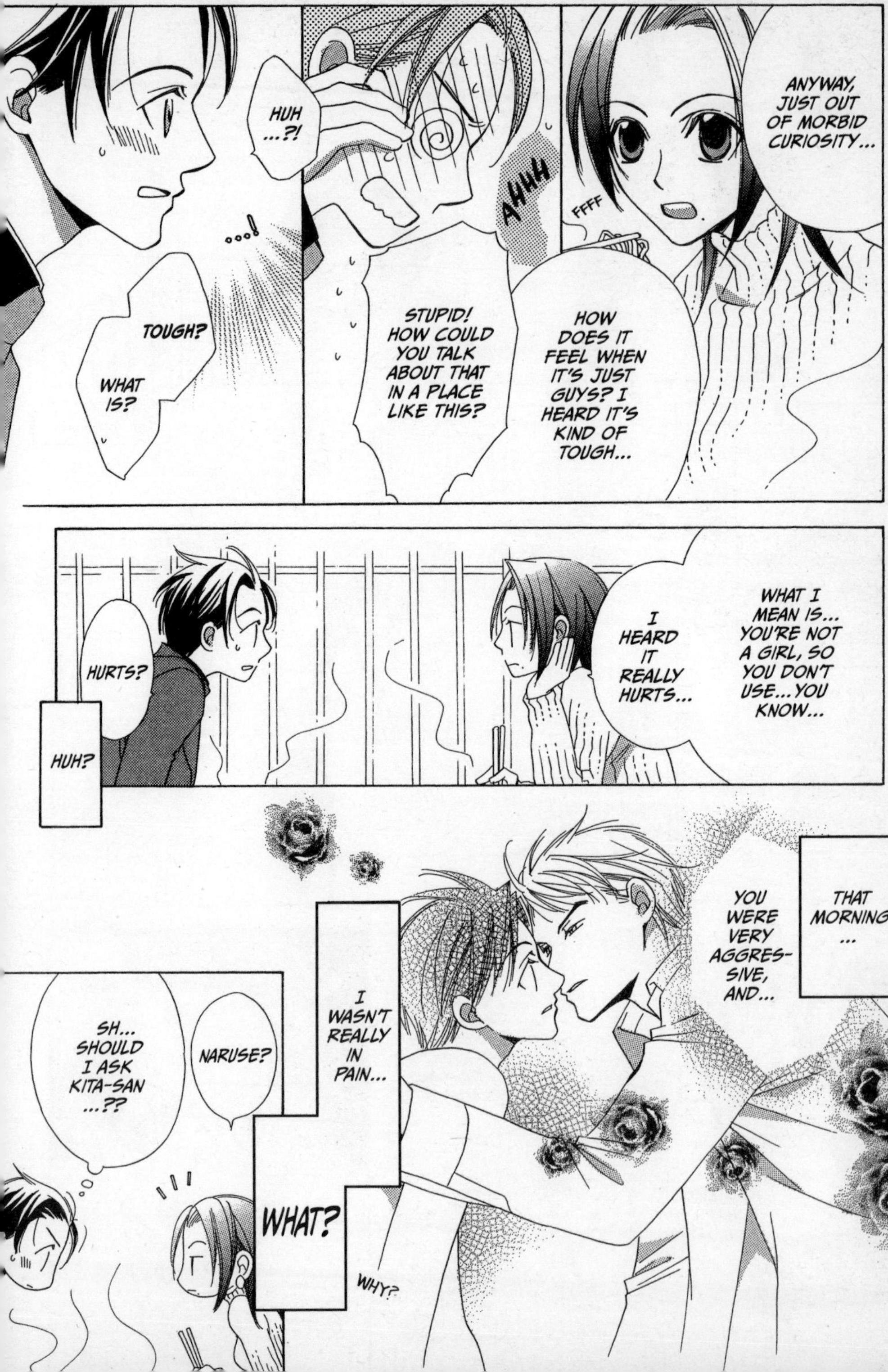
ANYWAY, JUST OUT OF MORBID CURIOSITY...
FFFF
HOW DOES IT FEEL WHEN IT'S JUST GUYS? I HEARD IT'S KIND OF TOUGH...
AHHH
STUPID! HOW COULD YOU TALK ABOUT THAT IN A PLACE LIKE THIS?
HUH ...?!
...!
TOUGH?
WHAT IS?
WHAT I MEAN IS... YOU'RE NOT A GIRL, SO YOU DON'T USE...YOU KNOW...
I HEARD IT REALLY HURTS...
HURTS?
HUH?
THAT MORNING...
YOU WERE VERY AGGRES-SIVE, AND...
I WASN'T REALLY IN PAIN...
WHAT?
WHY?
NARUSE?
SH... SHOULD I ASK KITA-SAN ...??

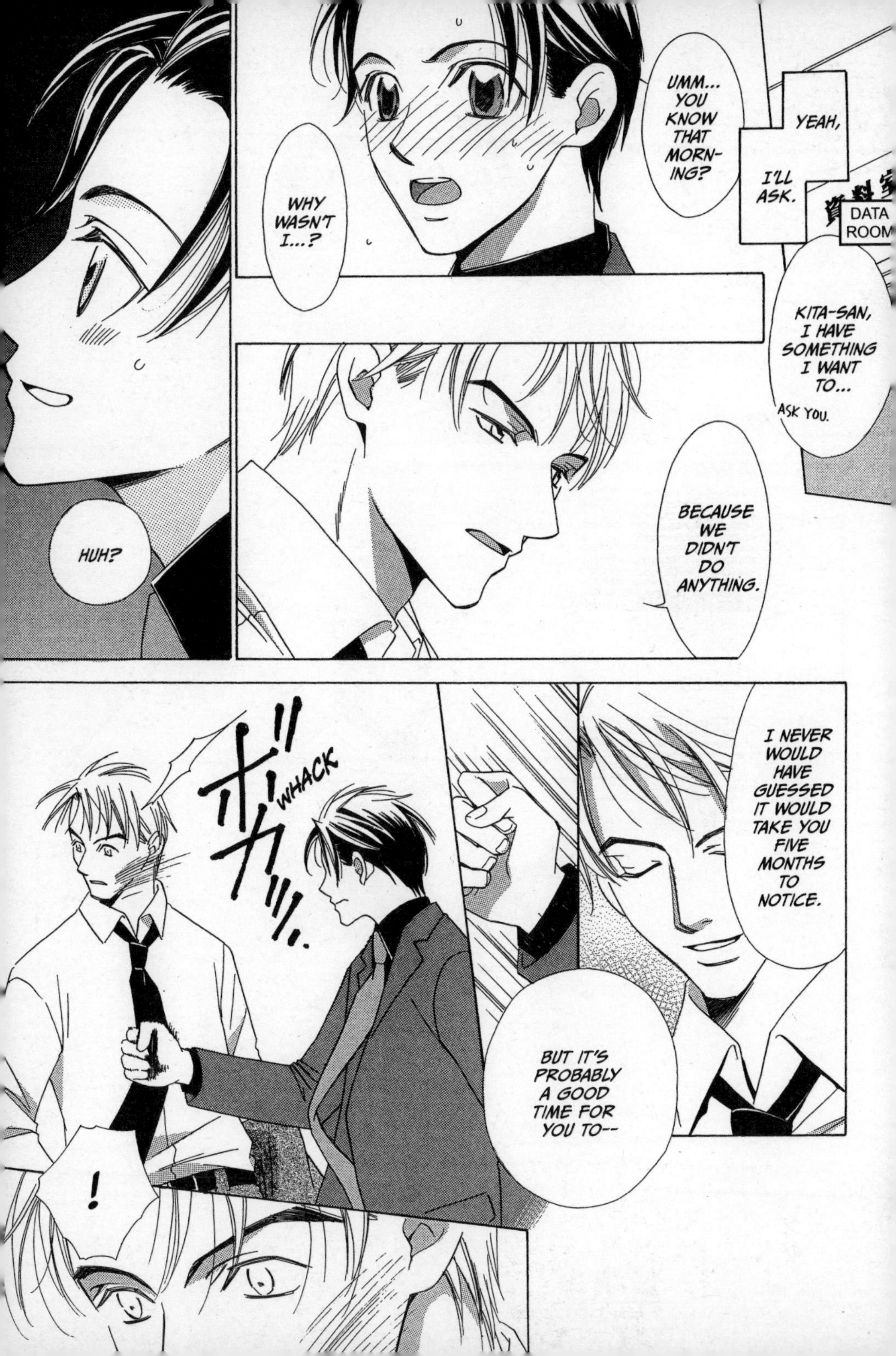
YEAH,
I'LL ASK.
DATA ROOM
KITA-SAN, I HAVE SOMETHING I WANT TO...
ASK YOU.
UMM... YOU KNOW THAT MORNING?
WHY WASN'T I...?
BECAUSE WE DIDN'T DO ANYTHING.
HUH?
I NEVER WOULD HAVE GUESSED IT WOULD TAKE YOU FIVE MONTHS TO NOTICE.
BUT IT'S PROBABLY A GOOD TIME FOR YOU TO--
WHACK
!

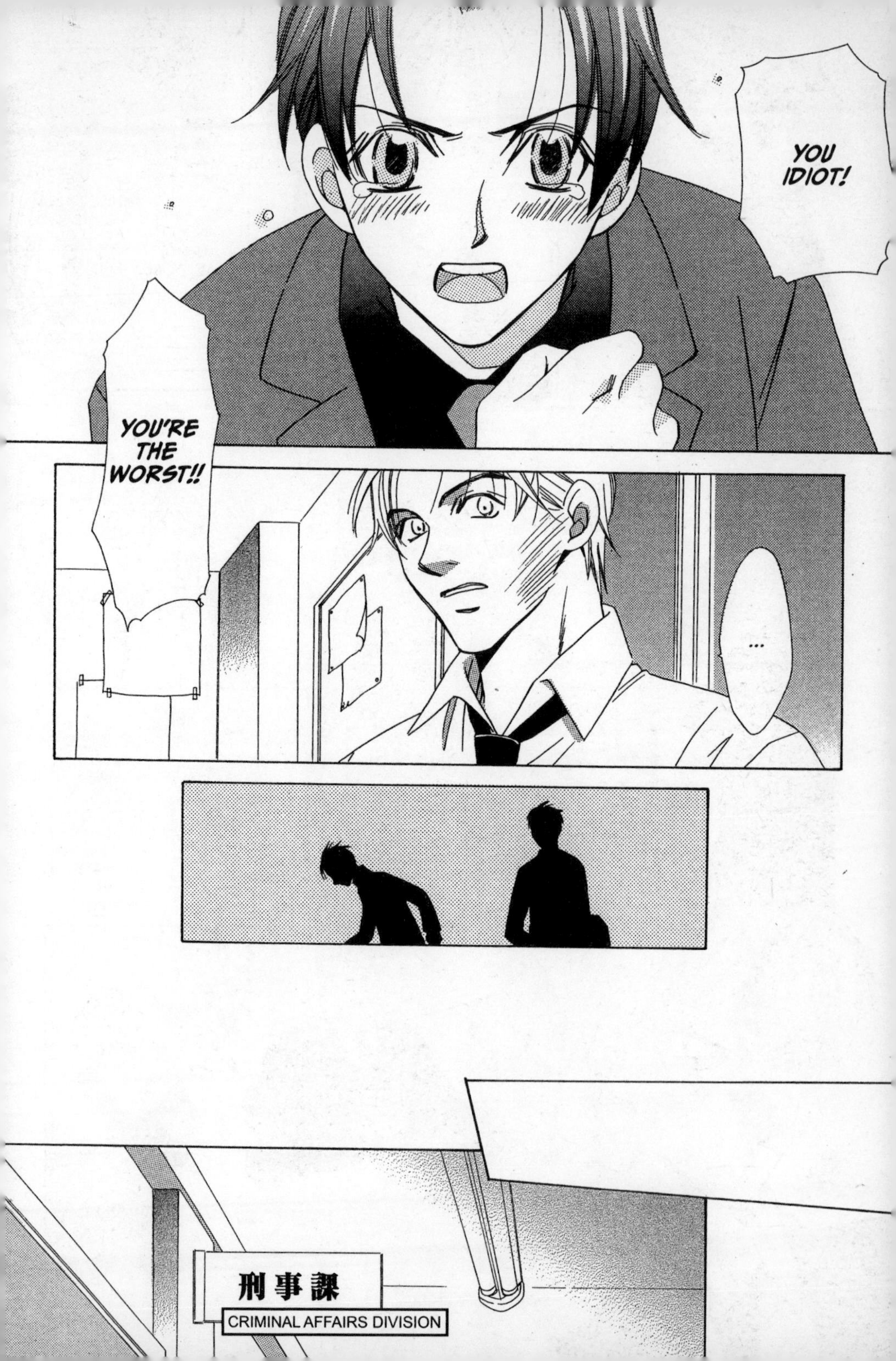
YOU IDIOT!
YOU'RE THE WORST!!
...
刑事課
CRIMINAL AFFAIRS DIVISION

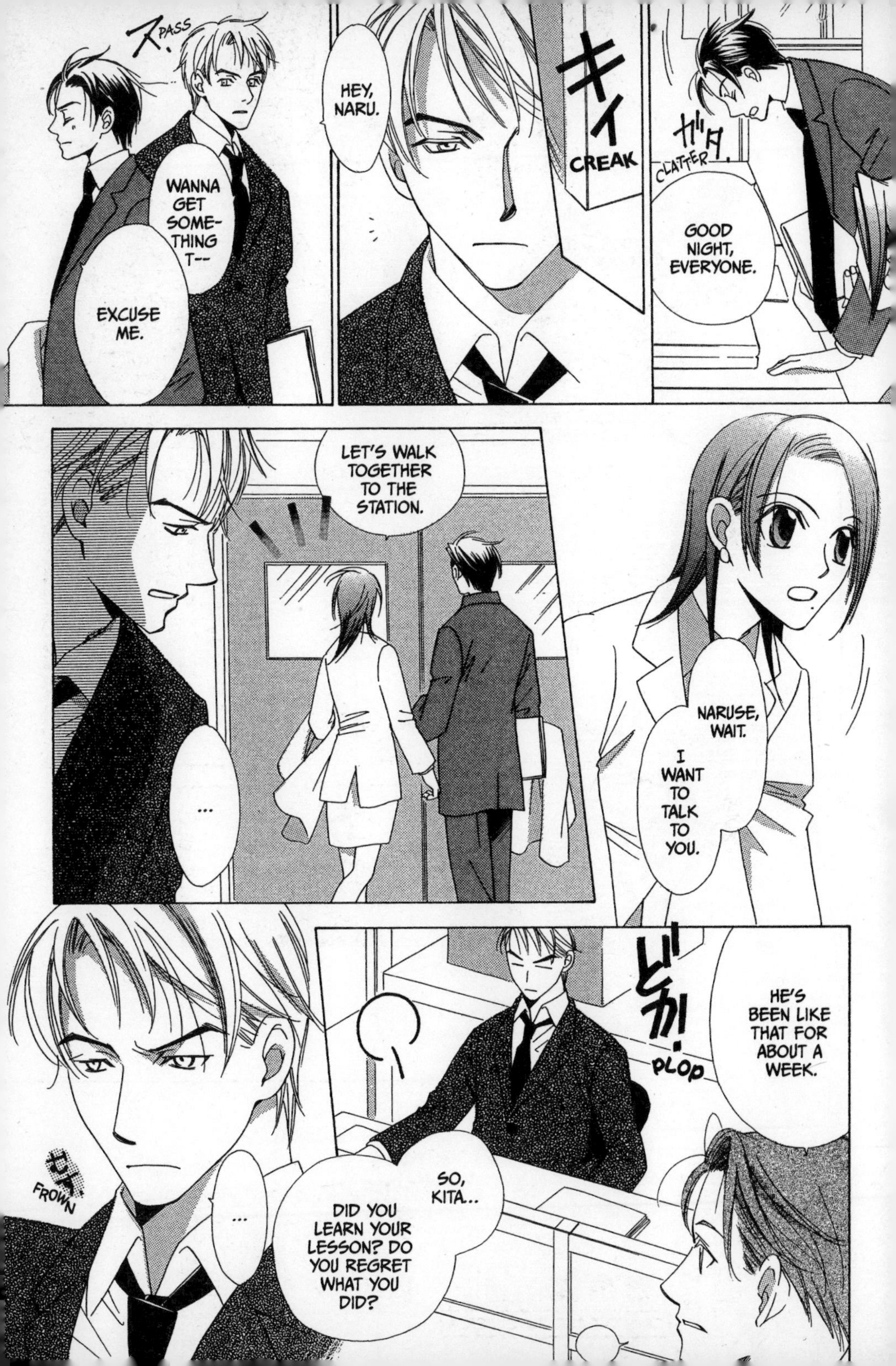
CLATTER
GOOD NIGHT, EVERYONE.
CREAK
HEY, NARU.
PASS
WANNA GET SOME-THING T--
EXCUSE ME.
NARUSE, WAIT.
I WANT TO TALK TO YOU.
LET'S WALK TOGETHER TO THE STATION.
...
HE'S BEEN LIKE THAT FOR ABOUT A WEEK.
PLOP
SO, KITA..
DID YOU LEARN YOUR LESSON? DO YOU REGRET WHAT YOU DID?
...
FROWN

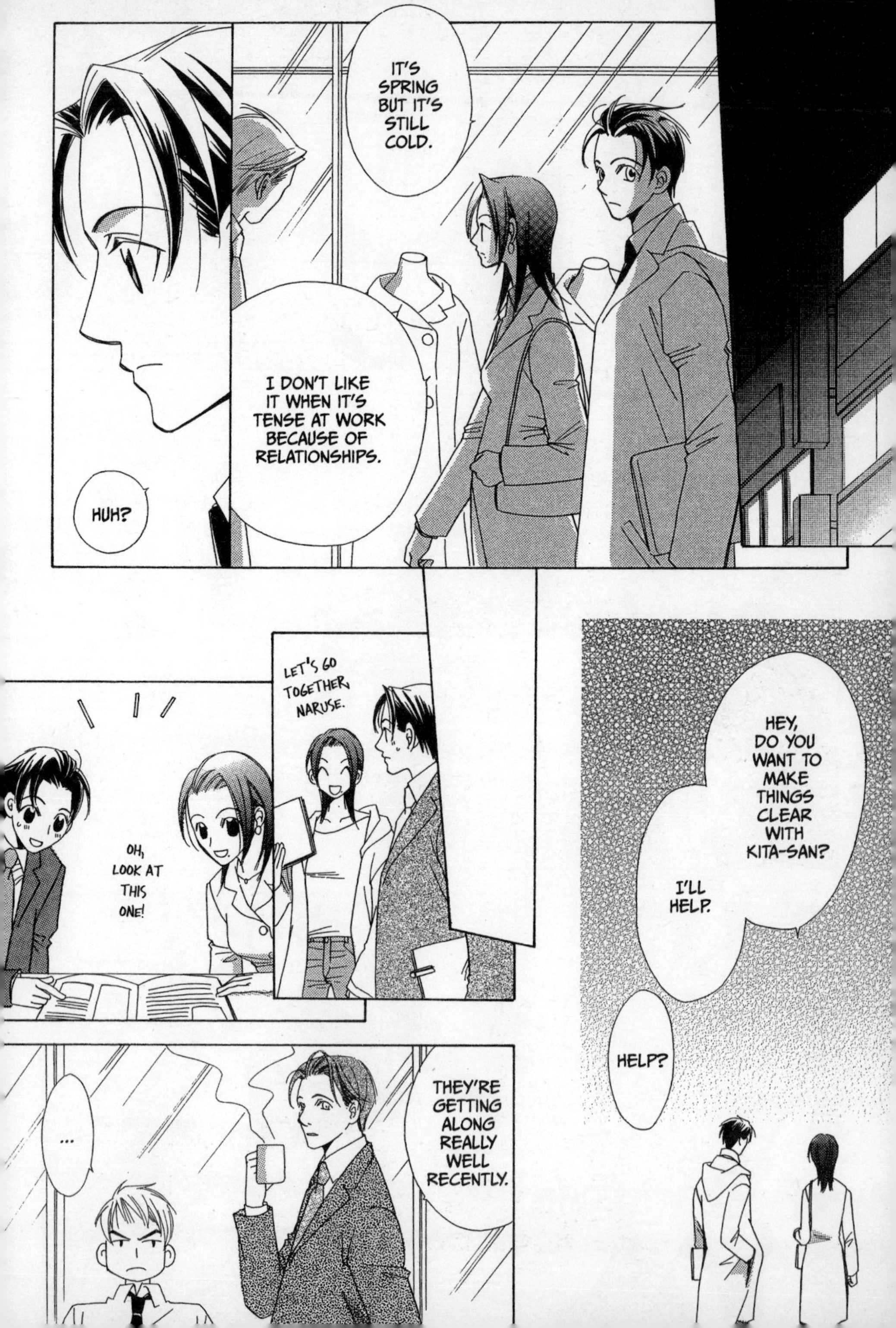
IT'S SPRING BUT IT'S STILL COLD.
I DON'T LIKE IT WHEN IT'S TENSE AT WORK BECAUSE OF RELATIONSHIPS.
HUH?
HEY, DO YOU WANT TO MAKE THINGS CLEAR WITH KITA-SAN?
I'LL HELP.
HELP?
LET'S GO TOGETHER, NARUSE.
OH, LOOK AT THIS ONE!
THEY'RE GETTING ALONG REALLY WELL RECENTLY.
...

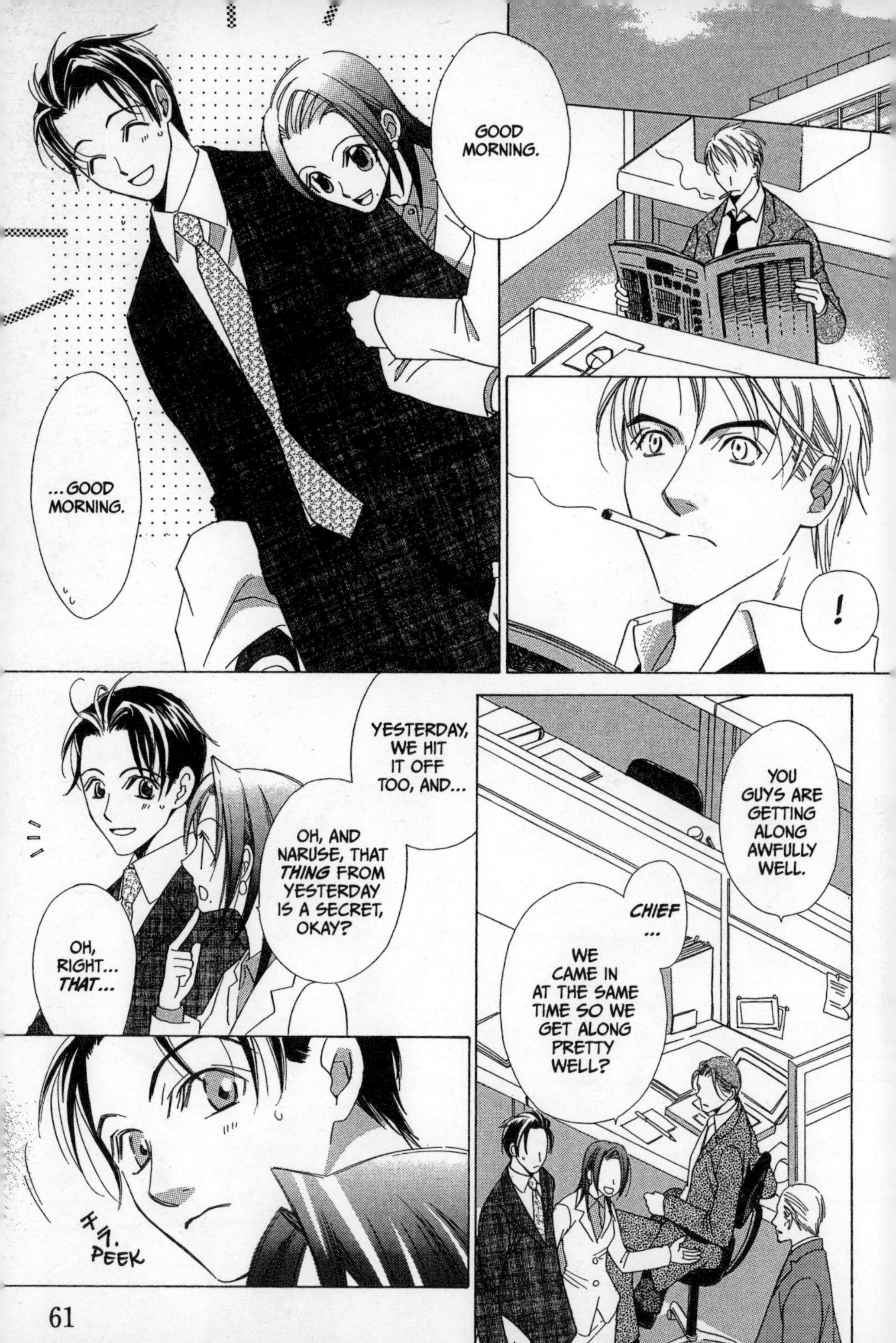
!
GOOD MORNING.
...GOOD MORNING.
YOU GUYS ARE GETTING ALONG AWFULLY WELL.
CHIEF...
WE CAME IN AT THE SAME TIME SO WE GET ALONG PRETTY WELL?
YESTERDAY, WE HIT IT OFF TOO, AND...
OH, AND NARUSE, THAT *THING* FROM YESTERDAY IS A SECRET, OKAY?
OH, RIGHT... *THAT*...
チラ
PEEK

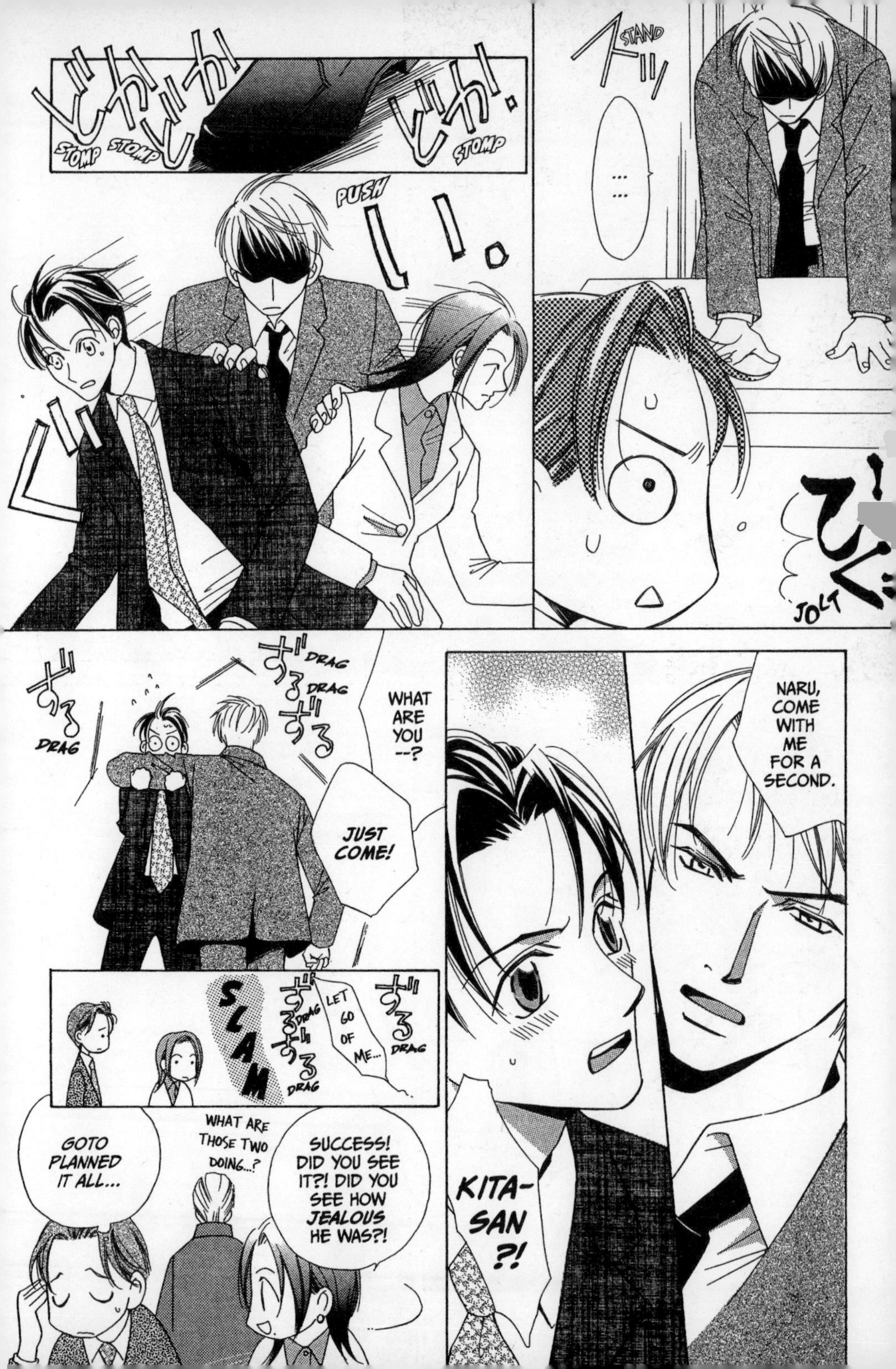
STAND
......
JOLT
STOMP STOMP
STOMP
PUSH
NARU, COME WITH ME FOR A SECOND.
KITA-SAN ?!
DRAG DRAG
DRAG
WHAT ARE YOU --?
JUST COME!
DRAG
LET GO OF ME...
SLAM
DRAG
DRAG
SUCCESS! DID YOU SEE IT?! DID YOU SEE HOW JEALOUS HE WAS?!
WHAT ARE THOSE TWO DOING...?
GOTO PLANNED IT ALL...

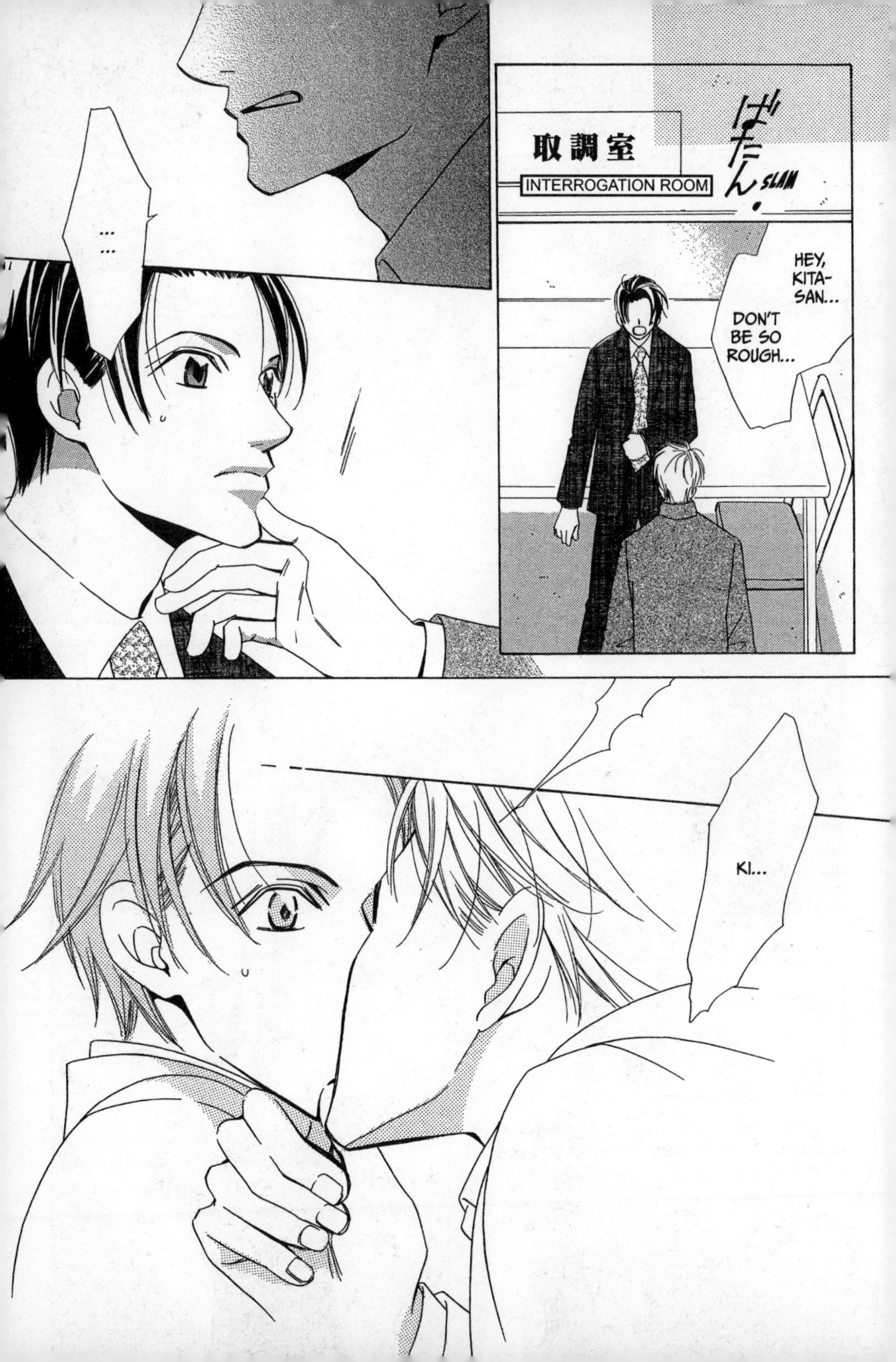
取調室
INTERROGATION ROOM
ばたん!
SLAM
HEY, KITA-SAN...
DON'T BE SO ROUGH...
......
KI...

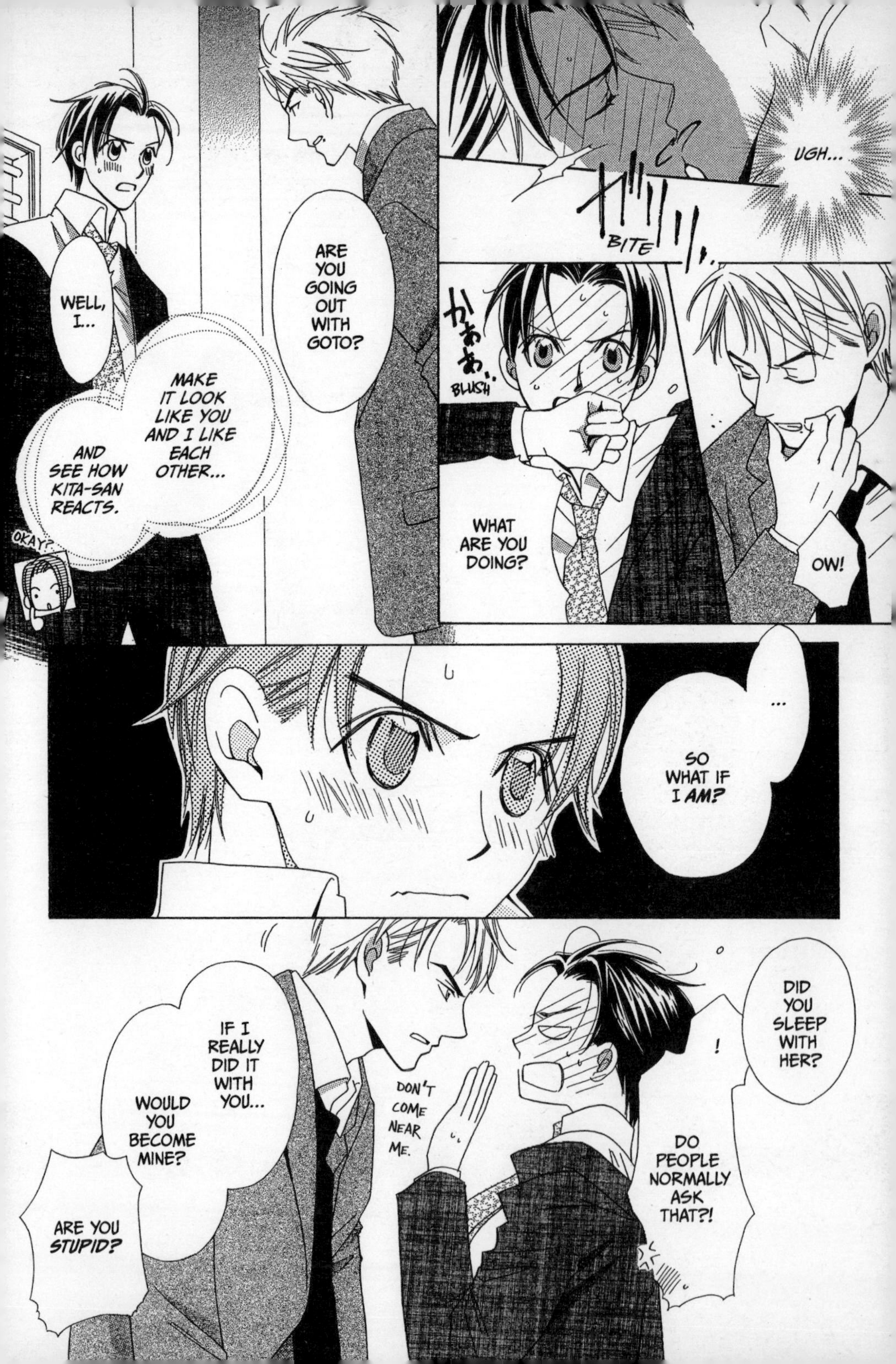
UGH...
BITE
かぁぁ
BLUSH
OW!
WHAT ARE YOU DOING?
ARE YOU GOING OUT WITH GOTO?
WELL, I...
MAKE IT LOOK LIKE YOU AND I LIKE EACH OTHER...
AND SEE HOW KITA-SAN REACTS.
OKAY?
...
SO WHAT IF I *AM*?
DID YOU SLEEP WITH HER?
!
DO PEOPLE NORMALLY ASK THAT?!
DON'T COME NEAR ME.
IF I REALLY DID IT WITH YOU...
WOULD YOU BECOME MINE?
ARE YOU *STUPID*?

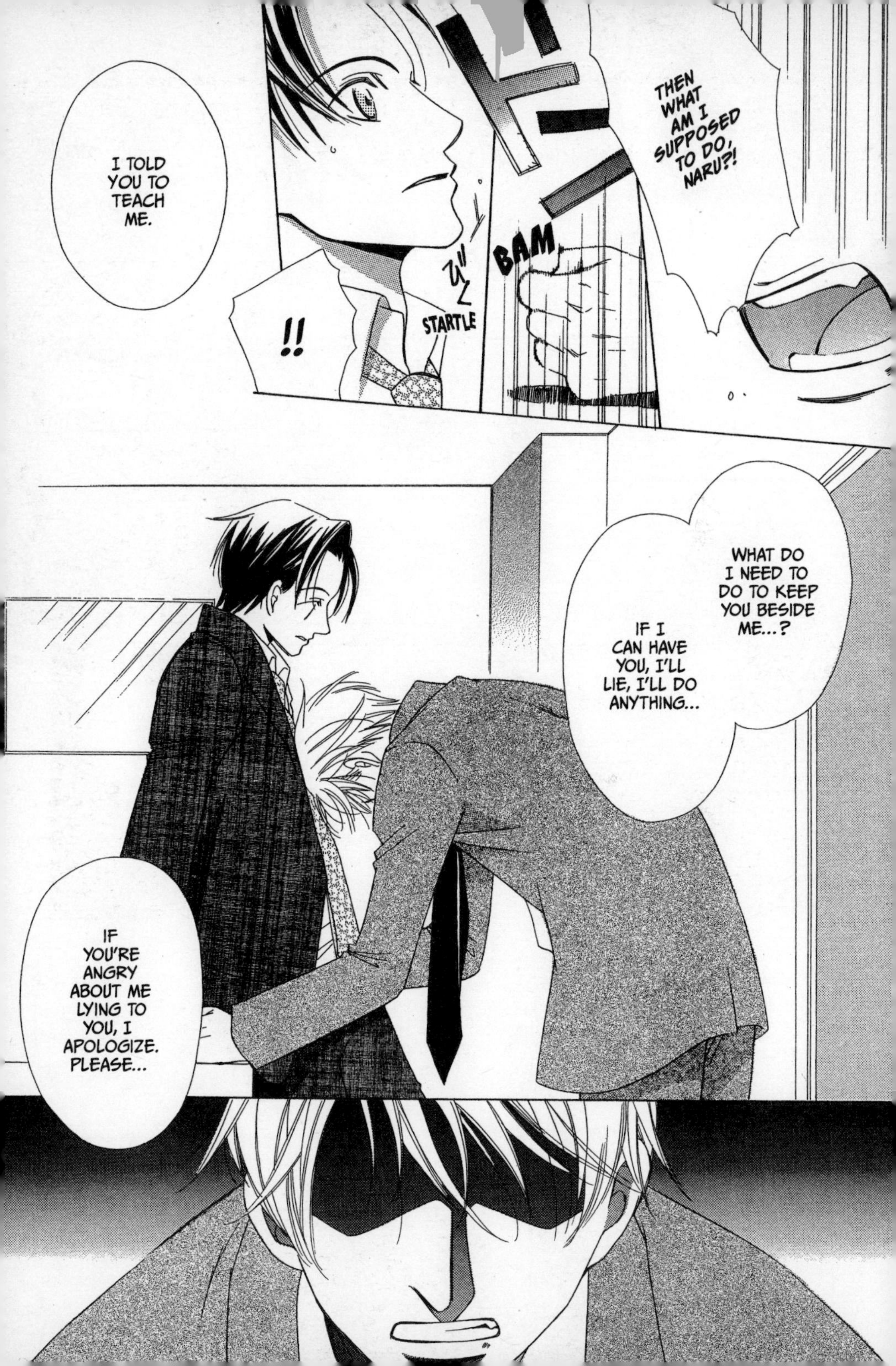
THEN WHAT AM I SUPPOSED TO DO, NARU?!
BAM
STARTLE
!!
I TOLD YOU TO TEACH ME.
WHAT DO I NEED TO DO TO KEEP YOU BESIDE ME...?
IF I CAN HAVE YOU, I'LL LIE, I'LL DO ANYTHING...
IF YOU'RE ANGRY ABOUT ME LYING TO YOU, I APOLOGIZE. PLEASE...

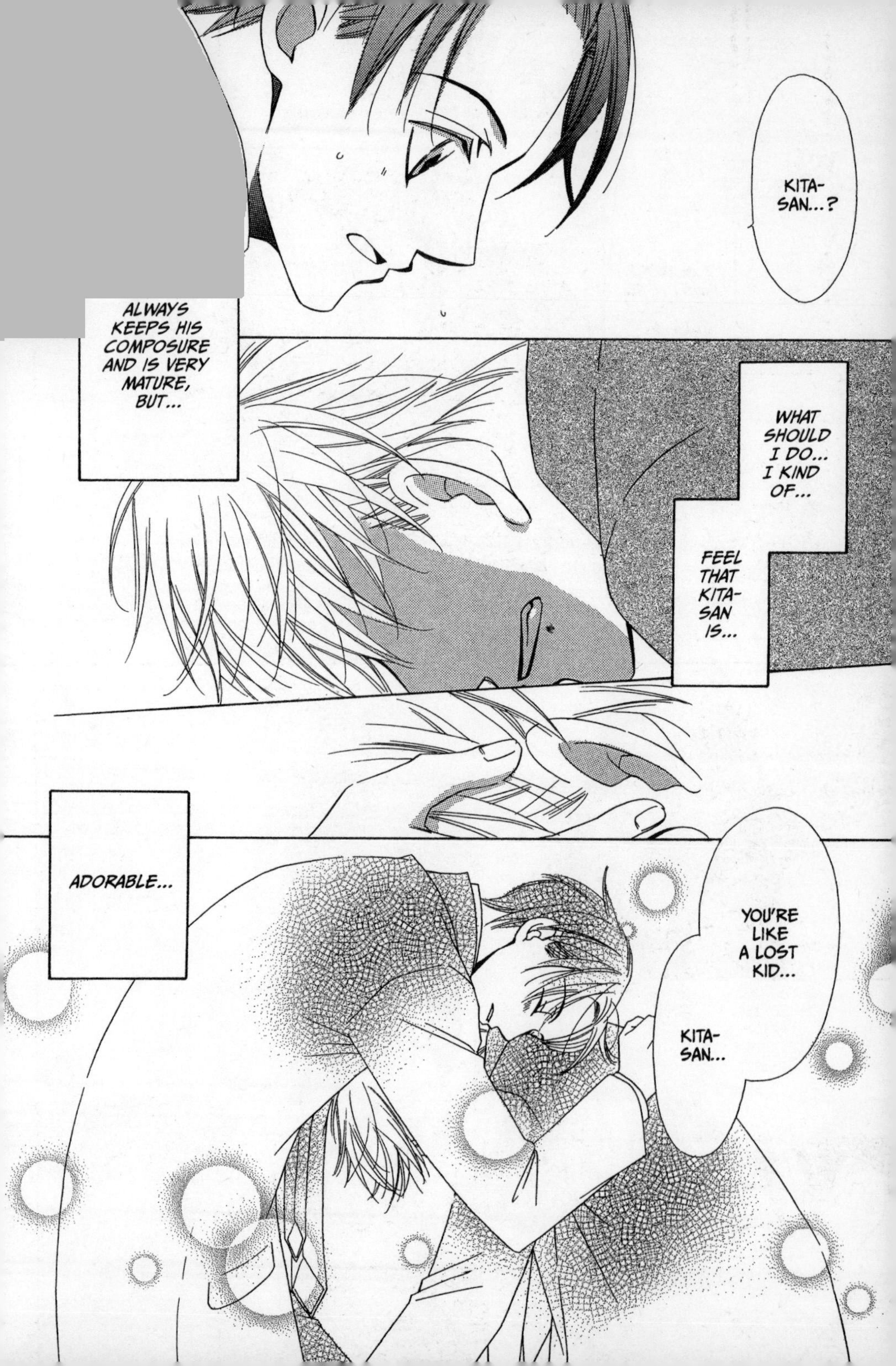
KITA-SAN...?
ALWAYS KEEPS HIS COMPOSURE AND IS VERY MATURE, BUT...
WHAT SHOULD I DO... I KIND OF...
FEEL THAT KITA-SAN IS...
YOU'RE LIKE A LOST KID...
KITA-SAN...
ADORABLE...

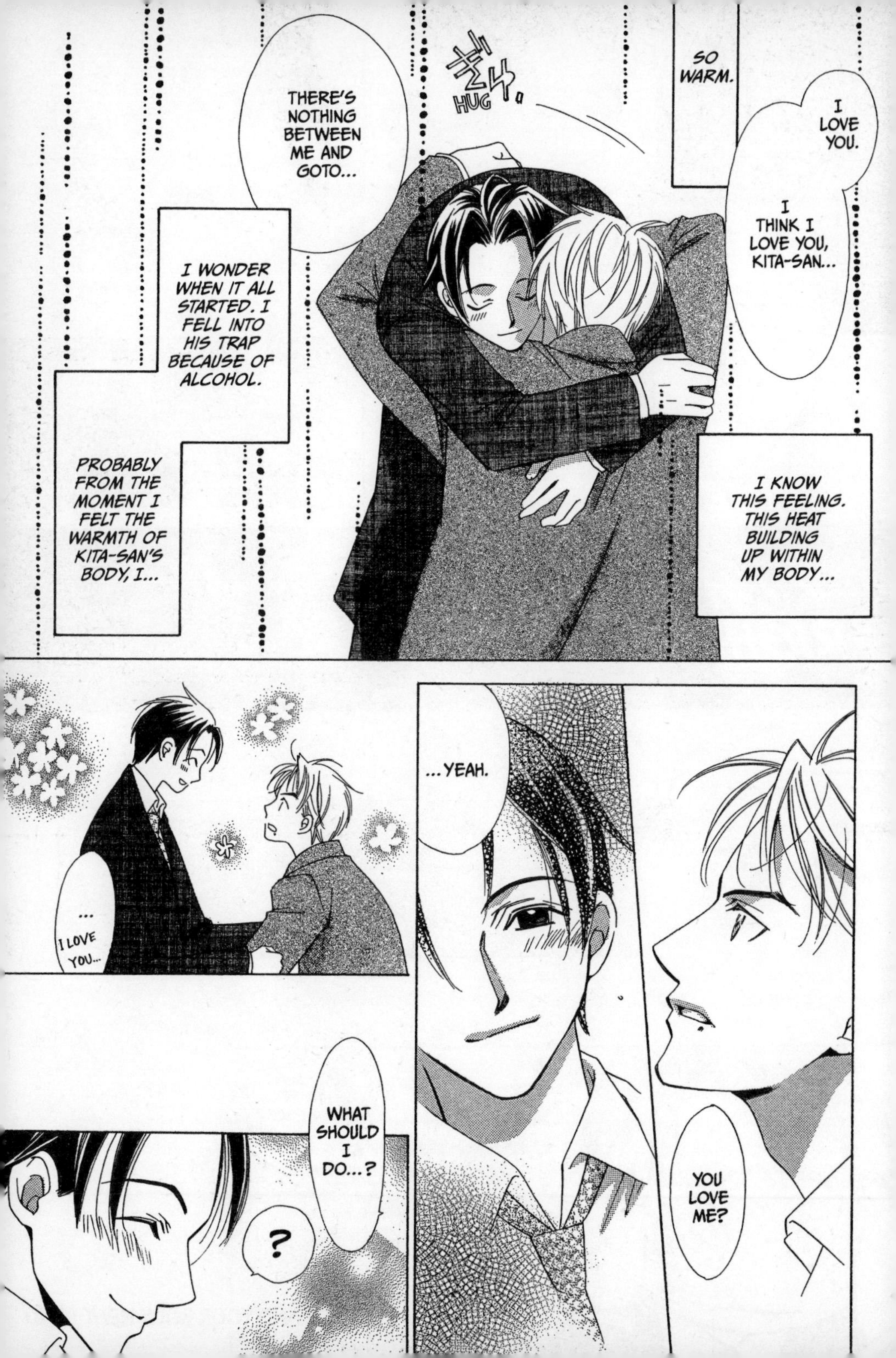
SO WARM.
I LOVE YOU.
I THINK I LOVE YOU, KITA-SAN...
HUG
THERE'S NOTHING BETWEEN ME AND GOTO...
I KNOW THIS FEELING. THIS HEAT BUILDING UP WITHIN MY BODY...
I WONDER WHEN IT ALL STARTED. I FELL INTO HIS TRAP BECAUSE OF ALCOHOL.
PROBABLY FROM THE MOMENT I FELT THE WARMTH OF KITA-SAN'S BODY, I...
YOU LOVE ME?
...YEAH.
... I LOVE YOU...
WHAT SHOULD I DO...?
?

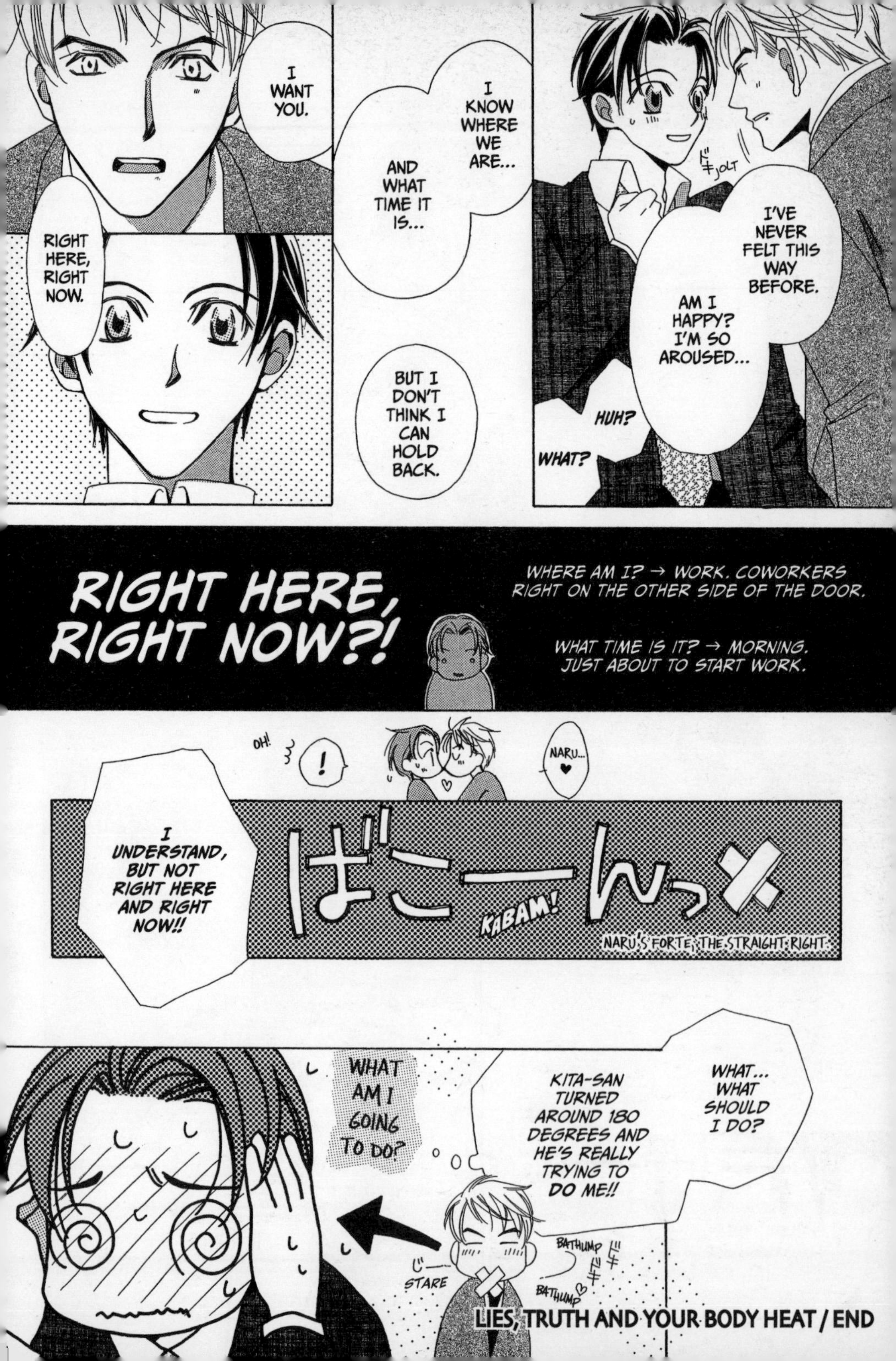
ドキ JOLT
I'VE NEVER FELT THIS WAY BEFORE.
AM I HAPPY? I'M SO AROUSED...
HUH?
WHAT?
I KNOW WHERE WE ARE...
AND WHAT TIME IT IS...
BUT I DON'T THINK I CAN HOLD BACK.
I WANT YOU.
RIGHT HERE, RIGHT NOW.
WHERE AM I? → WORK. COWORKERS RIGHT ON THE OTHER SIDE OF THE DOOR.
WHAT TIME IS IT? → MORNING. JUST ABOUT TO START WORK.
RIGHT HERE, RIGHT NOW?!
NARU... ♥
!
OH!
ばごーんっ
KABAM!
NARU'S FORTE, THE STRAIGHT RIGHT.
I UNDERSTAND, BUT NOT RIGHT HERE AND RIGHT NOW!!
WHAT... WHAT SHOULD I DO?
KITA-SAN TURNED AROUND 180 DEGREES AND HE'S REALLY TRYING TO DO ME!!
BATHUMP ドキドキ
BATHUMP ♡
じー STARE
WHAT AM I GOING TO DO?
LIES, TRUTH AND YOUR BODY HEAT / END

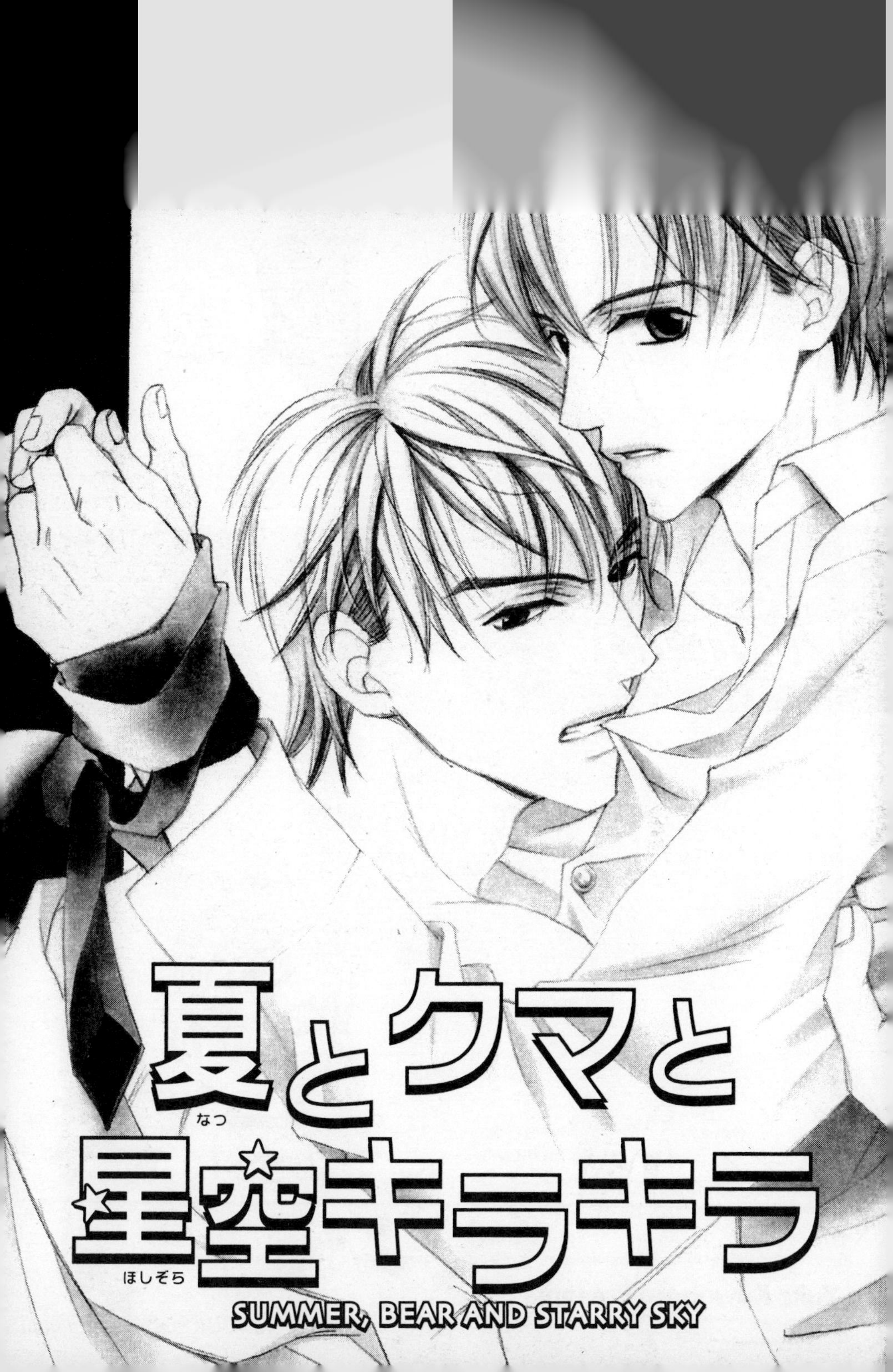
夏とクマと星空キラキラ
なつ
ほしぞら
SUMMER, BEAR AND STARRY SKY

THE FUNNIEST PERSON TO DRAW
THIS TIME AROUND WAS KITA!!

Yuko Kuwabara Presents

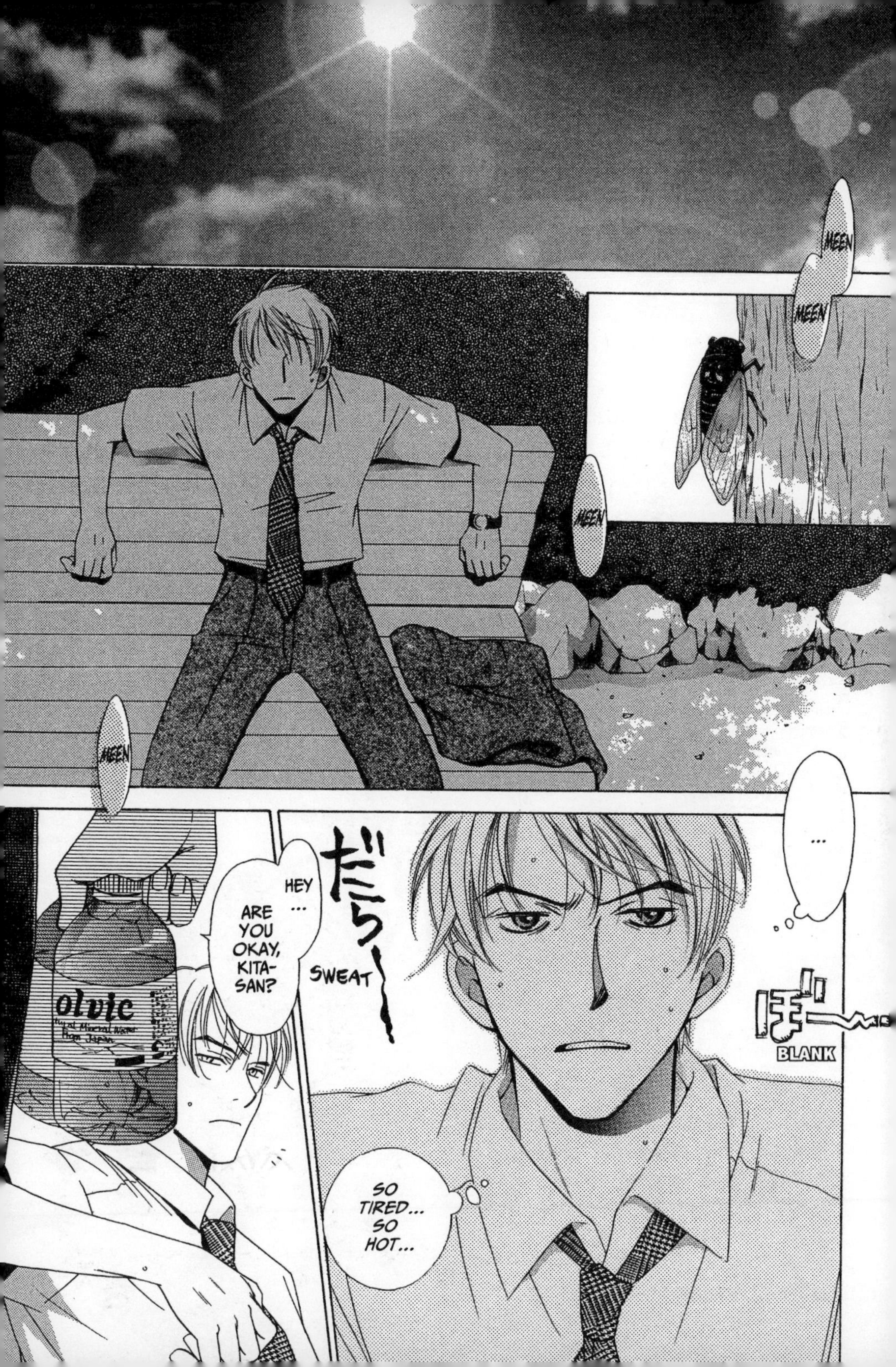
MEEN
MEEN
MEEN
MEEN
...
ぼーー
BLANK
SO TIRED... SO HOT...
だらー
SWEAT
HEY ... ARE YOU OKAY, KITA-SAN?
olvic

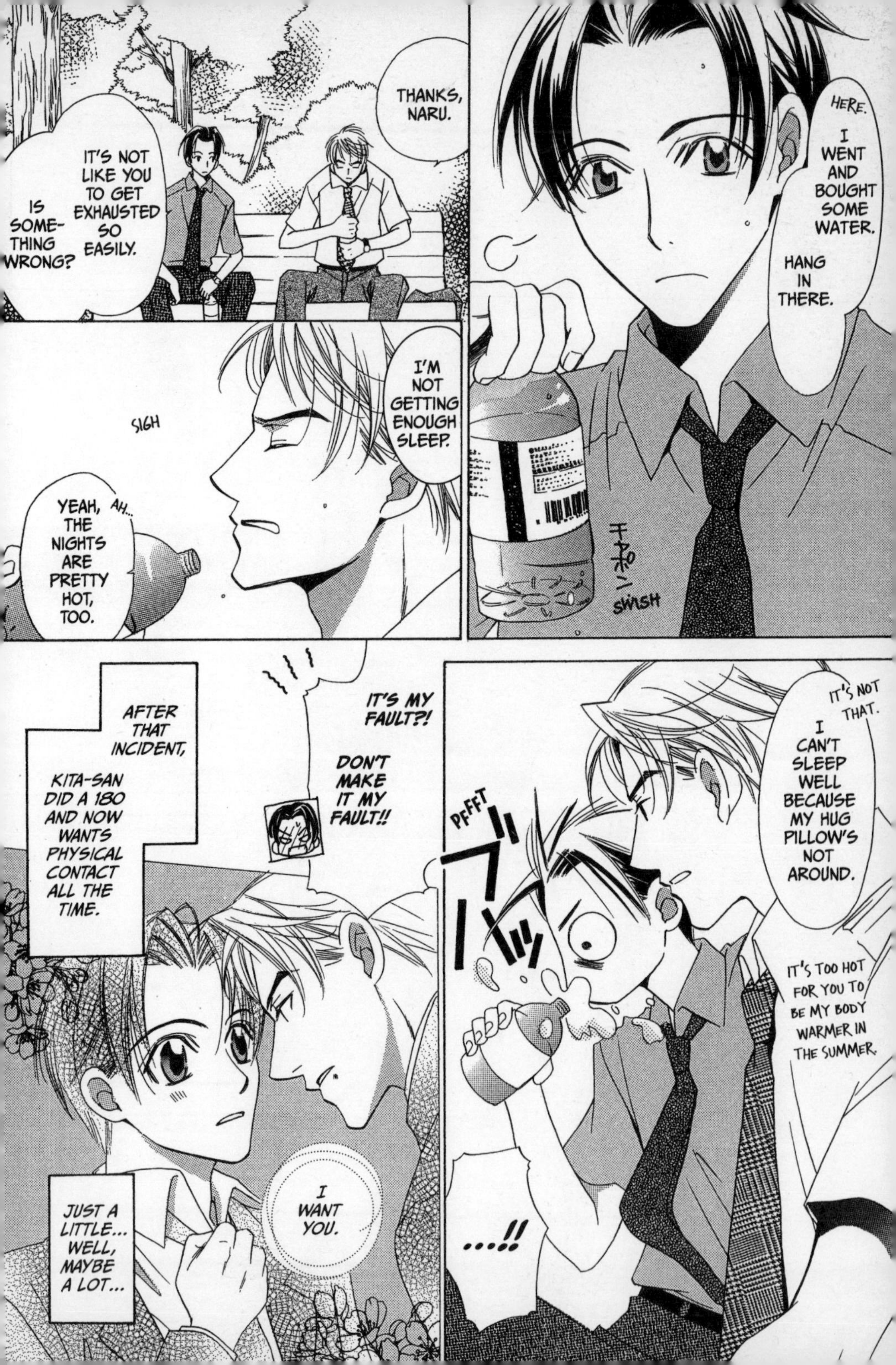
HERE.
I WENT AND BOUGHT SOME WATER.
HANG IN THERE.
チャポン
SWISH
THANKS, NARU.
IT'S NOT LIKE YOU TO GET EXHAUSTED SO EASILY.
IS SOME-THING WRONG?
I'M NOT GETTING ENOUGH SLEEP.
SIGH
AH...
YEAH, THE NIGHTS ARE PRETTY HOT, TOO.
IT'S NOT THAT.
I CAN'T SLEEP WELL BECAUSE MY HUG PILLOW'S NOT AROUND.
PFFFT
IT'S TOO HOT FOR YOU TO BE MY BODY WARMER IN THE SUMMER.
...!!
IT'S MY FAULT?!
DON'T MAKE IT MY FAULT!!
AFTER THAT INCIDENT, KITA-SAN DID A 180 AND NOW WANTS PHYSICAL CONTACT ALL THE TIME.
I WANT YOU.
JUST A LITTLE... WELL, MAYBE A LOT...

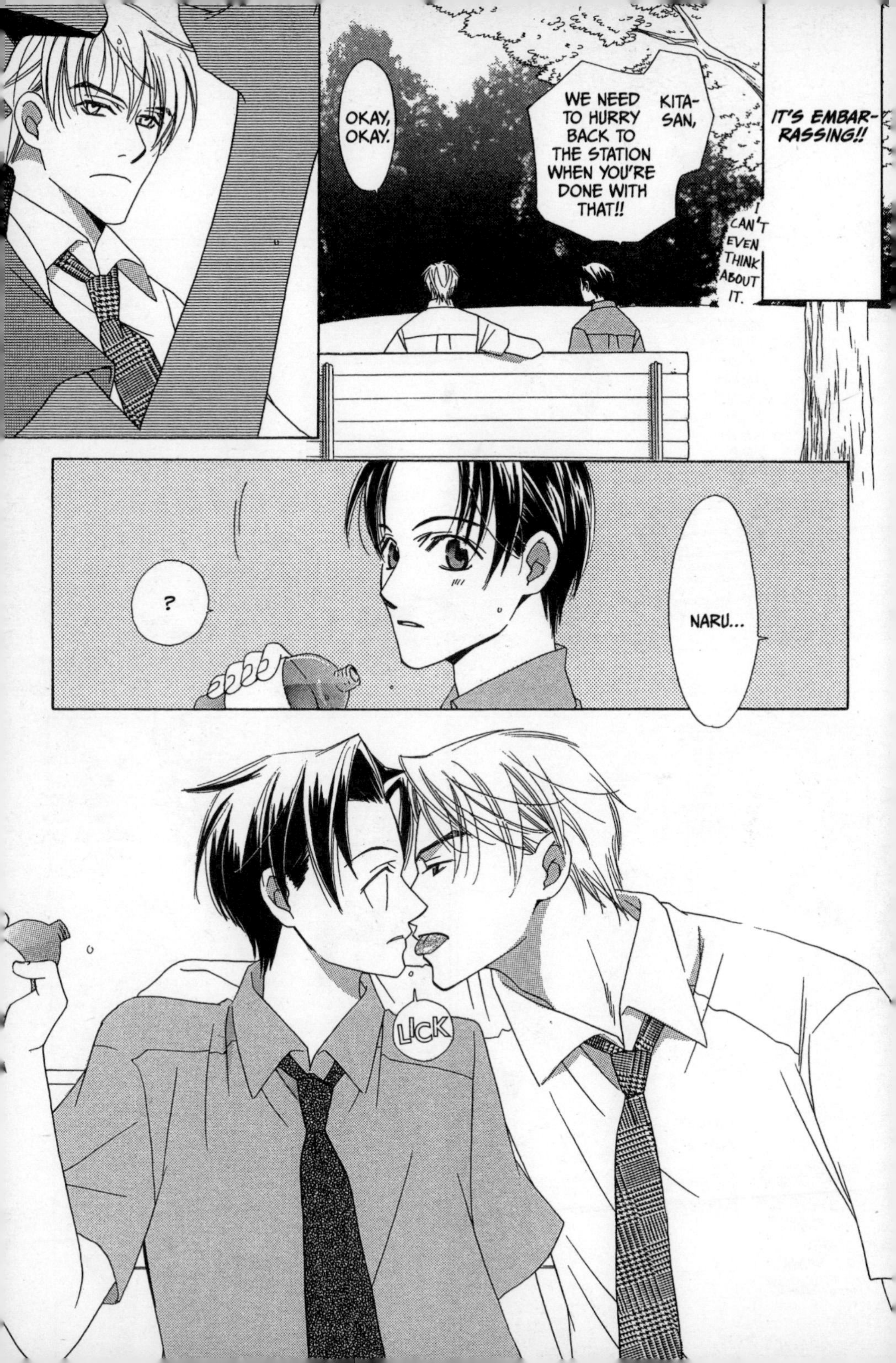
IT'S EMBARRASSING!!
I CAN'T EVEN THINK ABOUT IT.
KITA-SAN, WE NEED TO HURRY BACK TO THE STATION WHEN YOU'RE DONE WITH THAT!!
OKAY, OKAY.
NARU...
?
LICK

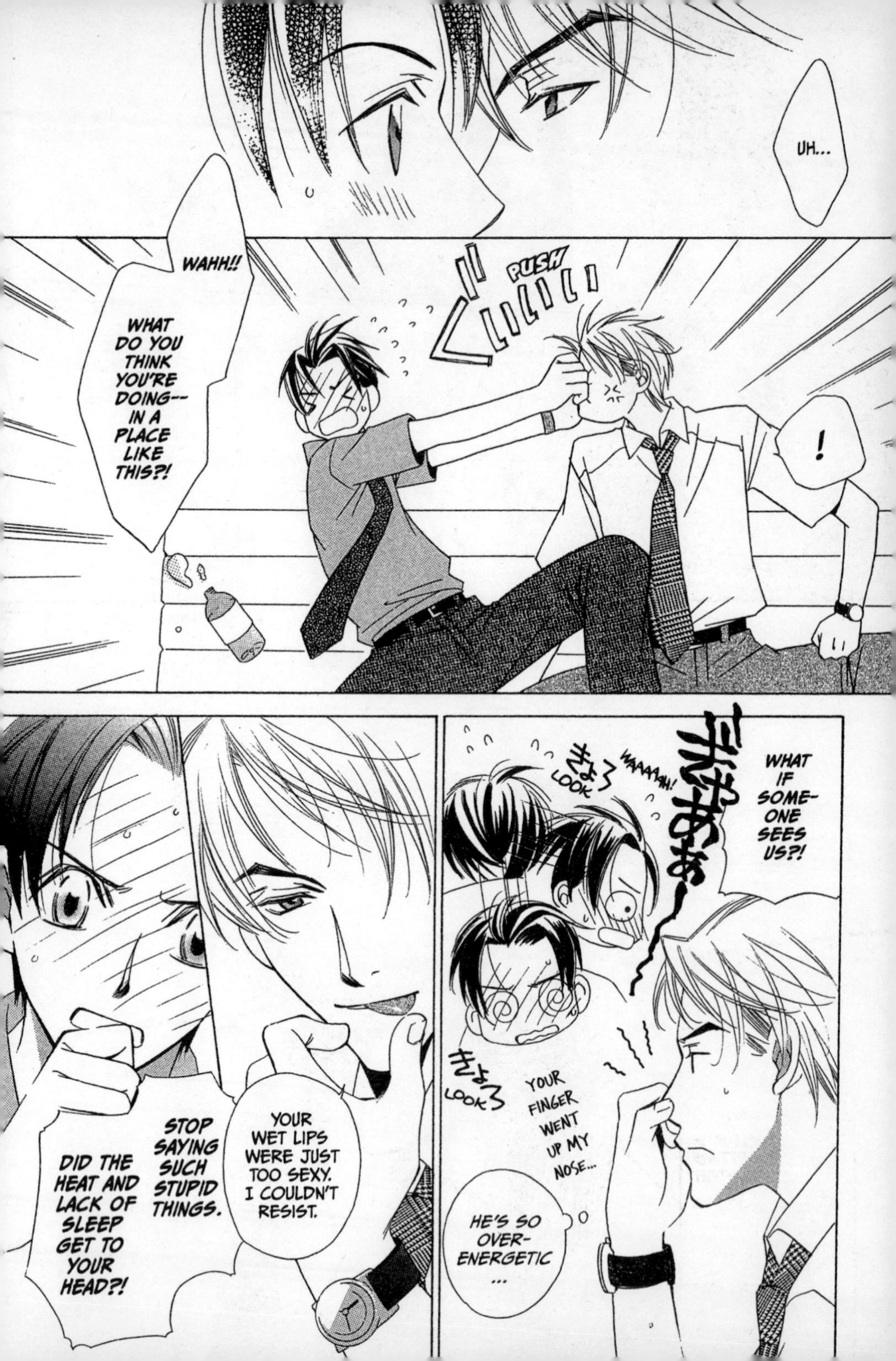
UH...
PUSH
WAHH!!
WHAT DO YOU THINK YOU'RE DOING--IN A PLACE LIKE THIS?!
!
WAAAAAH!
WHAT IF SOMEONE SEES US?!
きょろ LOOK
きょろ LOOK
YOUR FINGER WENT UP MY NOSE...
HE'S SO OVER-ENERGETIC...
YOUR WET LIPS WERE JUST TOO SEXY. I COULDN'T RESIST.
STOP SAYING SUCH STUPID THINGS.
DID THE HEAT AND LACK OF SLEEP GET TO YOUR HEAD?!

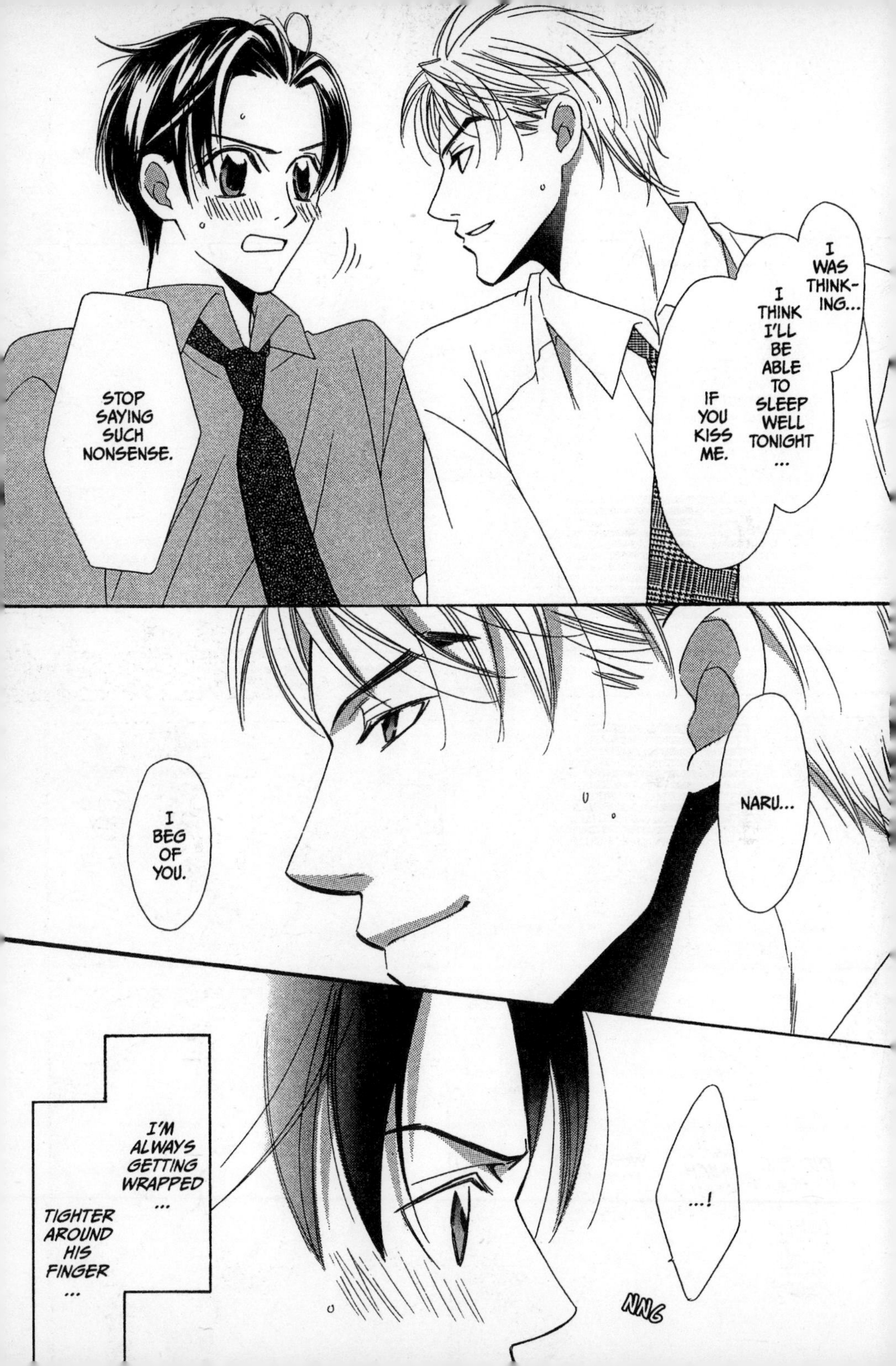
I WAS THINKING...
I THINK I'LL BE ABLE TO SLEEP WELL TONIGHT ...
IF YOU KISS ME.
STOP SAYING SUCH NONSENSE.
NARU...
I BEG OF YOU.
...!
NNG
I'M ALWAYS GETTING WRAPPED ...
TIGHTER AROUND HIS FINGER ...

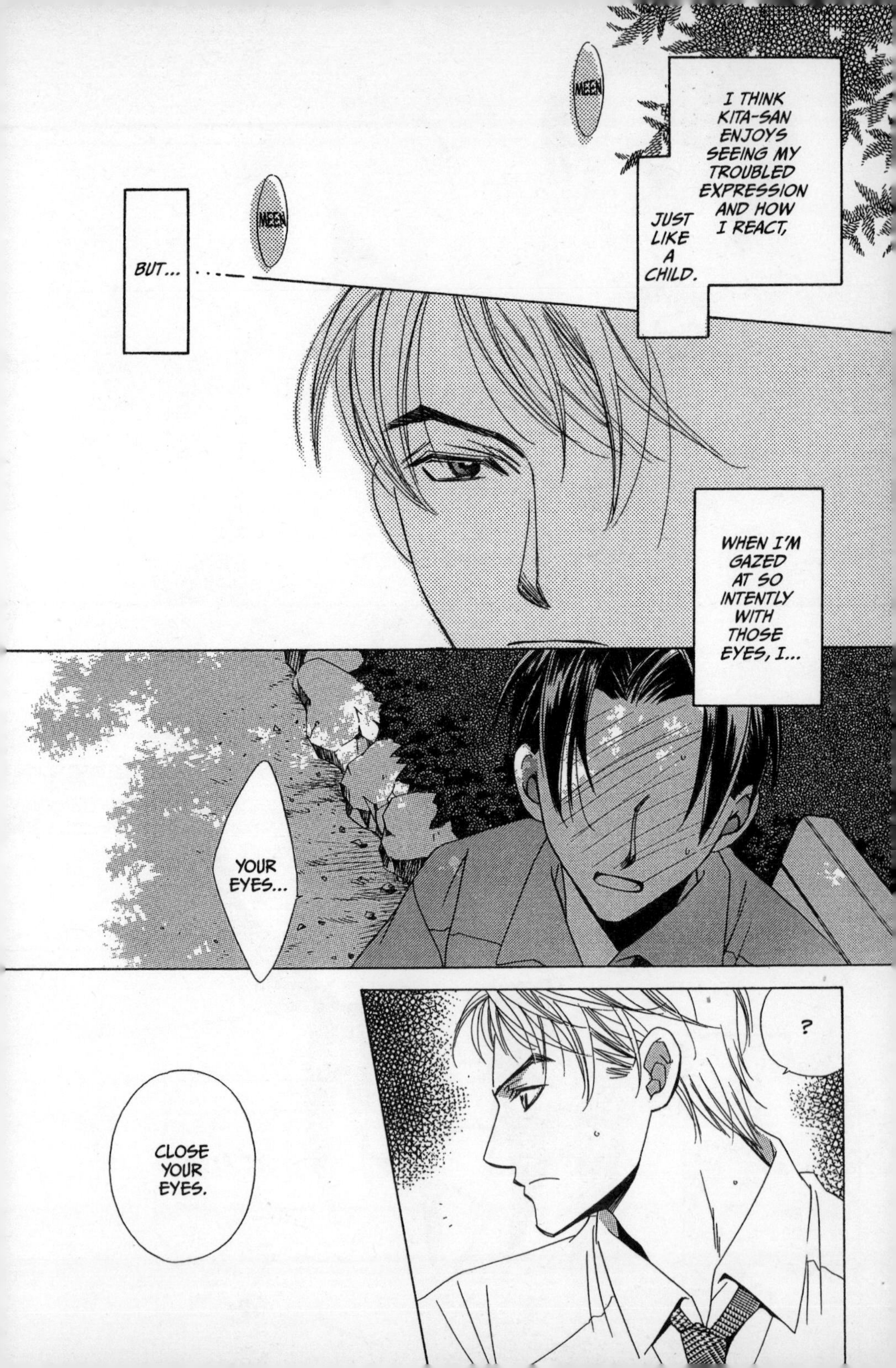
I THINK KITA-SAN ENJOYS SEEING MY TROUBLED EXPRESSION AND HOW I REACT,
JUST LIKE A CHILD.
MEEN
MEEN
BUT...
WHEN I'M GAZED AT SO INTENTLY WITH THOSE EYES, I...
YOUR EYES...
?
CLOSE YOUR EYES.

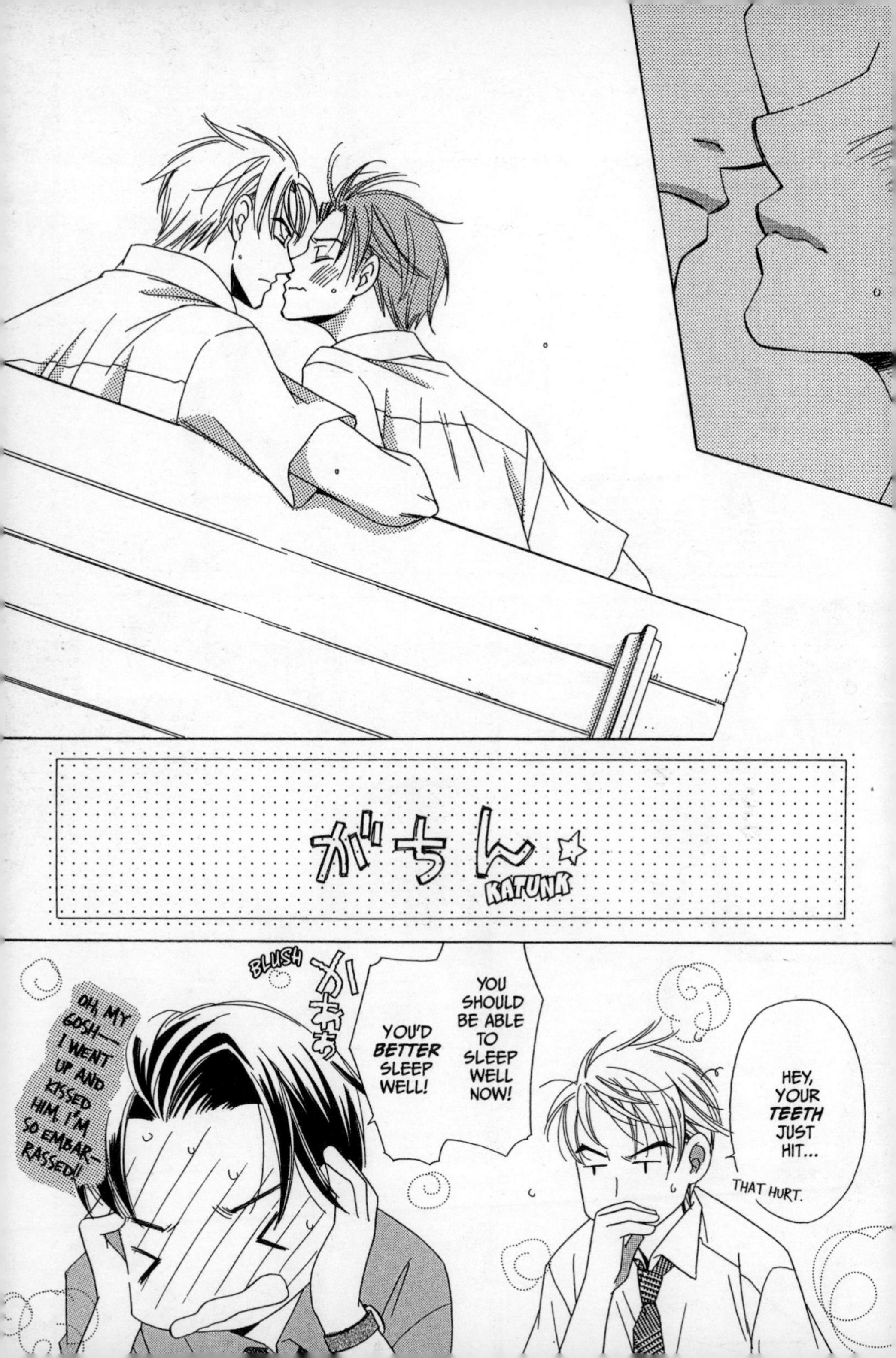

がちん
KATUNK
HEY, YOUR TEETH JUST HIT...
THAT HURT.
YOU SHOULD BE ABLE TO SLEEP WELL NOW!
YOU'D BETTER SLEEP WELL!
かぁぁ
BLUSH
OH, MY GOSH— I WENT UP AND KISSED HIM, I'M SO EMBARRASSED!!

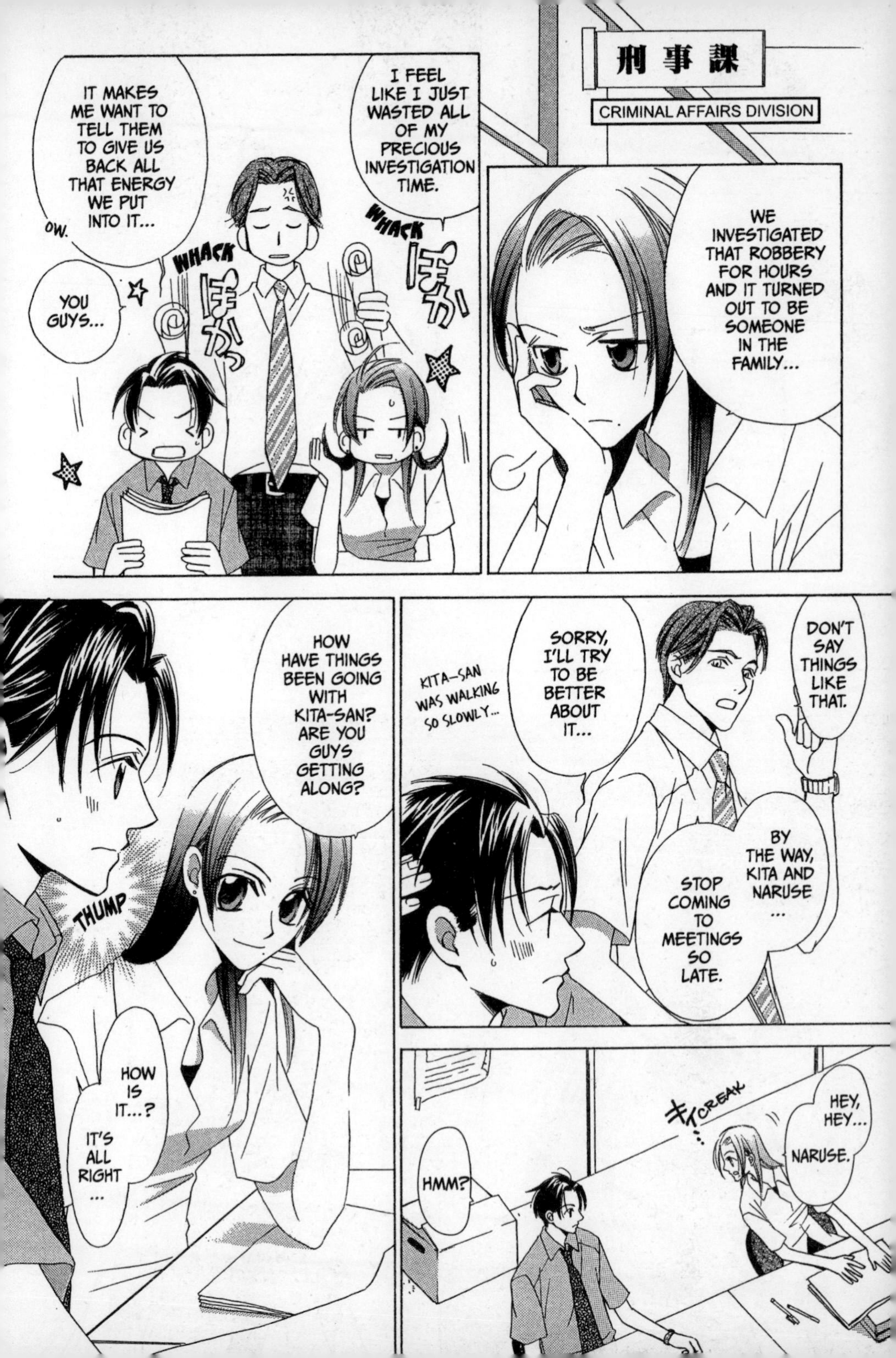

刑事課
CRIMINAL AFFAIRS DIVISION
WE INVESTIGATED THAT ROBBERY FOR HOURS AND IT TURNED OUT TO BE SOMEONE IN THE FAMILY...
I FEEL LIKE I JUST WASTED ALL OF MY PRECIOUS INVESTIGATION TIME.
WHACK
ぽか
IT MAKES ME WANT TO TELL THEM TO GIVE US BACK ALL THAT ENERGY WE PUT INTO IT...
WHACK
ぽかっ
OW.
YOU GUYS...
DON'T SAY THINGS LIKE THAT.
SORRY, I'LL TRY TO BE BETTER ABOUT IT...
KITA-SAN WAS WALKING SO SLOWLY...
BY THE WAY, KITA AND NARUSE...
STOP COMING TO MEETINGS SO LATE.
HEY, HEY...
NARUSE.
キィ
CREAK
HMM?
HOW HAVE THINGS BEEN GOING WITH KITA-SAN? ARE YOU GUYS GETTING ALONG?
THUMP
HOW IS IT...?
IT'S ALL RIGHT...

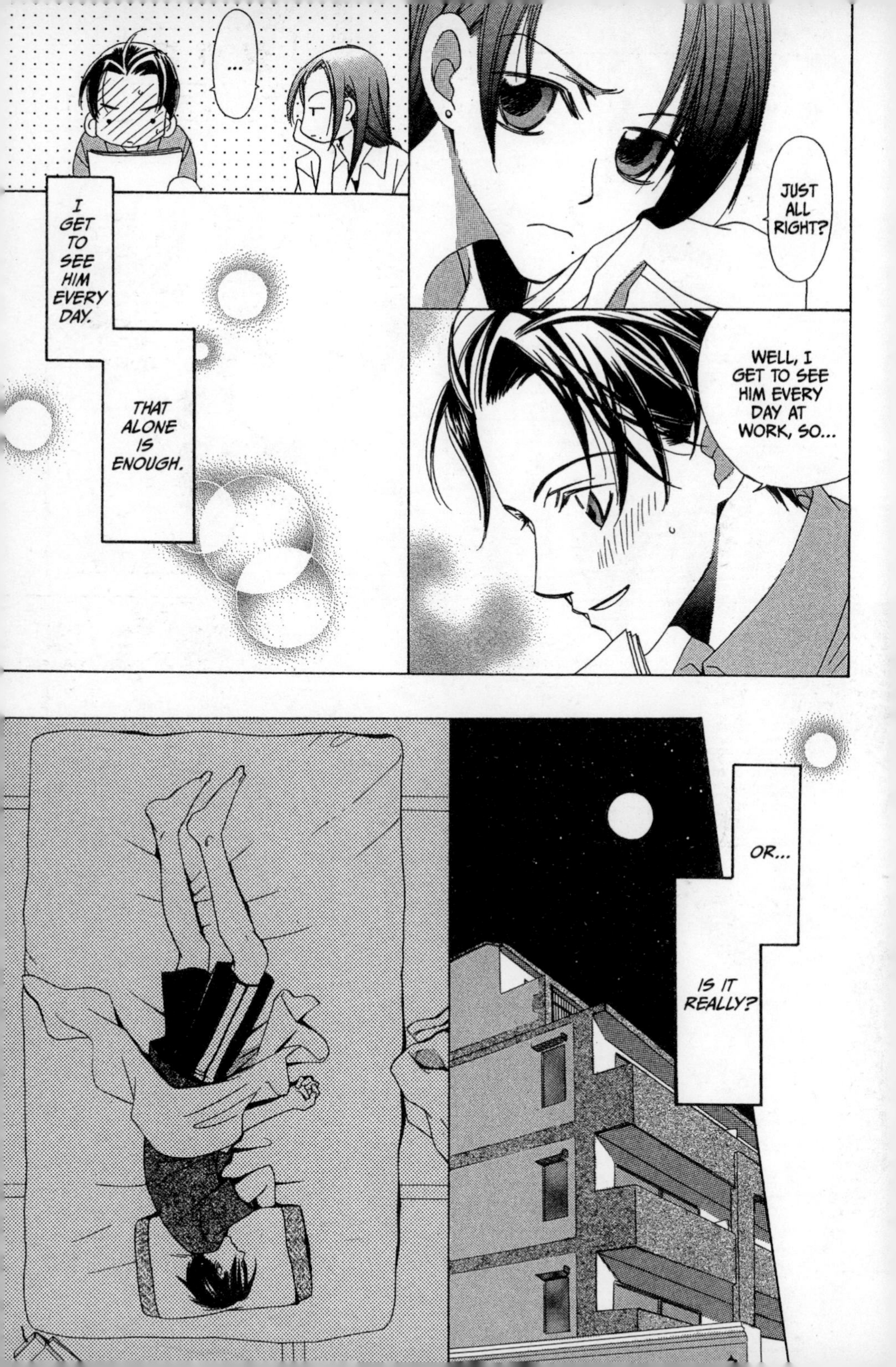
JUST ALL RIGHT?
...
WELL, I GET TO SEE HIM EVERY DAY AT WORK, SO...
I GET TO SEE HIM EVERY DAY.
THAT ALONE IS ENOUGH.
OR...
IS IT REALLY?

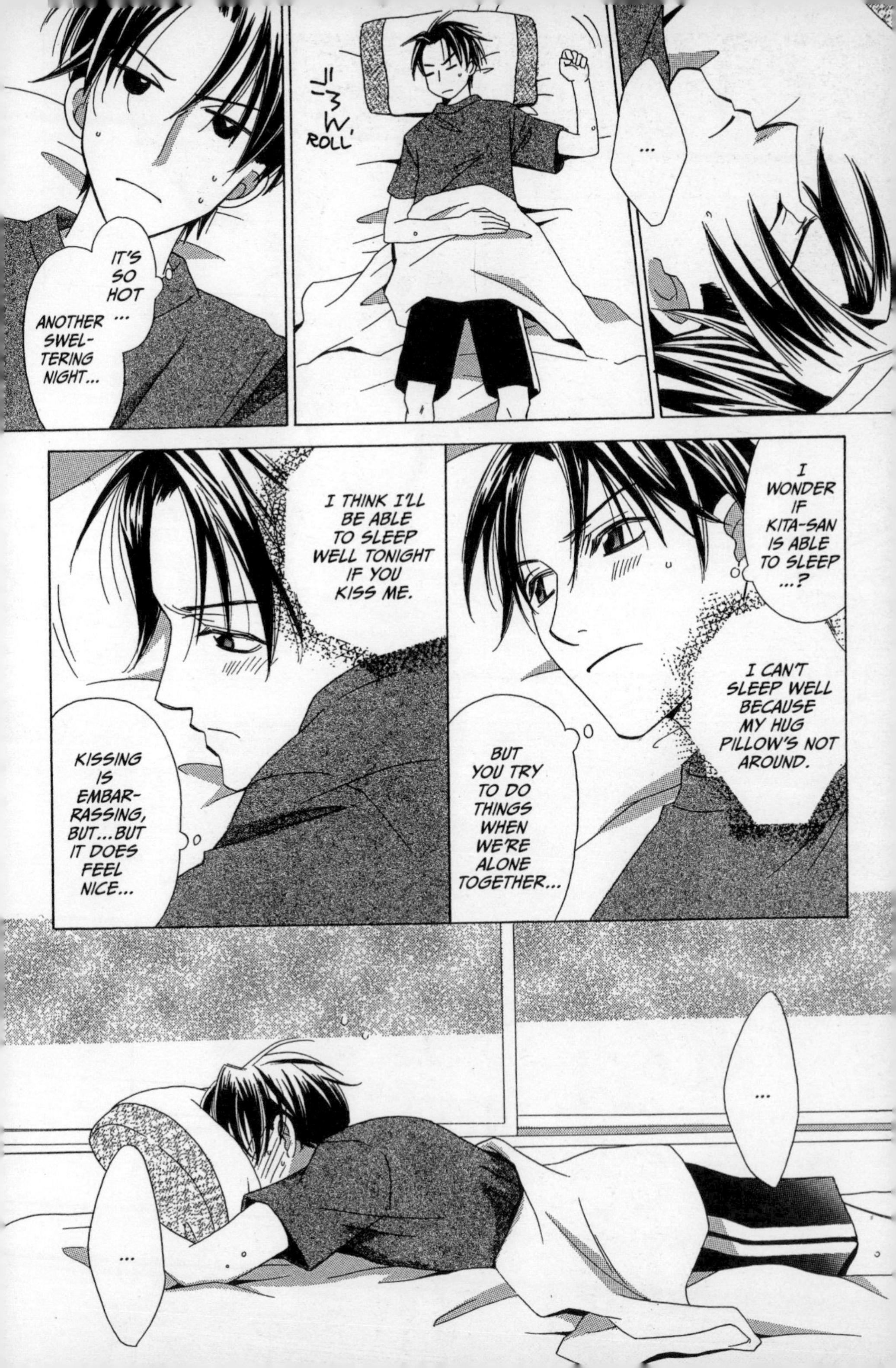
...
ROLL
IT'S SO HOT ...
ANOTHER SWEL-TERING NIGHT...
I WONDER IF KITA-SAN IS ABLE TO SLEEP ...?
I CAN'T SLEEP WELL BECAUSE MY HUG PILLOW'S NOT AROUND.
BUT YOU TRY TO DO THINGS WHEN WE'RE ALONE TOGETHER...
I THINK I'LL BE ABLE TO SLEEP WELL TONIGHT IF YOU KISS ME.
KISSING IS EMBAR-RASSING, BUT...BUT IT DOES FEEL NICE...
...
...

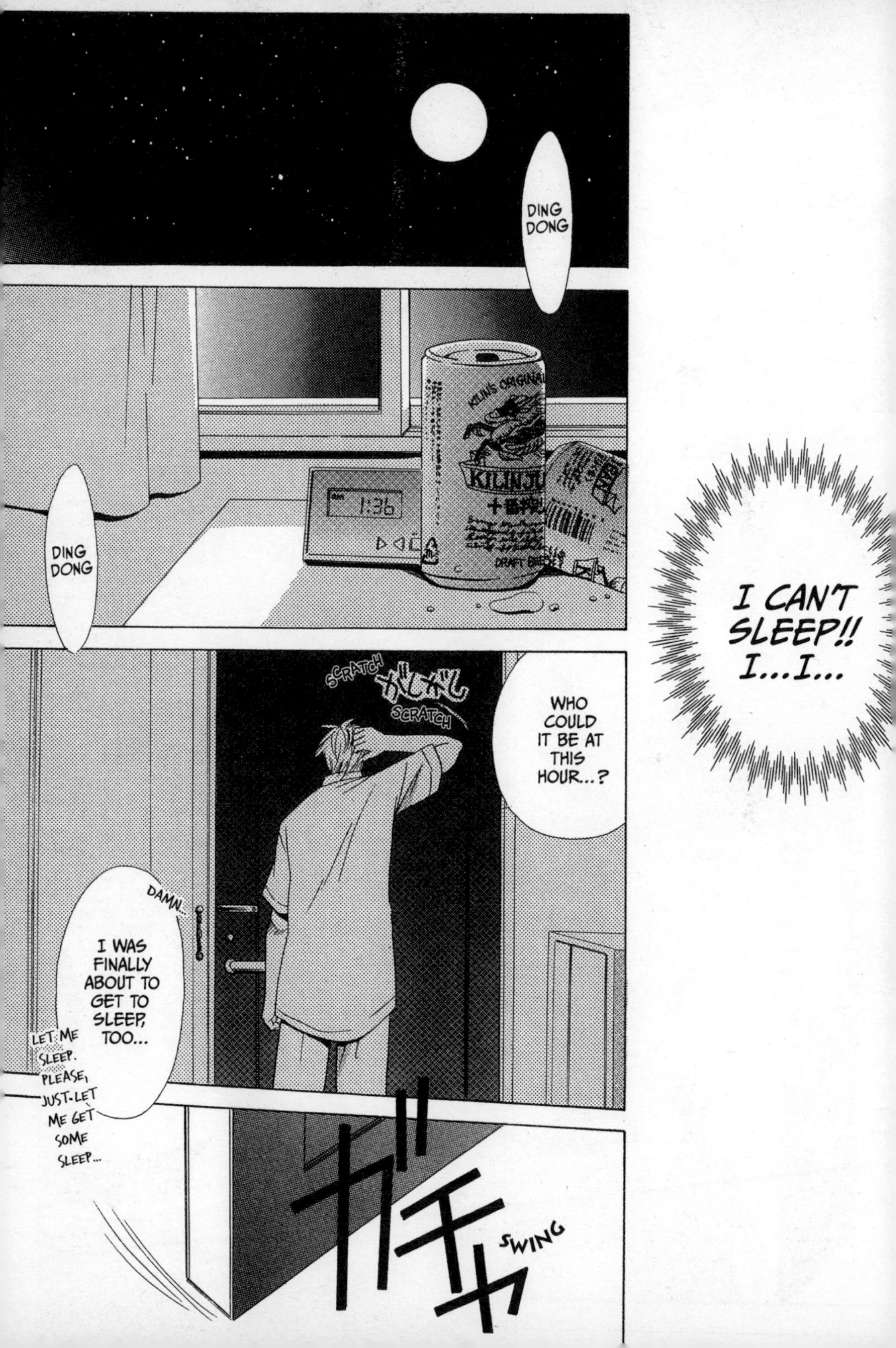
DING DONG
I CAN'T SLEEP!! I...I...
DING DONG
がしがし
SCRATCH SCRATCH
WHO COULD IT BE AT THIS HOUR...?
DAMN...
I WAS FINALLY ABOUT TO GET TO SLEEP, TOO...
LET ME SLEEP. PLEASE, JUST LET ME GET SOME SLEEP...
ガチャ
SWING

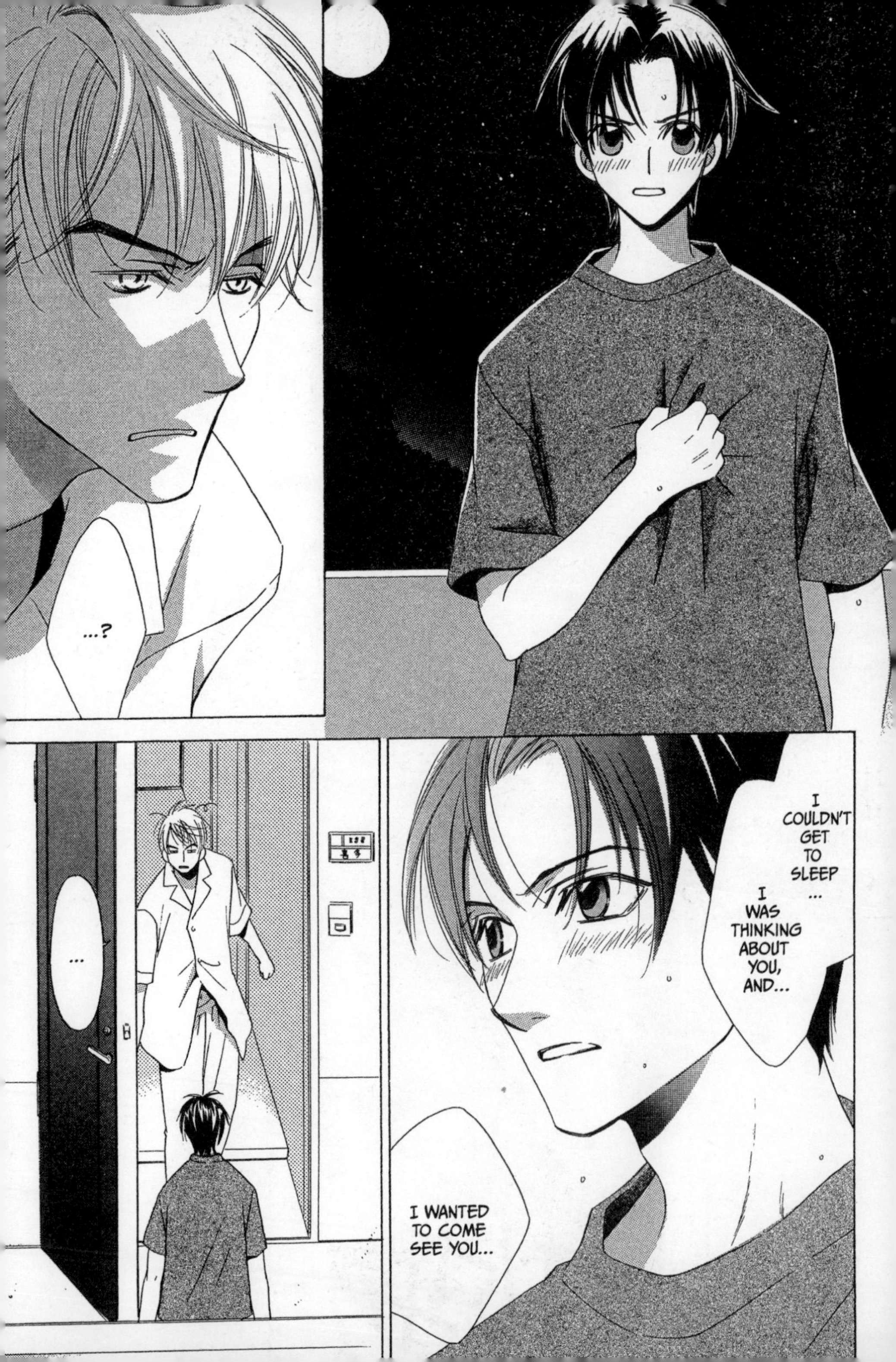
...?
I COULDN'T GET TO SLEEP ...
I WAS THINKING ABOUT YOU, AND...
I WANTED TO COME SEE YOU...
...

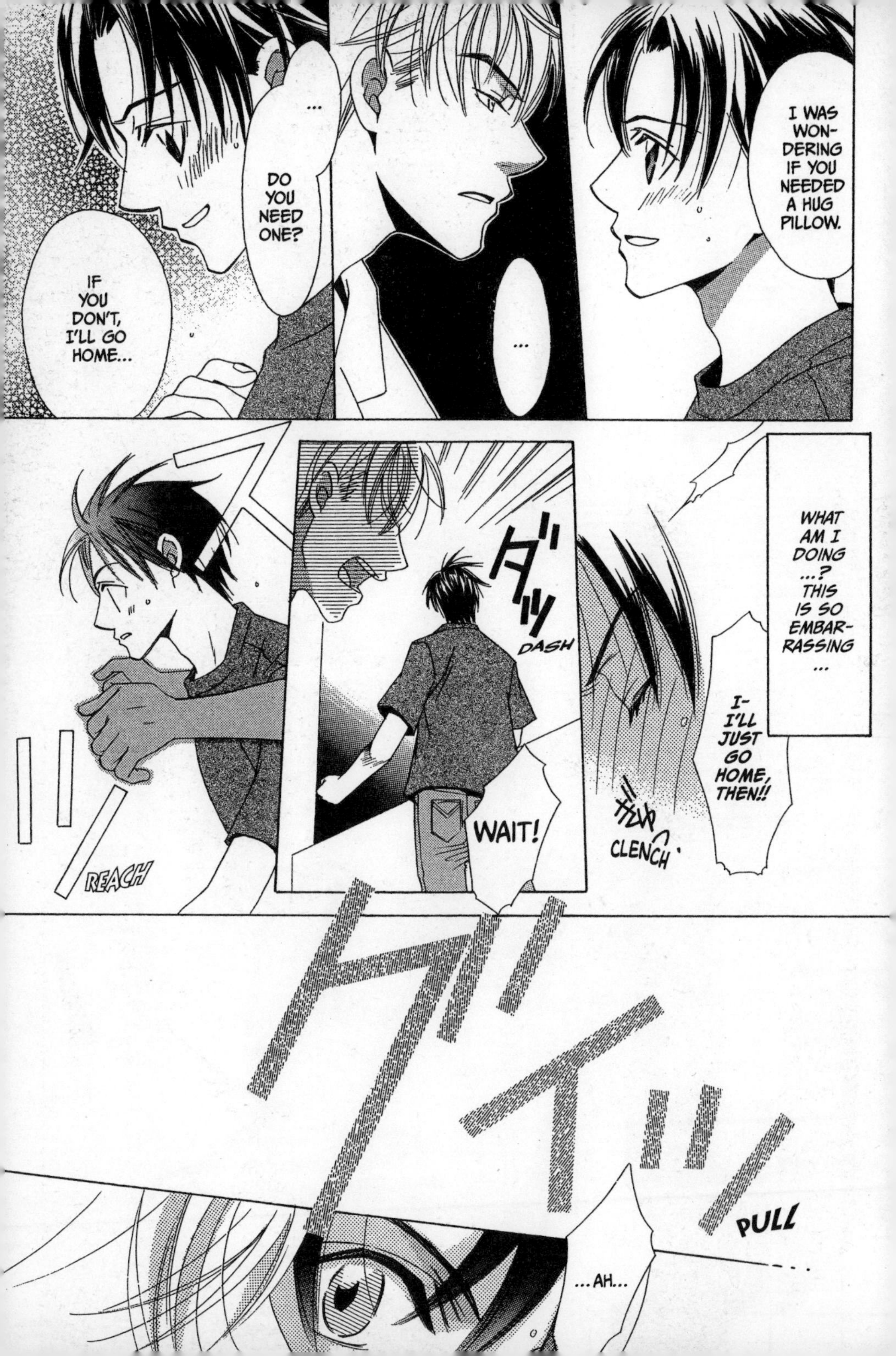
I WAS WONDERING IF YOU NEEDED A HUG PILLOW.
...
...
DO YOU NEED ONE?
IF YOU DON'T, I'LL GO HOME...
WHAT AM I DOING ...? THIS IS SO EMBARRASSING ...
I- I'LL JUST GO HOME, THEN!!
CLENCH
ダッ
DASH
WAIT!
REACH
グイッ
PULL
...AH...

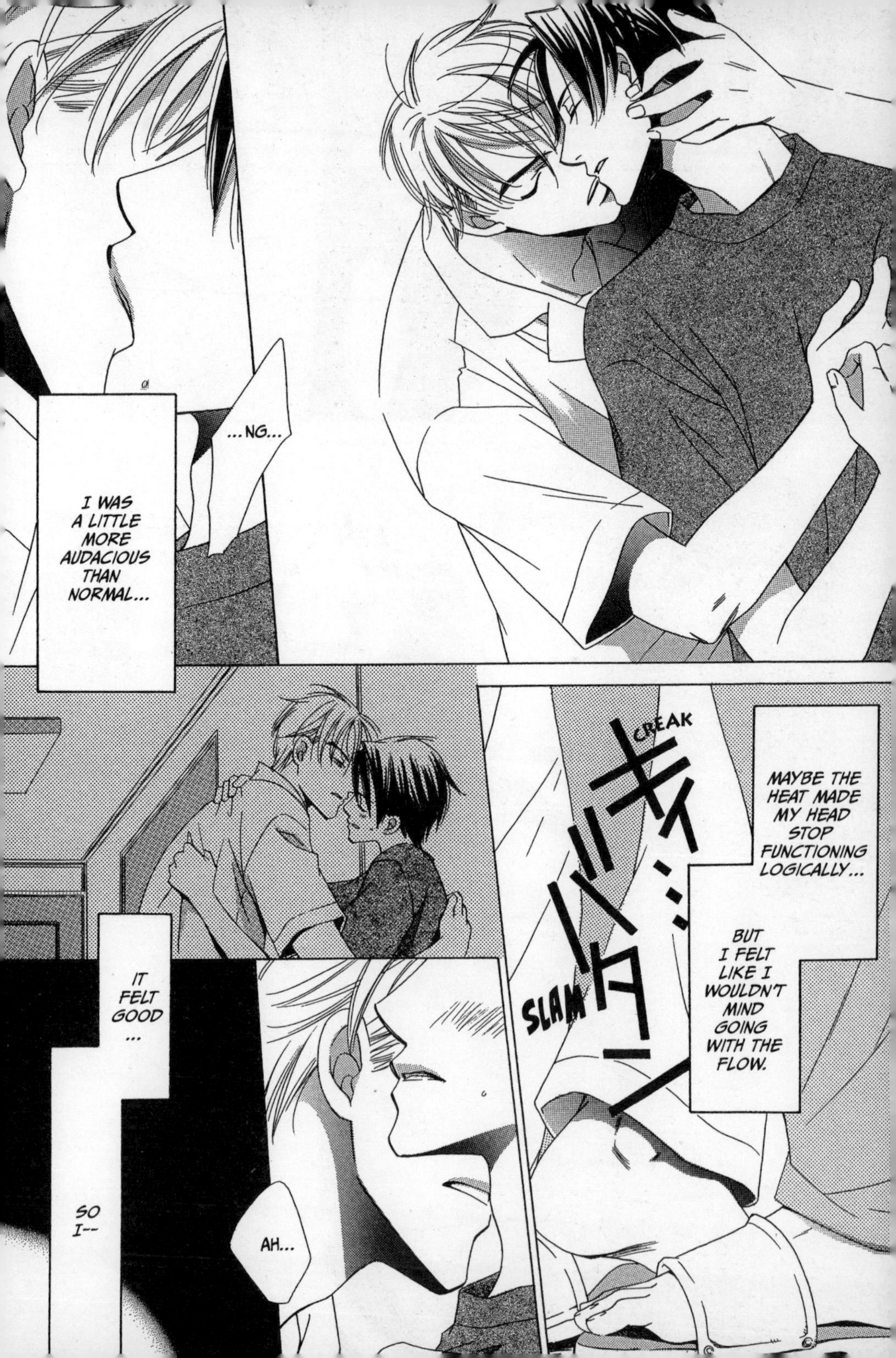

...NG...
I WAS A LITTLE MORE AUDACIOUS THAN NORMAL...
CREAK
MAYBE THE HEAT MADE MY HEAD STOP FUNCTIONING LOGICALLY...
BUT I FELT LIKE I WOULDN'T MIND GOING WITH THE FLOW.
SLAM
IT FELT GOOD...
AH...
SO I--

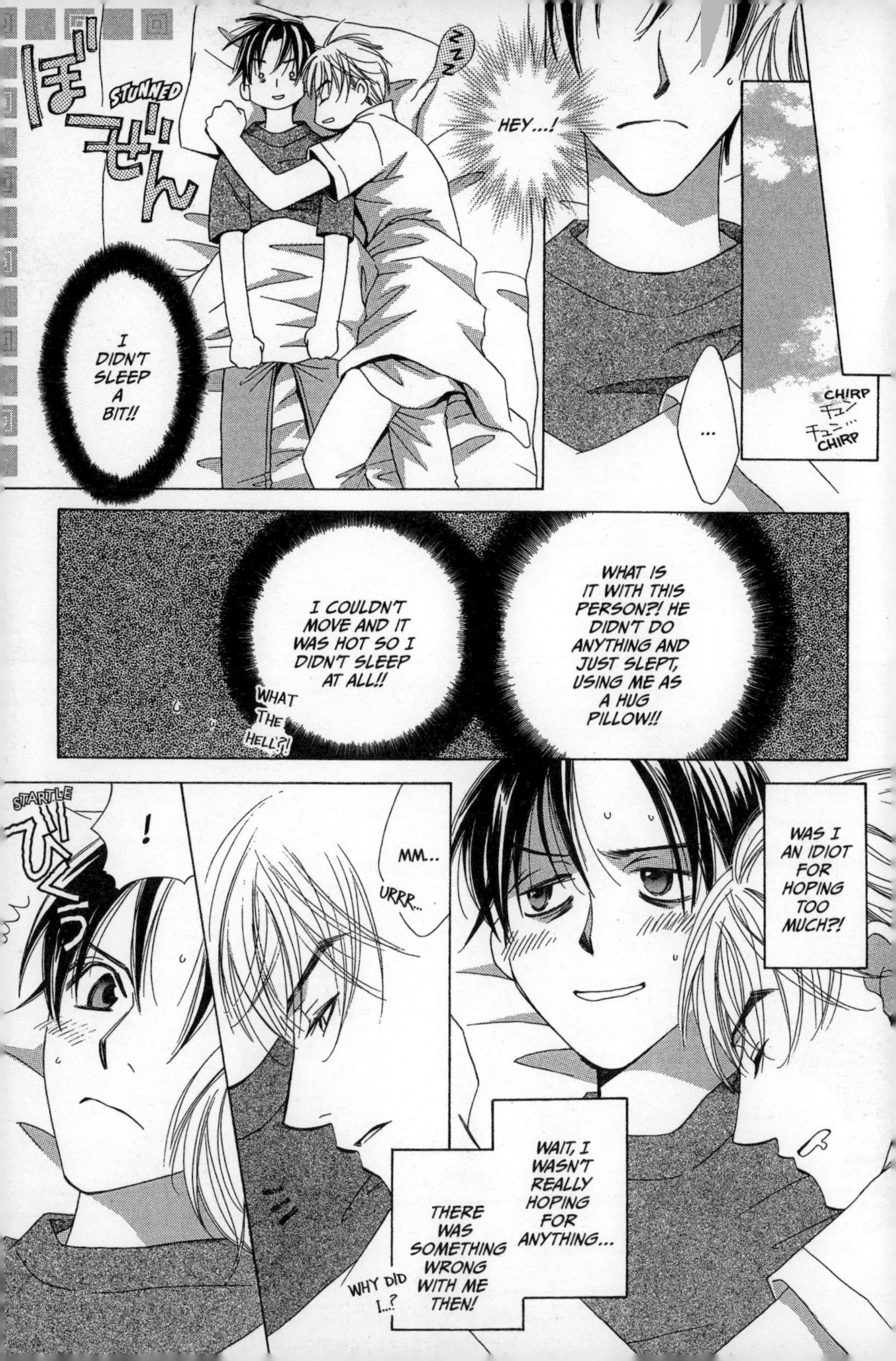

CHIRP
チュン
チュン…
CHIRP
...
HEY...!
ぼーぜん
STUNNED
I DIDN'T SLEEP A BIT!!
WHAT IS IT WITH THIS PERSON?! HE DIDN'T DO ANYTHING AND JUST SLEPT, USING ME AS A HUG PILLOW!!
I COULDN'T MOVE AND IT WAS HOT SO I DIDN'T SLEEP AT ALL!!
WHAT THE HELL?!
WAS I AN IDIOT FOR HOPING TOO MUCH?!
WAIT, I WASN'T REALLY HOPING FOR ANYTHING...
THERE WAS SOMETHING WRONG WITH ME THEN!
WHY DID I..?
MM...
URRR..
!
STARTLE

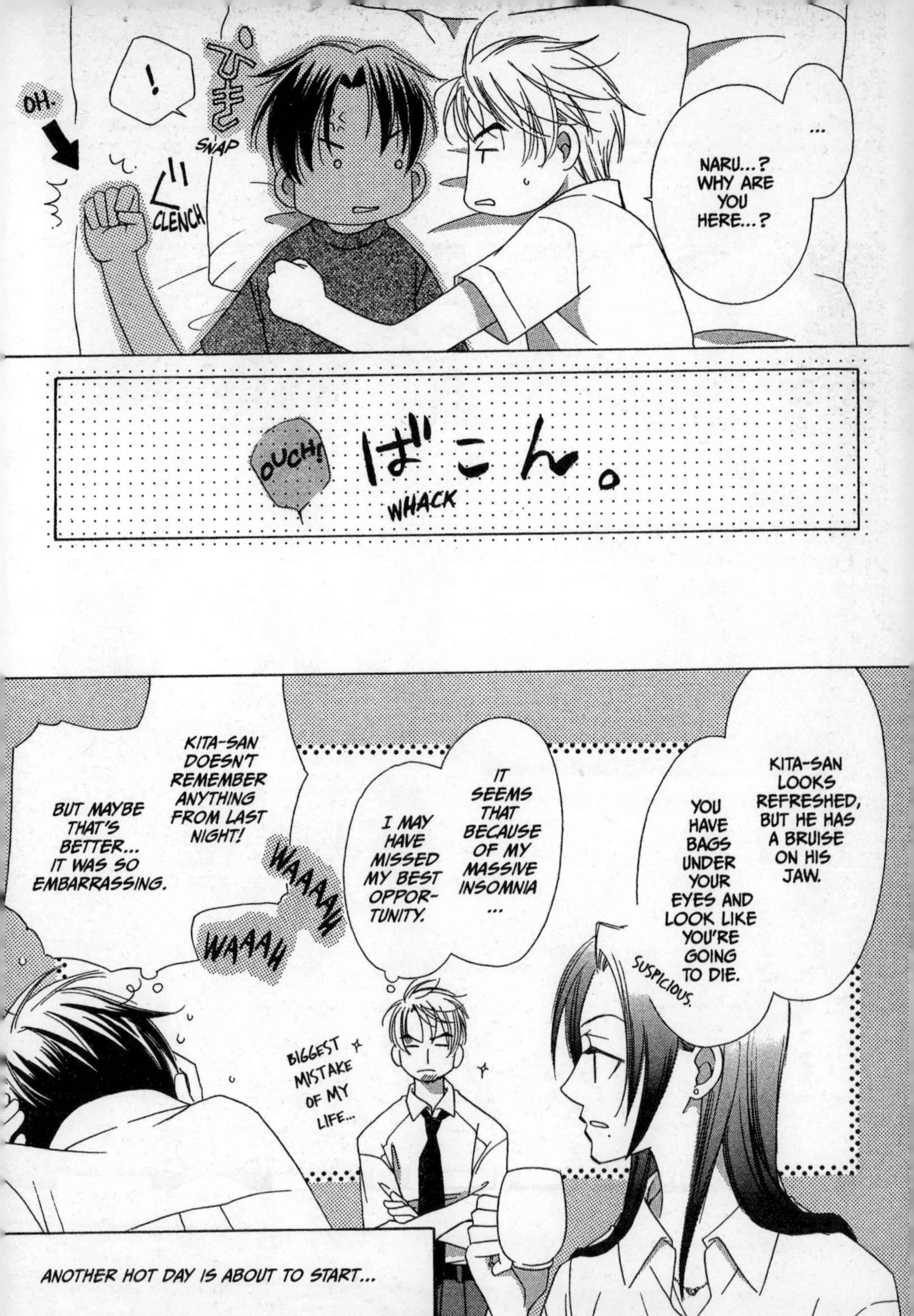
...
NARU...? WHY ARE YOU HERE...?
SNAP
!
OH.
CLENCH
ばこん。
WHACK
OUCH!
KITA-SAN LOOKS REFRESHED, BUT HE HAS A BRUISE ON HIS JAW.
YOU HAVE BAGS UNDER YOUR EYES AND LOOK LIKE YOU'RE GOING TO DIE.
SUSPICIOUS.
IT SEEMS THAT BECAUSE OF MY MASSIVE INSOMNIA ...
I MAY HAVE MISSED MY BEST OPPORTUNITY.
BIGGEST MISTAKE OF MY LIFE...
WAAAAAH
WAAAH
KITA-SAN DOESN'T REMEMBER ANYTHING FROM LAST NIGHT!
BUT MAYBE THAT'S BETTER... IT WAS SO EMBARRASSING.
ANOTHER HOT DAY IS ABOUT TO START...

SUMMER, BEAR AND STARRY SKY / END

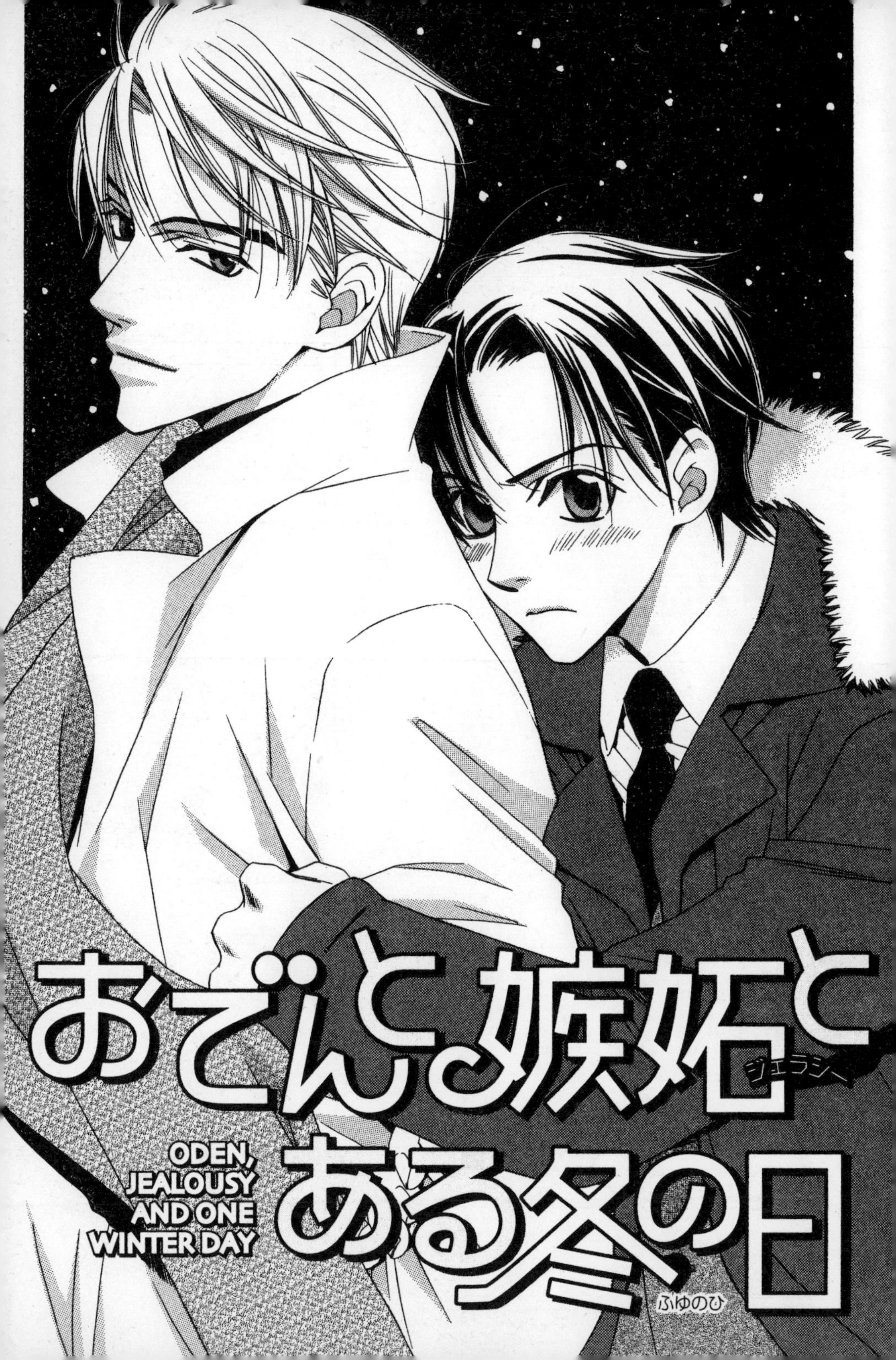
おでんと嫉妬と
ジェラシー
ある冬の日
ふゆのひ
ODEN, JEALOUSY AND ONE WINTER DAY

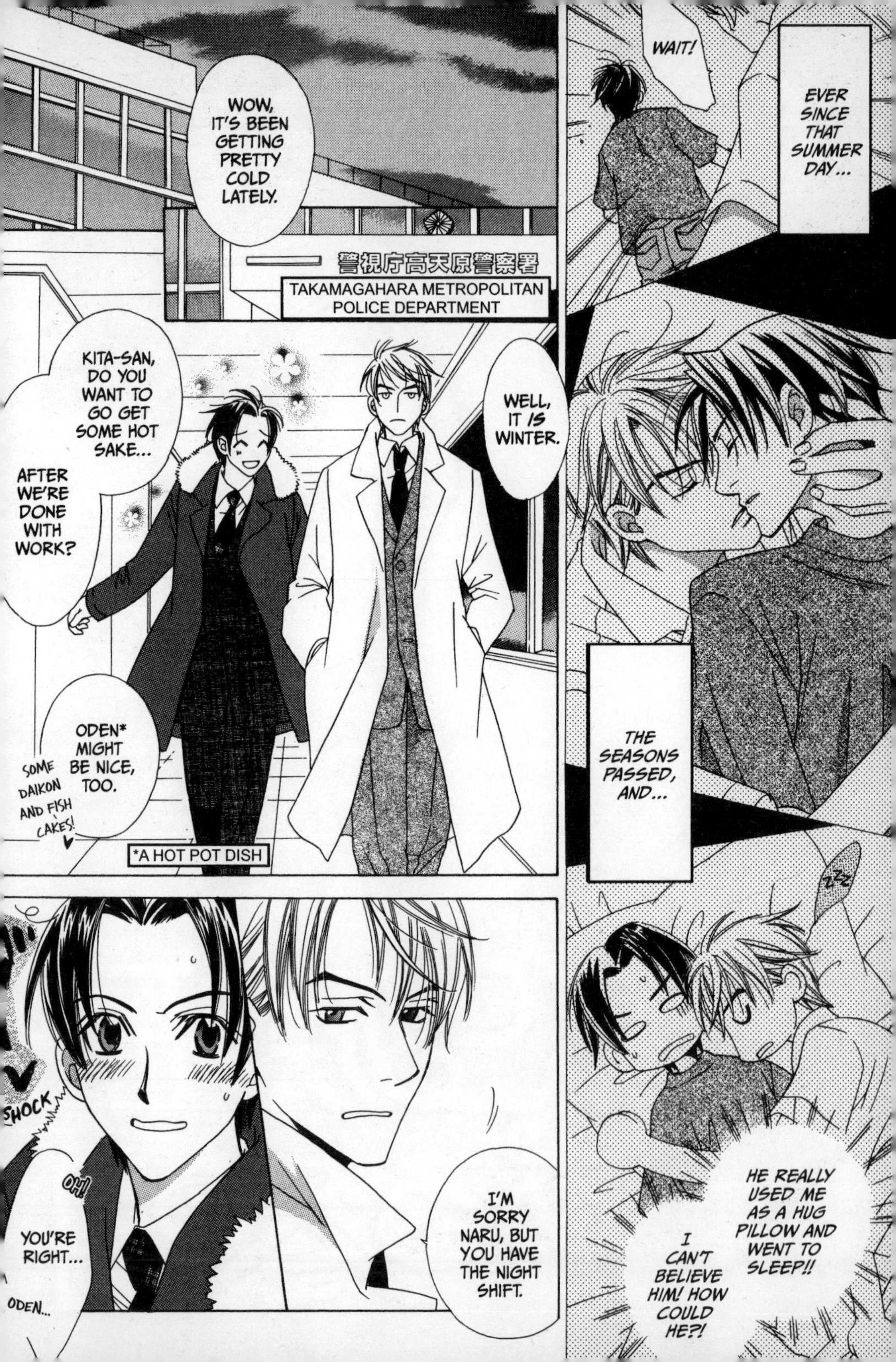
EVER SINCE THAT SUMMER DAY...
WAIT!
THE SEASONS PASSED, AND...
ZZZ
HE REALLY USED ME AS A HUG PILLOW AND WENT TO SLEEP!!
I CAN'T BELIEVE HIM! HOW COULD HE?!
WOW, IT'S BEEN GETTING PRETTY COLD LATELY.
警視庁高天原警察署
TAKAMAGAHARA METROPOLITAN POLICE DEPARTMENT
WELL, IT IS WINTER.
KITA-SAN, DO YOU WANT TO GO GET SOME HOT SAKE...
AFTER WE'RE DONE WITH WORK?
ODEN* MIGHT BE NICE, TOO.
SOME DAIKON AND FISH CAKES!
*A HOT POT DISH
SHOCK
I'M SORRY NARU, BUT YOU HAVE THE NIGHT SHIFT.
OH!
YOU'RE RIGHT...
ODEN...

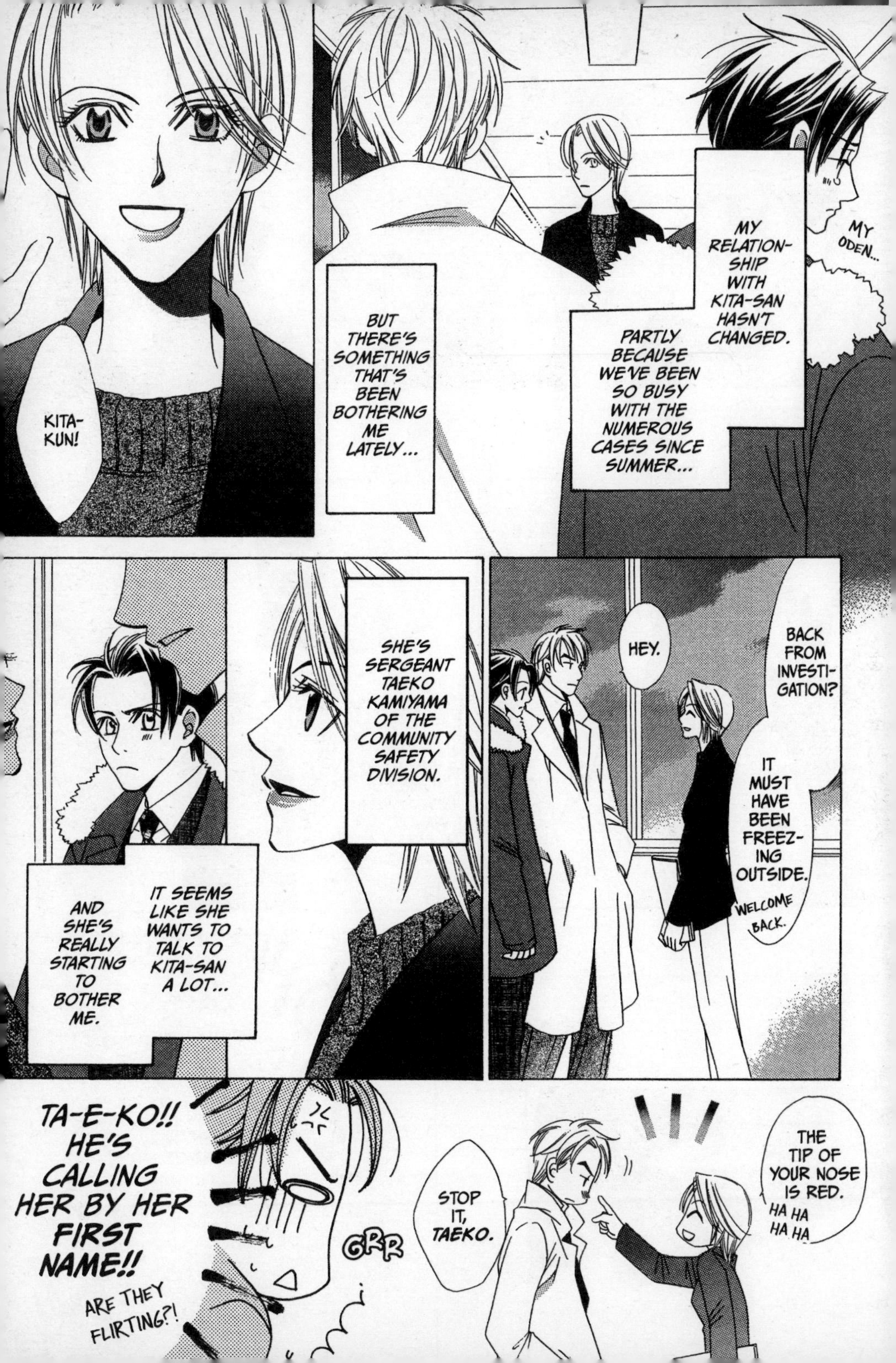
MY ODEN...
MY RELATIONSHIP WITH KITA-SAN HASN'T CHANGED.
PARTLY BECAUSE WE'VE BEEN SO BUSY WITH THE NUMEROUS CASES SINCE SUMMER...
BUT THERE'S SOMETHING THAT'S BEEN BOTHERING ME LATELY...
KITA-KUN!
BACK FROM INVESTIGATION?
IT MUST HAVE BEEN FREEZING OUTSIDE.
WELCOME BACK.
HEY.
SHE'S SERGEANT TAEKO KAMIYAMA OF THE COMMUNITY SAFETY DIVISION.
IT SEEMS LIKE SHE WANTS TO TALK TO KITA-SAN A LOT...
AND SHE'S REALLY STARTING TO BOTHER ME.
THE TIP OF YOUR NOSE IS RED.
HA HA HA HA
STOP IT, TAEKO.
TA-E-KO!! HE'S CALLING HER BY HER FIRST NAME!!
GRR
ARE THEY FLIRTING?!

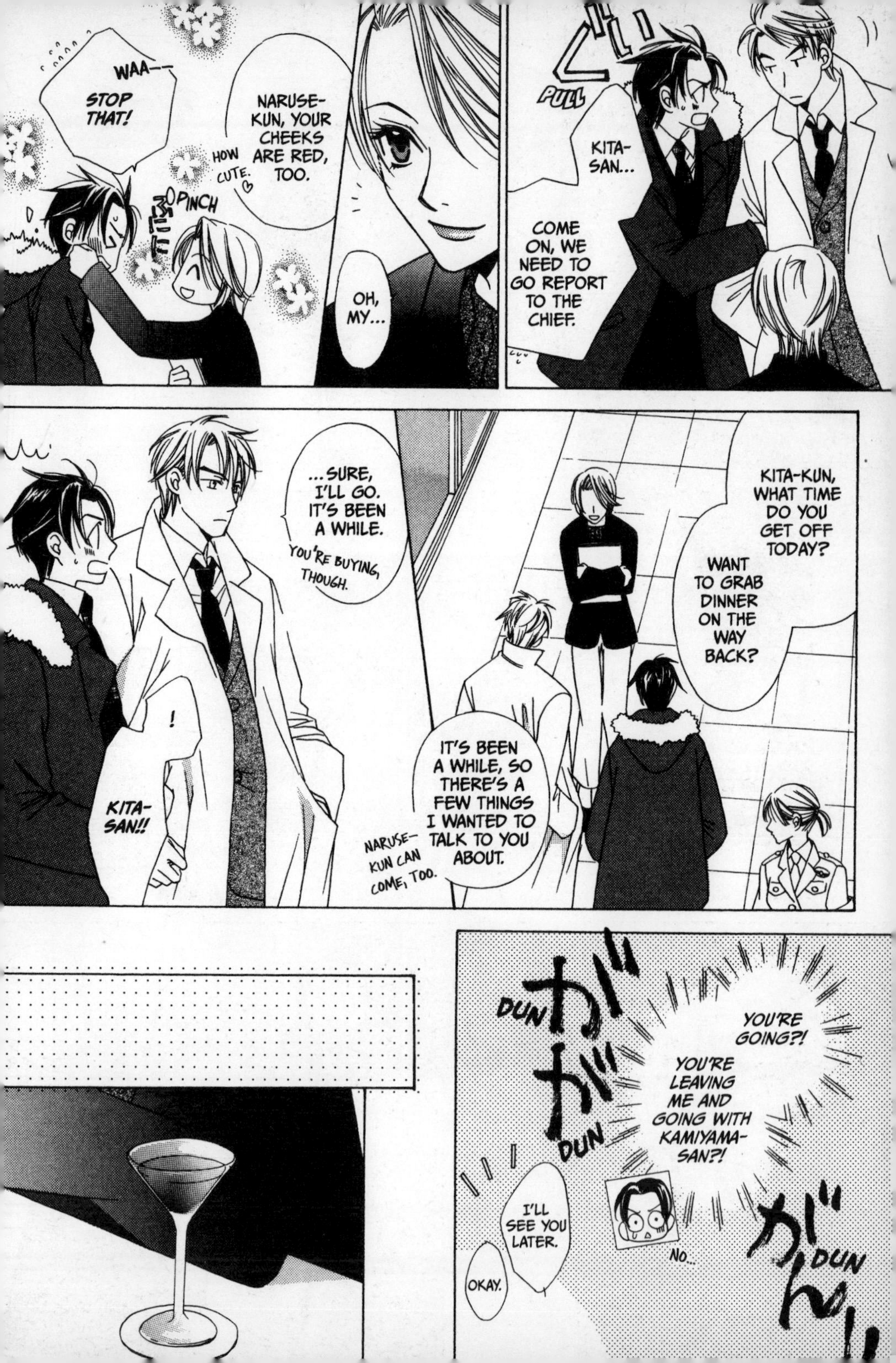
PULL
KITA-SAN...
COME ON, WE NEED TO GO REPORT TO THE CHIEF.
NARUSE-KUN, YOUR CHEEKS ARE RED, TOO.
OH, MY...
WAA--
STOP THAT!
HOW CUTE.
PINCH
KITA-KUN, WHAT TIME DO YOU GET OFF TODAY?
WANT TO GRAB DINNER ON THE WAY BACK?
IT'S BEEN A WHILE, SO THERE'S A FEW THINGS I WANTED TO TALK TO YOU ABOUT.
NARUSE-KUN CAN COME, TOO.
...SURE, I'LL GO. IT'S BEEN A WHILE.
YOU'RE BUYING, THOUGH.
!
KITA-SAN!!
DUN
YOU'RE GOING?!
YOU'RE LEAVING ME AND GOING WITH KAMIYAMA-SAN?!
DUN
I'LL SEE YOU LATER.
OKAY.
NO...
DUN

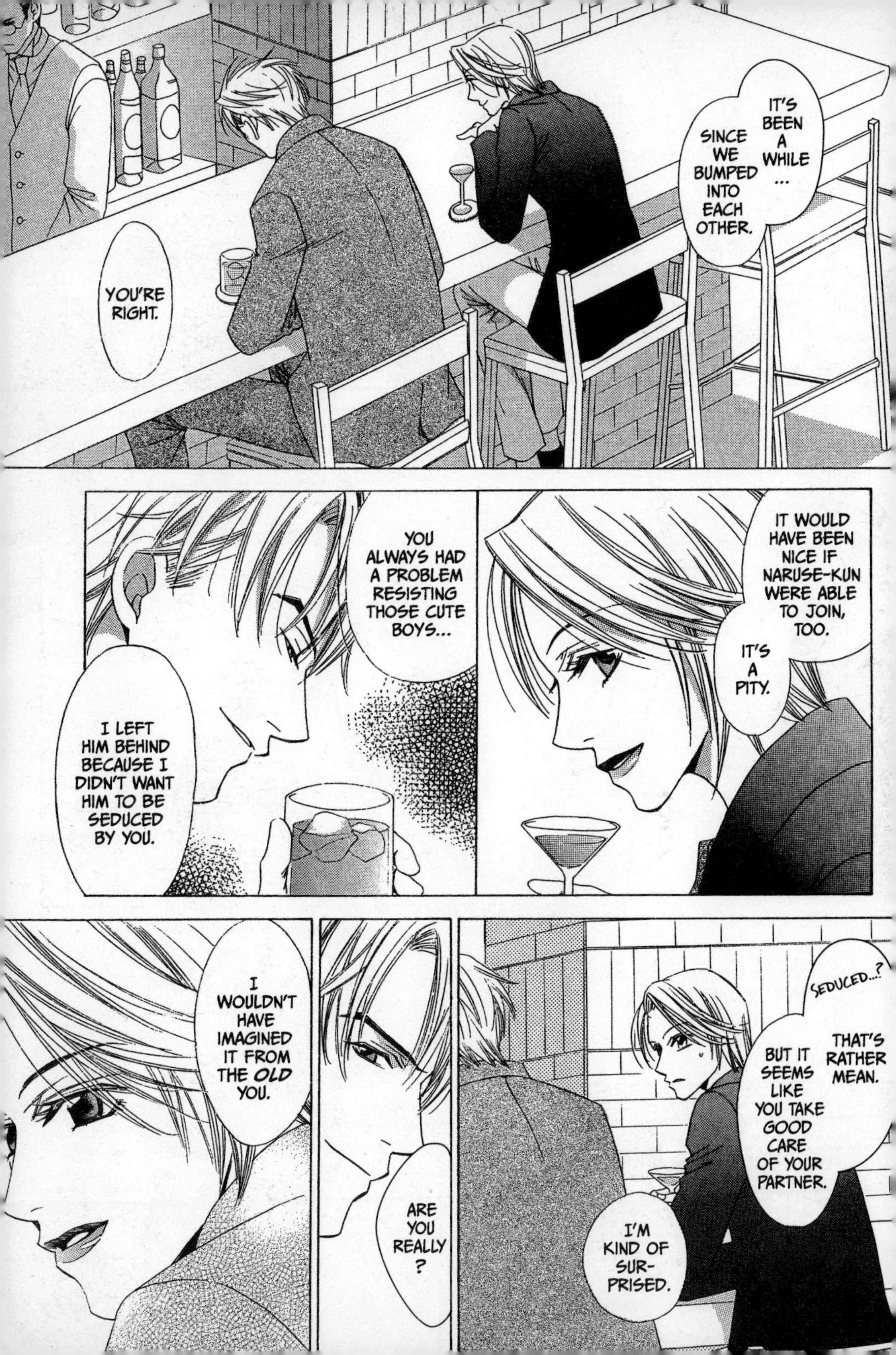
IT'S BEEN A WHILE...
SINCE WE BUMPED INTO EACH OTHER.
YOU'RE RIGHT.
IT WOULD HAVE BEEN NICE IF NARUSE-KUN WERE ABLE TO JOIN, TOO.
IT'S A PITY.
YOU ALWAYS HAD A PROBLEM RESISTING THOSE CUTE BOYS...
I LEFT HIM BEHIND BECAUSE I DIDN'T WANT HIM TO BE SEDUCED BY YOU.
SEDUCED...?
THAT'S RATHER MEAN.
BUT IT SEEMS LIKE YOU TAKE GOOD CARE OF YOUR PARTNER.
I'M KIND OF SUR-PRISED.
ARE YOU REALLY?
I WOULDN'T HAVE IMAGINED IT FROM THE *OLD* YOU.

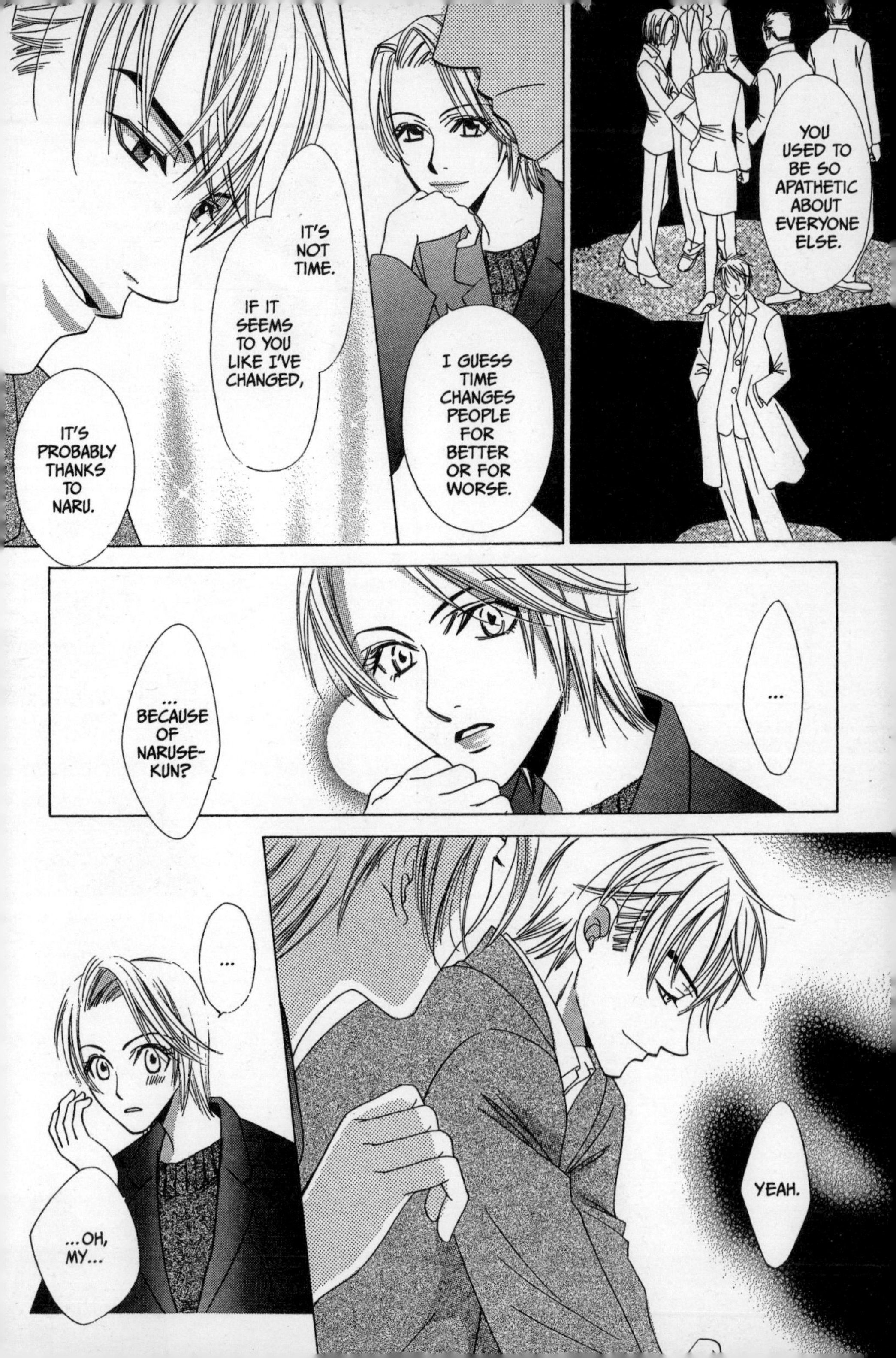
YOU USED TO BE SO APATHETIC ABOUT EVERYONE ELSE.
I GUESS TIME CHANGES PEOPLE FOR BETTER OR FOR WORSE.
IT'S NOT TIME.
IF IT SEEMS TO YOU LIKE I'VE CHANGED,
IT'S PROBABLY THANKS TO NARU.
...
...BECAUSE OF NARUSE-KUN?
YEAH.
...
...OH, MY...

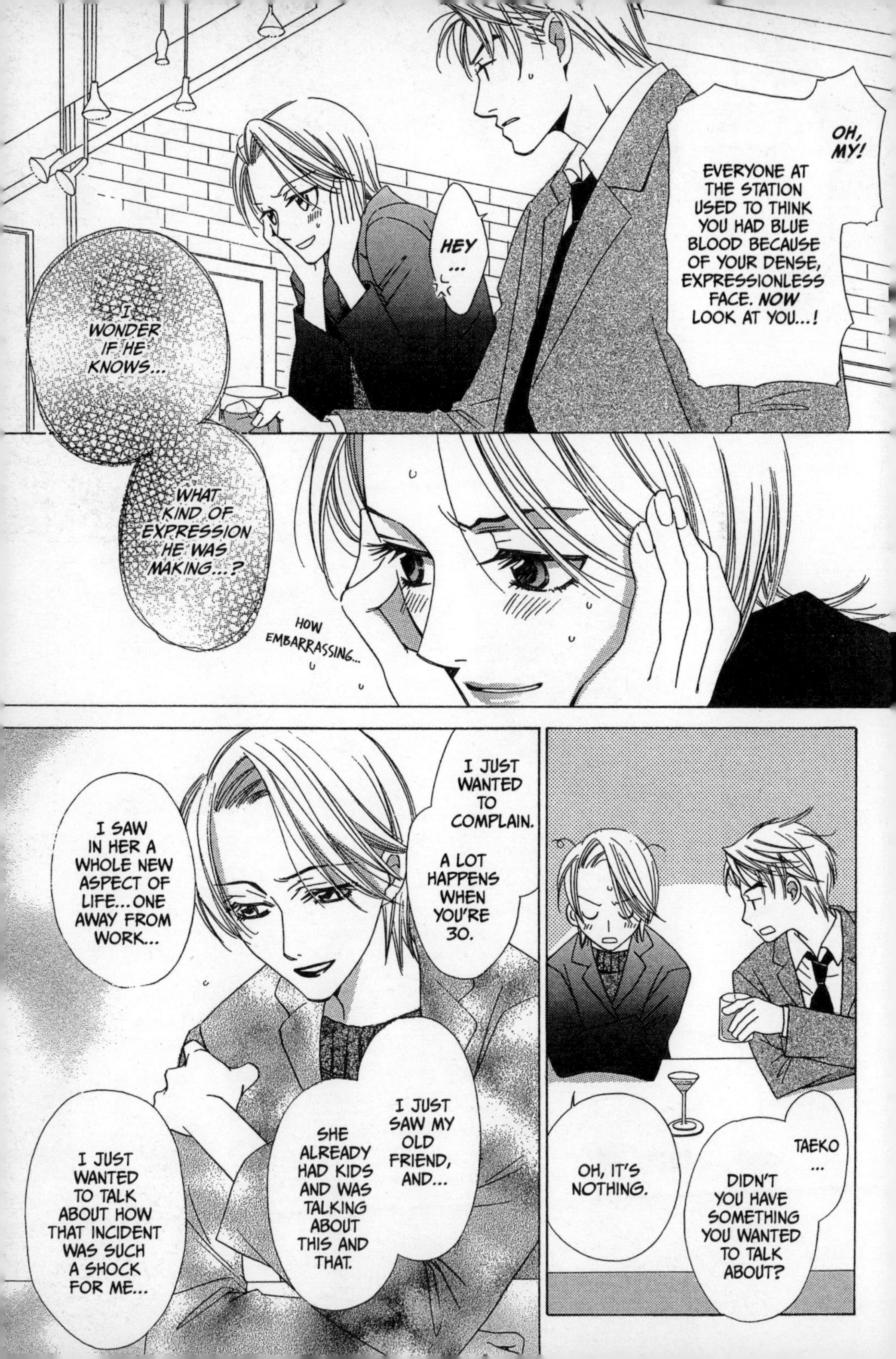
OH, MY!
EVERYONE AT THE STATION USED TO THINK YOU HAD BLUE BLOOD BECAUSE OF YOUR DENSE, EXPRESSIONLESS FACE. NOW LOOK AT YOU...!
HEY ...
I WONDER IF HE KNOWS...
WHAT KIND OF EXPRESSION HE WAS MAKING...?
HOW EMBARRASSING...
TAEKO ...
DIDN'T YOU HAVE SOMETHING YOU WANTED TO TALK ABOUT?
OH, IT'S NOTHING.
I JUST WANTED TO COMPLAIN.
A LOT HAPPENS WHEN YOU'RE 30.
I SAW IN HER A WHOLE NEW ASPECT OF LIFE...ONE AWAY FROM WORK...
I JUST SAW MY OLD FRIEND, AND...
SHE ALREADY HAD KIDS AND WAS TALKING ABOUT THIS AND THAT.
I JUST WANTED TO TALK ABOUT HOW THAT INCIDENT WAS SUCH A SHOCK FOR ME...

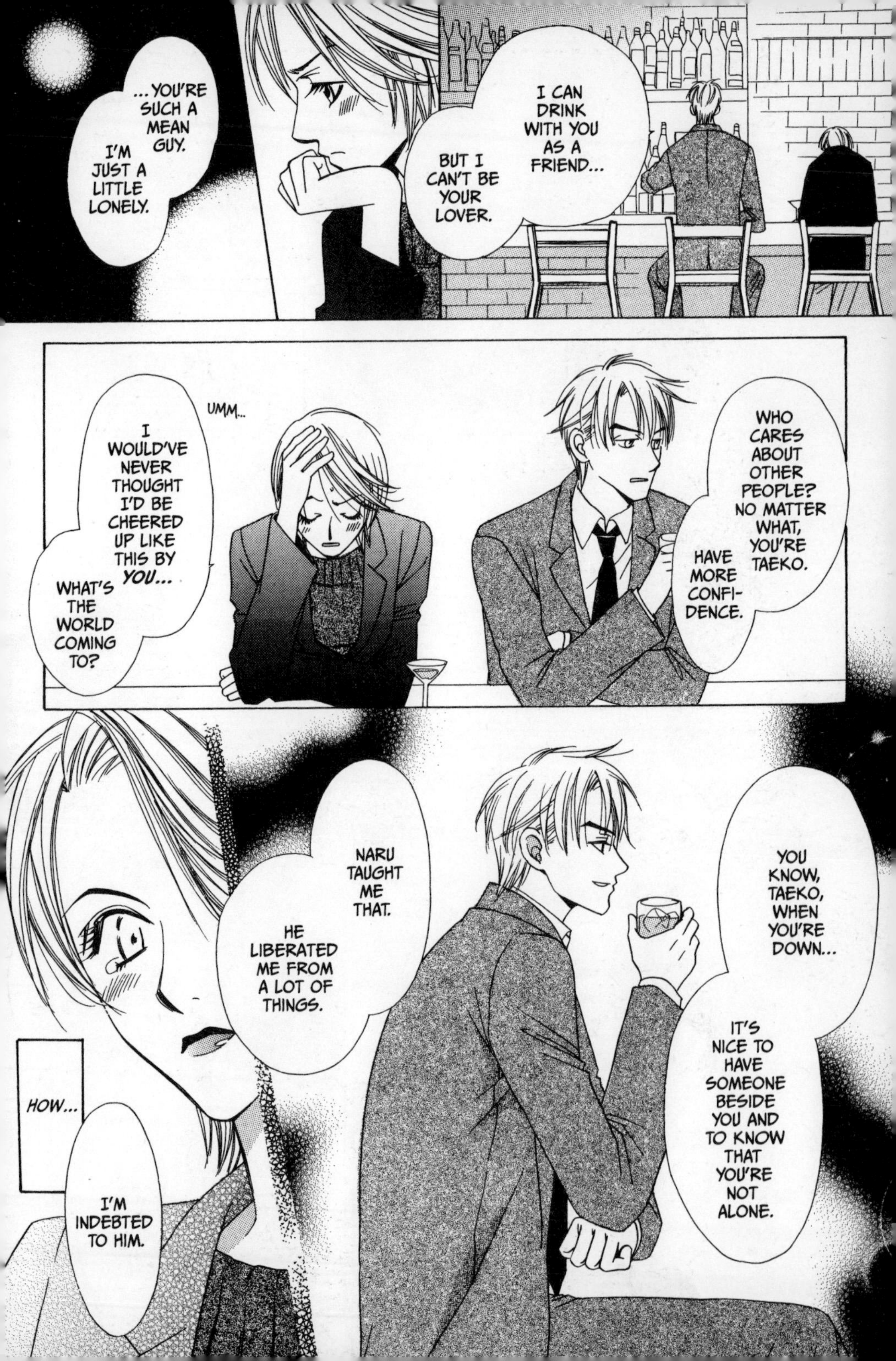
I CAN DRINK WITH YOU AS A FRIEND...
BUT I CAN'T BE YOUR LOVER.
...YOU'RE SUCH A MEAN GUY.
I'M JUST A LITTLE LONELY.
WHO CARES ABOUT OTHER PEOPLE? NO MATTER WHAT, YOU'RE TAEKO.
HAVE MORE CONFIDENCE.
UMM...
I WOULD'VE NEVER THOUGHT I'D BE CHEERED UP LIKE THIS BY *YOU*...
WHAT'S THE WORLD COMING TO?
YOU KNOW, TAEKO, WHEN YOU'RE DOWN...
IT'S NICE TO HAVE SOMEONE BESIDE YOU AND TO KNOW THAT YOU'RE NOT ALONE.
NARU TAUGHT ME THAT.
HE LIBERATED ME FROM A LOT OF THINGS.
HOW...
I'M INDEBTED TO HIM.

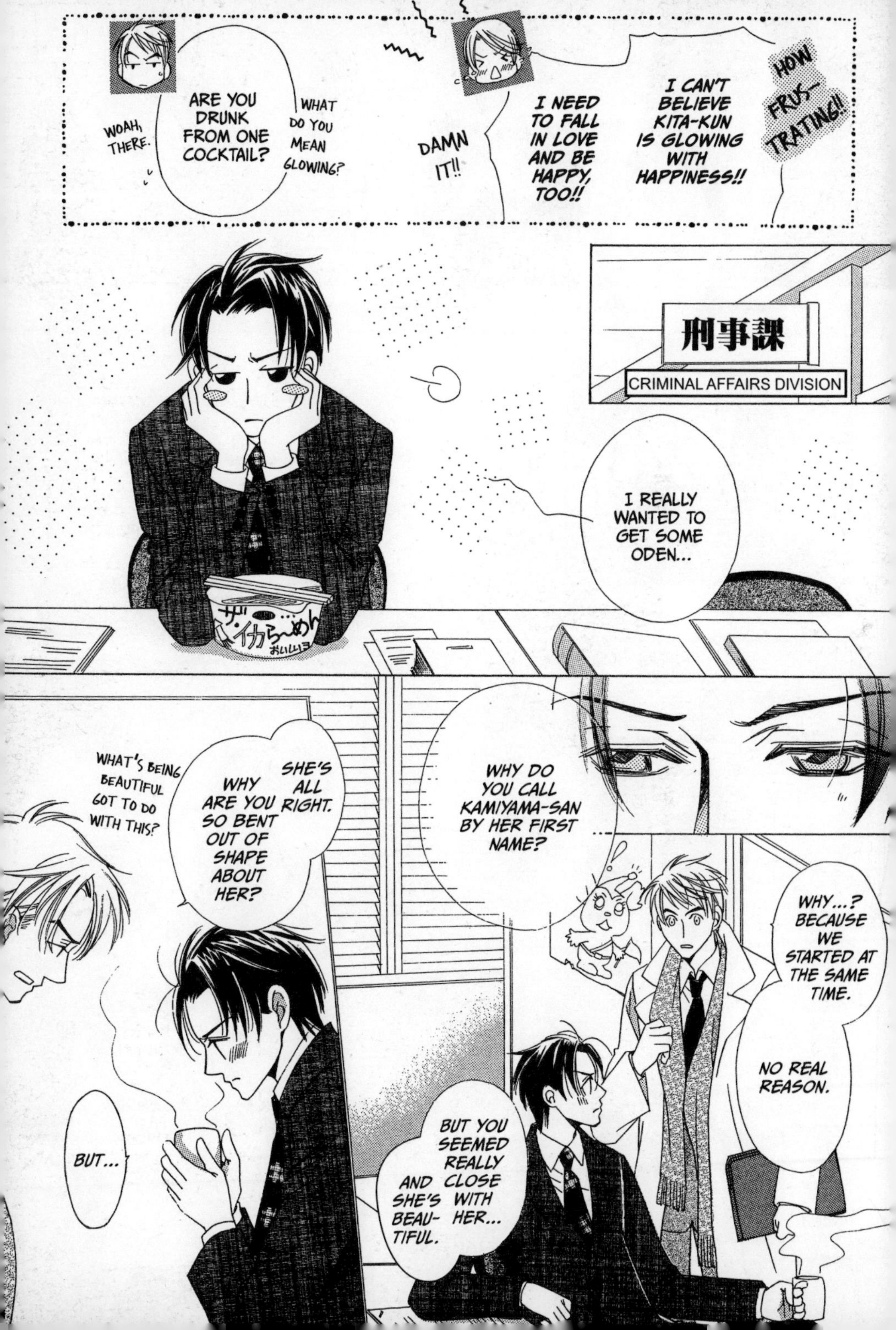
HOW FRUS-TRATING!!
I CAN'T BELIEVE KITA-KUN IS GLOWING WITH HAPPINESS!!
I NEED TO FALL IN LOVE AND BE HAPPY, TOO!!
DAMN IT!!
WHAT DO YOU MEAN GLOWING?
ARE YOU DRUNK FROM ONE COCKTAIL?
WOAH, THERE.
刑事課
CRIMINAL AFFAIRS DIVISION
I REALLY WANTED TO GET SOME ODEN...
WHY DO YOU CALL KAMIYAMA-SAN BY HER FIRST NAME?
WHY...? BECAUSE WE STARTED AT THE SAME TIME.
NO REAL REASON.
BUT YOU SEEMED REALLY CLOSE WITH HER...
AND SHE'S BEAUTIFUL.
SHE'S ALL RIGHT.
WHY ARE YOU SO BENT OUT OF SHAPE ABOUT HER?
WHAT'S BEING BEAUTIFUL GOT TO DO WITH THIS?
BUT...

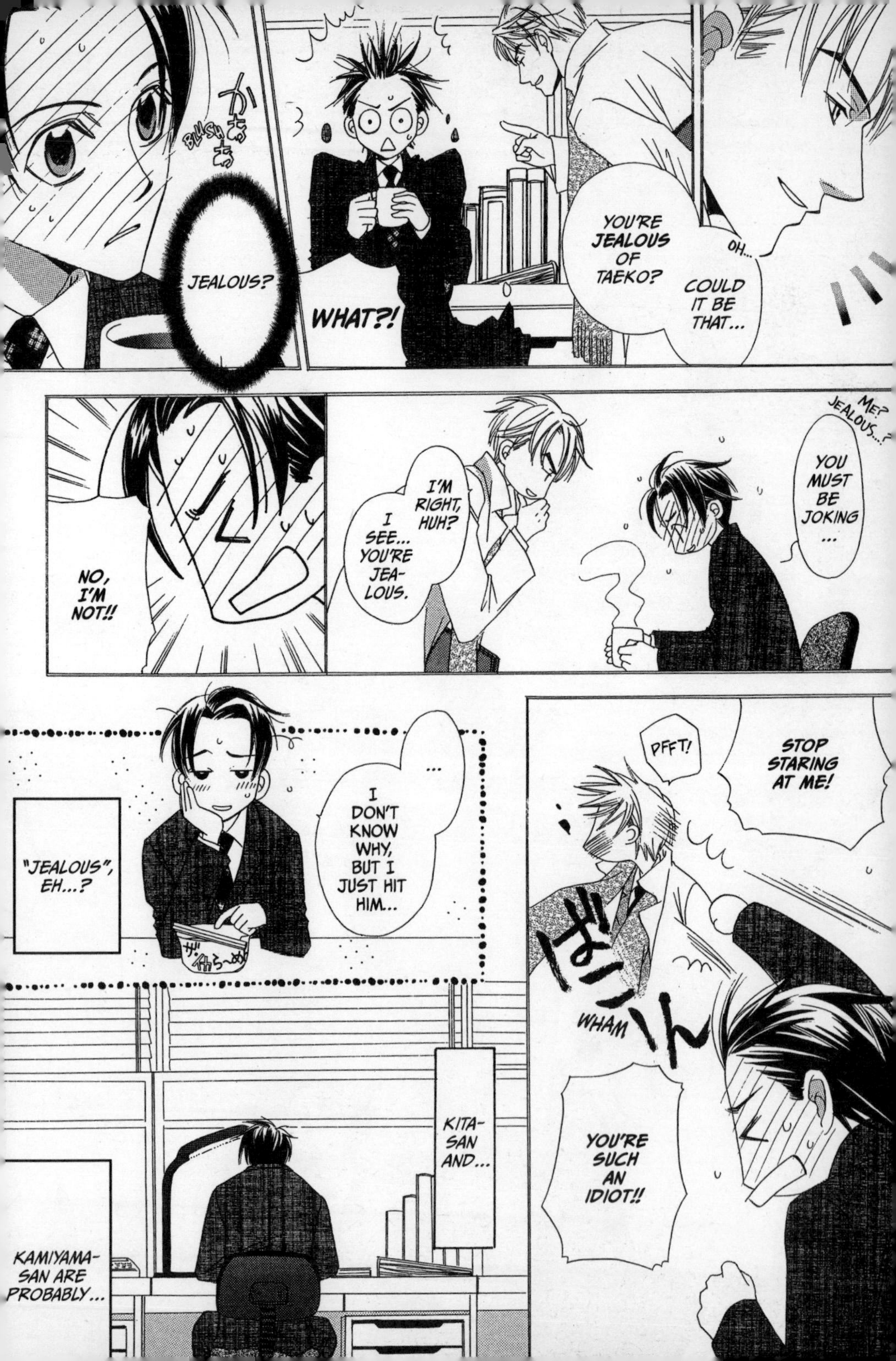
OH...
COULD IT BE THAT...
YOU'RE JEALOUS OF TAEKO?
WHAT?!
BLUSH
JEALOUS?
ME? JEALOUS...?
YOU MUST BE JOKING...
I'M RIGHT, HUH?
I SEE... YOU'RE JEA-LOUS.
NO, I'M NOT!!
PFFT!
STOP STARING AT ME!
WHAM
YOU'RE SUCH AN IDIOT!!
...
I DON'T KNOW WHY, BUT I JUST HIT HIM...
"JEALOUS", EH...?
KITA-SAN AND...
KAMIYAMA-SAN ARE PROBABLY...

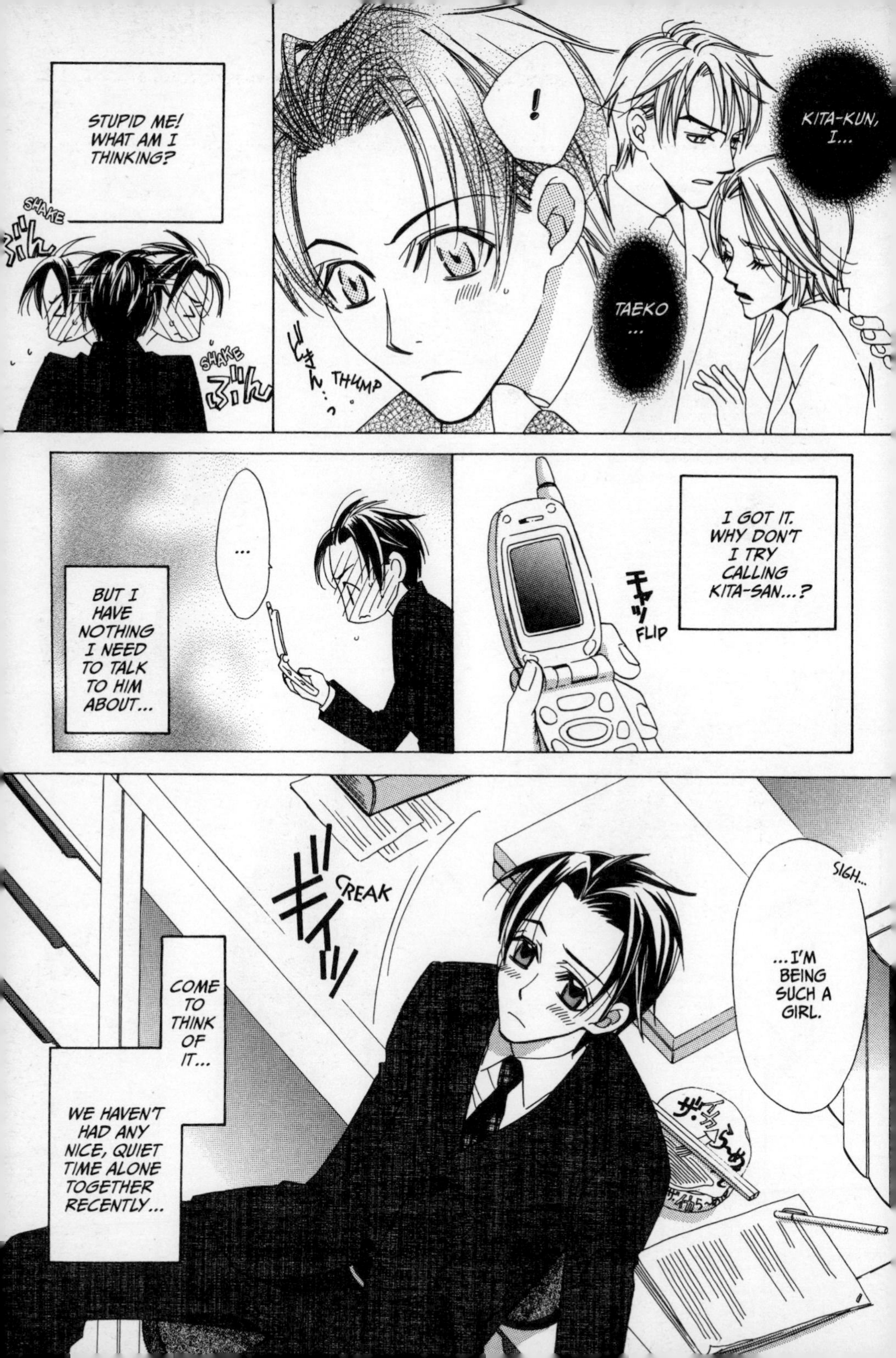
!
KITA-KUN, I...
TAEKO ...
THUMP
STUPID ME! WHAT AM I THINKING?
SHAKE
SHAKE
I GOT IT. WHY DON'T I TRY CALLING KITA-SAN...?
FLIP
...
BUT I HAVE NOTHING I NEED TO TALK TO HIM ABOUT...
SIGH...
...I'M BEING SUCH A GIRL.
CREAK
COME TO THINK OF IT...
WE HAVEN'T HAD ANY NICE, QUIET TIME ALONE TOGETHER RECENTLY...

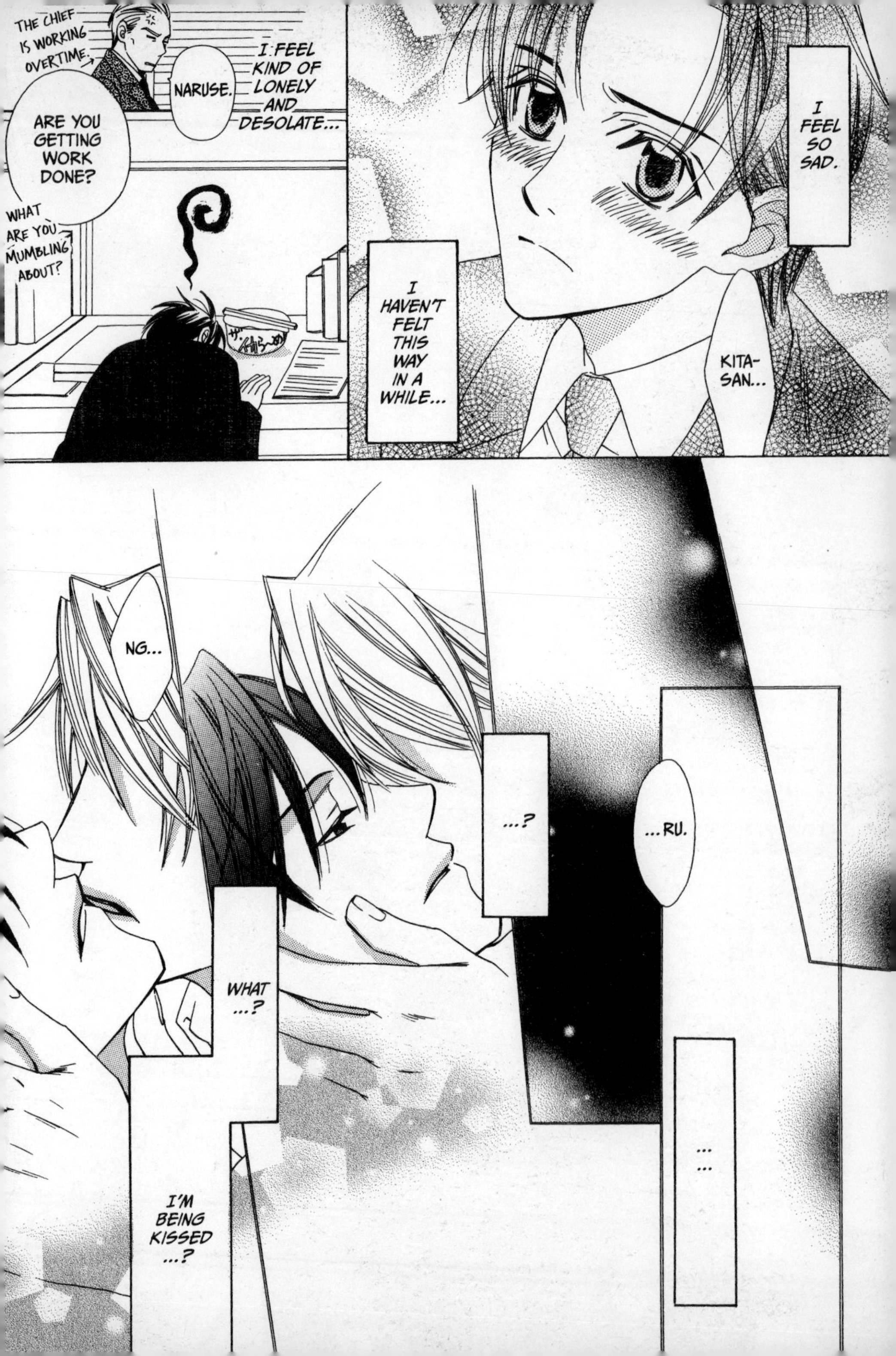
I FEEL SO SAD.
KITA-SAN...
I HAVEN'T FELT THIS WAY IN A WHILE...
I FEEL KIND OF LONELY AND DESOLATE...
NARUSE.
THE CHIEF IS WORKING OVERTIME.
ARE YOU GETTING WORK DONE?
WHAT ARE YOU MUMBLING ABOUT?
...RU.
... ...
...?
NG...
WHAT ...?
I'M BEING KISSED ...?

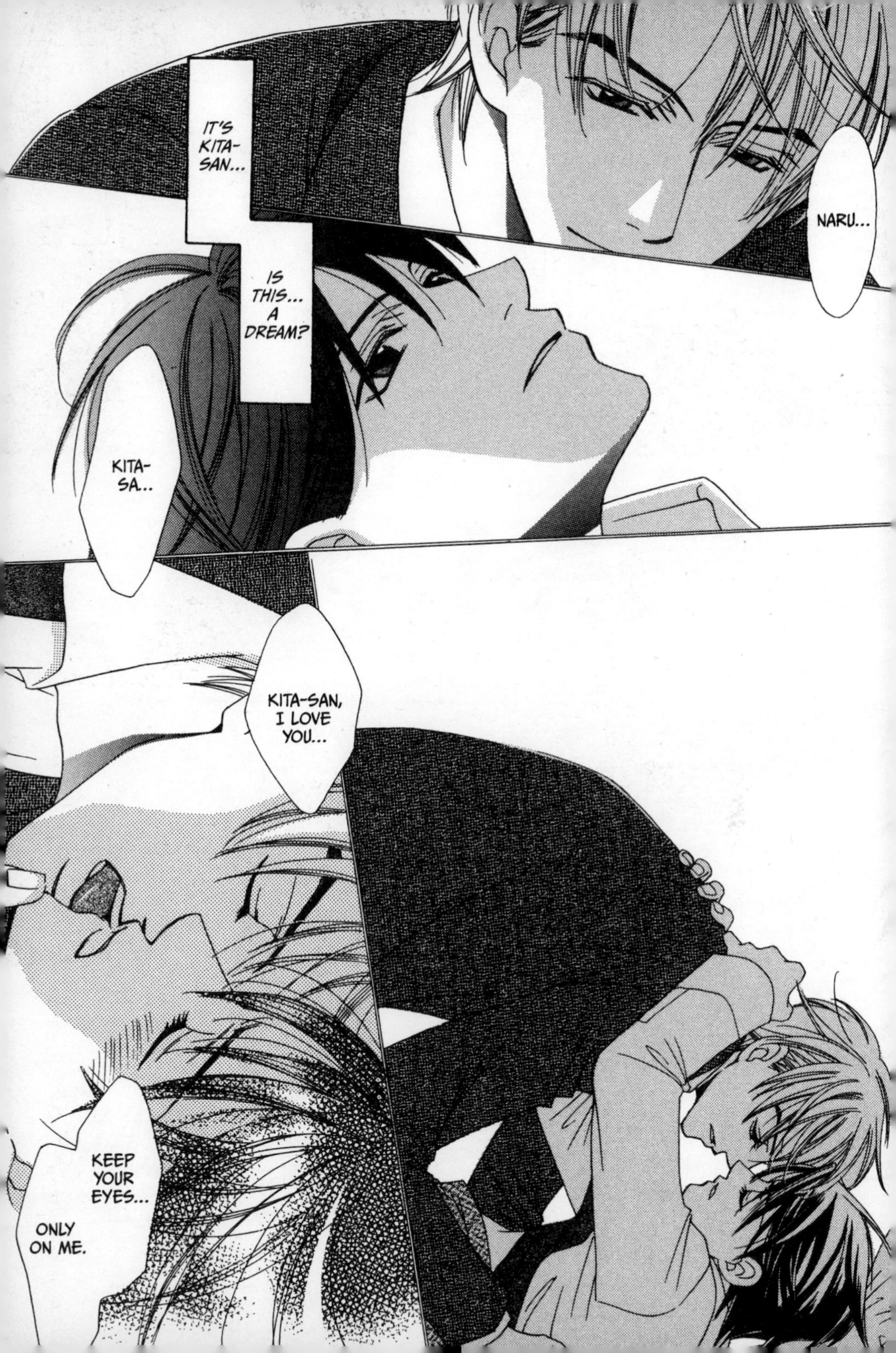
NARU...
IT'S KITA-SAN...
IS THIS... A DREAM?
KITA-SA...
KITA-SAN, I LOVE YOU...
KEEP YOUR EYES...
ONLY ON ME.

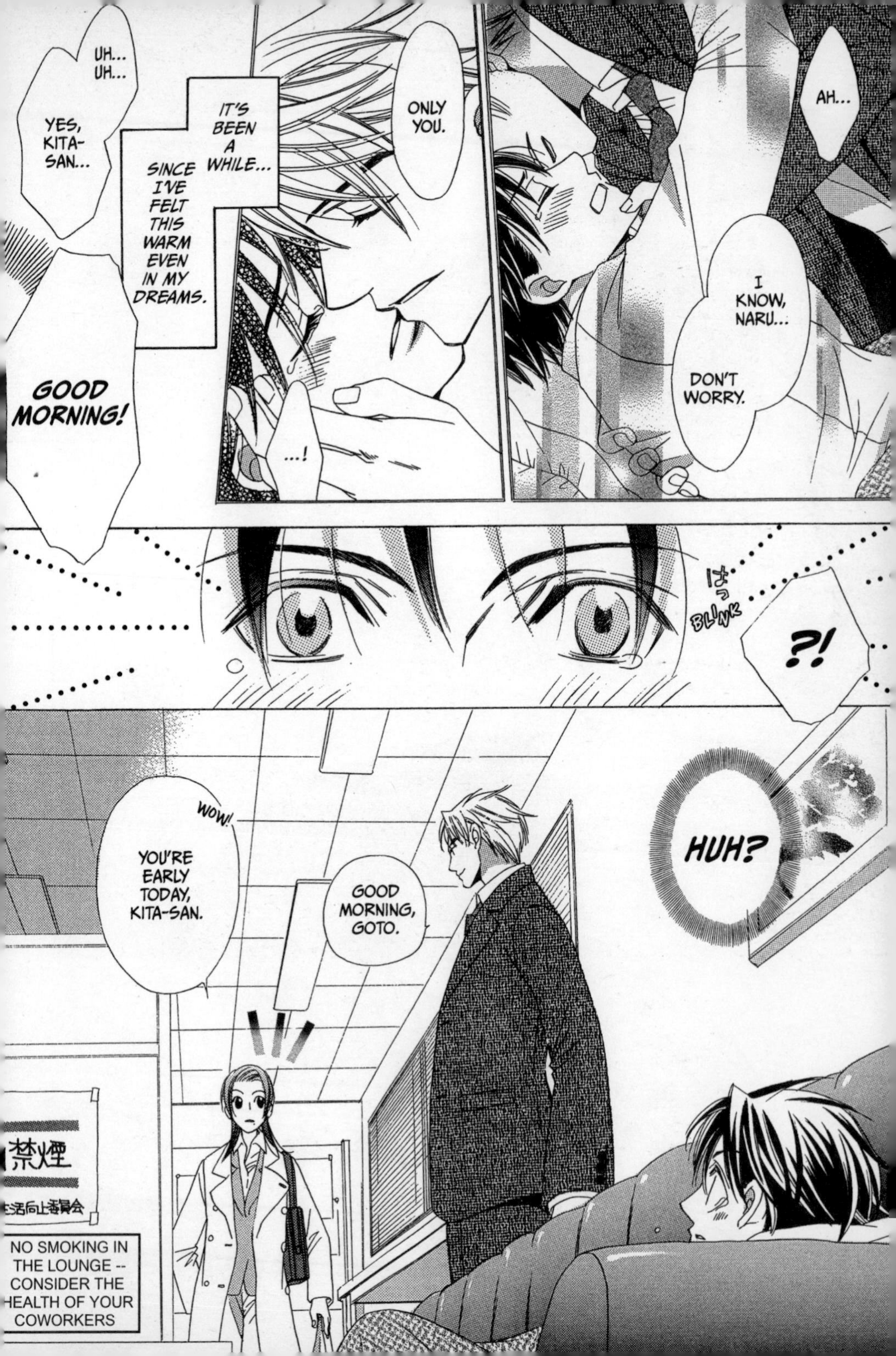
AH...
I KNOW, NARU...
DON'T WORRY.
ONLY YOU.
IT'S BEEN A WHILE...
SINCE I'VE FELT THIS WARM EVEN IN MY DREAMS.
...!
UH... UH...
YES, KITA-SAN...
GOOD MORNING!
はっ
BLINK
?!
HUH?
GOOD MORNING, GOTO.
WOW!
YOU'RE EARLY TODAY, KITA-SAN.
禁煙
活向上委員会
NO SMOKING IN THE LOUNGE -- CONSIDER THE HEALTH OF YOUR COWORKERS

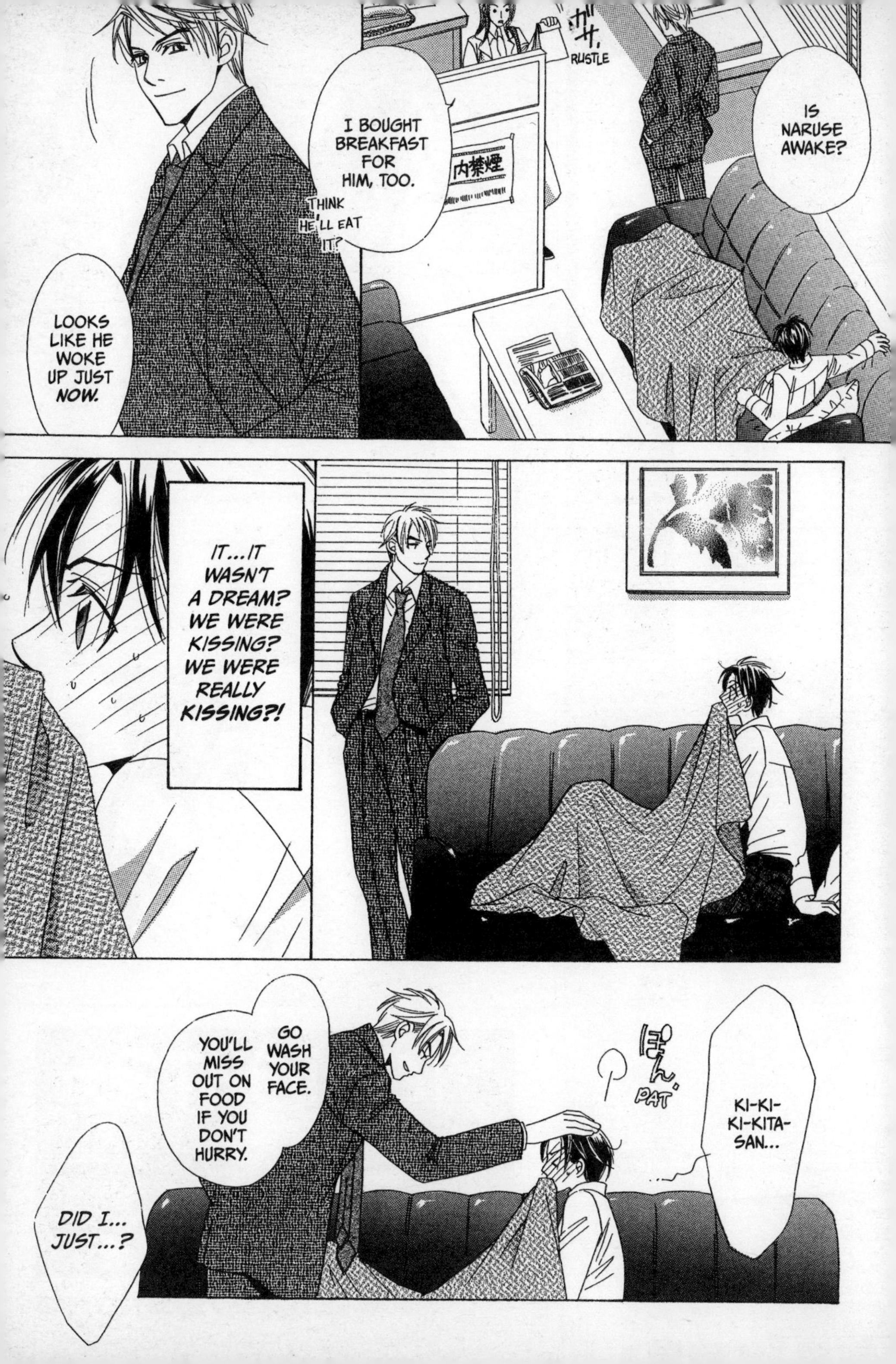

ガサ
RUSTLE
IS NARUSE AWAKE?
内禁煙
I BOUGHT BREAKFAST FOR HIM, TOO.
THINK HE'LL EAT IT?
LOOKS LIKE HE WOKE UP JUST NOW.
IT...IT WASN'T A DREAM? WE WERE KISSING? WE WERE REALLY KISSING?!
KI-KI-KI-KITA-SAN...
ぽん
PAT
GO WASH YOUR FACE.
YOU'LL MISS OUT ON FOOD IF YOU DON'T HURRY.
DID I... JUST...?

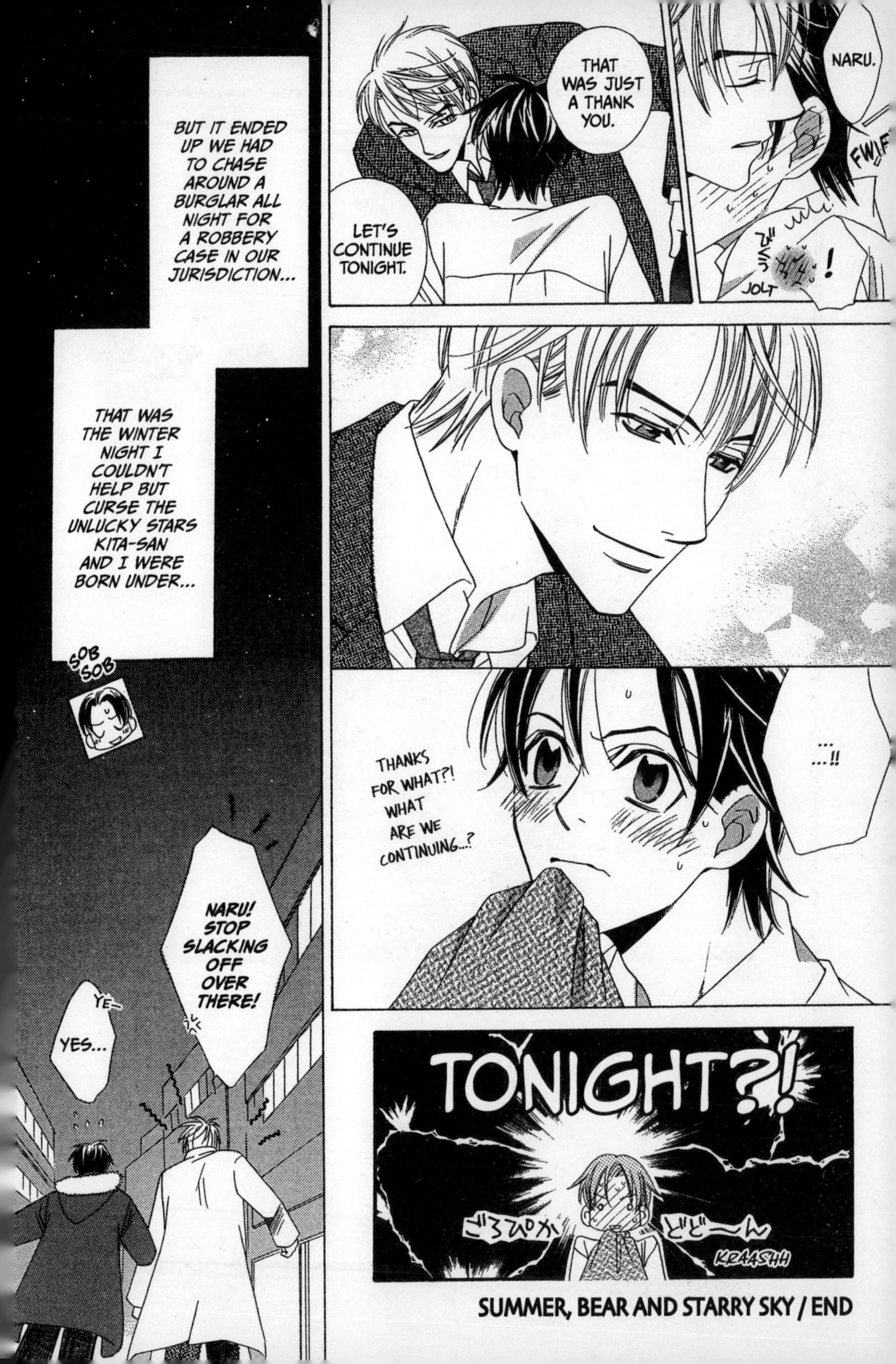
NARU.
FWIF
JOLT
!
THAT WAS JUST A THANK YOU.
LET'S CONTINUE TONIGHT.
... ...!!
THANKS FOR WHAT?! WHAT ARE WE CONTINUING...?
TONIGHT?!
KRAASHH
BUT IT ENDED UP WE HAD TO CHASE AROUND A BURGLAR ALL NIGHT FOR A ROBBERY CASE IN OUR JURISDICTION...
THAT WAS THE WINTER NIGHT I COULDN'T HELP BUT CURSE THE UNLUCKY STARS KITA-SAN AND I WERE BORN UNDER...
SOB SOB
NARU! STOP SLACKING OFF OVER THERE!
YE-
YES...
SUMMER, BEAR AND STARRY SKY / END

Kita & Naru series

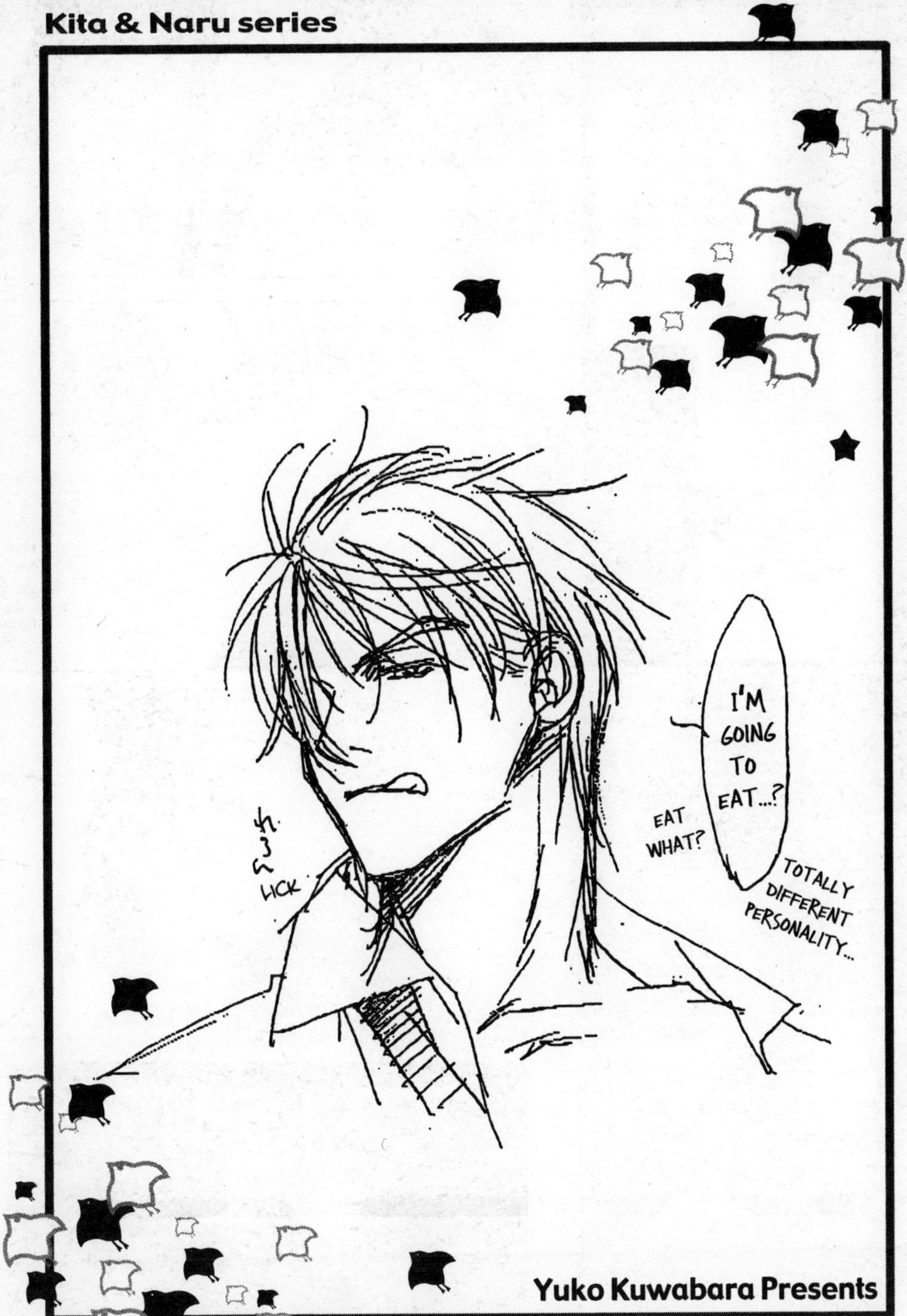

Yuko Kuwabara Presents

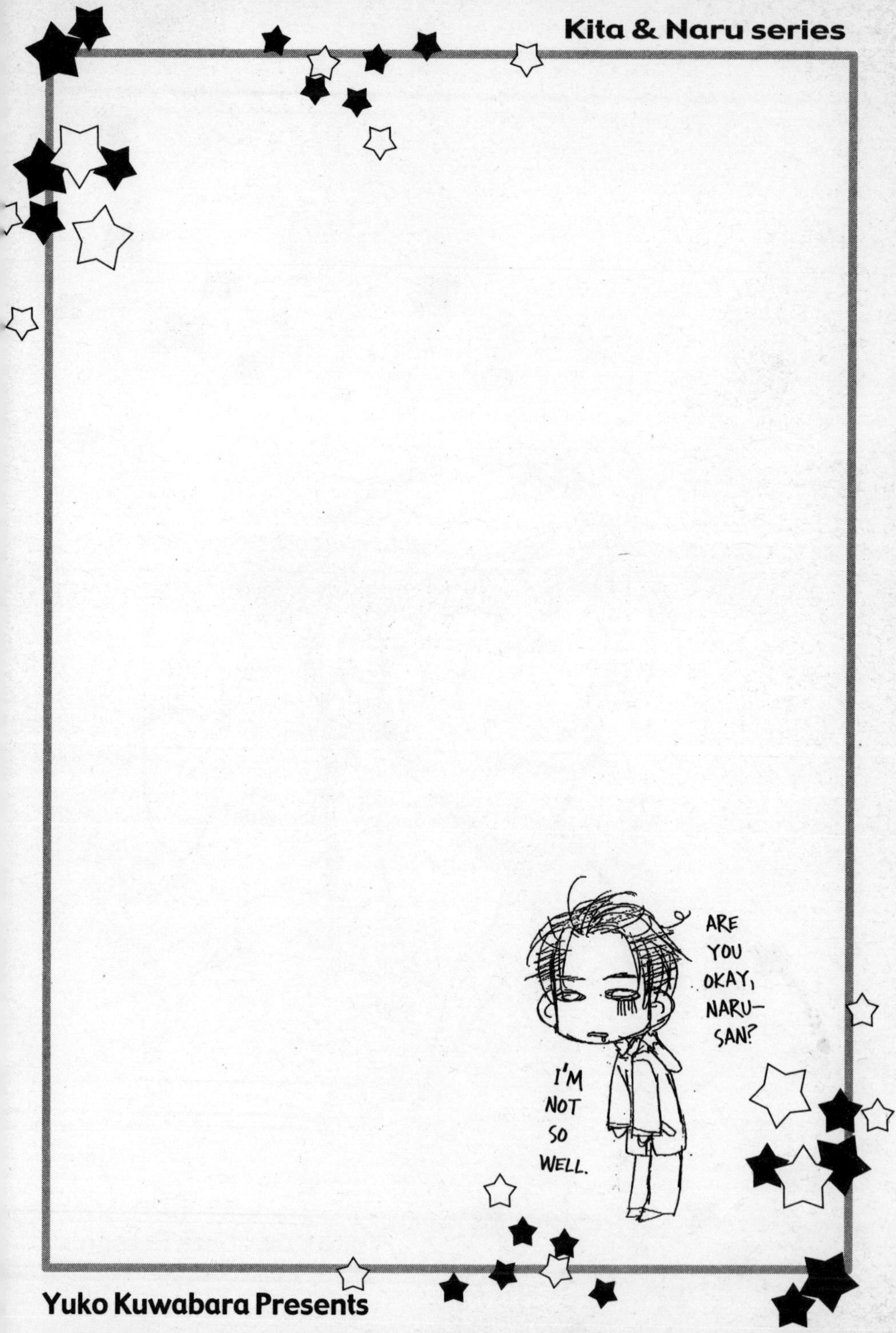
ARE YOU OKAY, NARU-SAN?
I'M NOT SO WELL.

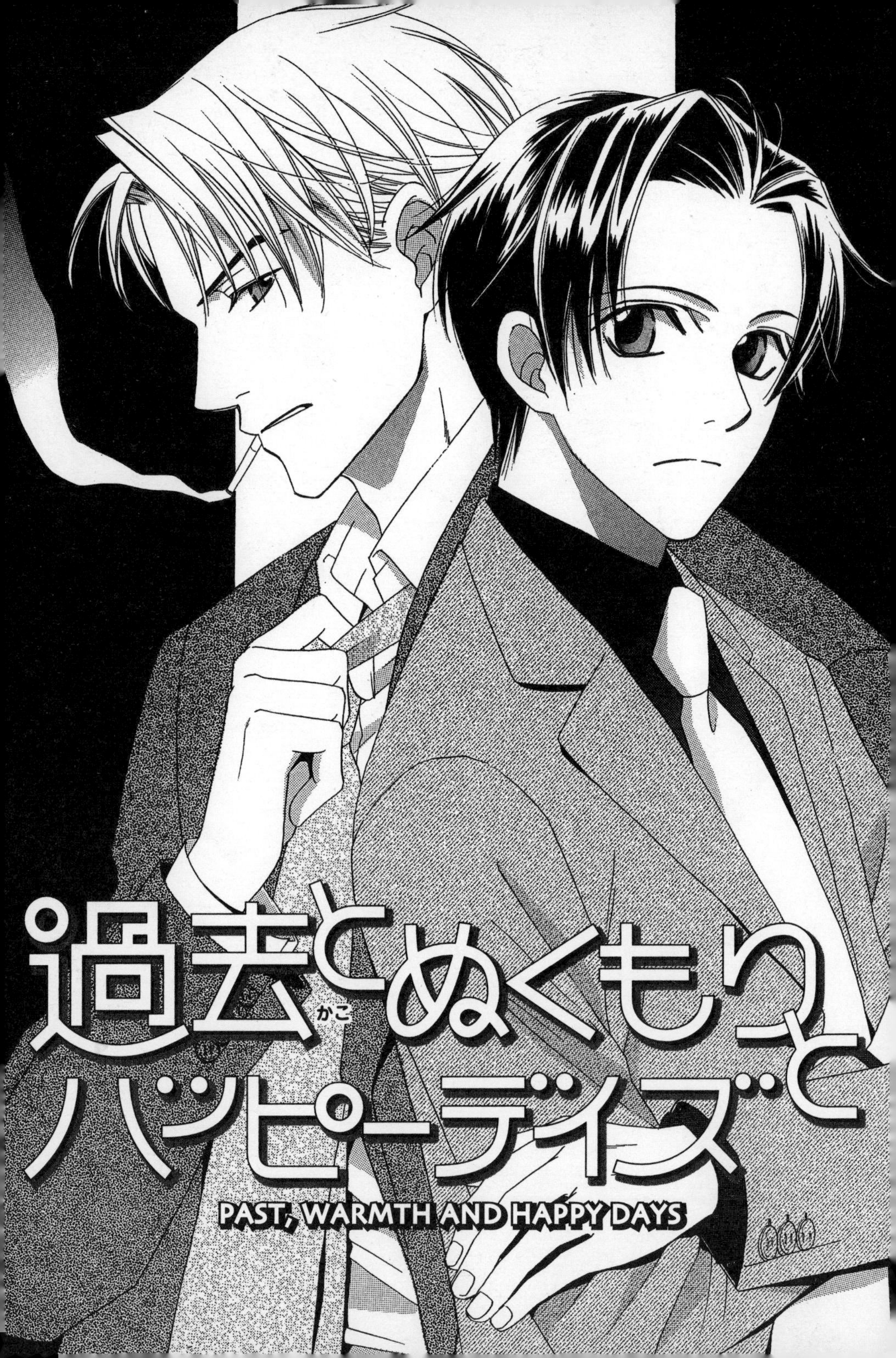
過去とぬくもりとハッピーデイズ
かこ
PAST, WARMTH AND HAPPY DAYS

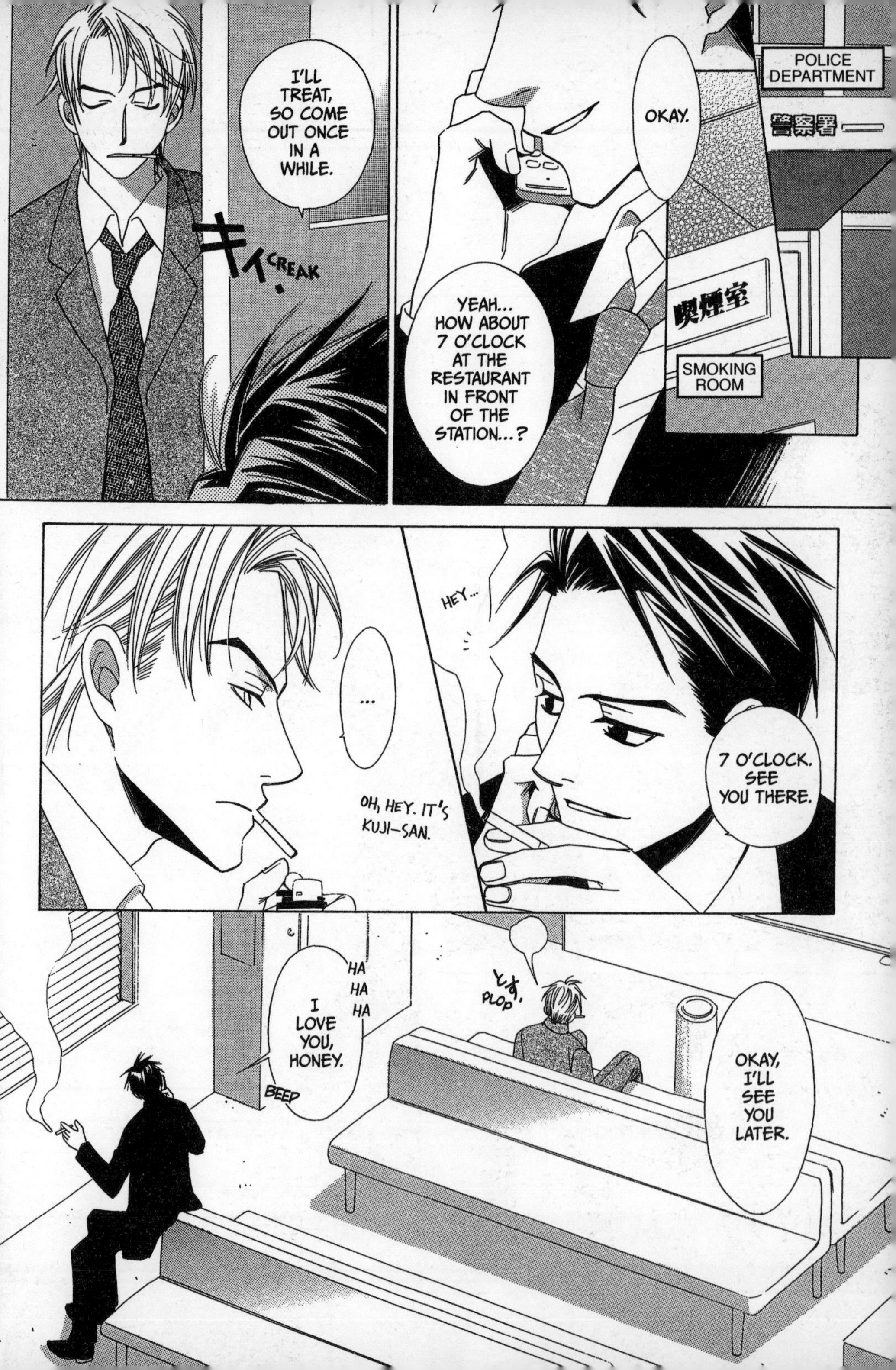
POLICE DEPARTMENT
警察署
OKAY.
YEAH... HOW ABOUT 7 O'CLOCK AT THE RESTAURANT IN FRONT OF THE STATION...?
喫煙室
SMOKING ROOM
I'LL TREAT, SO COME OUT ONCE IN A WHILE.
キイ
CREAK
HEY...
7 O'CLOCK. SEE YOU THERE.
...
OH, HEY. IT'S KUJI-SAN.
OKAY, I'LL SEE YOU LATER.
とす
PLOP
HA HA HA
I LOVE YOU, HONEY.
BEEP
...

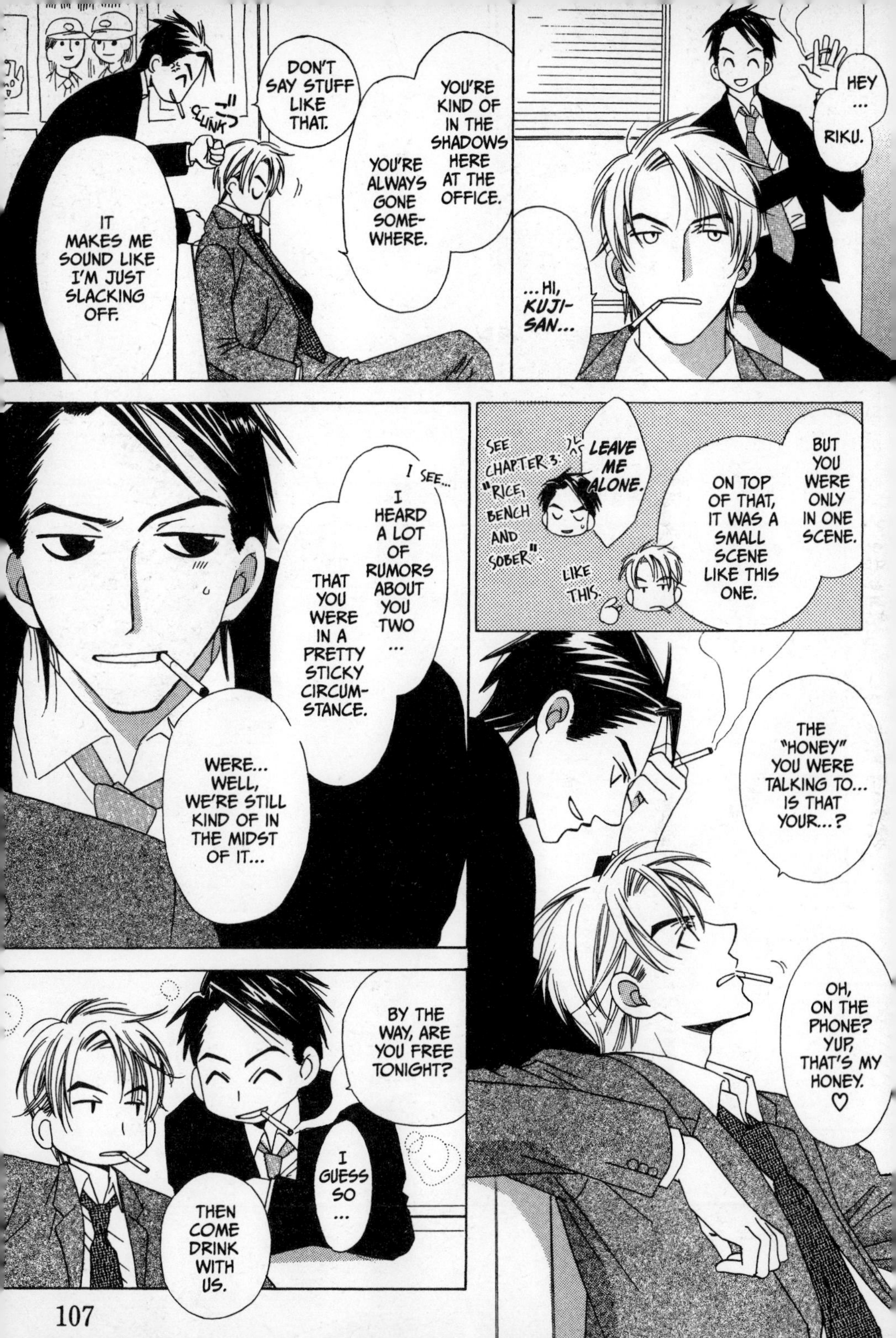
HEY ... RIKU.
...HI, KUJI-SAN...
YOU'RE KIND OF IN THE SHADOWS HERE AT THE OFFICE.
YOU'RE ALWAYS GONE SOMEWHERE.
DON'T SAY STUFF LIKE THAT.
CLUNK
IT MAKES ME SOUND LIKE I'M JUST SLACKING OFF.
BUT YOU WERE ONLY IN ONE SCENE.
ON TOP OF THAT, IT WAS A SMALL SCENE LIKE THIS ONE.
LIKE THIS.
LEAVE ME ALONE.
SEE CHAPTER 3: "RICE, BENCH AND SOBER".
THE "HONEY" YOU WERE TALKING TO... IS THAT YOUR...?
OH, ON THE PHONE? YUP, THAT'S MY HONEY. ♡
I HEARD A LOT OF RUMORS ABOUT YOU TWO ...
THAT YOU WERE IN A PRETTY STICKY CIRCUMSTANCE.
I SEE...
WERE... WELL, WE'RE STILL KIND OF IN THE MIDST OF IT...
BY THE WAY, ARE YOU FREE TONIGHT?
I GUESS SO ...
THEN COME DRINK WITH US.

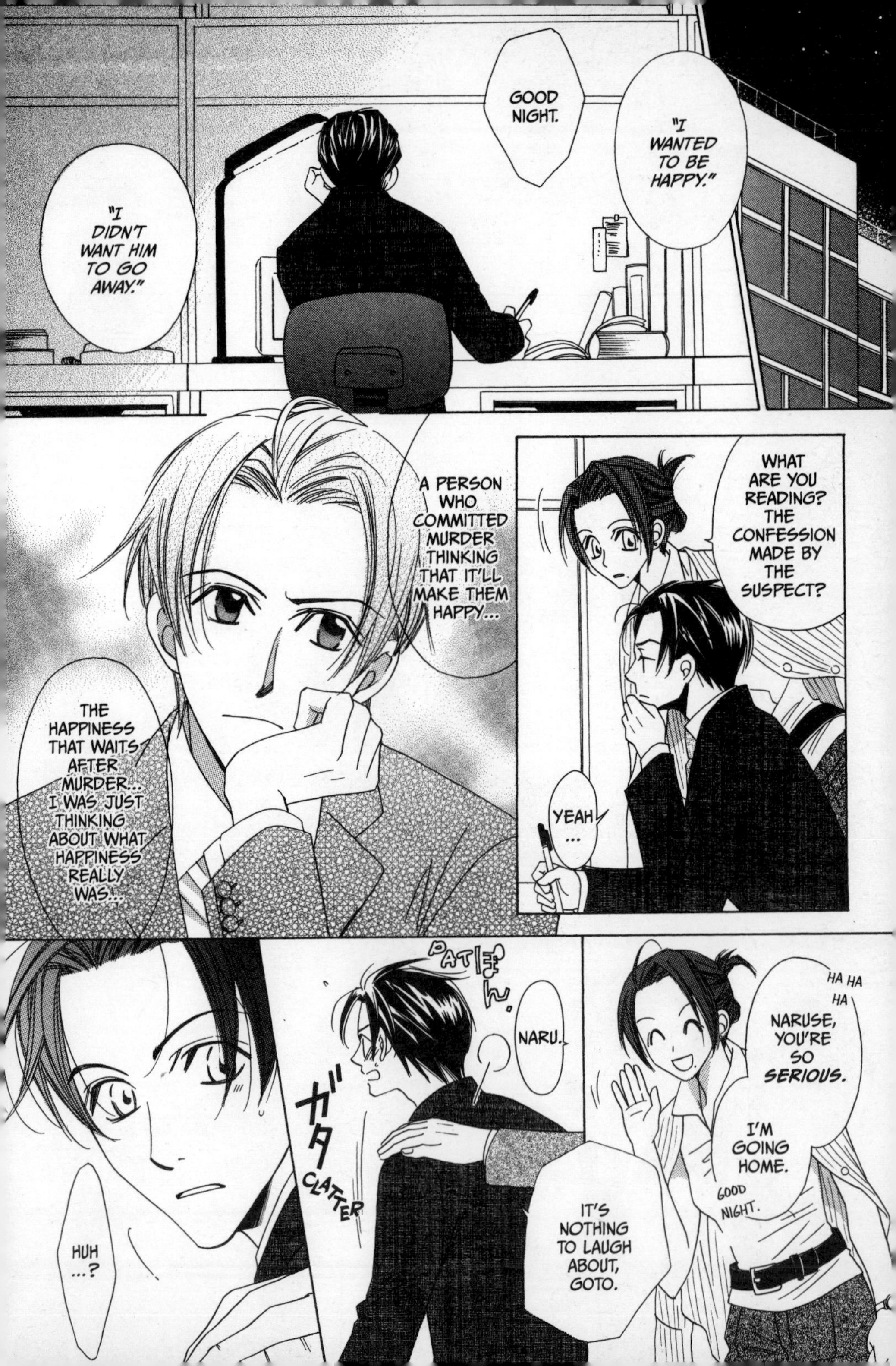
"I WANTED TO BE HAPPY."
GOOD NIGHT.
"I DIDN'T WANT HIM TO GO AWAY."
WHAT ARE YOU READING? THE CONFESSION MADE BY THE SUSPECT?
YEAH...
A PERSON WHO COMMITTED MURDER THINKING THAT IT'LL MAKE THEM HAPPY...
THE HAPPINESS THAT WAITS AFTER MURDER... I WAS JUST THINKING ABOUT WHAT HAPPINESS REALLY WAS...
HA HA HA
NARUSE, YOU'RE SO **SERIOUS.**
I'M GOING HOME.
GOOD NIGHT.
IT'S NOTHING TO LAUGH ABOUT, GOTO.
PAT ぽん。
NARU..
ガタ
CLATTER
HUH ...?

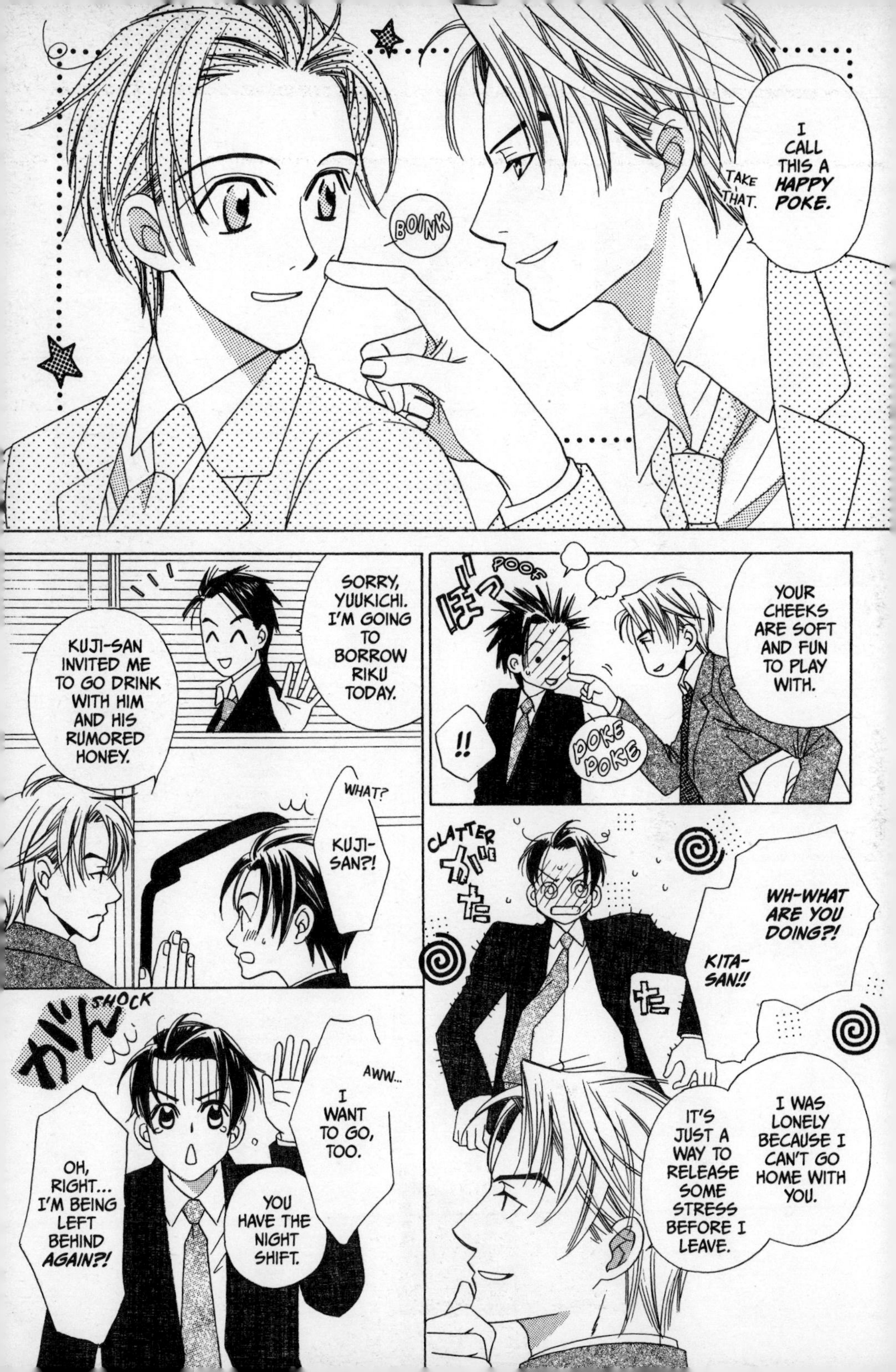
I CALL THIS A HAPPY POKE.
TAKE THAT.
BOINK
POOF
YOUR CHEEKS ARE SOFT AND FUN TO PLAY WITH.
!!
POKE POKE
SORRY, YUUKICHI. I'M GOING TO BORROW RIKU TODAY.
KUJI-SAN INVITED ME TO GO DRINK WITH HIM AND HIS RUMORED HONEY.
WHAT?
KUJI-SAN?!
CLATTER
WH-WHAT ARE YOU DOING?!
KITA-SAN!!
I WAS LONELY BECAUSE I CAN'T GO HOME WITH YOU.
IT'S JUST A WAY TO RELEASE SOME STRESS BEFORE I LEAVE.
SHOCK
AWW... I WANT TO GO, TOO.
YOU HAVE THE NIGHT SHIFT.
OH, RIGHT... I'M BEING LEFT BEHIND AGAIN?!

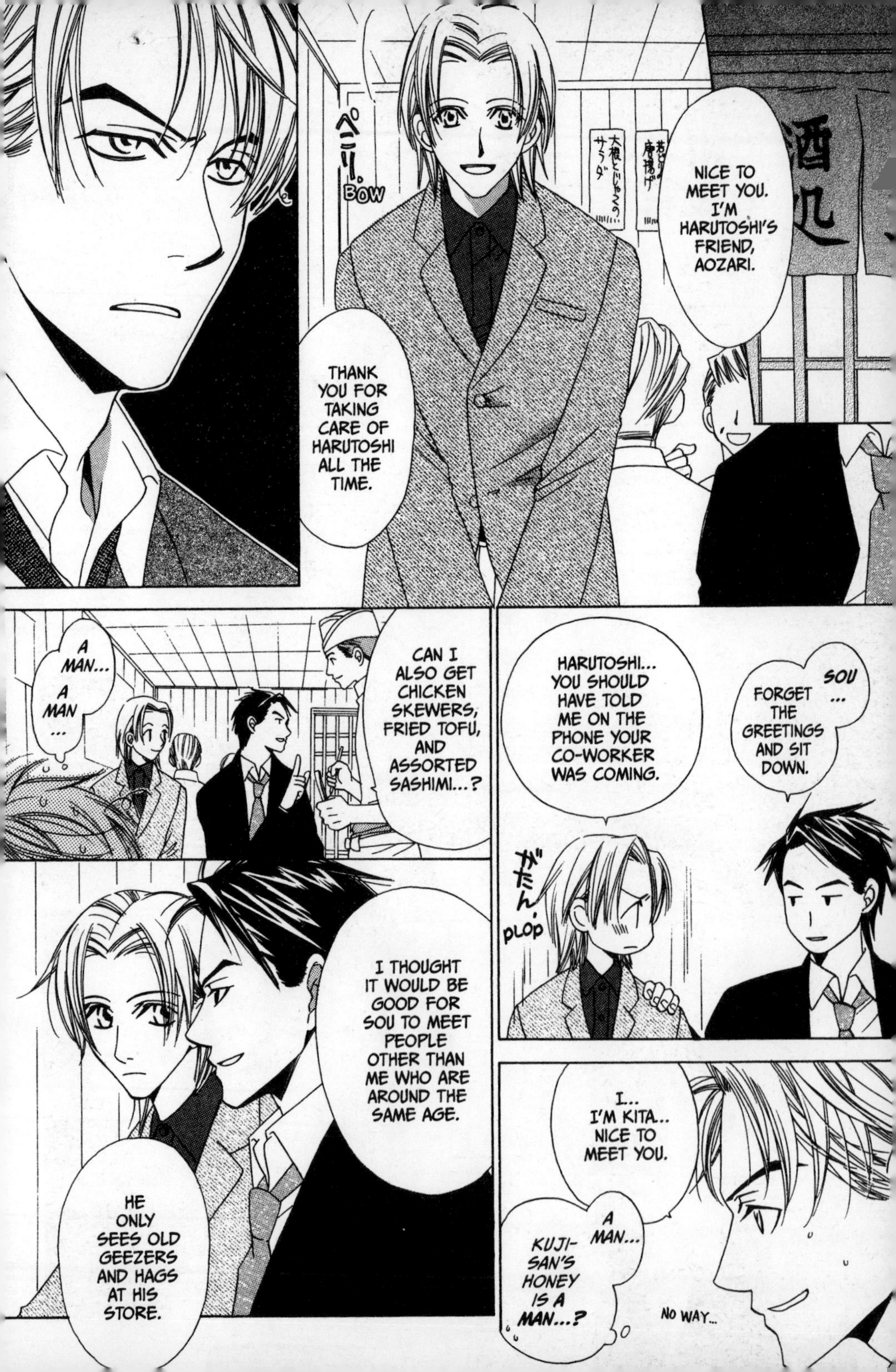
NICE TO MEET YOU. I'M HARUTOSHI'S FRIEND, AOZARI.
ペこり。
BOW
THANK YOU FOR TAKING CARE OF HARUTOSHI ALL THE TIME.
SOU... FORGET THE GREETINGS AND SIT DOWN.
HARUTOSHI... YOU SHOULD HAVE TOLD ME ON THE PHONE YOUR CO-WORKER WAS COMING.
がたん。
PLOP
CAN I ALSO GET CHICKEN SKEWERS, FRIED TOFU, AND ASSORTED SASHIMI...?
A MAN... A MAN...
I THOUGHT IT WOULD BE GOOD FOR SOU TO MEET PEOPLE OTHER THAN ME WHO ARE AROUND THE SAME AGE.
HE ONLY SEES OLD GEEZERS AND HAGS AT HIS STORE.
I... I'M KITA... NICE TO MEET YOU.
A MAN...
KUJI-SAN'S HONEY IS A MAN...?
NO WAY...

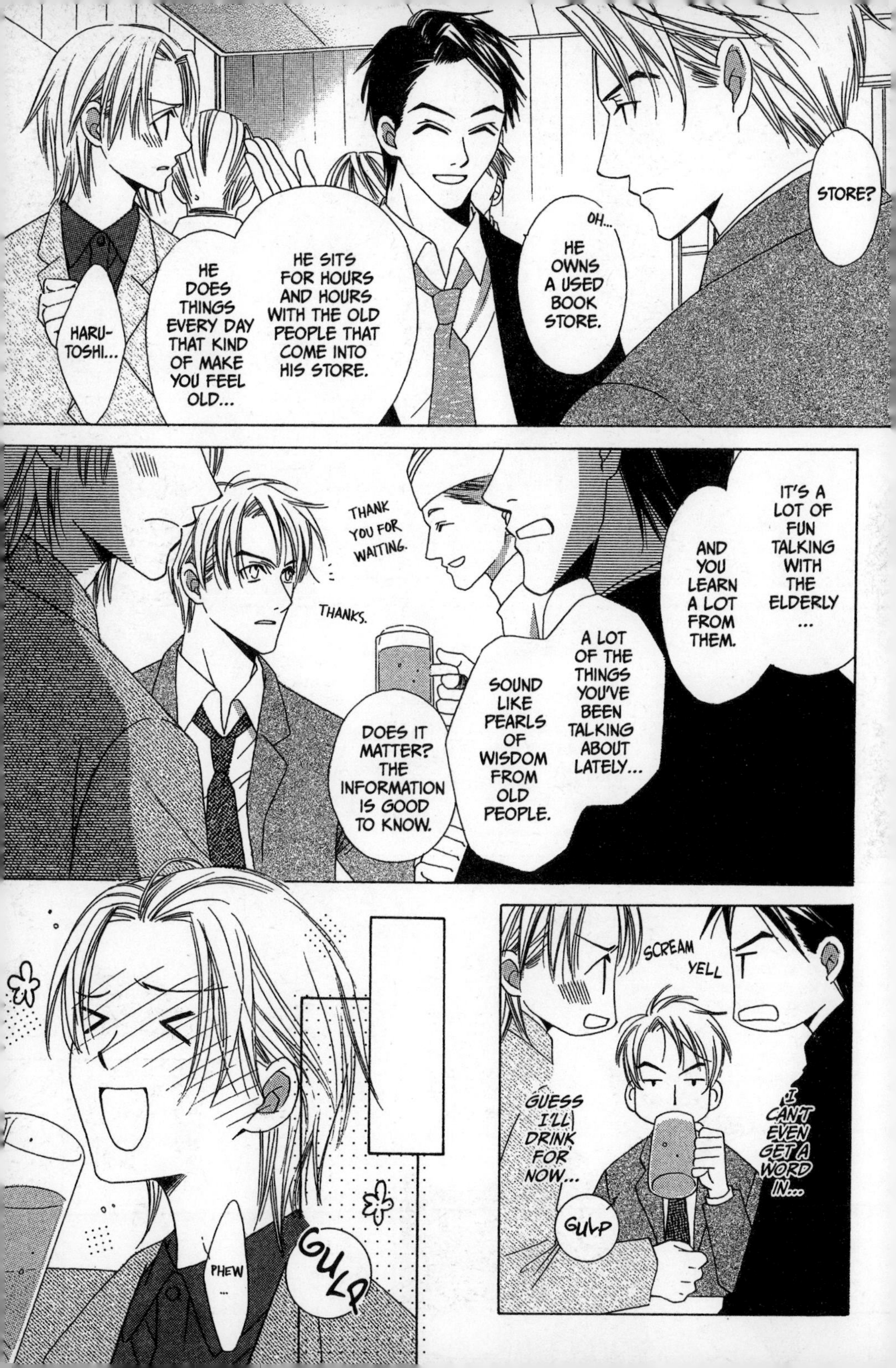
STORE?
OH... HE OWNS A USED BOOK STORE.
HE SITS FOR HOURS AND HOURS WITH THE OLD PEOPLE THAT COME INTO HIS STORE.
HE DOES THINGS EVERY DAY THAT KIND OF MAKE YOU FEEL OLD...
HARU-TOSHI...
IT'S A LOT OF FUN TALKING WITH THE ELDERLY ...
AND YOU LEARN A LOT FROM THEM.
A LOT OF THE THINGS YOU'VE BEEN TALKING ABOUT LATELY...
SOUND LIKE PEARLS OF WISDOM FROM OLD PEOPLE.
THANK YOU FOR WAITING.
THANKS.
DOES IT MATTER? THE INFORMATION IS GOOD TO KNOW.
YELL
SCREAM
I CAN'T EVEN GET A WORD IN...
GUESS I'LL DRINK FOR NOW...
GULP
GULP
PHEW ...

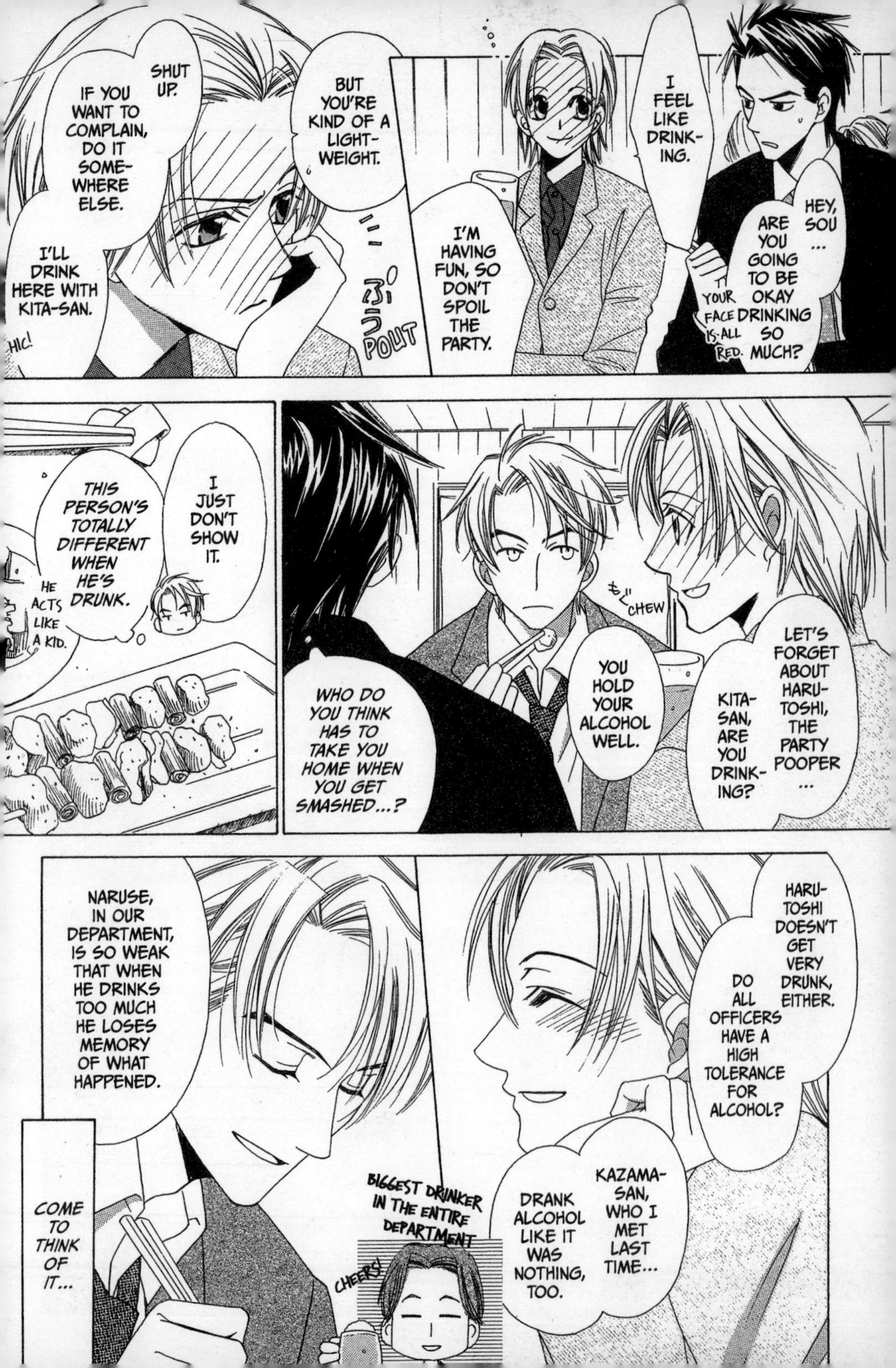
HEY, SOU ... ARE YOU GOING TO BE OKAY DRINKING SO MUCH?
YOUR FACE IS ALL RED.
I FEEL LIKE DRINKING.
I'M HAVING FUN, SO DON'T SPOIL THE PARTY.
BUT YOU'RE KIND OF A LIGHT-WEIGHT.
SHUT UP.
IF YOU WANT TO COMPLAIN, DO IT SOME-WHERE ELSE.
ぷう POUT
I'LL DRINK HERE WITH KITA-SAN.
HIC!
LET'S FORGET ABOUT HARU-TOSHI, THE PARTY POOPER ...
KITA-SAN, ARE YOU DRINK-ING?
もぐ CHEW
YOU HOLD YOUR ALCOHOL WELL.
WHO DO YOU THINK HAS TO TAKE YOU HOME WHEN YOU GET SMASHED...?
I JUST DON'T SHOW IT.
THIS PERSON'S TOTALLY DIFFERENT WHEN HE'S DRUNK.
HE ACTS LIKE A KID.
HARU-TOSHI DOESN'T GET VERY DRUNK, EITHER.
DO ALL OFFICERS HAVE A HIGH TOLERANCE FOR ALCOHOL?
KAZAMA-SAN, WHO I MET LAST TIME...
DRANK ALCOHOL LIKE IT WAS NOTHING, TOO.
BIGGEST DRINKER IN THE ENTIRE DEPARTMENT
CHEERS!
NARUSE, IN OUR DEPARTMENT, IS SO WEAK THAT WHEN HE DRINKS TOO MUCH HE LOSES MEMORY OF WHAT HAPPENED.
COME TO THINK OF IT...

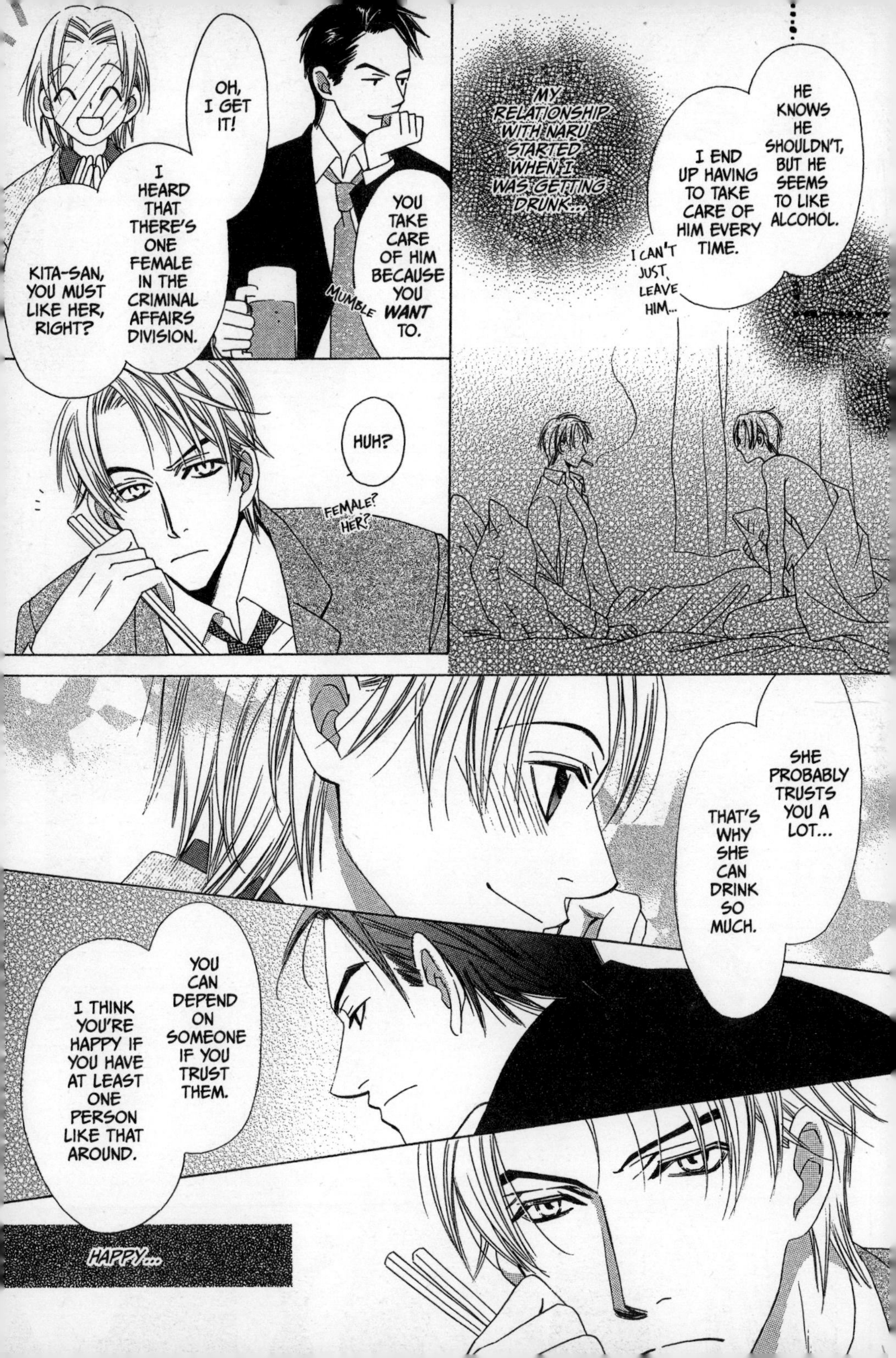

MY RELATIONSHIP WITH NARU STARTED WHEN I WAS GETTING DRUNK...
HE KNOWS HE SHOULDN'T, BUT HE SEEMS TO LIKE ALCOHOL.
I END UP HAVING TO TAKE CARE OF HIM EVERY TIME.
I CAN'T JUST LEAVE HIM...
OH, I GET IT!
YOU TAKE CARE OF HIM BECAUSE YOU *WANT* TO.
MUMBLE
I HEARD THAT THERE'S ONE FEMALE IN THE CRIMINAL AFFAIRS DIVISION.
KITA-SAN, YOU MUST LIKE HER, RIGHT?
HUH?
FEMALE? HER?
SHE PROBABLY TRUSTS YOU A LOT...
THAT'S WHY SHE CAN DRINK SO MUCH.
YOU CAN DEPEND ON SOMEONE IF YOU TRUST THEM.
I THINK YOU'RE HAPPY IF YOU HAVE AT LEAST ONE PERSON LIKE THAT AROUND.
HAPPY...

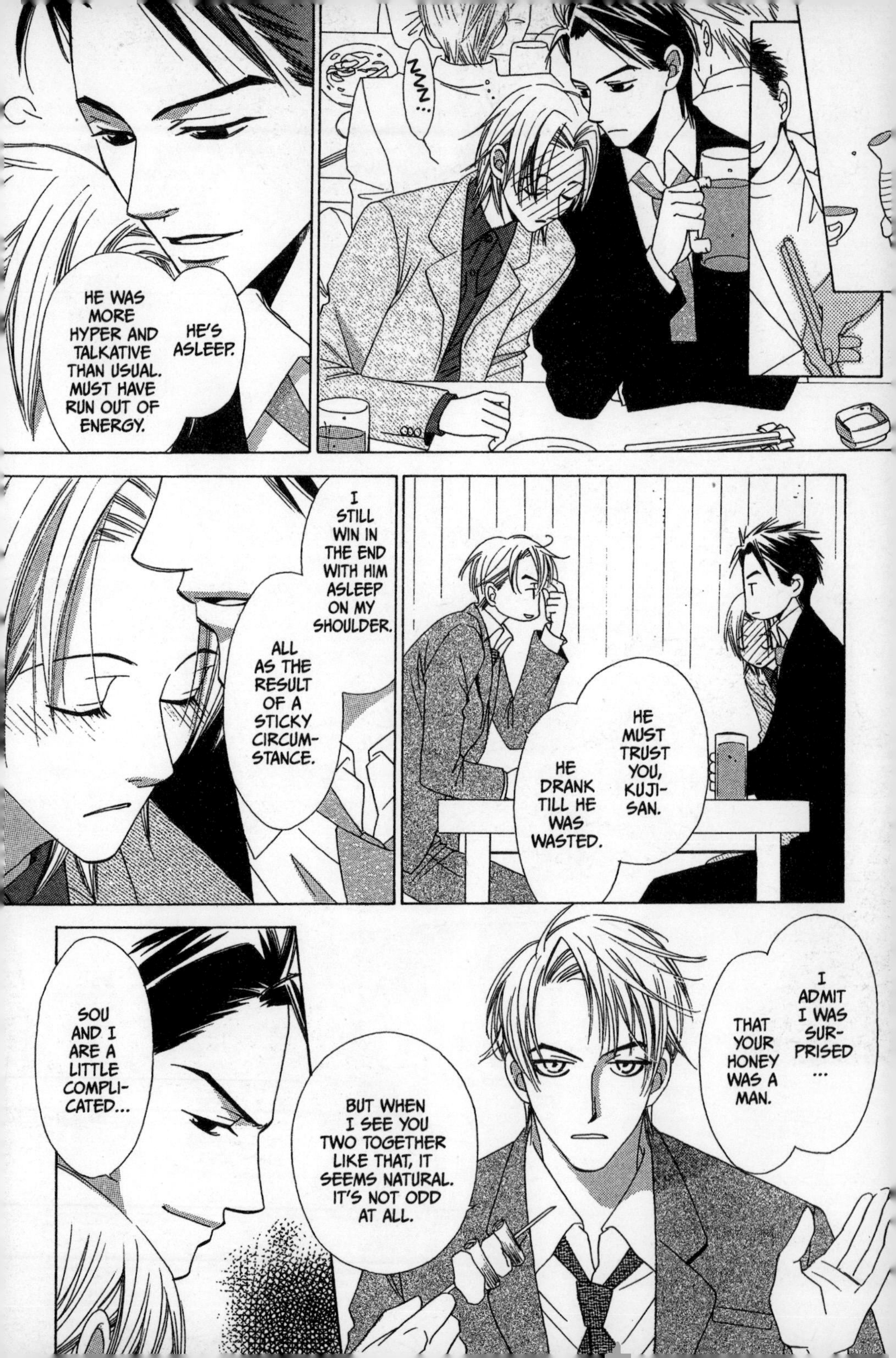
ZZZ...
HE'S ASLEEP.
HE WAS MORE HYPER AND TALKATIVE THAN USUAL. MUST HAVE RUN OUT OF ENERGY.
HE MUST TRUST YOU, KUJI-SAN.
HE DRANK TILL HE WAS WASTED.
I STILL WIN IN THE END WITH HIM ASLEEP ON MY SHOULDER.
ALL AS THE RESULT OF A STICKY CIRCUM-STANCE.
I ADMIT I WAS SUR-PRISED...
THAT YOUR HONEY WAS A MAN.
BUT WHEN I SEE YOU TWO TOGETHER LIKE THAT, IT SEEMS NATURAL. IT'S NOT ODD AT ALL.
SOU AND I ARE A LITTLE COMPLI-CATED...

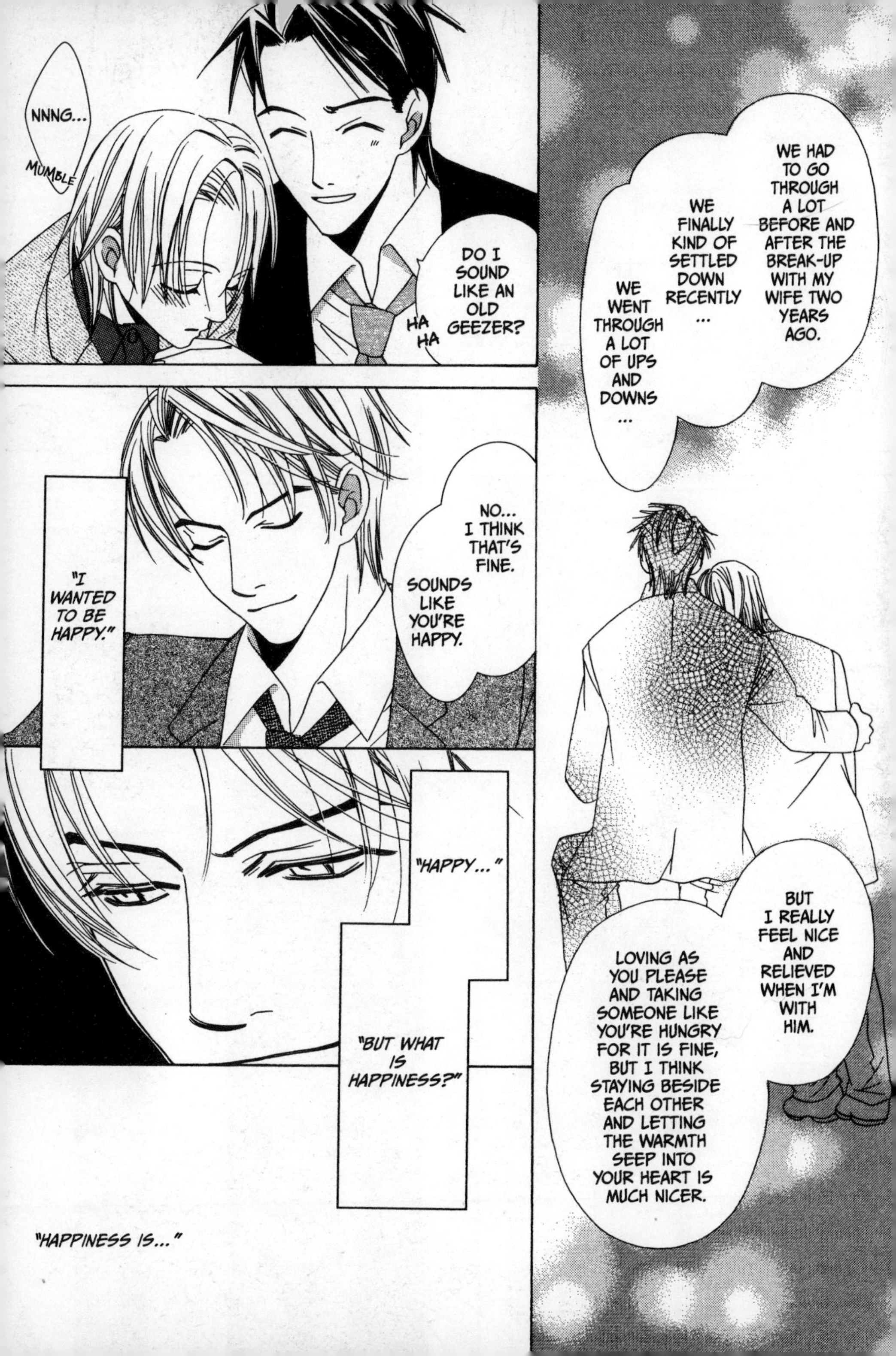
WE HAD TO GO THROUGH A LOT BEFORE AND AFTER THE BREAK-UP WITH MY WIFE TWO YEARS AGO.
WE FINALLY KIND OF SETTLED DOWN RECENTLY ...
WE WENT THROUGH A LOT OF UPS AND DOWNS ...
BUT I REALLY FEEL NICE AND RELIEVED WHEN I'M WITH HIM.
LOVING AS YOU PLEASE AND TAKING SOMEONE LIKE YOU'RE HUNGRY FOR IT IS FINE, BUT I THINK STAYING BESIDE EACH OTHER AND LETTING THE WARMTH SEEP INTO YOUR HEART IS MUCH NICER.
DO I SOUND LIKE AN OLD GEEZER?
HA HA
NNNG...
MUMBLE
NO... I THINK THAT'S FINE.
SOUNDS LIKE YOU'RE HAPPY.
"I WANTED TO BE HAPPY."
"HAPPY..."
"BUT WHAT IS HAPPINESS?"
"HAPPINESS IS..."

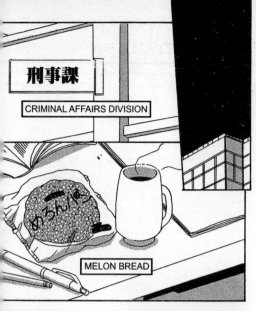

OF MY MIND...

SORRY, KUJI-SAN. I'M GONNA GO BACK.

I REMEMBERED SOMETHING I HAVE TO DO.

OH, YOU DID?

ALL RIGHT. I'M GOING TO LET HIM REST A LITTLE MORE BEFORE I LEAVE.

COMING TO THE "HAPPINESS" THAT WAS PUT BEFORE ME.

SEE YOU LATER, THEN.

SOMETHING IS BURNING.

I HEAR AWFUL SOUNDS...

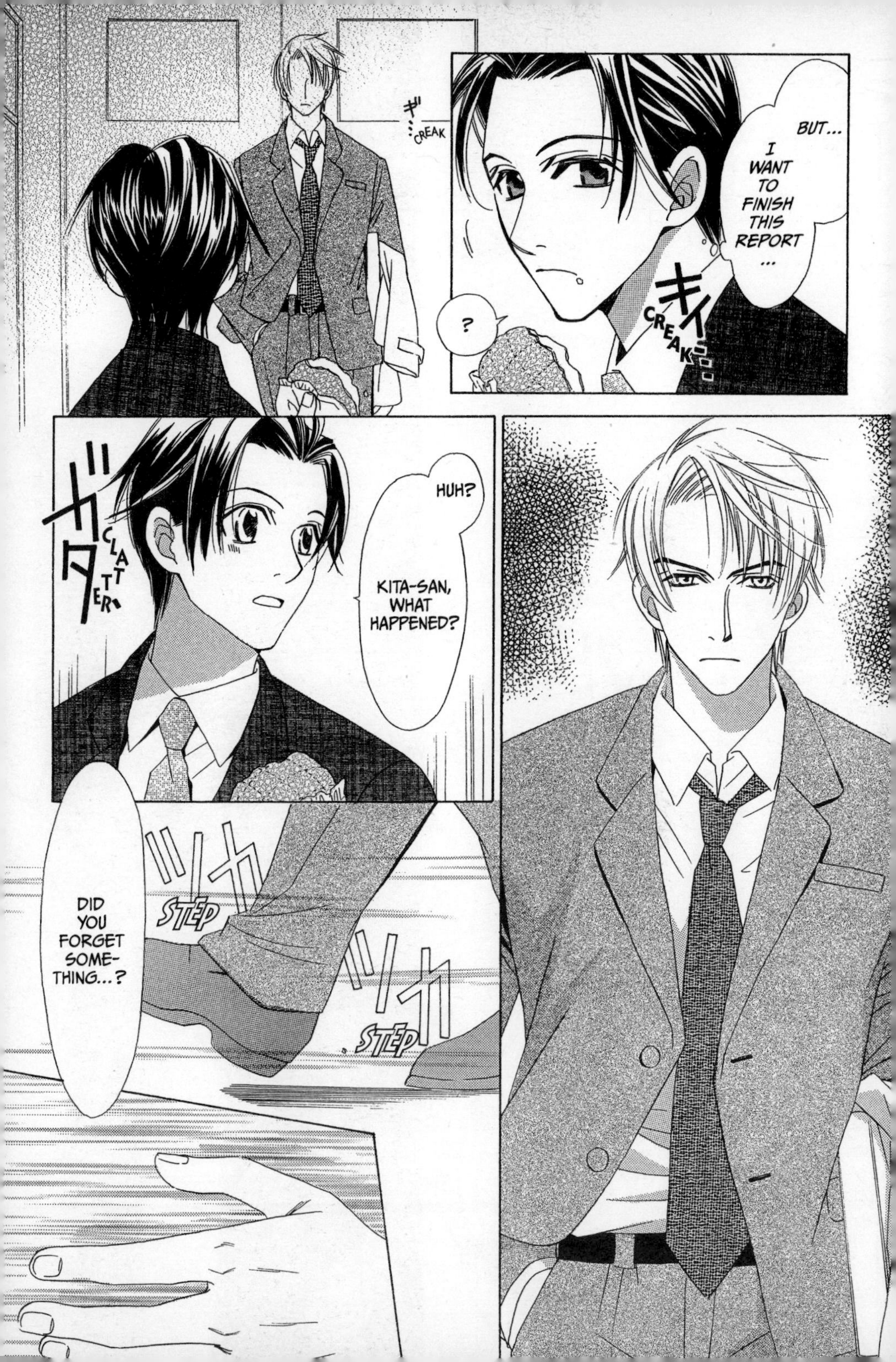
BUT... I WANT TO FINISH THIS REPORT...
CREAK
?
CREAK
HUH?
KITA-SAN, WHAT HAPPENED?
CLATTER
DID YOU FORGET SOMETHING...?
STEP
STEP

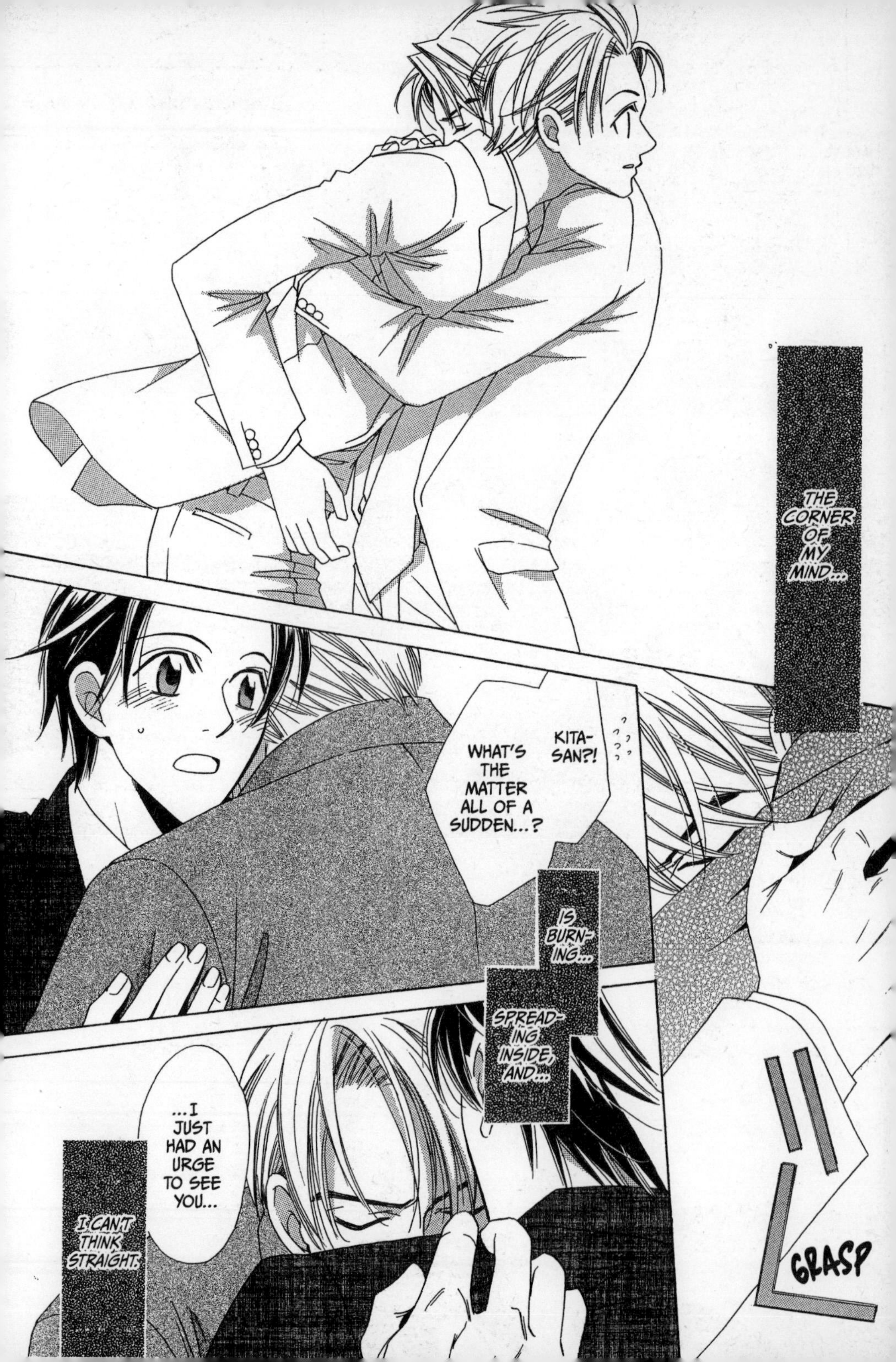
THE CORNER OF MY MIND...
KITA-SAN?!
WHAT'S THE MATTER ALL OF A SUDDEN...?
IS BURNING...
SPREADING INSIDE, AND...
GRASP
...I JUST HAD AN URGE TO SEE YOU...
I CAN'T THINK STRAIGHT.

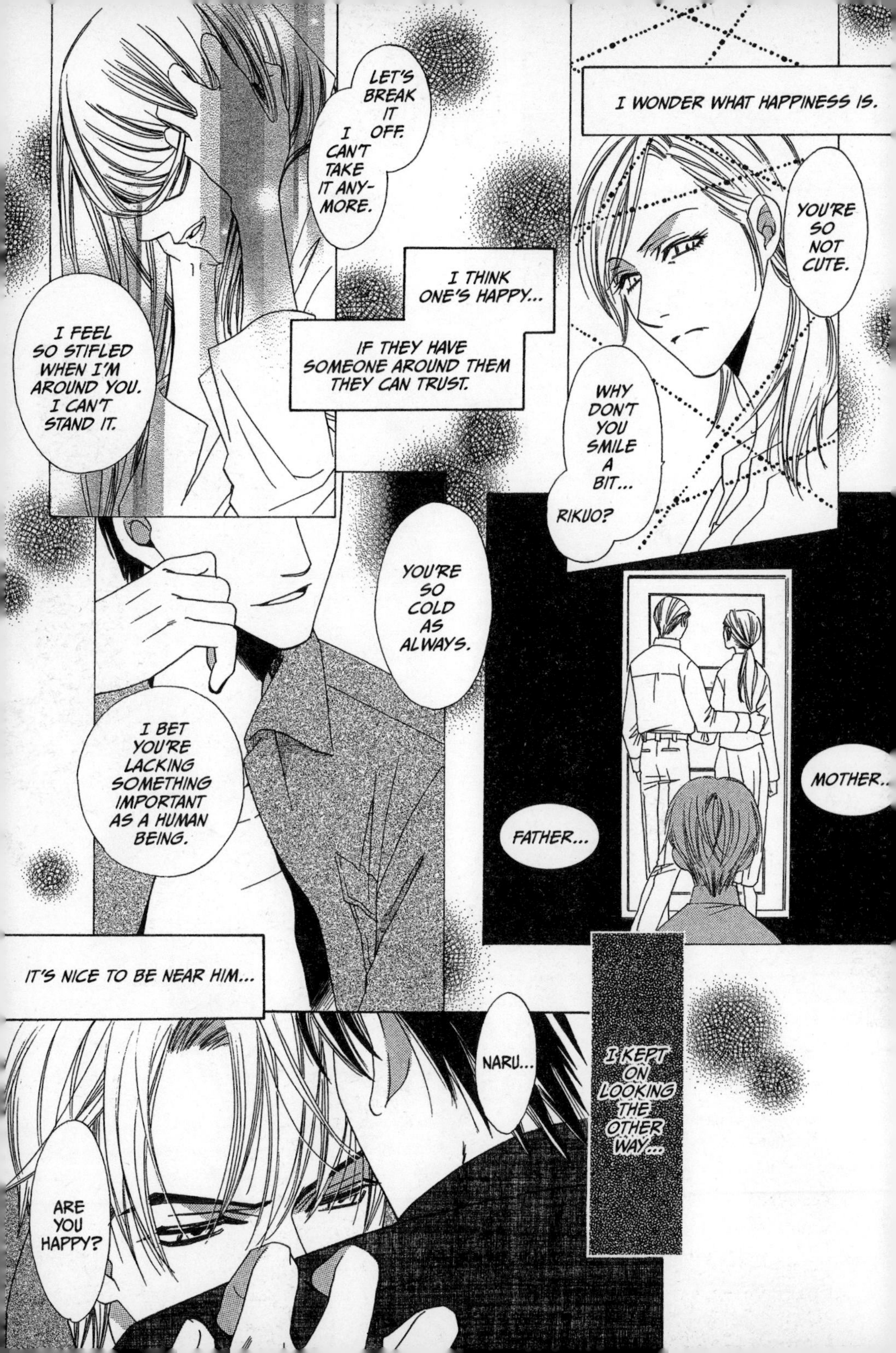
I WONDER WHAT HAPPINESS IS.
YOU'RE SO NOT CUTE.
WHY DON'T YOU SMILE A BIT... RIKUO?
LET'S BREAK IT OFF. I CAN'T TAKE IT ANYMORE.
I FEEL SO STIFLED WHEN I'M AROUND YOU. I CAN'T STAND IT.
I THINK ONE'S HAPPY...
IF THEY HAVE SOMEONE AROUND THEM THEY CAN TRUST.
MOTHER...
FATHER...
YOU'RE SO COLD AS ALWAYS.
I BET YOU'RE LACKING SOMETHING IMPORTANT AS A HUMAN BEING.
IT'S NICE TO BE NEAR HIM...
I KEPT ON LOOKING THE OTHER WAY...
NARU...
ARE YOU HAPPY?

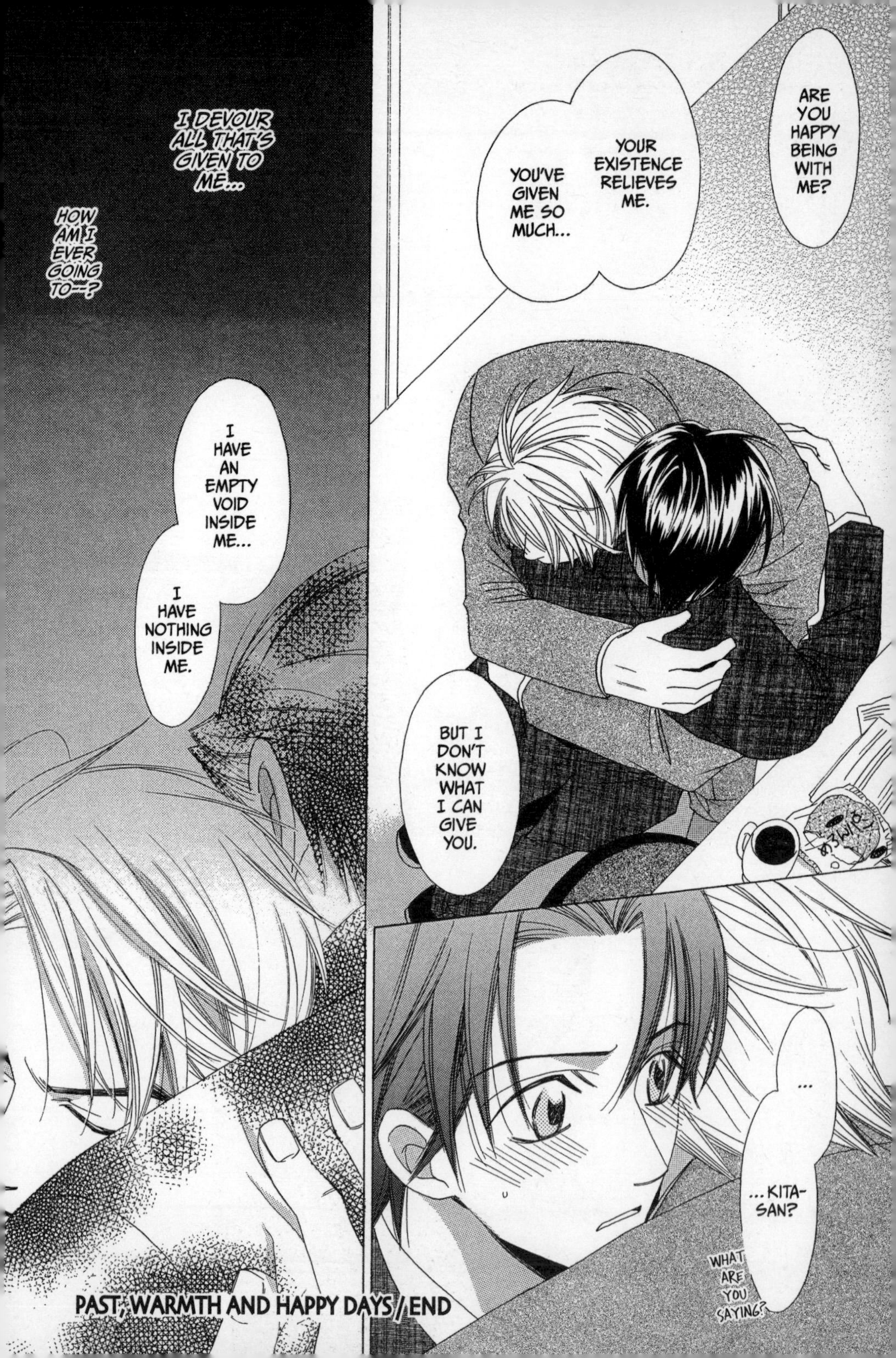
ARE YOU HAPPY BEING WITH ME?
YOUR EXISTENCE RELIEVES ME.
YOU'VE GIVEN ME SO MUCH...
BUT I DON'T KNOW WHAT I CAN GIVE YOU.
...
...KITA-SAN?
WHAT ARE YOU SAYING?
I DEVOUR ALL THAT'S GIVEN TO ME...
HOW AM I EVER GOING TO--?
I HAVE AN EMPTY VOID INSIDE ME...
I HAVE NOTHING INSIDE ME.
PAST, WARMTH AND HAPPY DAYS / END

Kita & Naru series

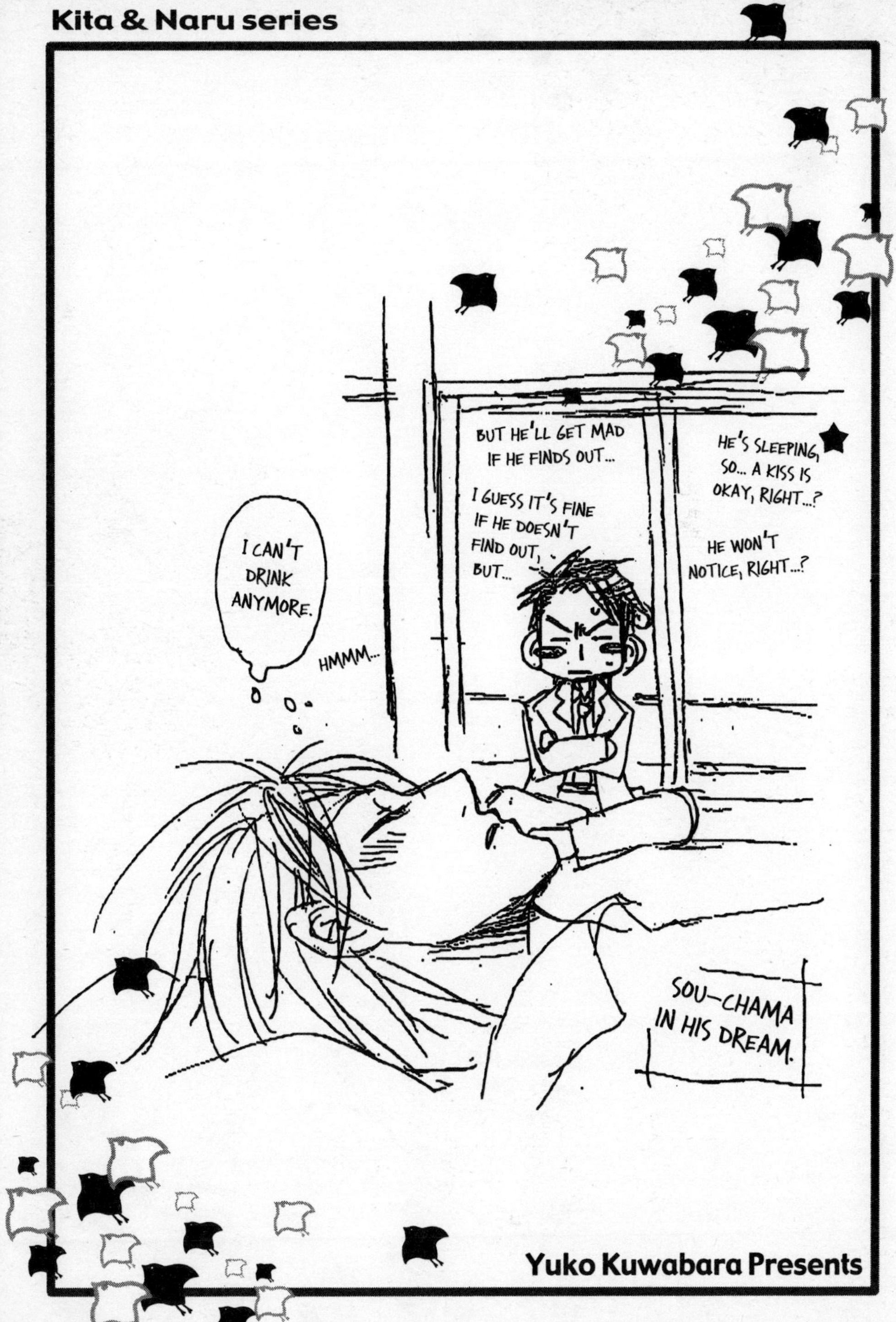
HE'S SLEEPING, SO... A KISS IS OKAY, RIGHT...?
HE WON'T NOTICE, RIGHT...?
BUT HE'LL GET MAD IF HE FINDS OUT...
I GUESS IT'S FINE IF HE DOESN'T FIND OUT, BUT...
I CAN'T DRINK ANYMORE.
HMMM...
SOU-CHAMA IN HIS DREAM.

Yuko Kuwabara Presents

HER HAIR GREW
LONGER SINCE THE
LAST EPISODE. →

Yuko Kuwabara Presents

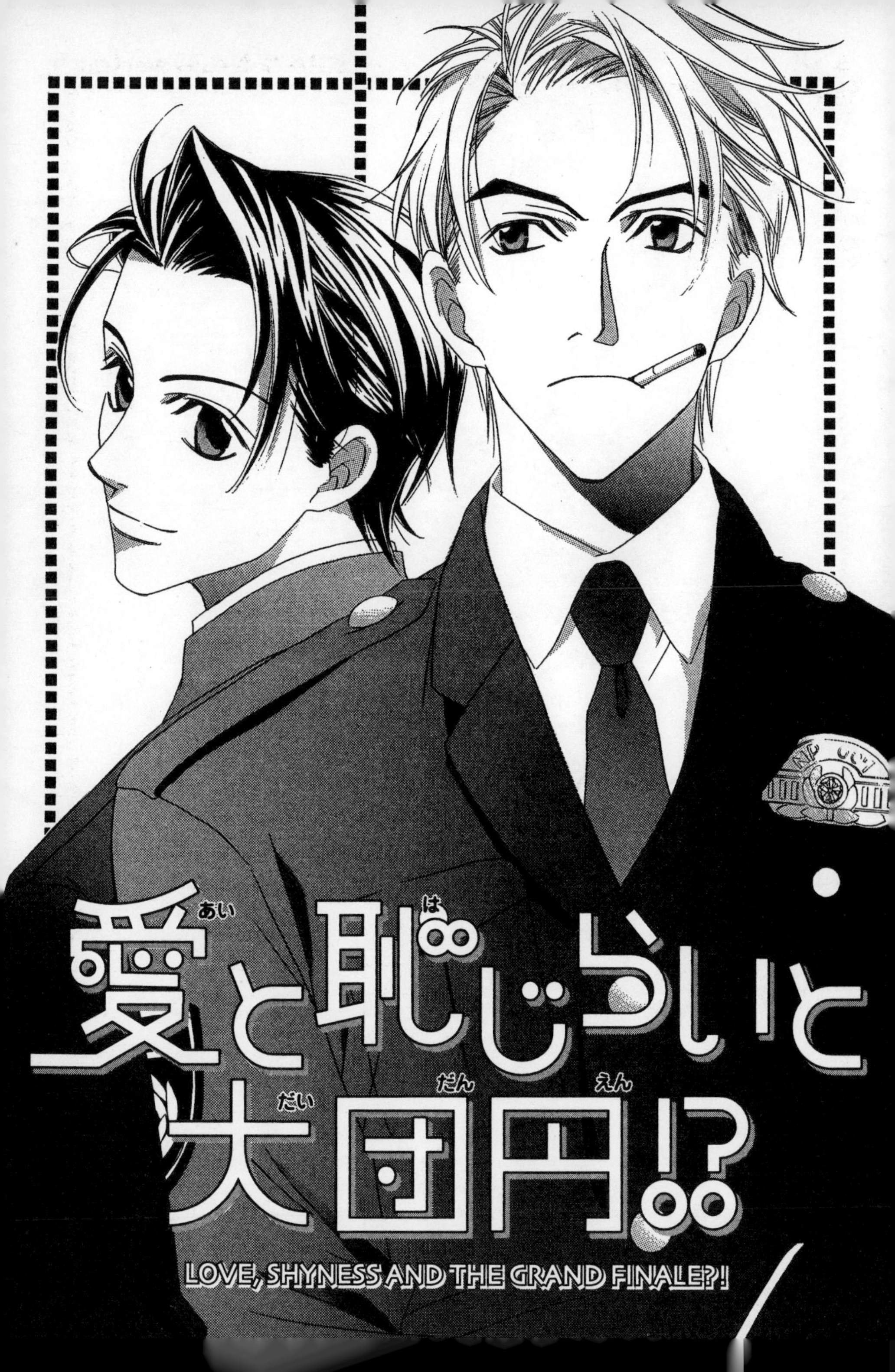
愛と恥じらいと大団円!?
LOVE, SHYNESS AND THE GRAND FINALE?!

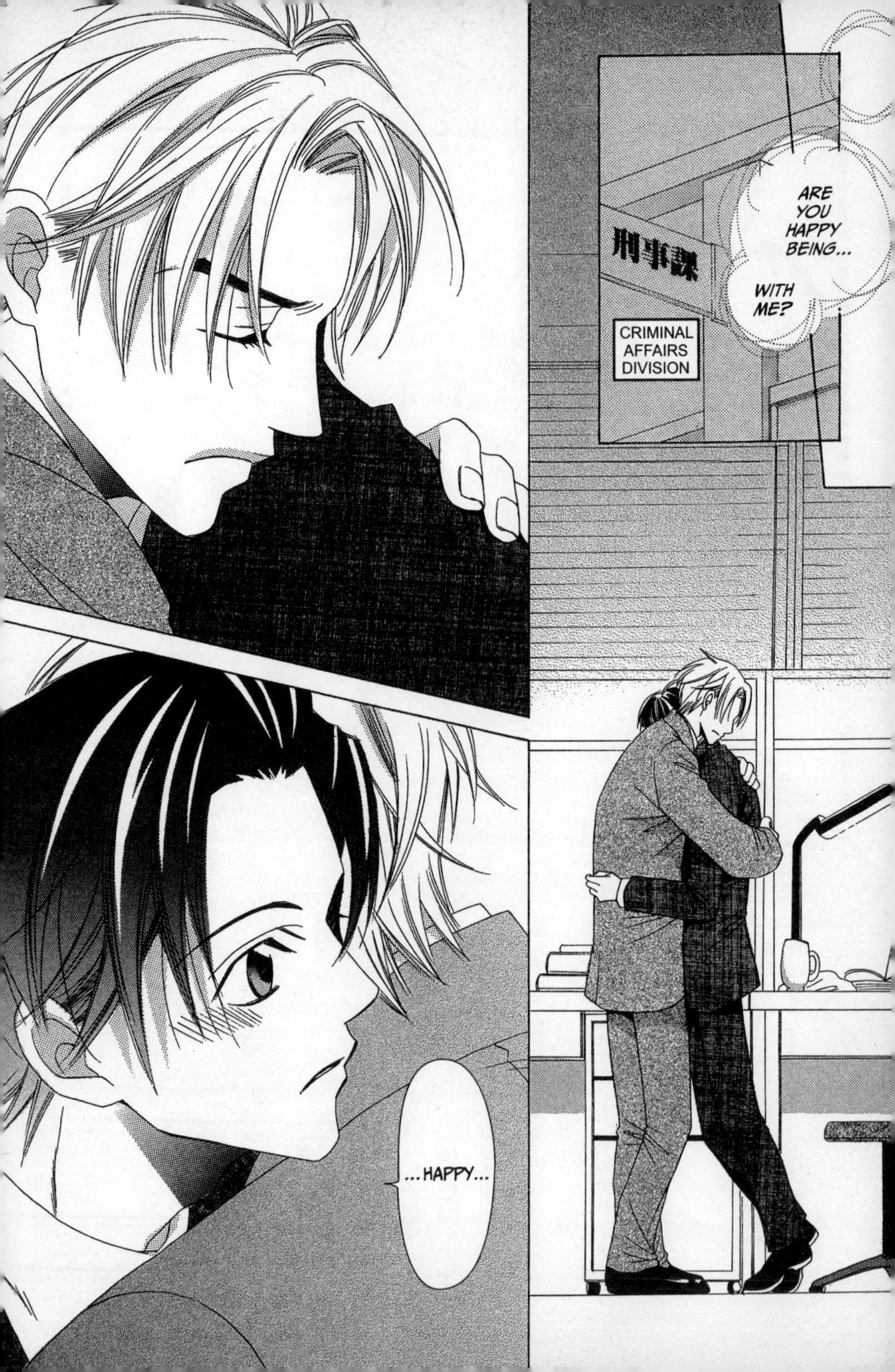
刑事課
CRIMINAL AFFAIRS DIVISION
ARE YOU HAPPY BEING...
WITH ME?
...HAPPY...

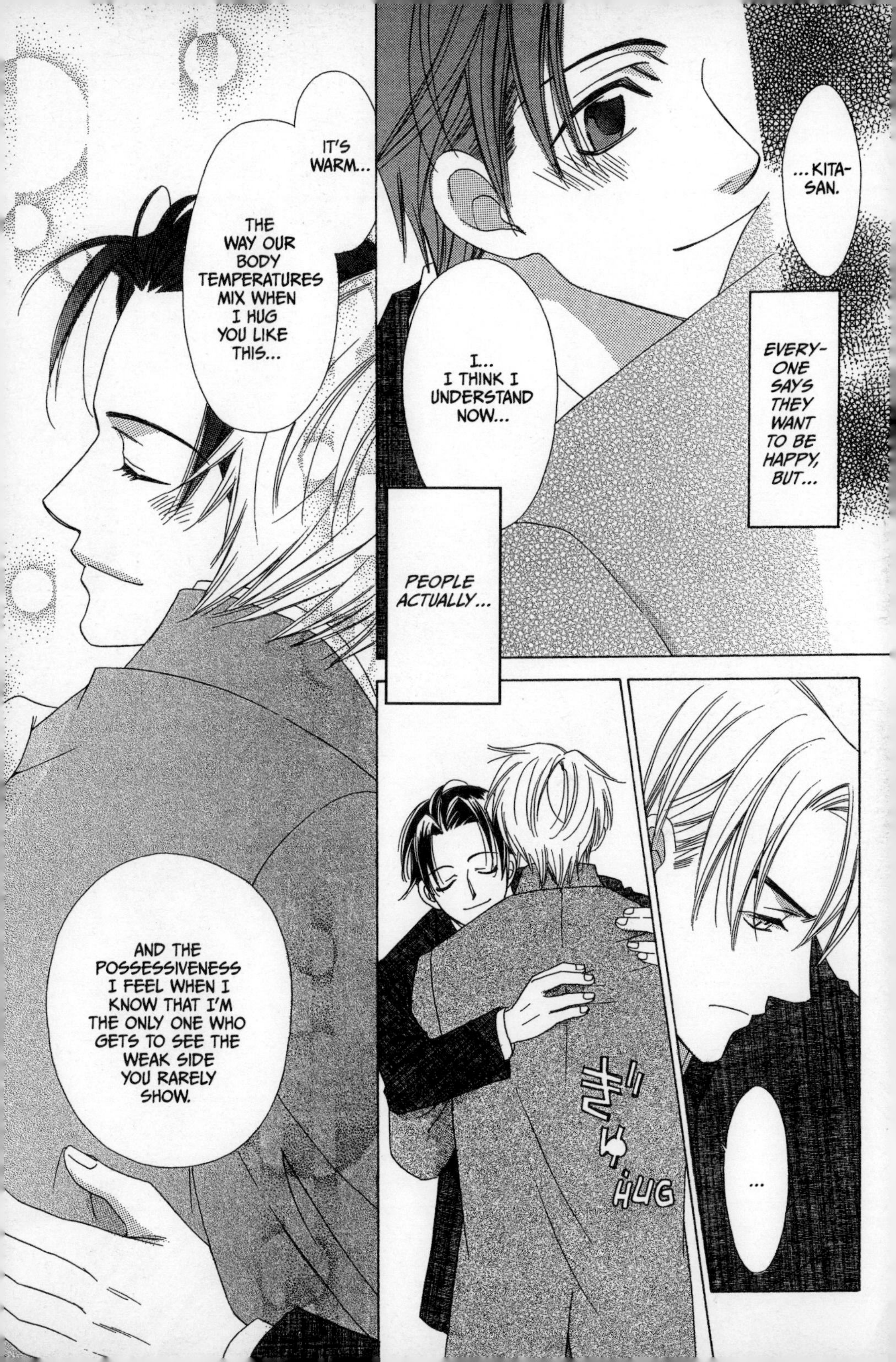
...KITA-SAN.
EVERY-ONE SAYS THEY WANT TO BE HAPPY, BUT...
I... I THINK I UNDERSTAND NOW...
PEOPLE ACTUALLY...
...
ぎゅっ HUG
IT'S WARM...
THE WAY OUR BODY TEMPERATURES MIX WHEN I HUG YOU LIKE THIS...
AND THE POSSESSIVENESS I FEEL WHEN I KNOW THAT I'M THE ONLY ONE WHO GETS TO SEE THE WEAK SIDE YOU RARELY SHOW.

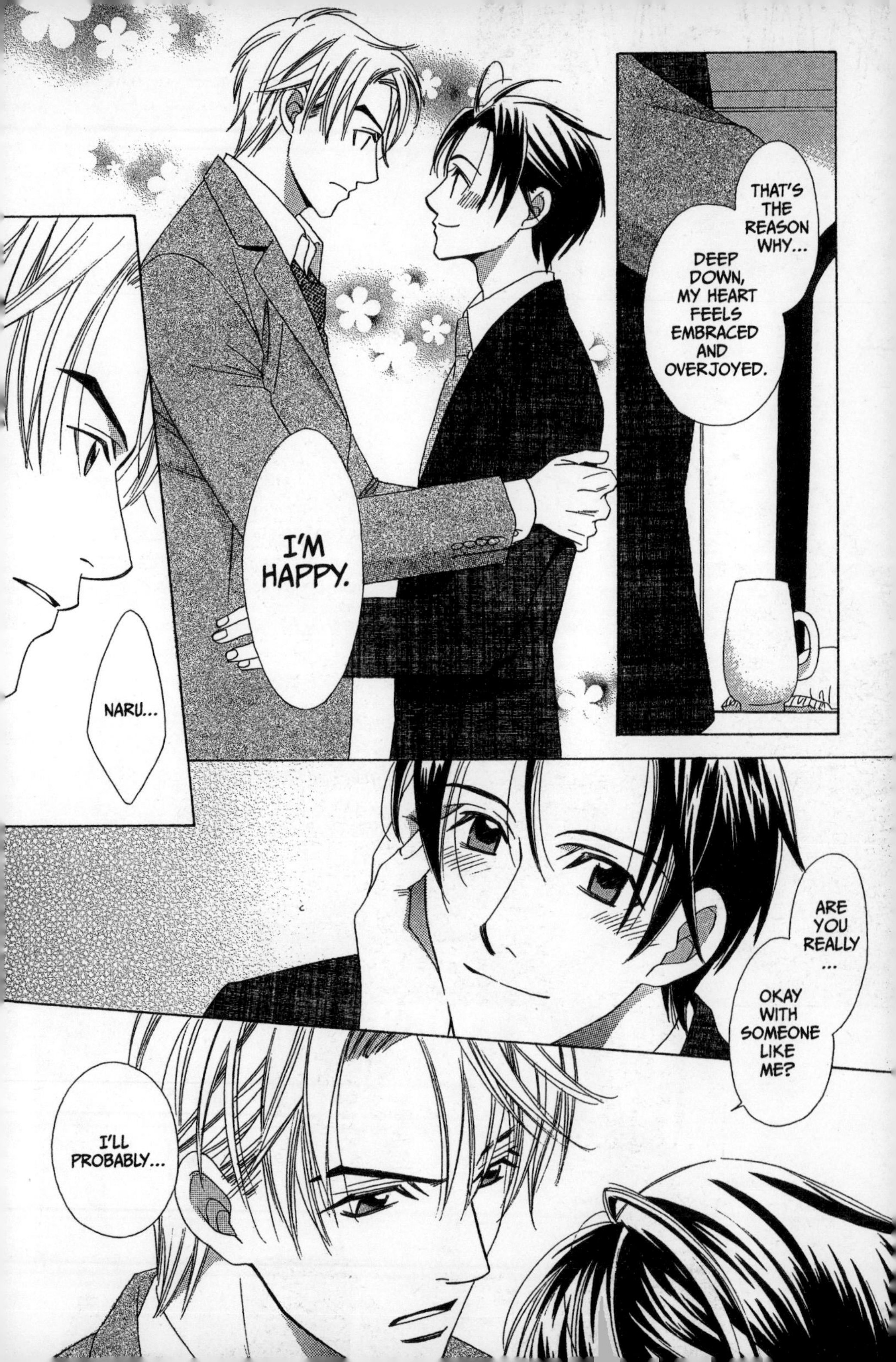
THAT'S THE REASON WHY...
DEEP DOWN, MY HEART FEELS EMBRACED AND OVERJOYED.
I'M HAPPY.
NARU...
ARE YOU REALLY ...
OKAY WITH SOMEONE LIKE ME?
I'LL PROBABLY...

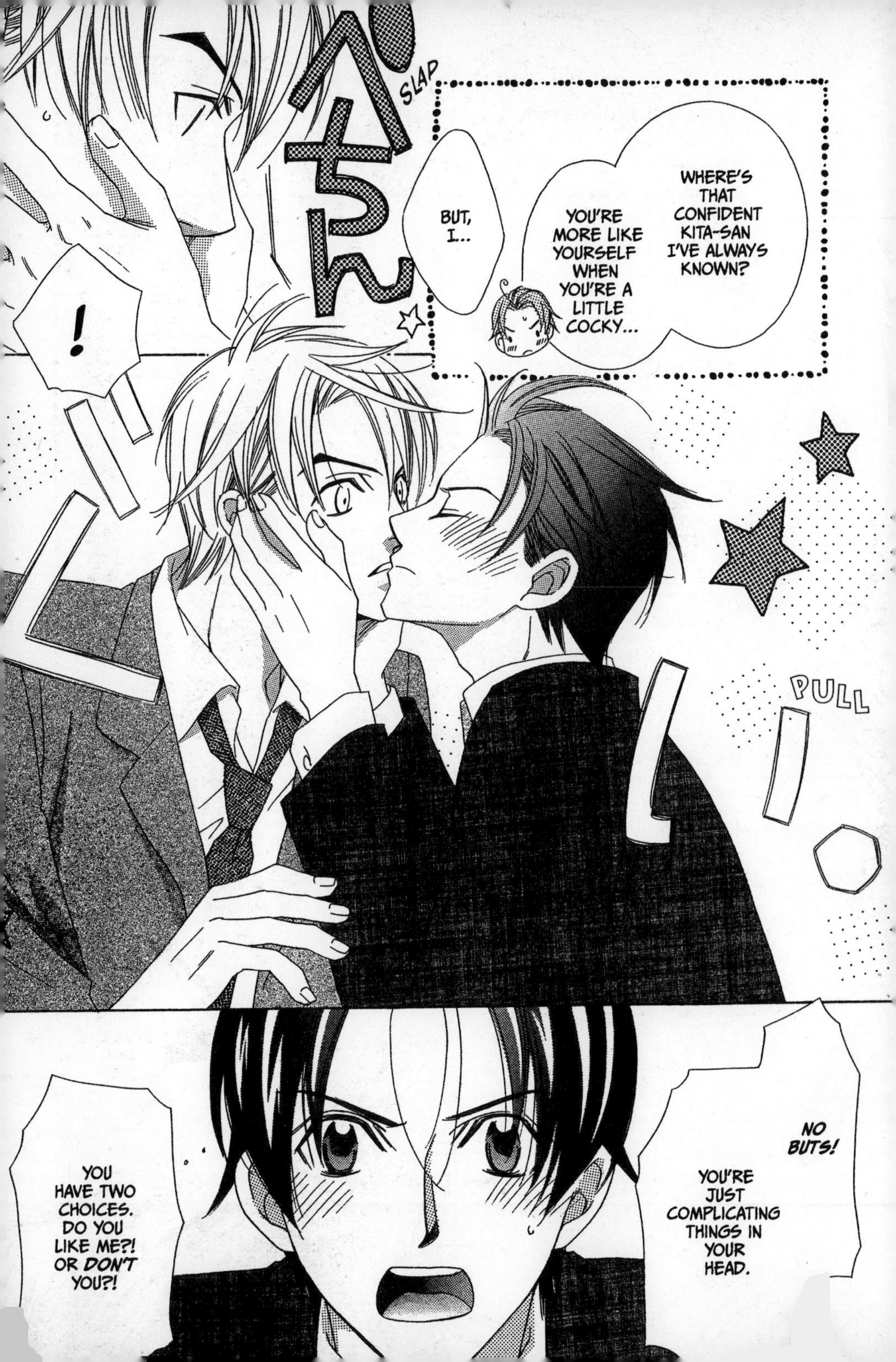

ぺちん
SLAP
WHERE'S THAT CONFIDENT KITA-SAN I'VE ALWAYS KNOWN?
YOU'RE MORE LIKE YOURSELF WHEN YOU'RE A LITTLE COCKY...
BUT, I...
!
PULL
NO BUTS!
YOU'RE JUST COMPLICATING THINGS IN YOUR HEAD.
YOU HAVE TWO CHOICES. DO YOU LIKE ME?! OR *DON'T* YOU?!

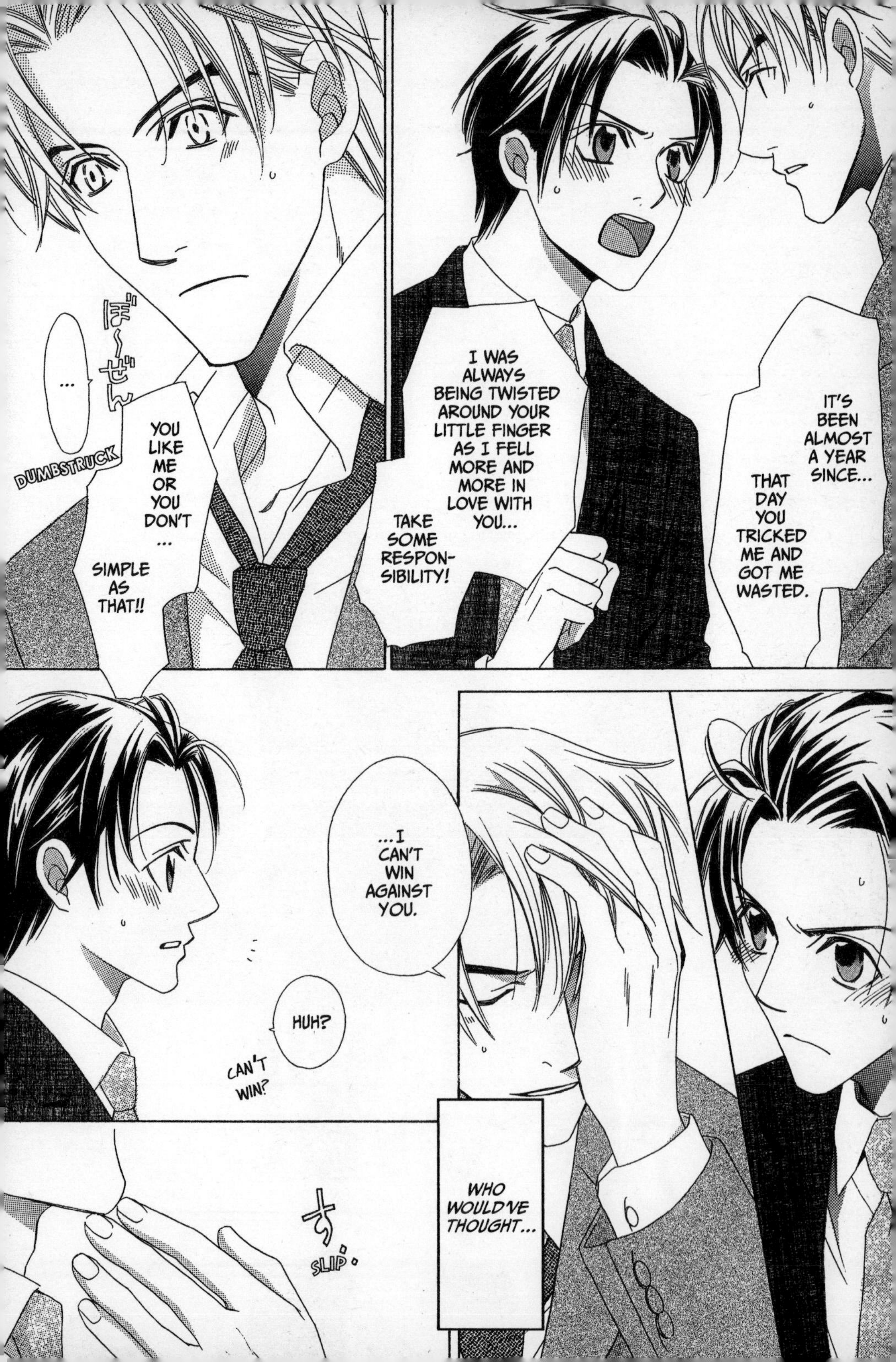
IT'S BEEN ALMOST A YEAR SINCE...
THAT DAY YOU TRICKED ME AND GOT ME WASTED.
I WAS ALWAYS BEING TWISTED AROUND YOUR LITTLE FINGER AS I FELL MORE AND MORE IN LOVE WITH YOU...
TAKE SOME RESPON-SIBILITY!
YOU LIKE ME OR YOU DON'T ...
SIMPLE AS THAT!!
...
ぼ〜ぜん
DUMBSTRUCK
...I CAN'T WIN AGAINST YOU.
HUH?
CAN'T WIN?
WHO WOULD'VE THOUGHT...
す
SLIP

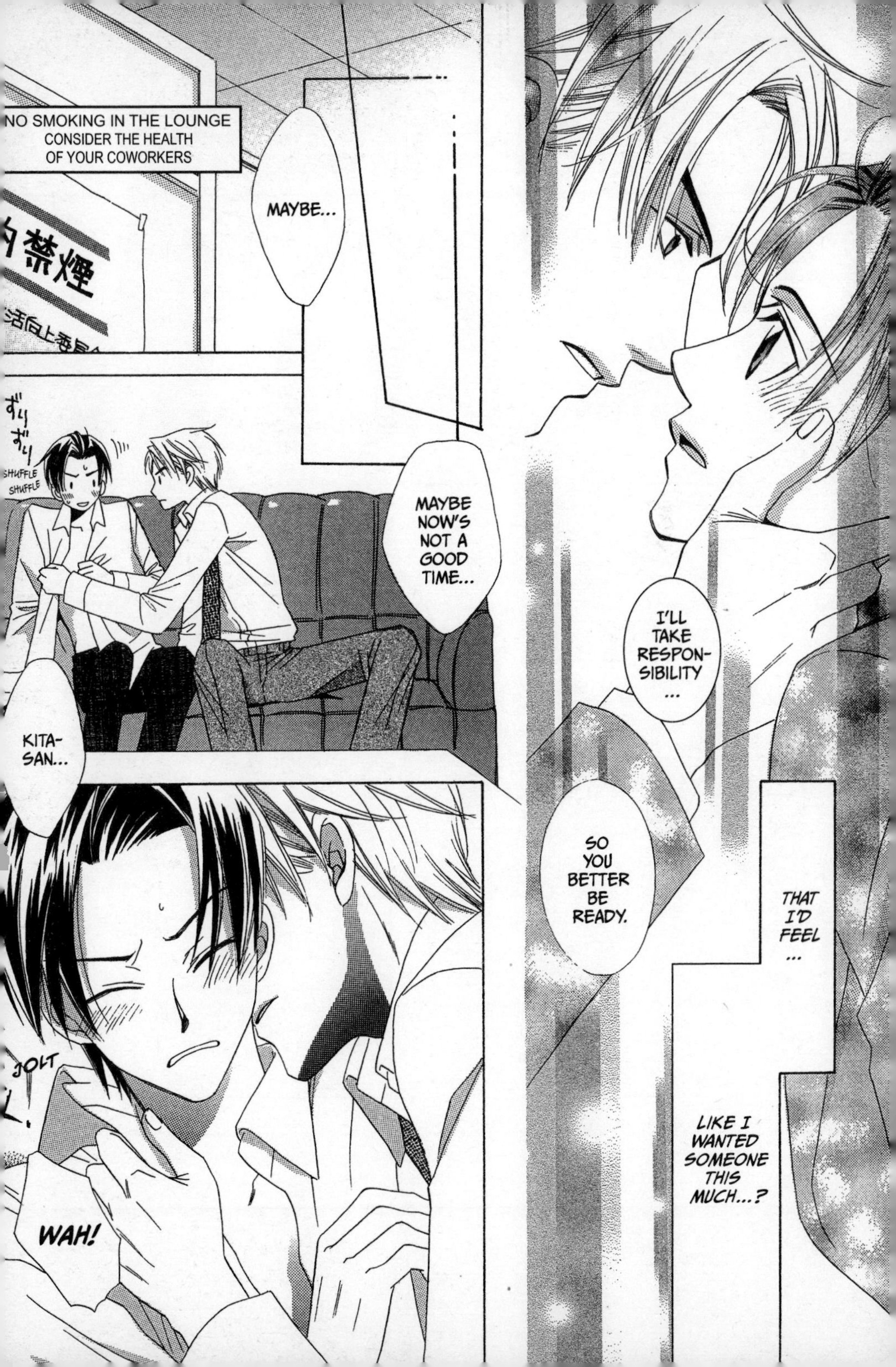
I'LL TAKE RESPON-SIBILITY...
SO YOU BETTER BE READY.
THAT I'D FEEL...
LIKE I WANTED SOMEONE THIS MUCH...?
NO SMOKING IN THE LOUNGE
CONSIDER THE HEALTH OF YOUR COWORKERS
MAYBE...
ずりずり
SHUFFLE SHUFFLE
MAYBE NOW'S NOT A GOOD TIME...
KITA-SAN...
JOLT
WAH!

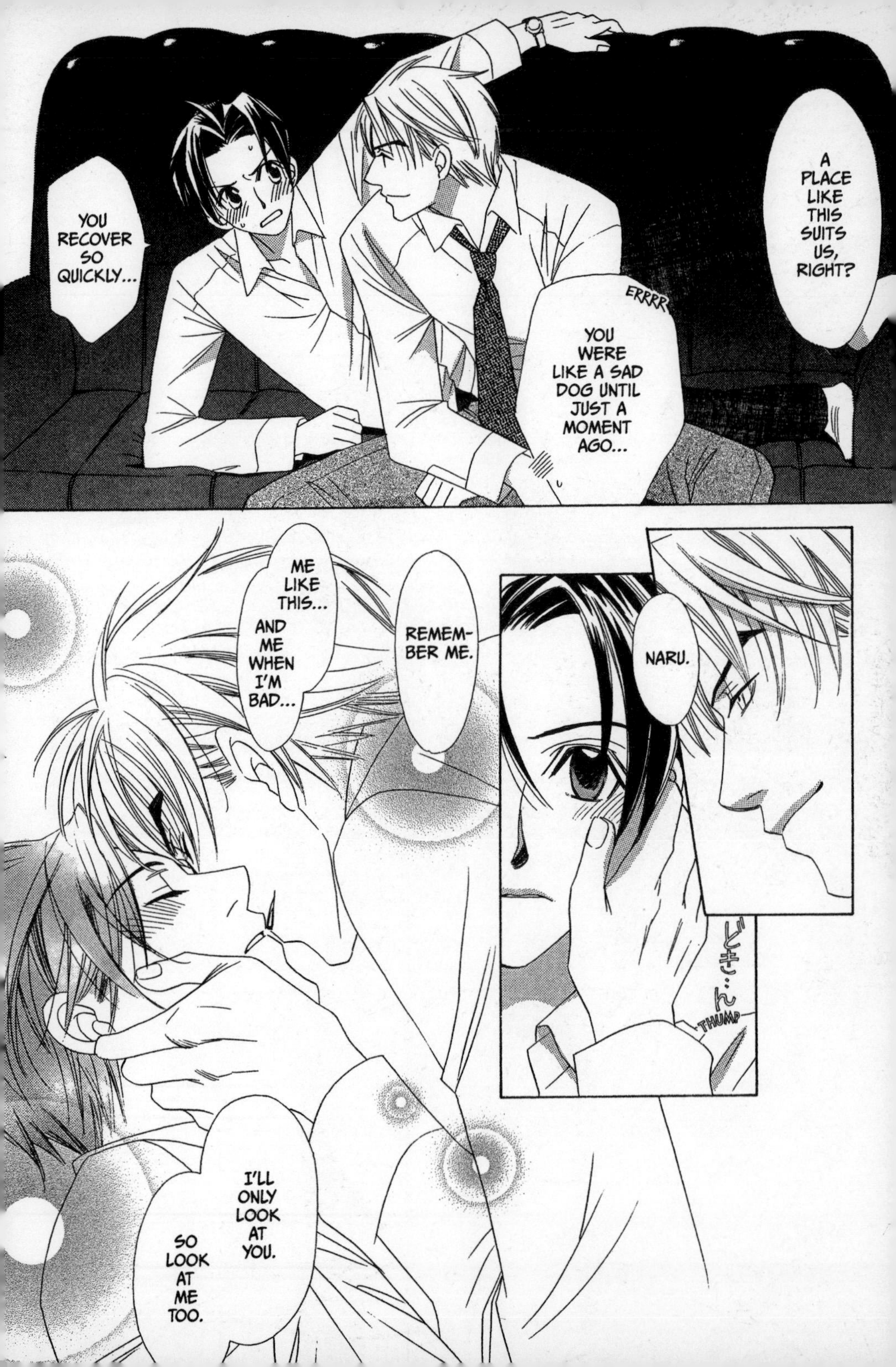
A PLACE LIKE THIS SUITS US, RIGHT?
ERRRR
YOU WERE LIKE A SAD DOG UNTIL JUST A MOMENT AGO...
YOU RECOVER SO QUICKLY...
NARU.
どき…ん
THUMP
REMEM-BER ME.
ME LIKE THIS...
AND ME WHEN I'M BAD...
I'LL ONLY LOOK AT YOU.
SO LOOK AT ME TOO.

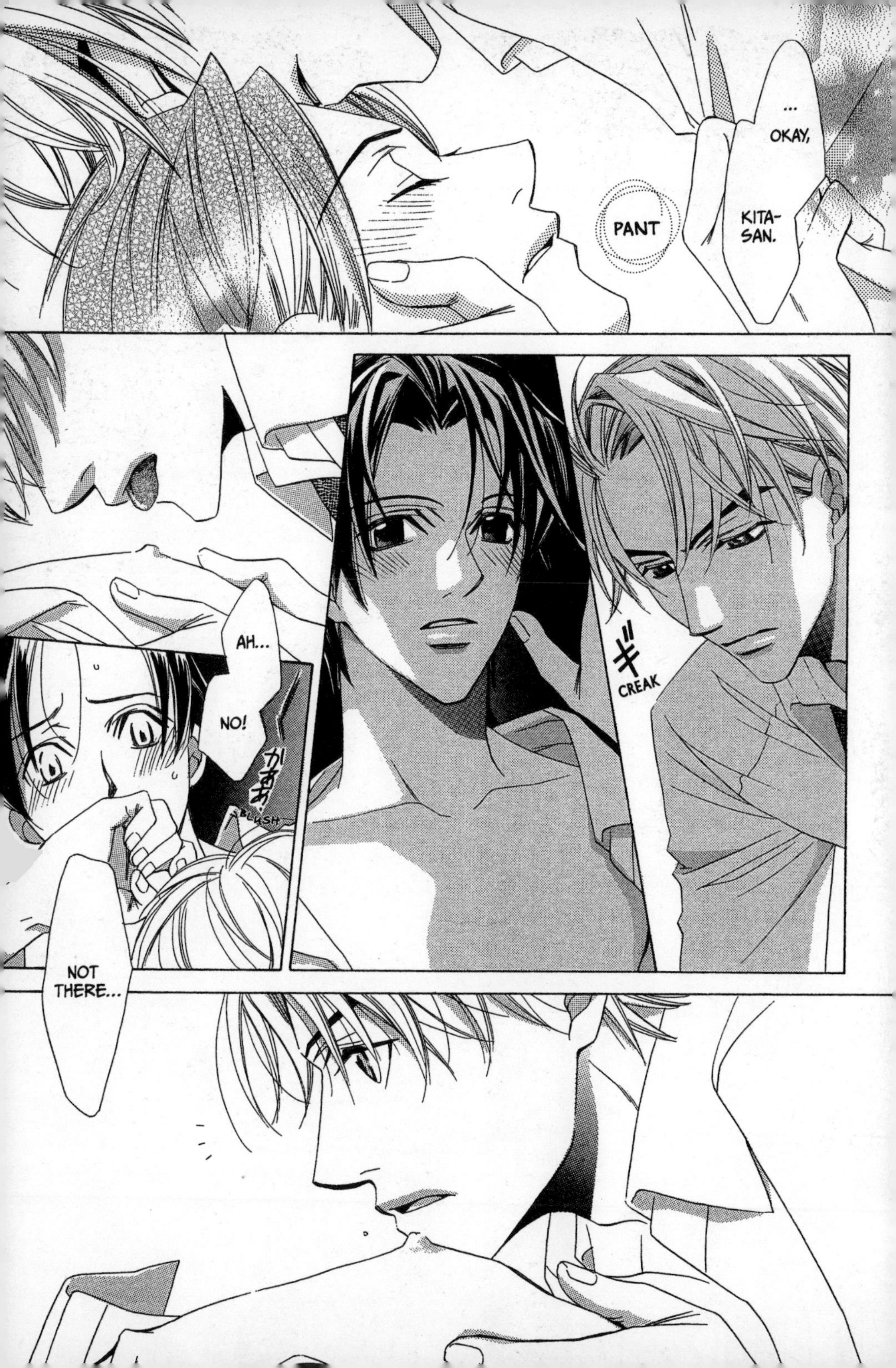

... OKAY, KITA-SAN.
PANT
ギ
CREAK
AH... NO!
BLUSH
NOT THERE...

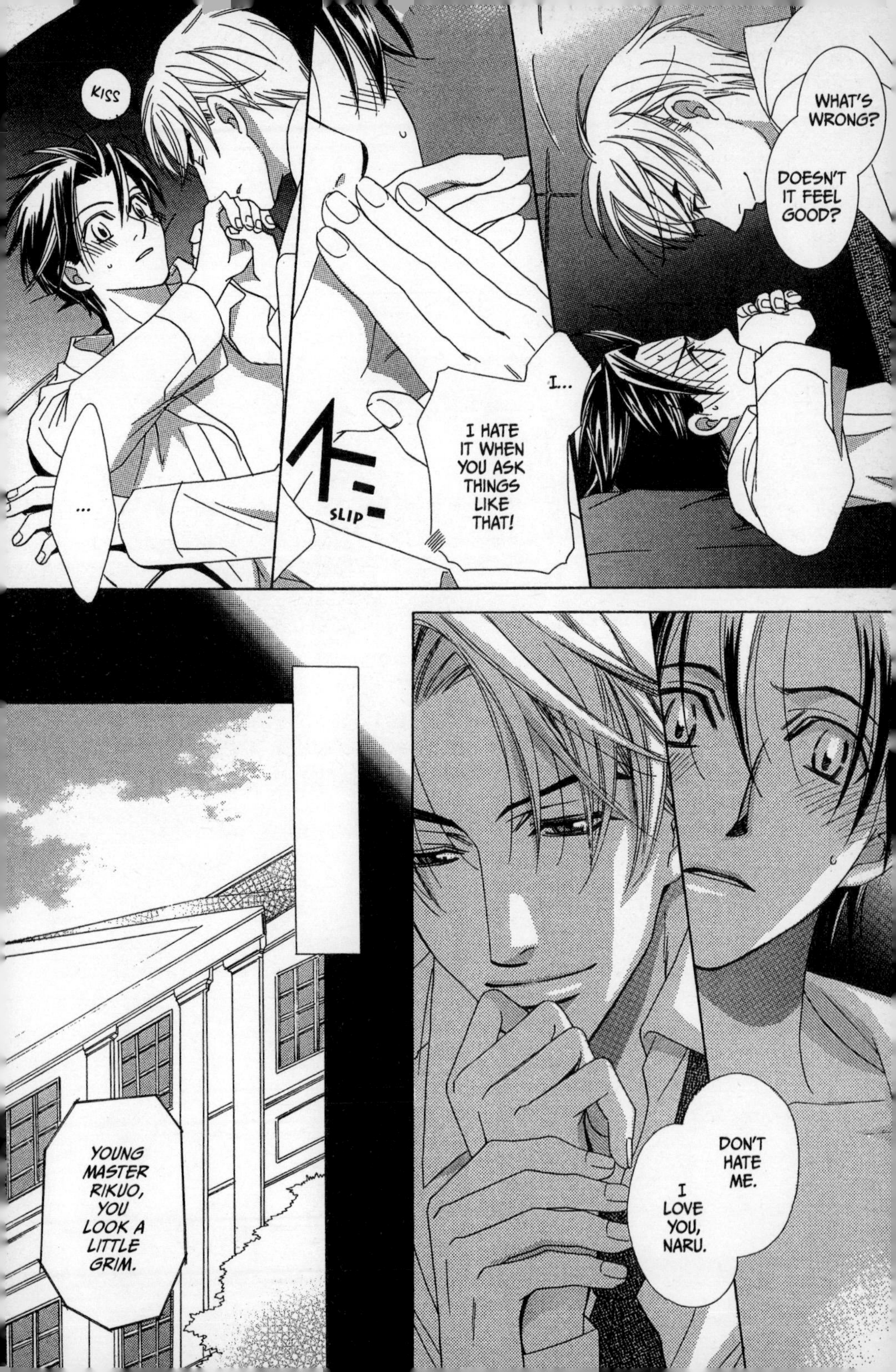
WHAT'S WRONG?
DOESN'T IT FEEL GOOD?
I...
I HATE IT WHEN YOU ASK THINGS LIKE THAT!
SLIP
KISS
...
DON'T HATE ME.
I LOVE YOU, NARU.
YOUNG MASTER RIKUO, YOU LOOK A LITTLE GRIM.

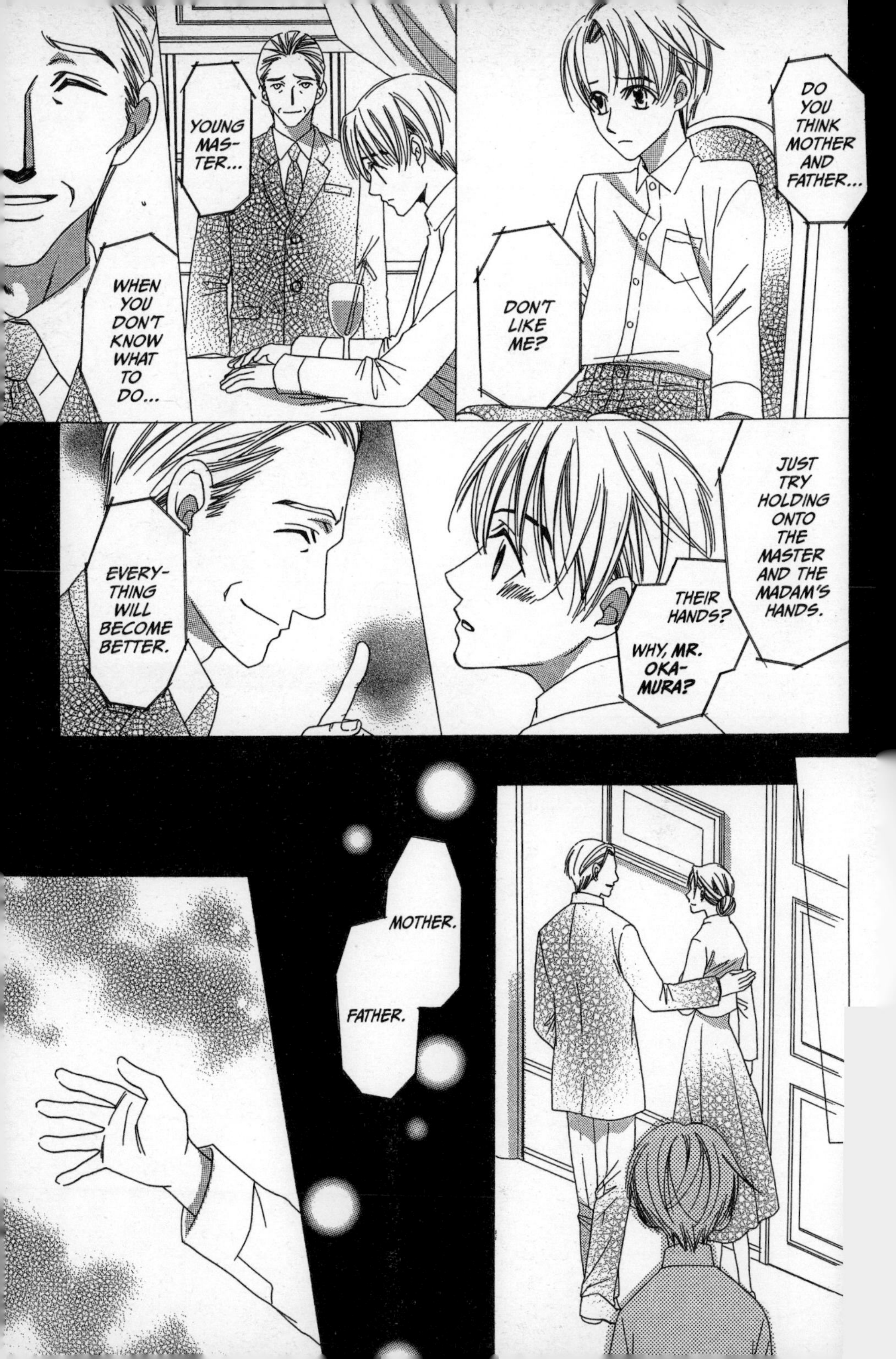
DO YOU THINK MOTHER AND FATHER...
DON'T LIKE ME?
YOUNG MASTER...
WHEN YOU DON'T KNOW WHAT TO DO...
JUST TRY HOLDING ONTO THE MASTER AND THE MADAM'S HANDS.
THEIR HANDS?
WHY, MR. OKAMURA?
EVERYTHING WILL BECOME BETTER.
MOTHER.
FATHER.

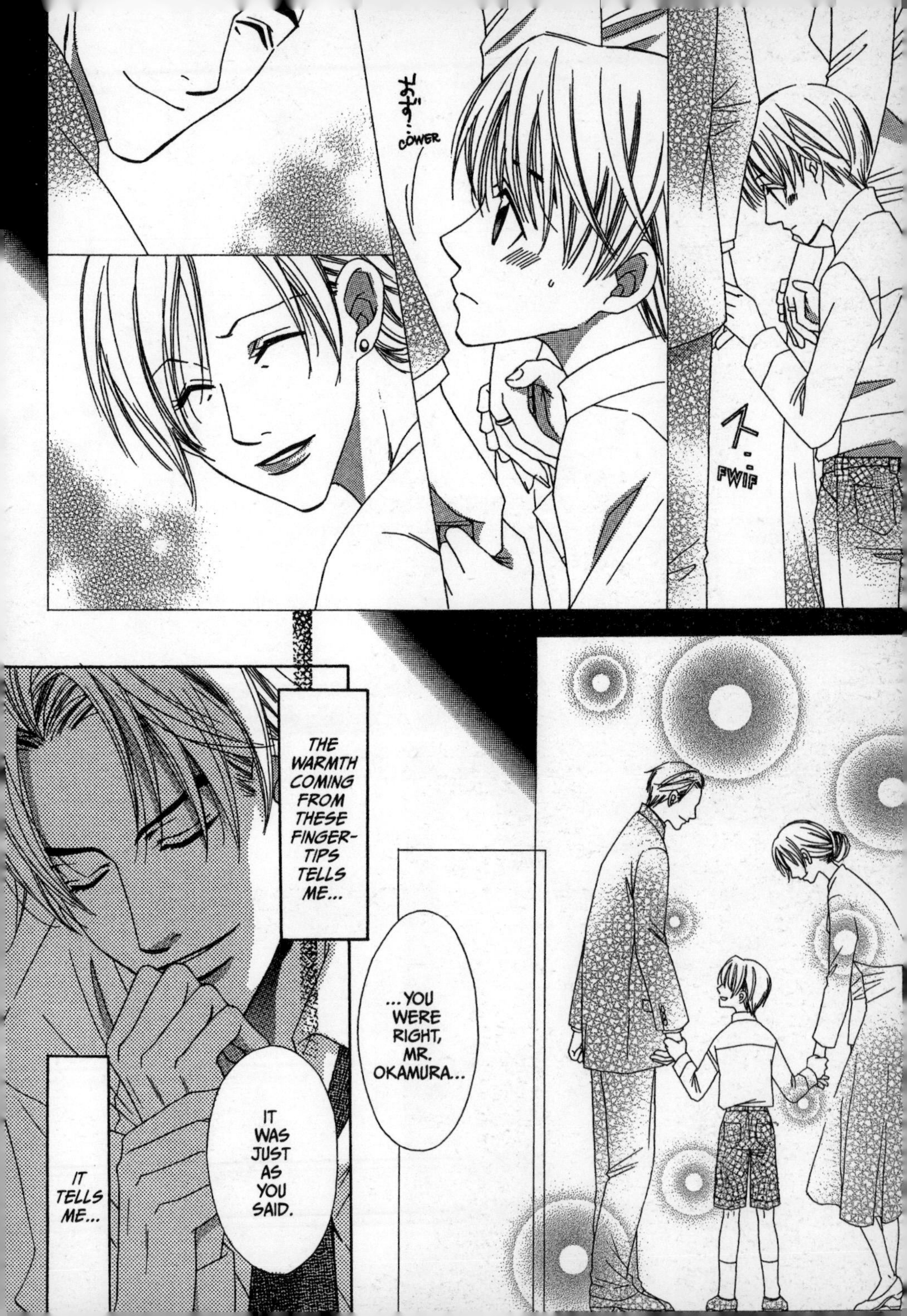
FWIF
COWER
...YOU WERE RIGHT, MR. OKAMURA...
IT WAS JUST AS YOU SAID.
THE WARMTH COMING FROM THESE FINGER-TIPS TELLS ME...
IT TELLS ME...

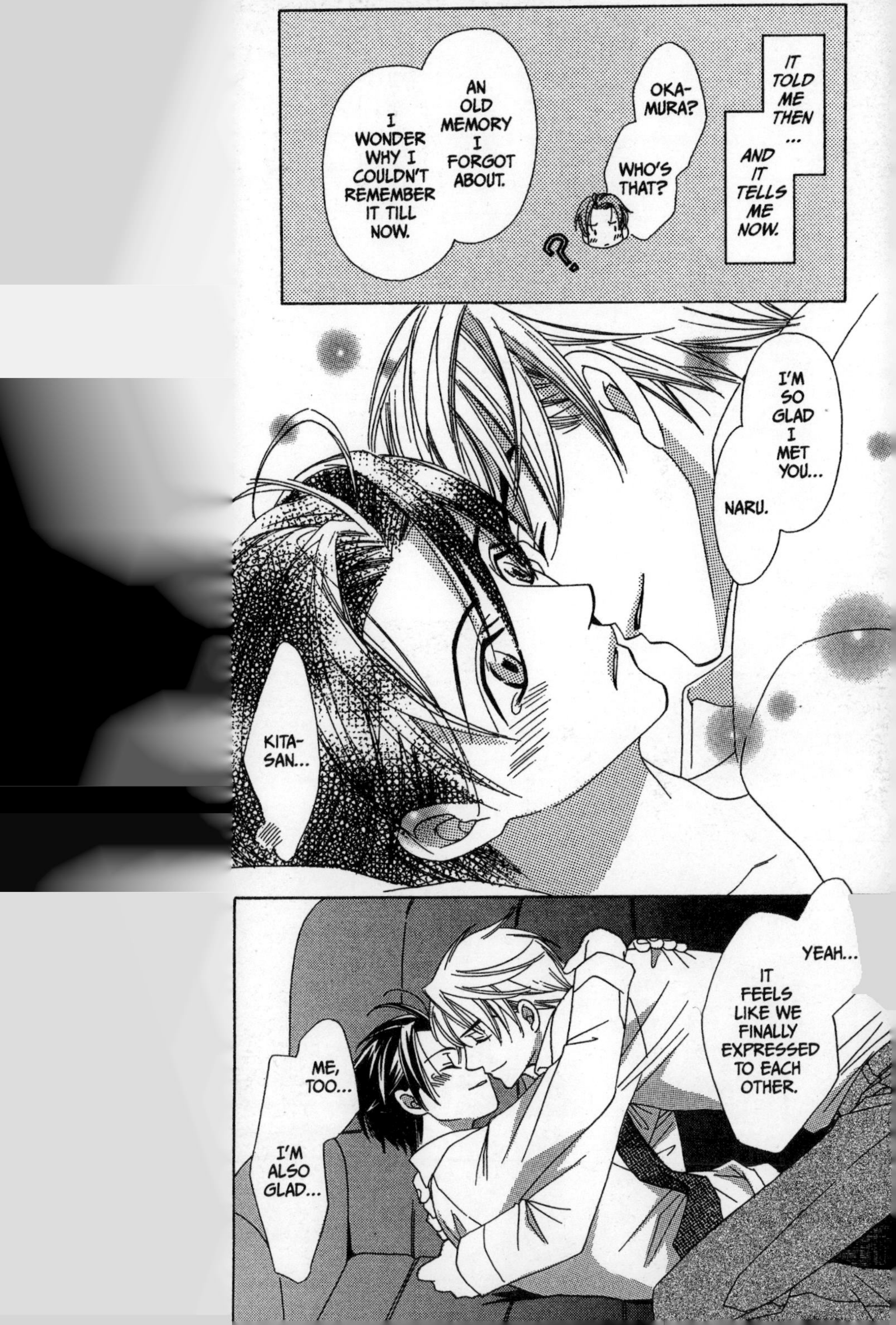
IT TOLD ME THEN ... AND IT TELLS ME NOW.
OKA-MURA?
WHO'S THAT?
AN OLD MEMORY I FORGOT ABOUT.
I WONDER WHY I COULDN'T REMEMBER IT TILL NOW.
I'M SO GLAD I MET YOU...
NARU.
KITA-SAN...
YEAH...
IT FEELS LIKE WE FINALLY EXPRESSED TO EACH OTHER.
ME, TOO...
I'M ALSO GLAD...

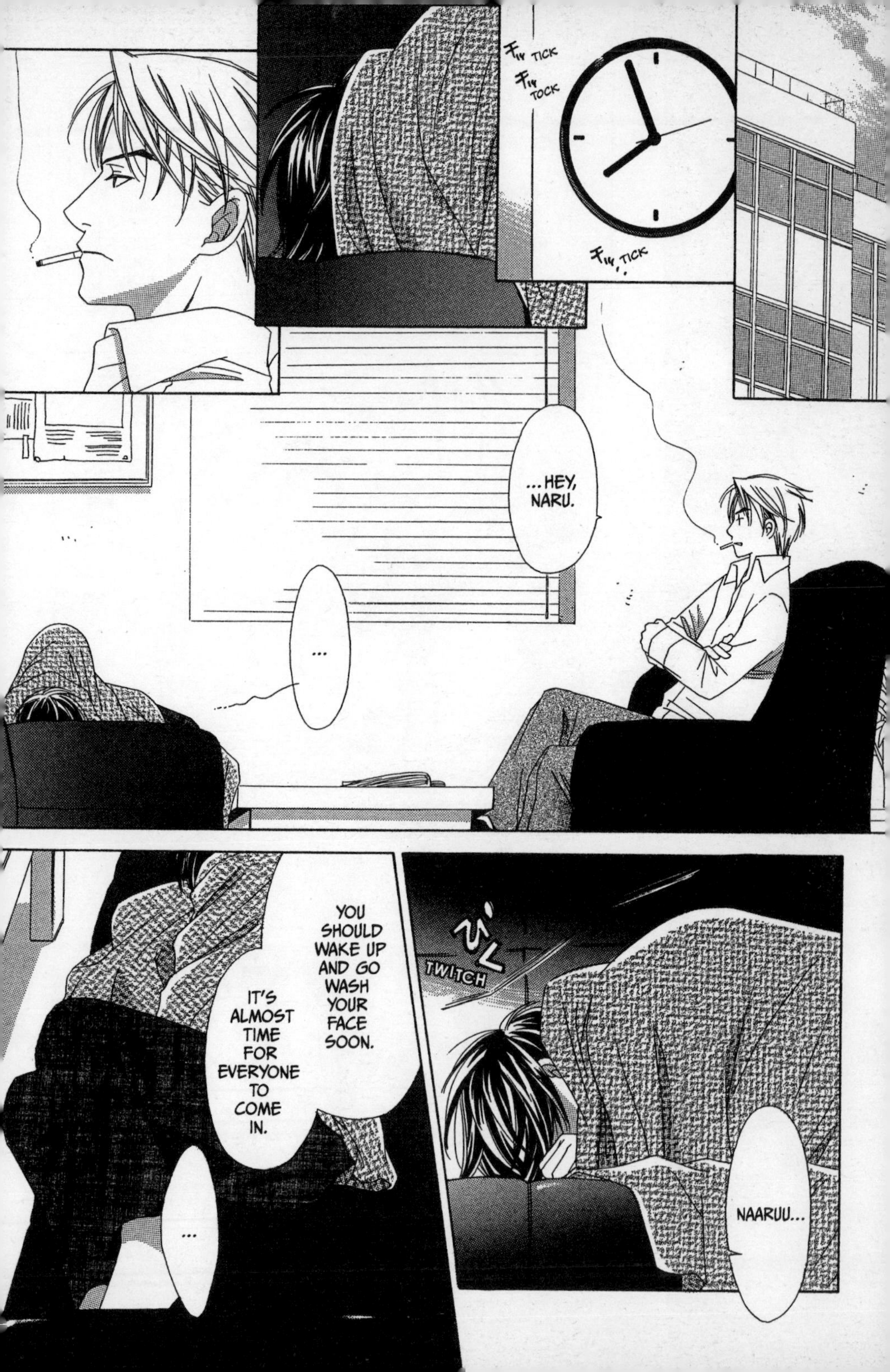
TICK
TOCK
TICK
...HEY, NARU.
...
TWITCH
NAARUU...
YOU SHOULD WAKE UP AND GO WASH YOUR FACE SOON.
IT'S ALMOST TIME FOR EVERYONE TO COME IN.
...

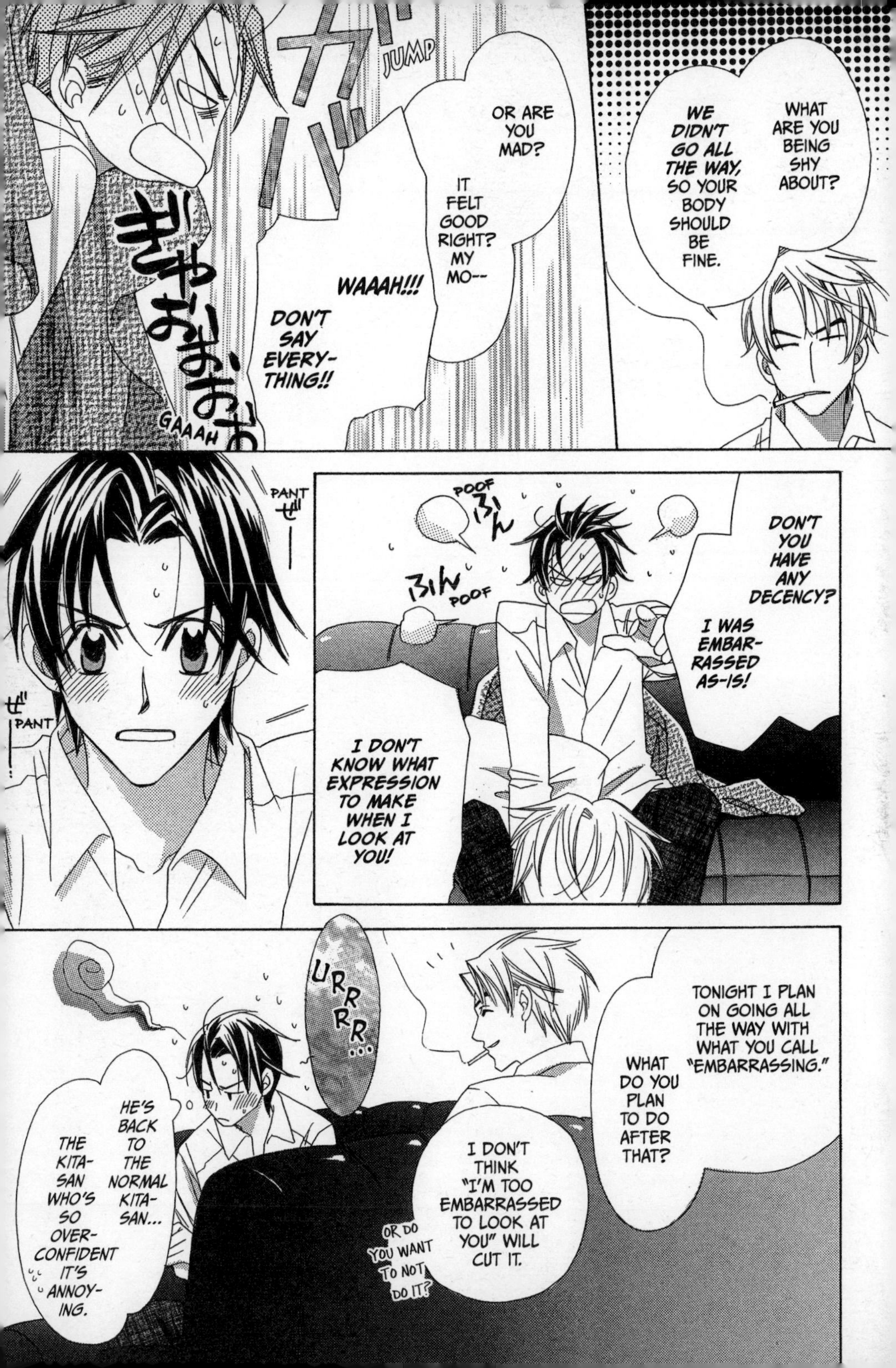

WHAT ARE YOU BEING SHY ABOUT?
WE DIDN'T GO ALL THE WAY, SO YOUR BODY SHOULD BE FINE.
OR ARE YOU MAD?
IT FELT GOOD RIGHT? MY MO--
JUMP
WAAAH!!!
DON'T SAY EVERY-THING!!
GAAAH
DON'T YOU HAVE ANY DECENCY?
I WAS EMBARRASSED AS-IS!
POOF
POOF
I DON'T KNOW WHAT EXPRESSION TO MAKE WHEN I LOOK AT YOU!
PANT
PANT
TONIGHT I PLAN ON GOING ALL THE WAY WITH WHAT YOU CALL "EMBARRASSING."
WHAT DO YOU PLAN TO DO AFTER THAT?
I DON'T THINK "I'M TOO EMBARRASSED TO LOOK AT YOU" WILL CUT IT.
OR DO YOU WANT TO NOT DO IT?
URRR...
HE'S BACK TO THE NORMAL KITA-SAN...
THE KITA-SAN WHO'S SO OVER-CONFIDENT IT'S ANNOYING.

WILL—DEFINITELY—DO-IT-TONIGHT AURA

...

YOU'RE SO CRUEL!!

I'M A MAN, TOO.

I'LL BE READY FOR IT. JUST GIVE IT TO ME!

PFFT

WHY DID YOU LAUGH?

I'M BEING SERIOUS. I'M TRYING TO GET READY FOR IT AS THOUGH MY LIFE DEPENDED ON IT!

TONIGHT ...

WILL BE FUN.

WHAT FATE SHALL AWAIT THESE TWO TONIGHT?

HA HA HA HA

NARU, YOU'RE SO CUTE.

YOU'RE SO MANLY, REALLY.

KITA-SAN!

KUJI-SAN!

GRAB!

GOOD MORNING.

HEY, YOU GUYS ...

IT'S MORNING. CUT IT OUT.

SHOCK

LOVE, SHYNESS AND THE GRAND FINALE?! / END

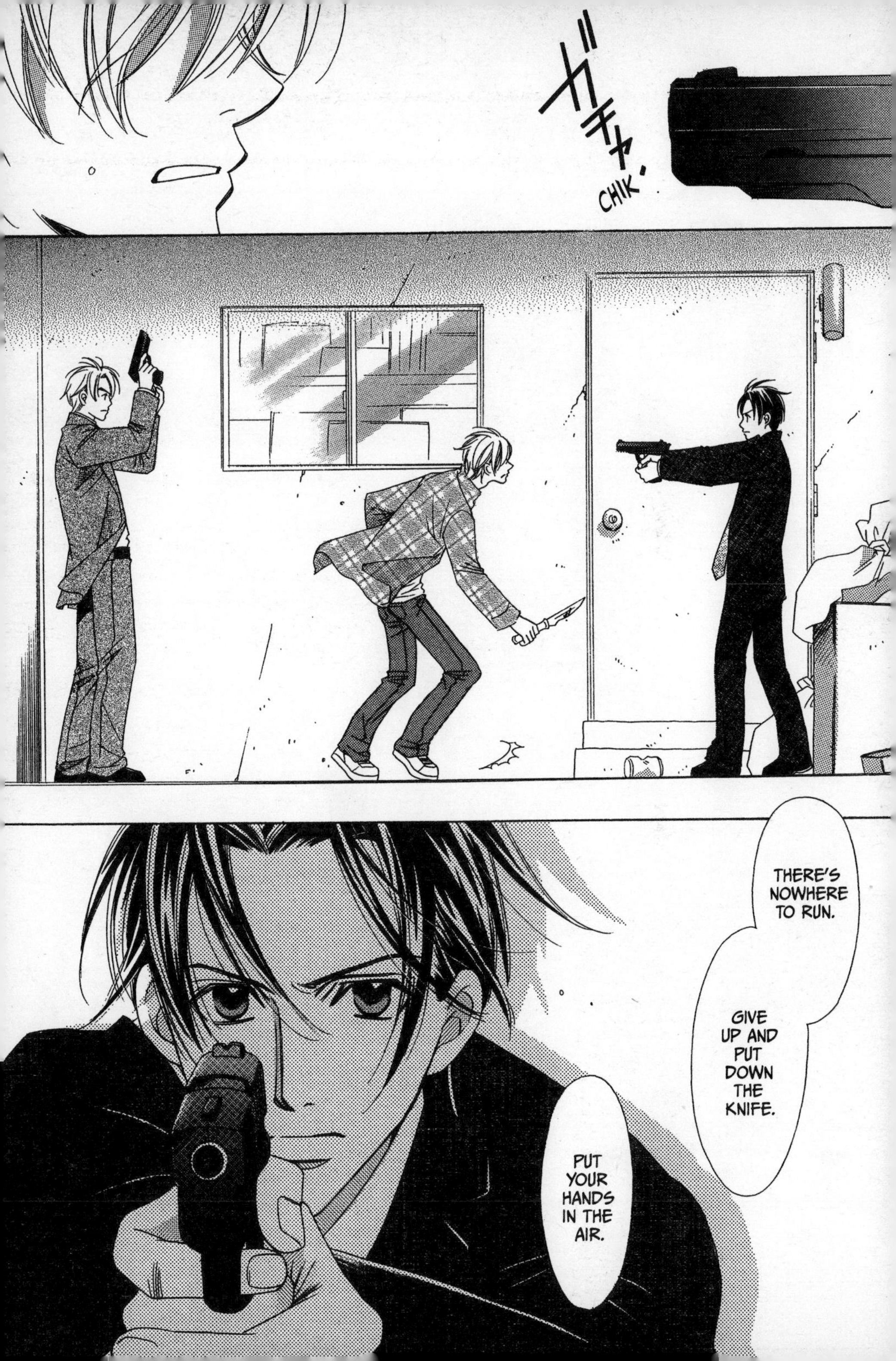
ガチャ
CHIK
THERE'S NOWHERE TO RUN.
GIVE UP AND PUT DOWN THE KNIFE.
PUT YOUR HANDS IN THE AIR.

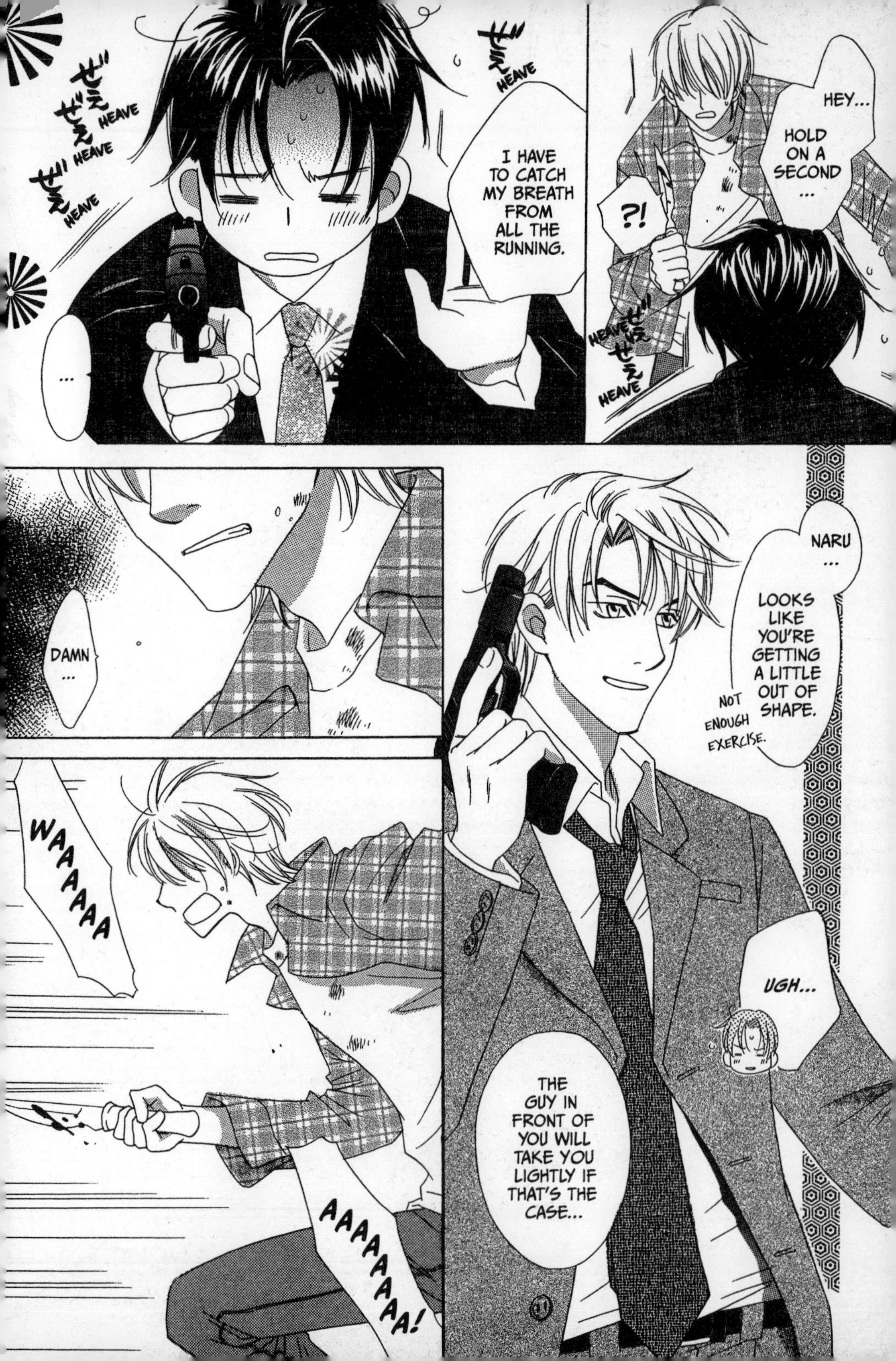
HEY...
HOLD ON A SECOND ...
?!
ぜぇ HEAVE
ぜぇ HEAVE
ぜぇ HEAVE
I HAVE TO CATCH MY BREATH FROM ALL THE RUNNING.
ぜぇ HEAVE
ぜぇ HEAVE
ぜぇ HEAVE
...
NARU ...
LOOKS LIKE YOU'RE GETTING A LITTLE OUT OF SHAPE.
NOT ENOUGH EXERCISE.
UGH...
THE GUY IN FRONT OF YOU WILL TAKE YOU LIGHTLY IF THAT'S THE CASE...
DAMN ...
WAAAAAAA
AAAAAAAA!

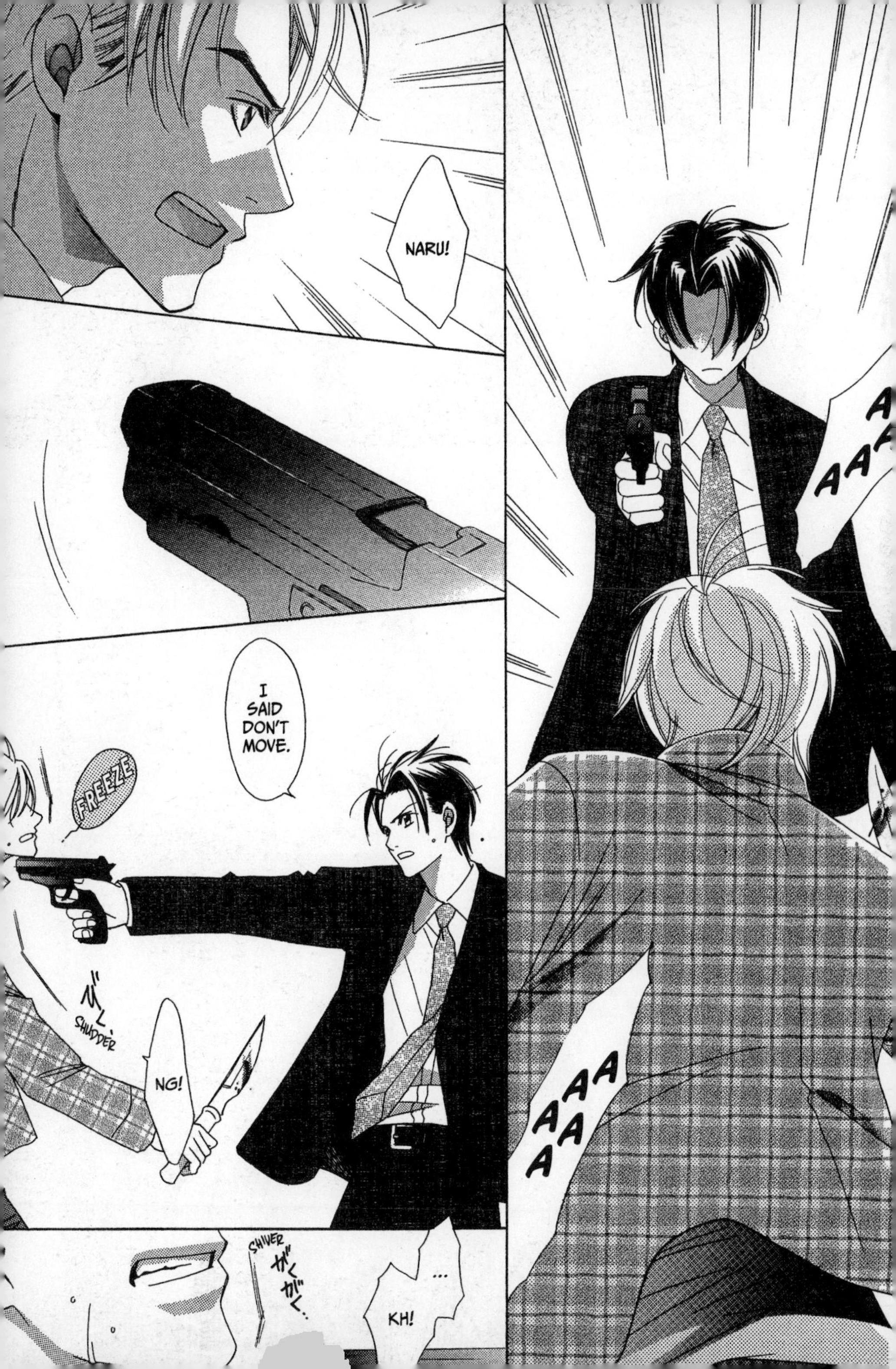
AAAA
AAAAAAA
NARU!
I SAID DON'T MOVE.
FREEZE
SHUDDER
NG!
SHIVER
がくがく...
...
KH!

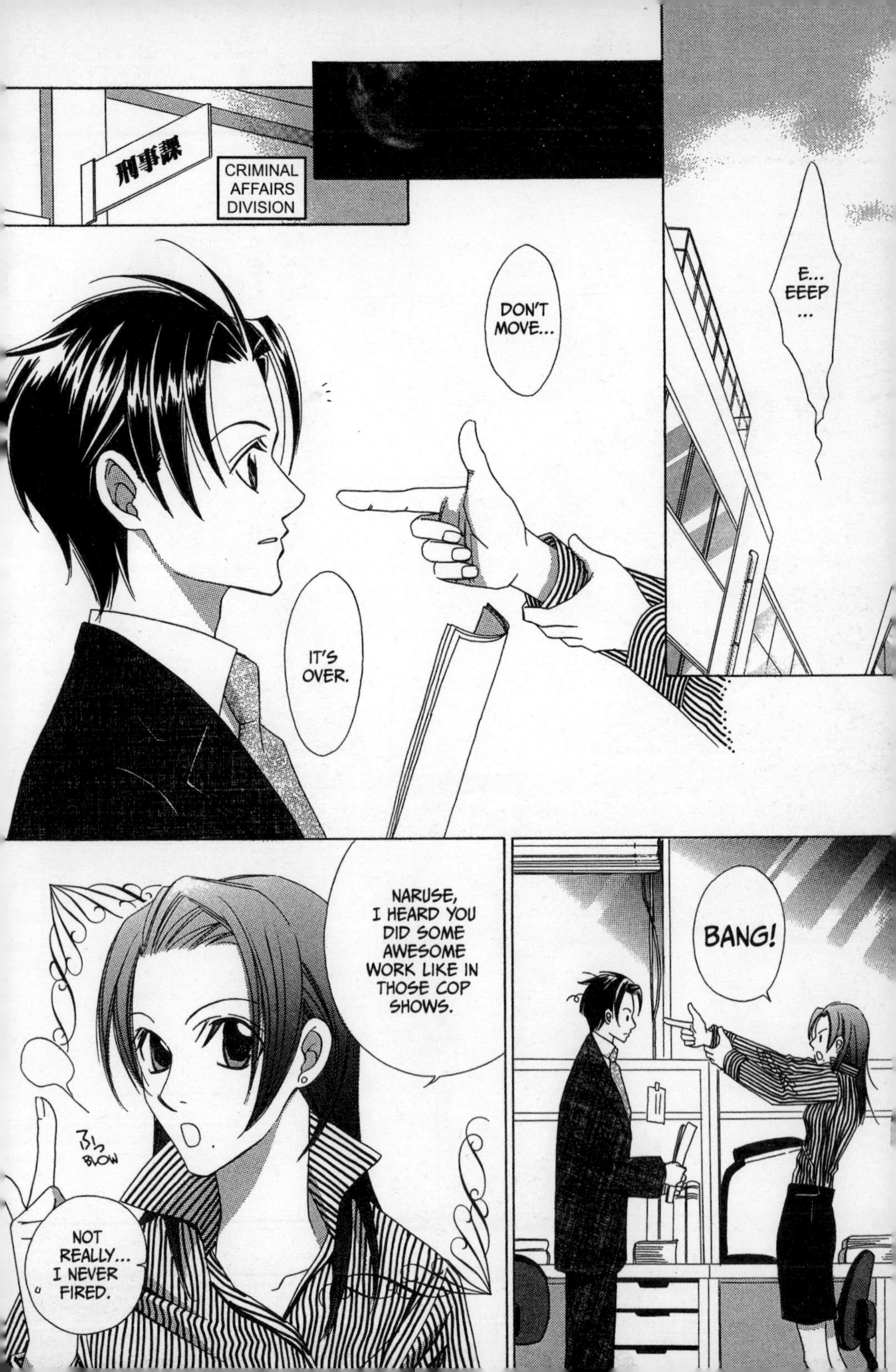
E... EEEP ...
刑事課
CRIMINAL AFFAIRS DIVISION
DON'T MOVE...
IT'S OVER.
BANG!
NARUSE, I HEARD YOU DID SOME AWESOME WORK LIKE IN THOSE COP SHOWS.
ふぅっ BLOW
NOT REALLY... I NEVER FIRED.

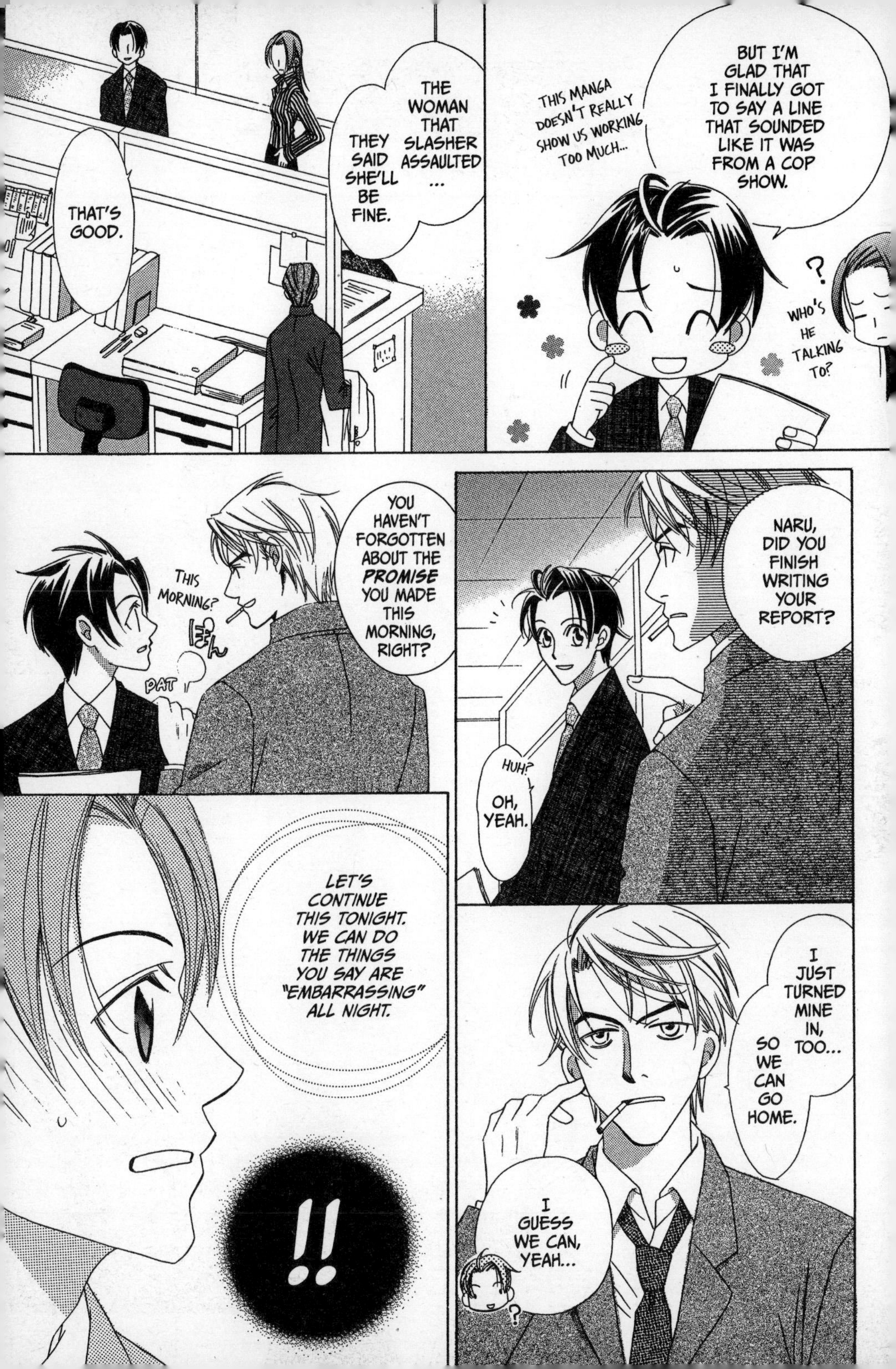
BUT I'M GLAD THAT I FINALLY GOT TO SAY A LINE THAT SOUNDED LIKE IT WAS FROM A COP SHOW.
THIS MANGA DOESN'T REALLY SHOW US WORKING TOO MUCH...
?
WHO'S HE TALKING TO?
THE WOMAN THAT SLASHER ASSAULTED...
THEY SAID SHE'LL BE FINE.
THAT'S GOOD.
NARU, DID YOU FINISH WRITING YOUR REPORT?
HUH?
OH, YEAH.
I JUST TURNED MINE IN, TOO... SO WE CAN GO HOME.
I GUESS WE CAN, YEAH...
?
YOU HAVEN'T FORGOTTEN ABOUT THE PROMISE YOU MADE THIS MORNING, RIGHT?
THIS MORNING?
PAT
LET'S CONTINUE THIS TONIGHT. WE CAN DO THE THINGS YOU SAY ARE "EMBARRASSING" ALL NIGHT.
!!

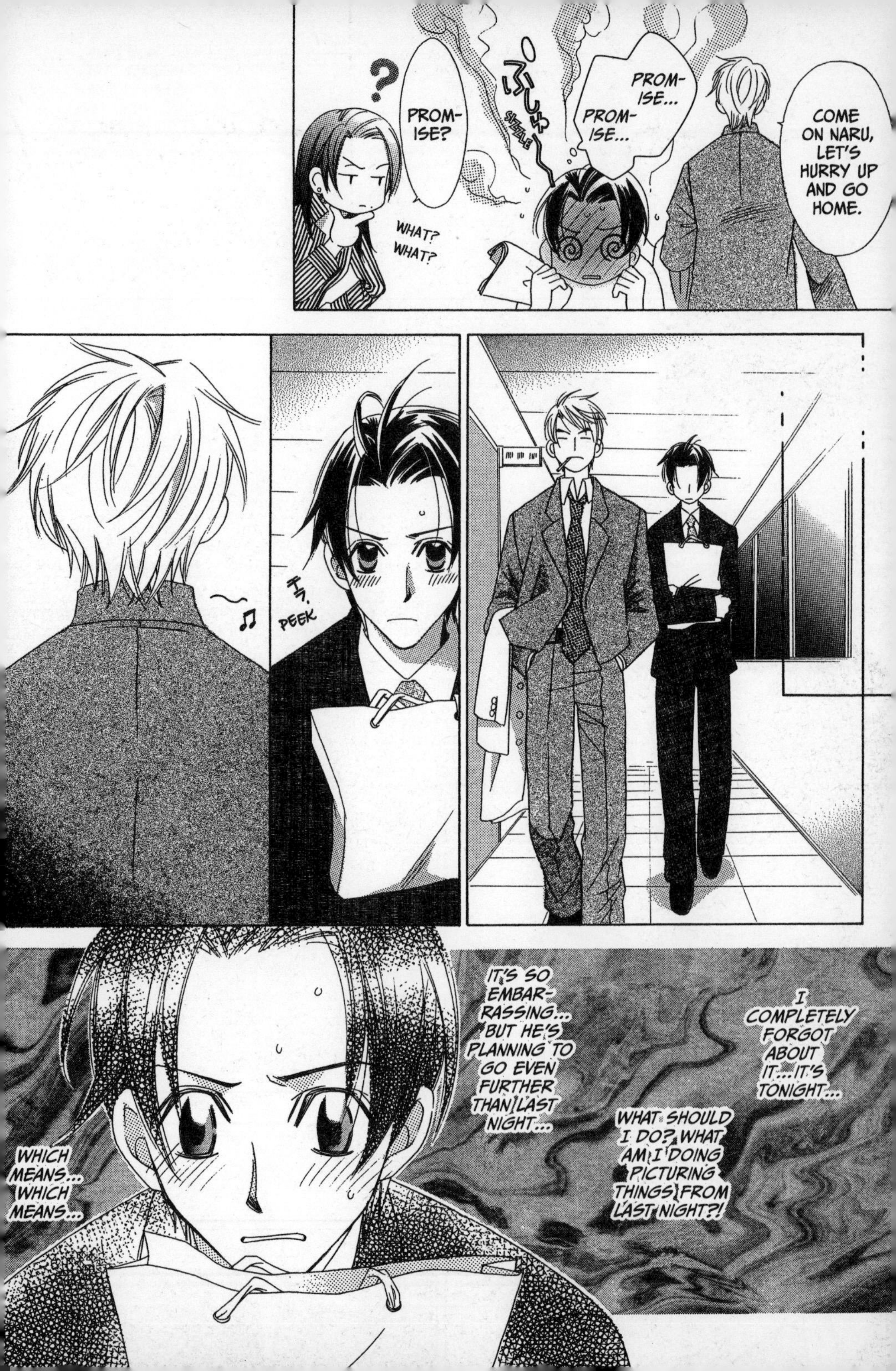
COME ON NARU, LET'S HURRY UP AND GO HOME.
PROM-ISE...
PROM-ISE...
ふしゅ~
SIZZLE
PROM-ISE?
?
WHAT? WHAT?
チラ
PEEK
I COMPLETELY FORGOT ABOUT IT... IT'S TONIGHT...
WHAT SHOULD I DO? WHAT AM I DOING PICTURING THINGS FROM LAST NIGHT?!
IT'S SO EMBAR-RASSING... BUT HE'S PLANNING TO GO EVEN FURTHER THAN LAST NIGHT...
WHICH MEANS... WHICH MEANS...

KI... KITA-SAN...

WOBBLE

NARU?

KITA-SAN, LET'S GO DRINK FIRST!

HUH?

DESPERATE

THE NIGHT'S PRETTY LONG. LET'S DRINK!

PLEASE!

IF NOT, MAYBE WE CAN GET SOME CANNED BEERS AND DRINK AT *YOUR* PLACE...

NOOO! I CAN'T...! I CAN'T DO THIS! I FEEL LIKE MY HEART IS GOING TO JUMP OUT!!!

DOOOOOM

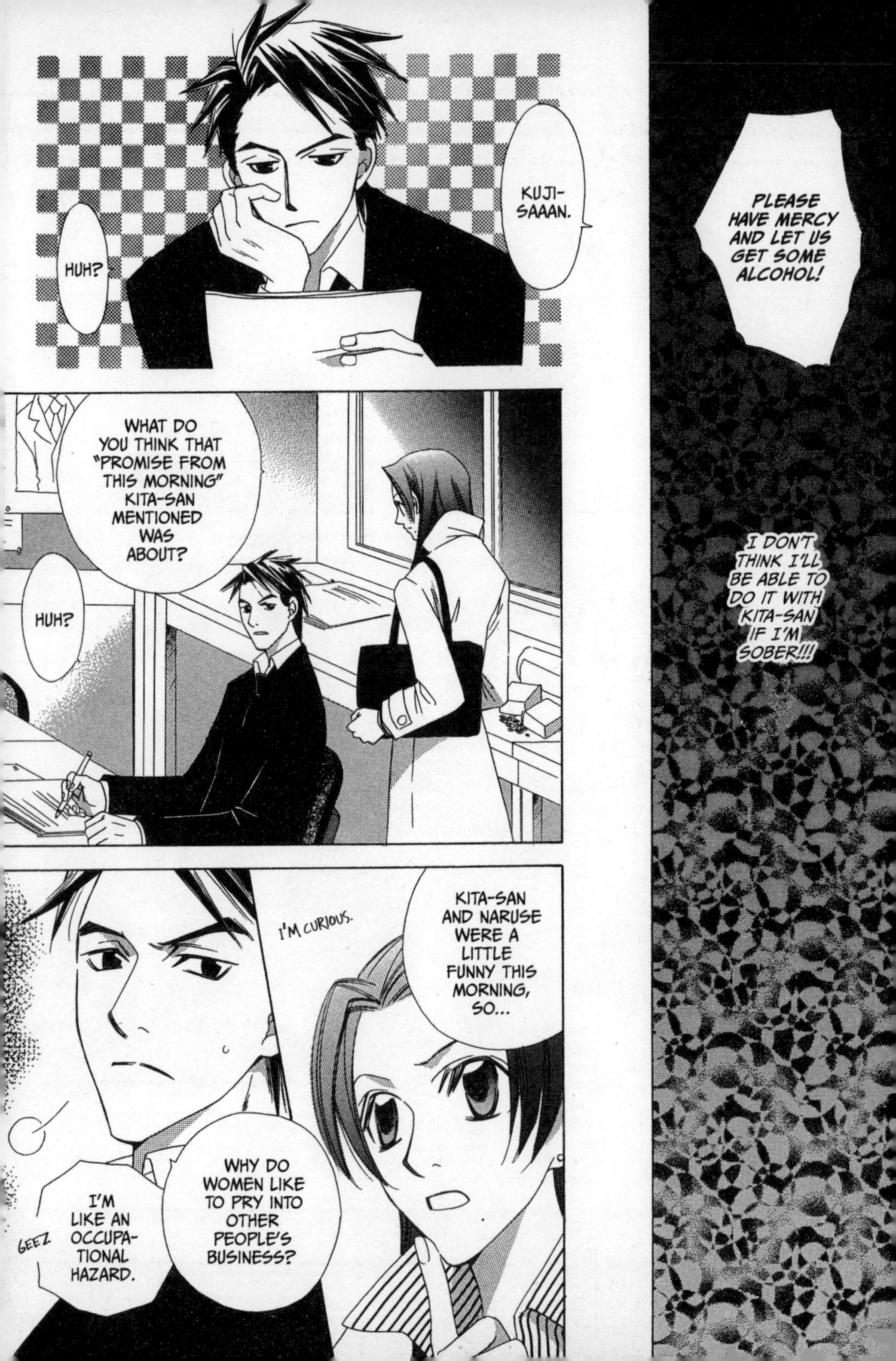
PLEASE HAVE MERCY AND LET US GET SOME ALCOHOL!
I DON'T THINK I'LL BE ABLE TO DO IT WITH KITA-SAN IF I'M SOBER!!!
KUJI-SAAAN.
HUH?
WHAT DO YOU THINK THAT "PROMISE FROM THIS MORNING" KITA-SAN MENTIONED WAS ABOUT?
HUH?
KITA-SAN AND NARUSE WERE A LITTLE FUNNY THIS MORNING, SO...
I'M CURIOUS.
WHY DO WOMEN LIKE TO PRY INTO OTHER PEOPLE'S BUSINESS?
I'M LIKE AN OCCUPA-TIONAL HAZARD.
GEEZ

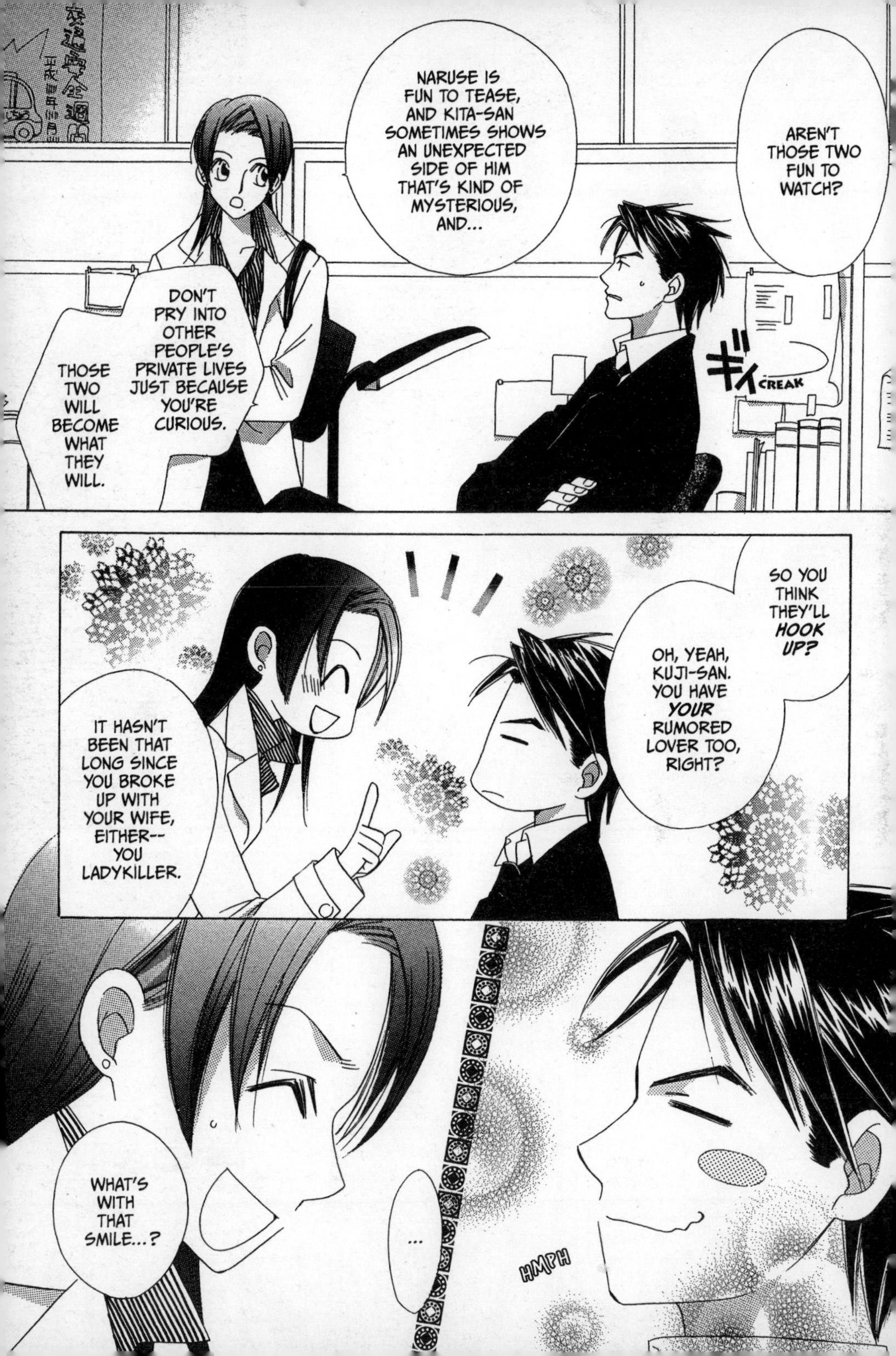
AREN'T THOSE TWO FUN TO WATCH?
NARUSE IS FUN TO TEASE, AND KITA-SAN SOMETIMES SHOWS AN UNEXPECTED SIDE OF HIM THAT'S KIND OF MYSTERIOUS, AND...
ギィ CREAK
DON'T PRY INTO OTHER PEOPLE'S PRIVATE LIVES JUST BECAUSE YOU'RE CURIOUS.
THOSE TWO WILL BECOME WHAT THEY WILL.
SO YOU THINK THEY'LL *HOOK UP?*
OH, YEAH, KUJI-SAN. YOU HAVE *YOUR* RUMORED LOVER TOO, RIGHT?
IT HASN'T BEEN THAT LONG SINCE YOU BROKE UP WITH YOUR WIFE, EITHER-- YOU LADYKILLER.
HMPH
...
WHAT'S WITH THAT SMILE...?

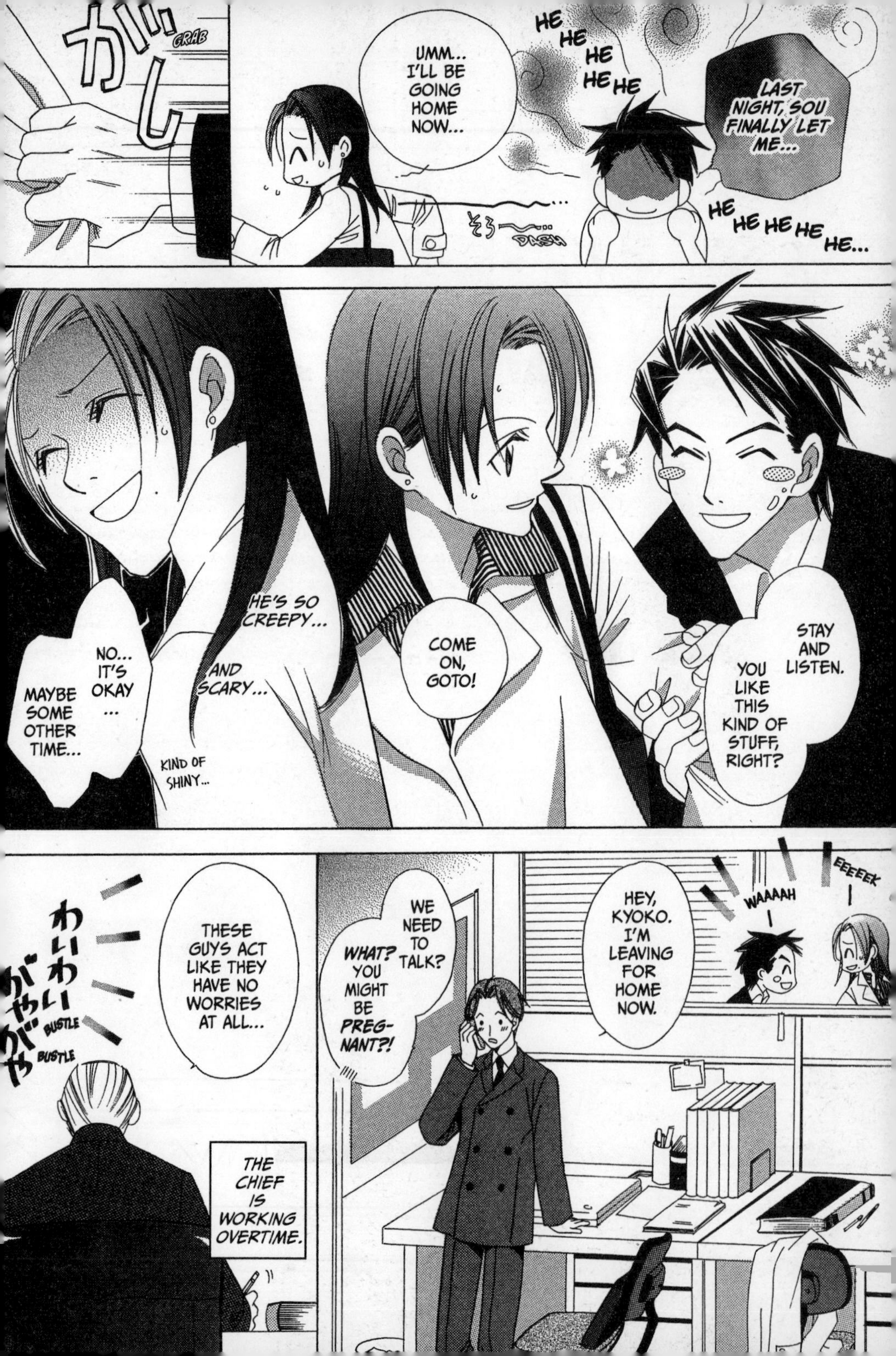
HE HE HE HE HE
LAST NIGHT, SOU FINALLY LET ME...
HE HE HE HE HE...
UMM... I'LL BE GOING HOME NOW...
そろ〜 DASH
がし GRAB
STAY AND LISTEN.
YOU LIKE THIS KIND OF STUFF, RIGHT?
COME ON, GOTO!
HE'S SO CREEPY...
AND SCARY...
KIND OF SHINY...
NO... IT'S OKAY...
MAYBE SOME OTHER TIME...
EEEEEK
WAAAAH
HEY, KYOKO. I'M LEAVING FOR HOME NOW.
WE NEED TO TALK?
WHAT? YOU MIGHT BE PREGNANT?!
わいわい BUSTLE
がやがや BUSTLE
THESE GUYS ACT LIKE THEY HAVE NO WORRIES AT ALL...
THE CHIEF IS WORKING OVERTIME.

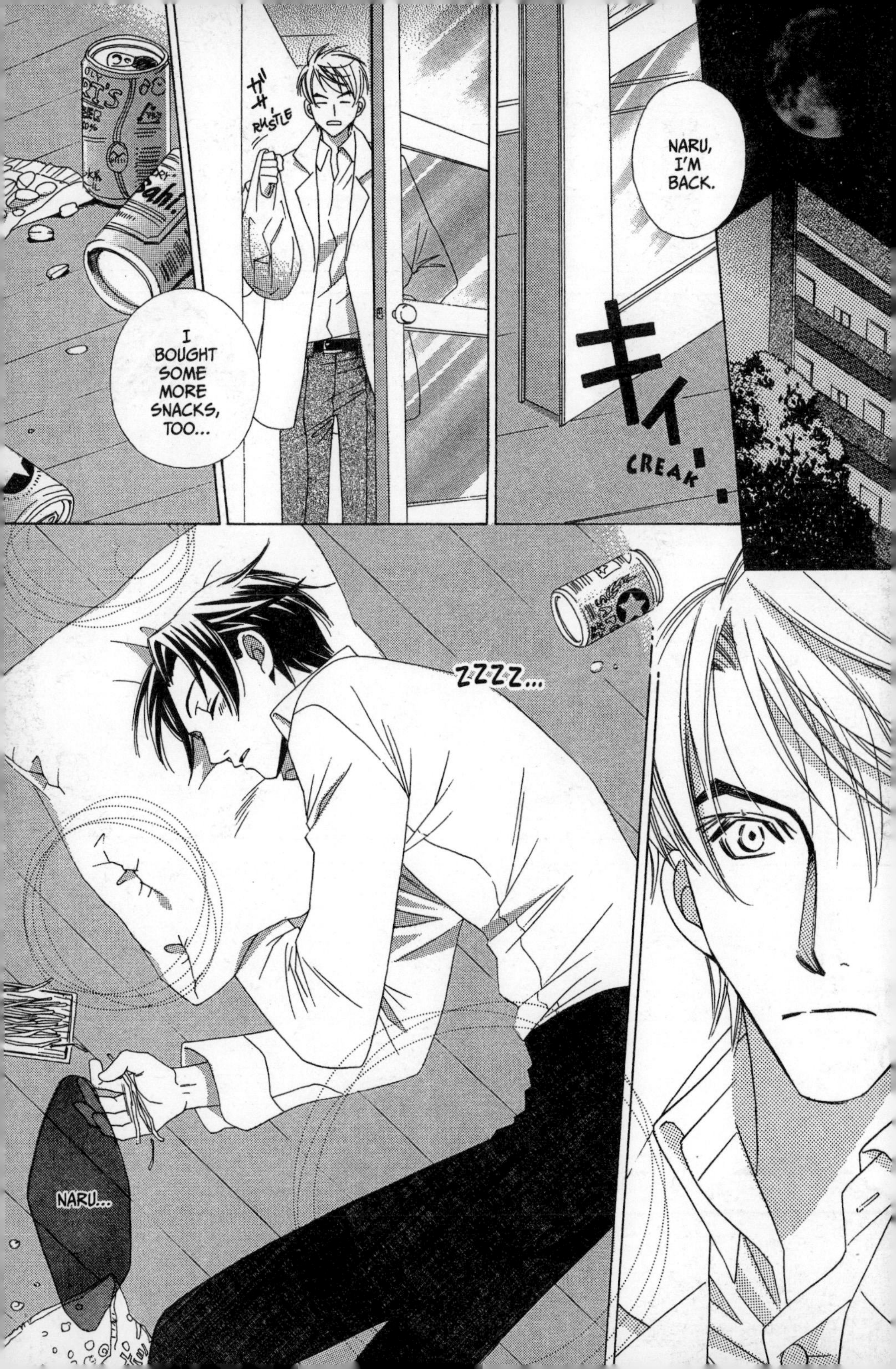
NARU, I'M BACK.
キイ
CREAK
ガサ
RUSTLE
I BOUGHT SOME MORE SNACKS, TOO...
ZZZZ...
NARU...

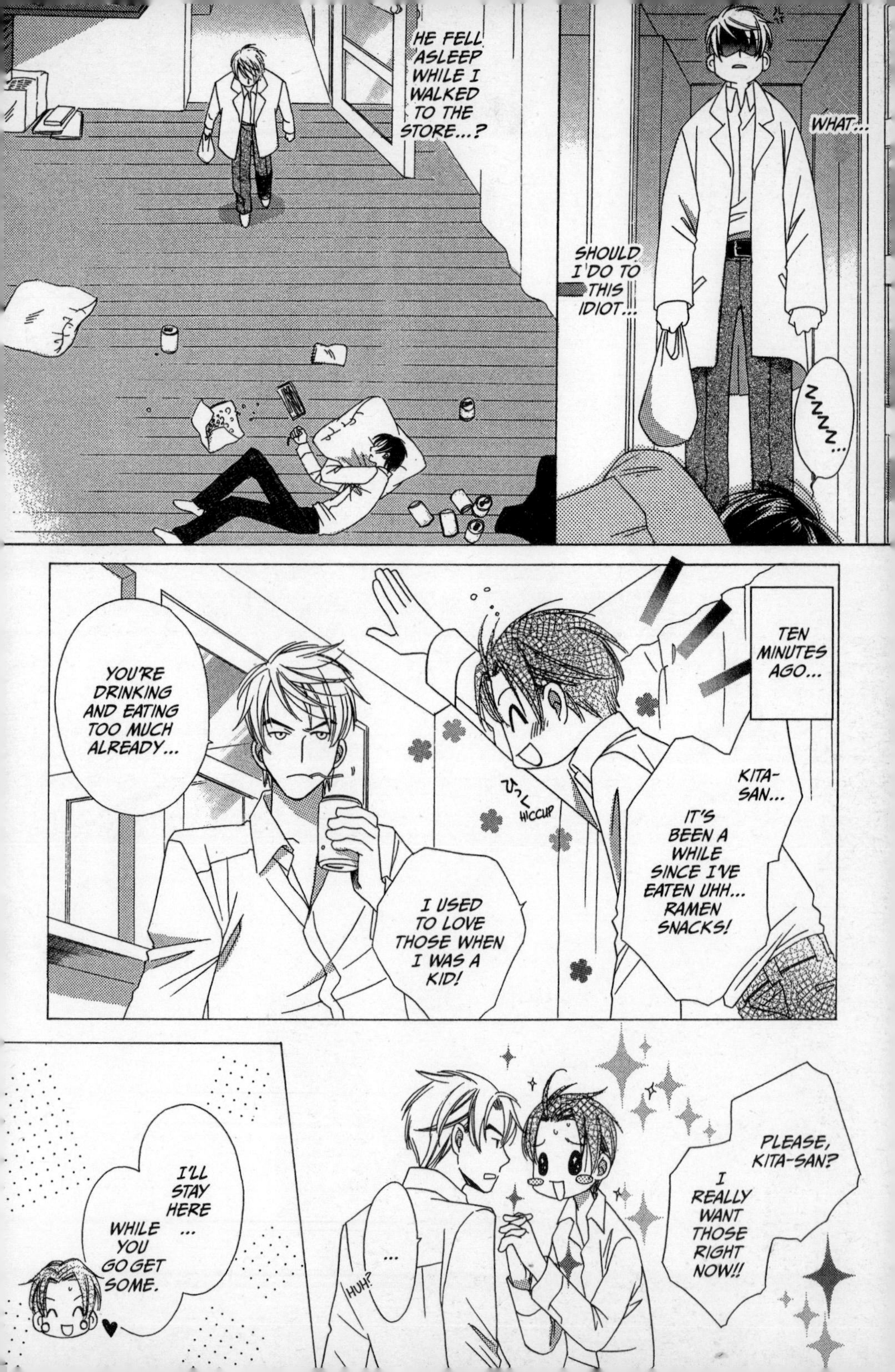
WHAT...
SHOULD I DO TO THIS IDIOT...
ZZZZ...
HE FELL ASLEEP WHILE I WALKED TO THE STORE...?
TEN MINUTES AGO...
KITA-SAN...
IT'S BEEN A WHILE SINCE I'VE EATEN UHH... RAMEN SNACKS!
HICCUP
I USED TO LOVE THOSE WHEN I WAS A KID!
YOU'RE DRINKING AND EATING TOO MUCH ALREADY...
PLEASE, KITA-SAN?
I REALLY WANT THOSE RIGHT NOW!!
...
HUH?
I'LL STAY HERE ...
WHILE YOU GO GET SOME.

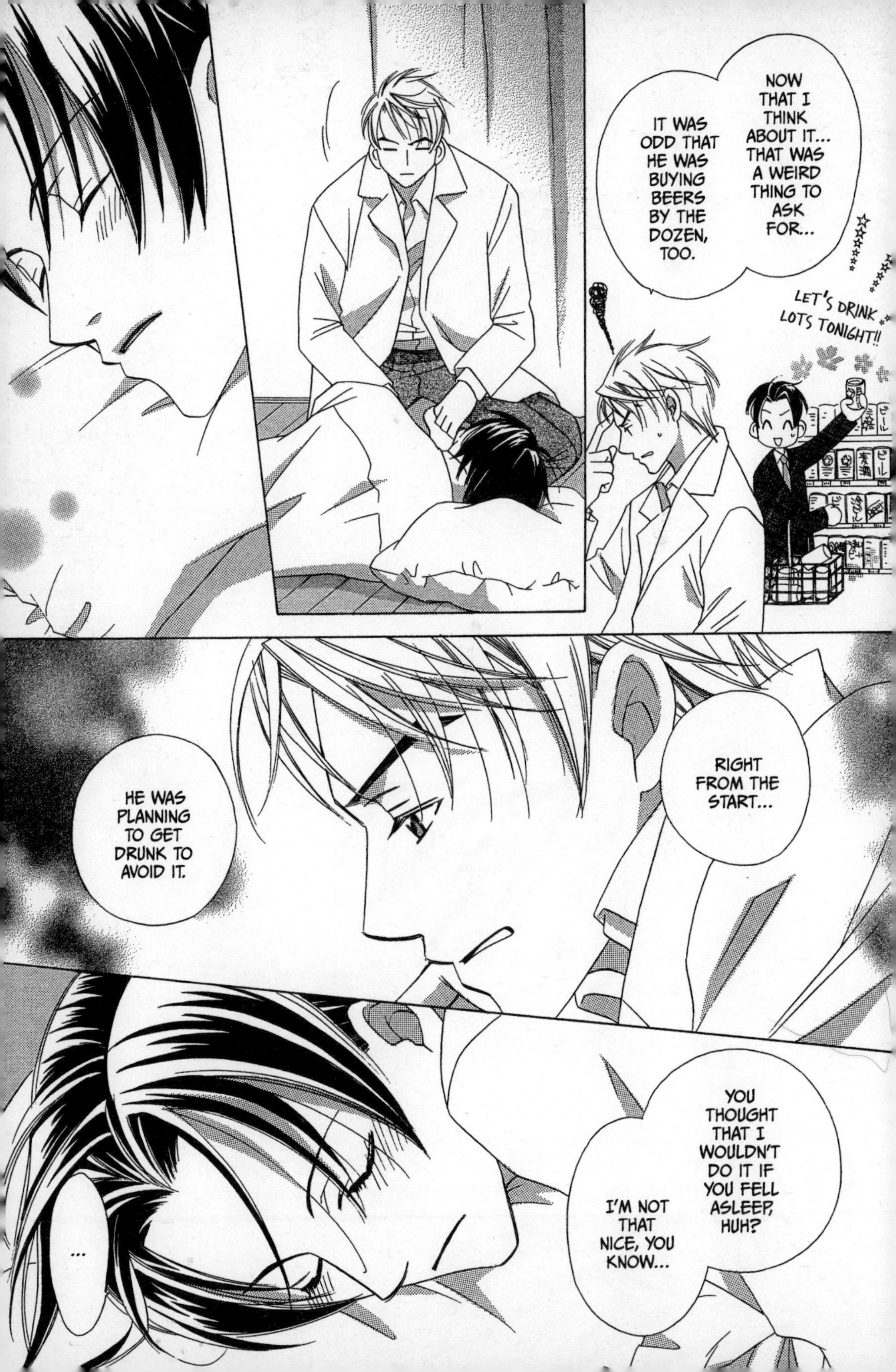
NOW THAT I THINK ABOUT IT... THAT WAS A WEIRD THING TO ASK FOR...
IT WAS ODD THAT HE WAS BUYING BEERS BY THE DOZEN, TOO.
LET'S DRINK LOTS TONIGHT!!
RIGHT FROM THE START...
HE WAS PLANNING TO GET DRUNK TO AVOID IT.
YOU THOUGHT THAT I WOULDN'T DO IT IF YOU FELL ASLEEP, HUH?
I'M NOT THAT NICE, YOU KNOW...
...

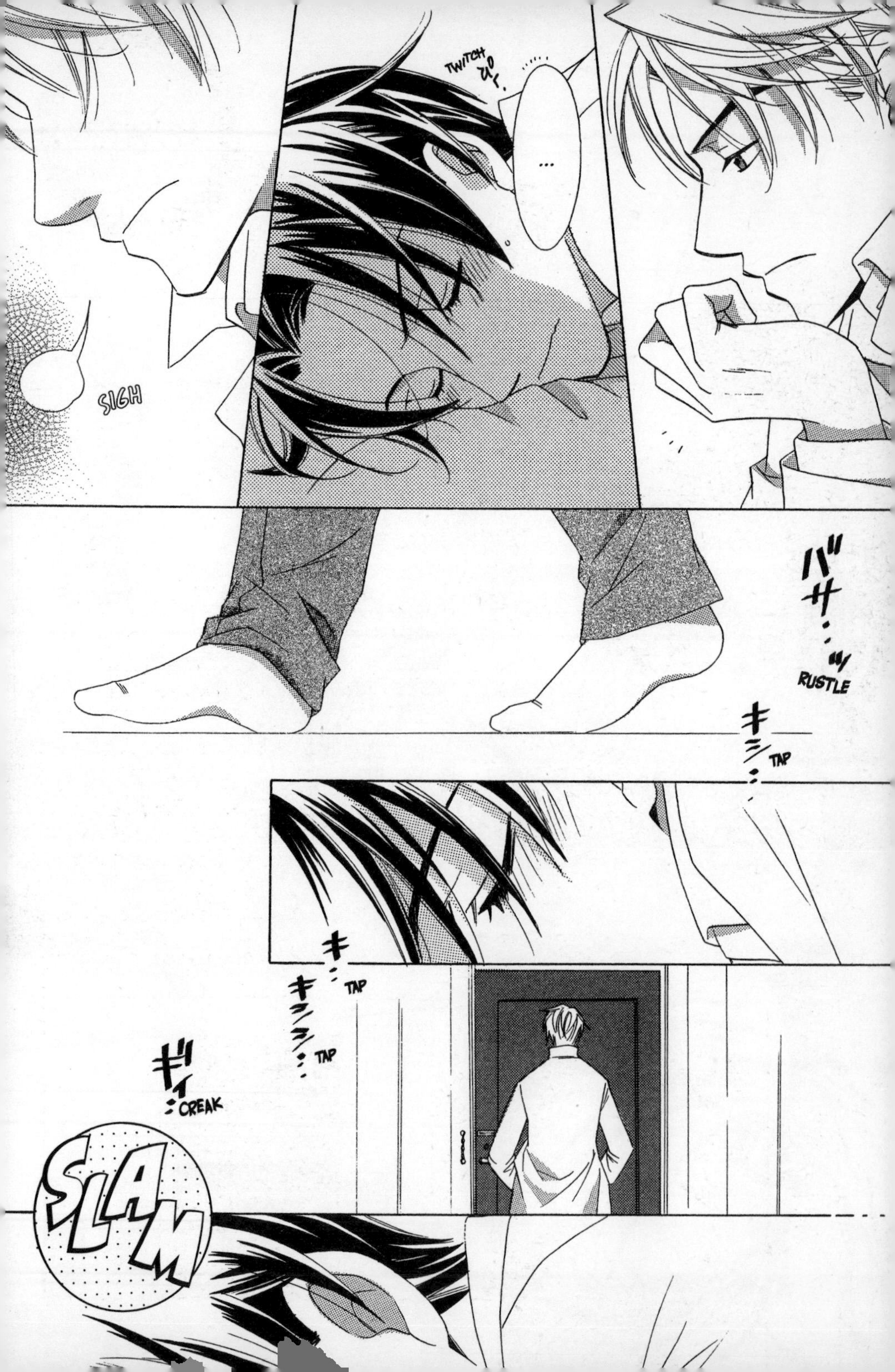

TWITCH
ぴく.
...
SIGH
バサ…
RUSTLE
キシ…
TAP
キ…
TAP
キシシ…
TAP
ギイ…
CREAK
SLAM

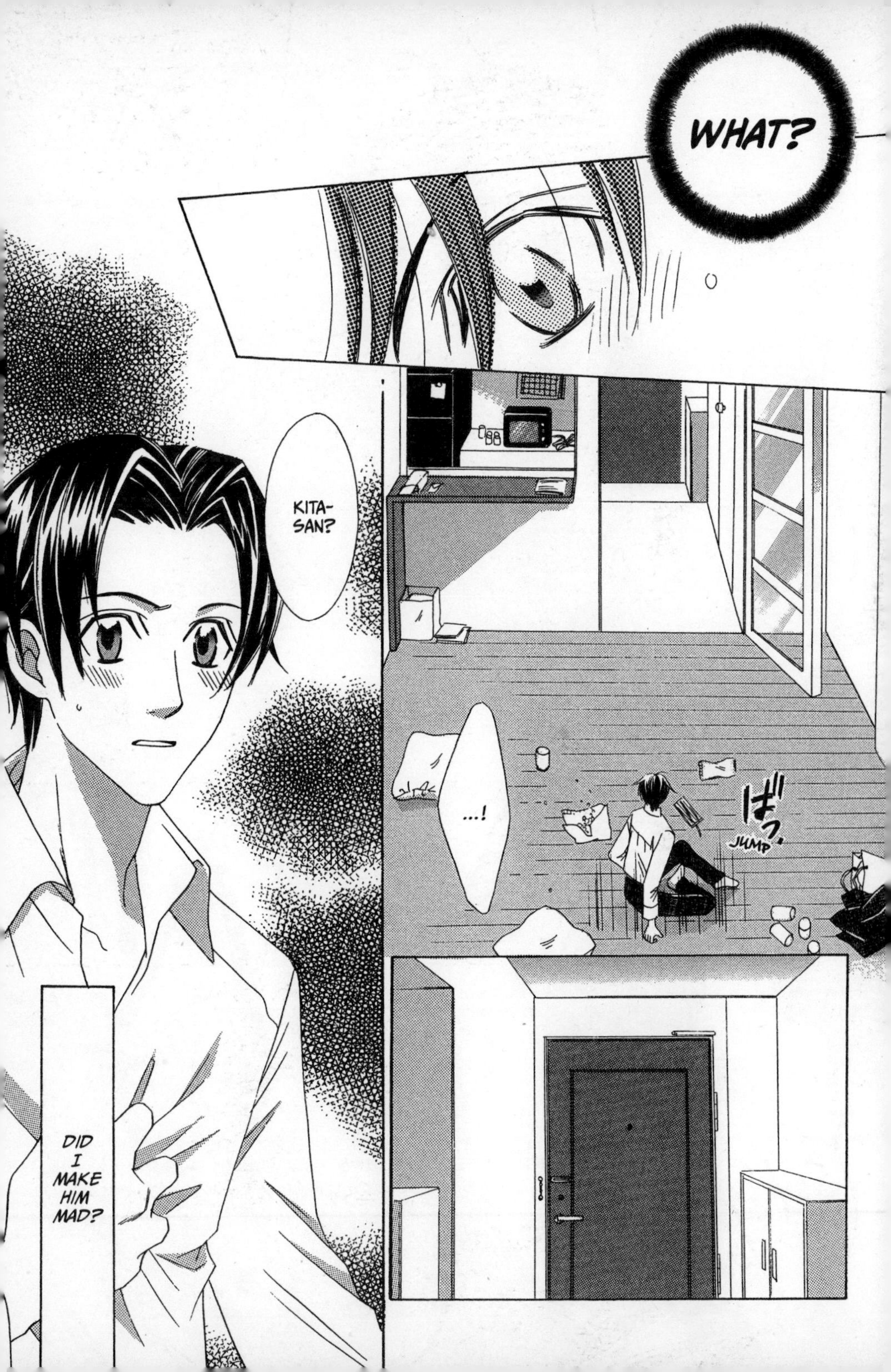
WHAT?
...!
ばっ
JUMP
KITA-SAN?
DID I MAKE HIM MAD?

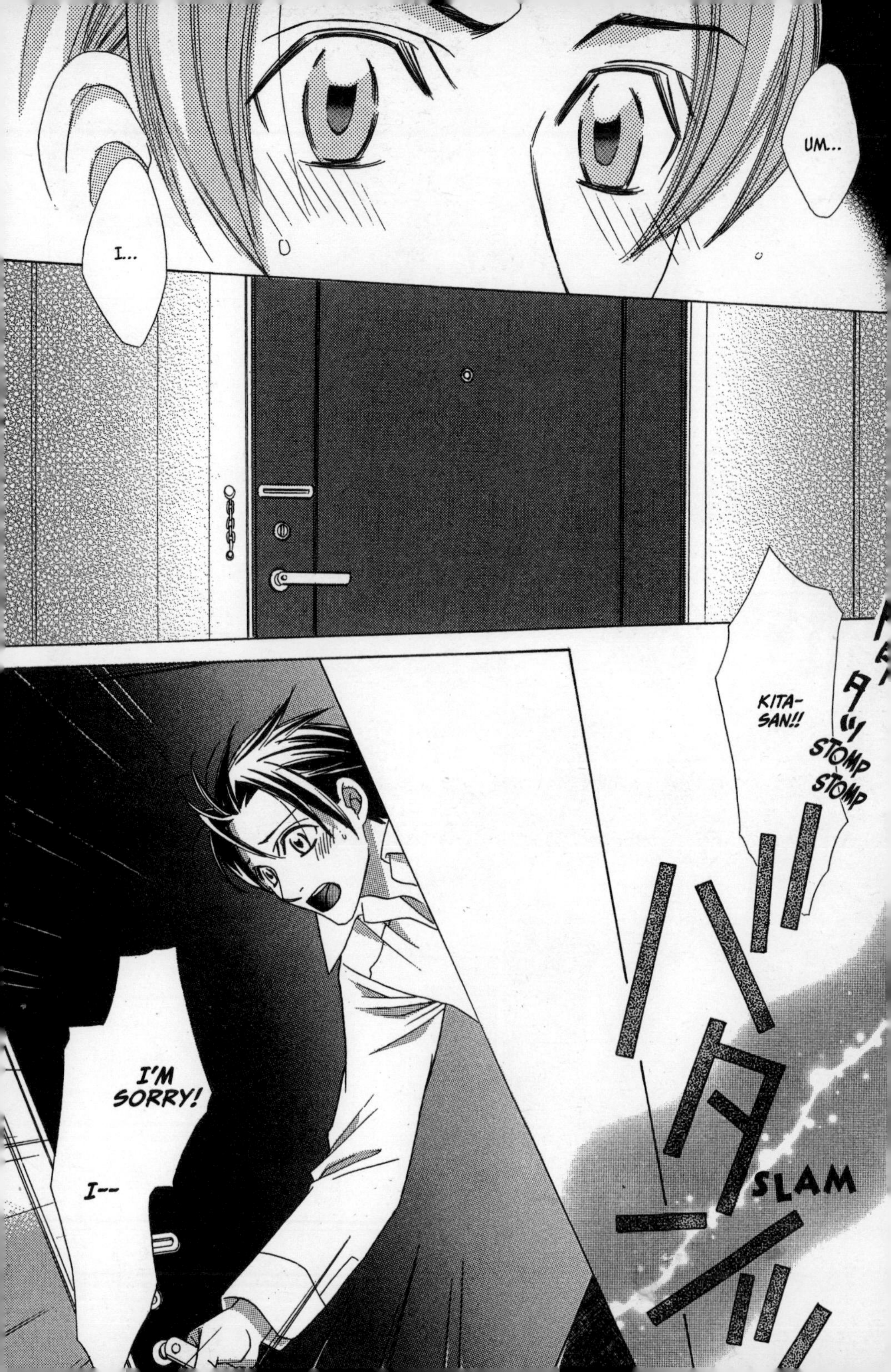
UM...
I...
KITA-SAN!!
STOMP STOMP
SLAM
I'M SORRY!
I--

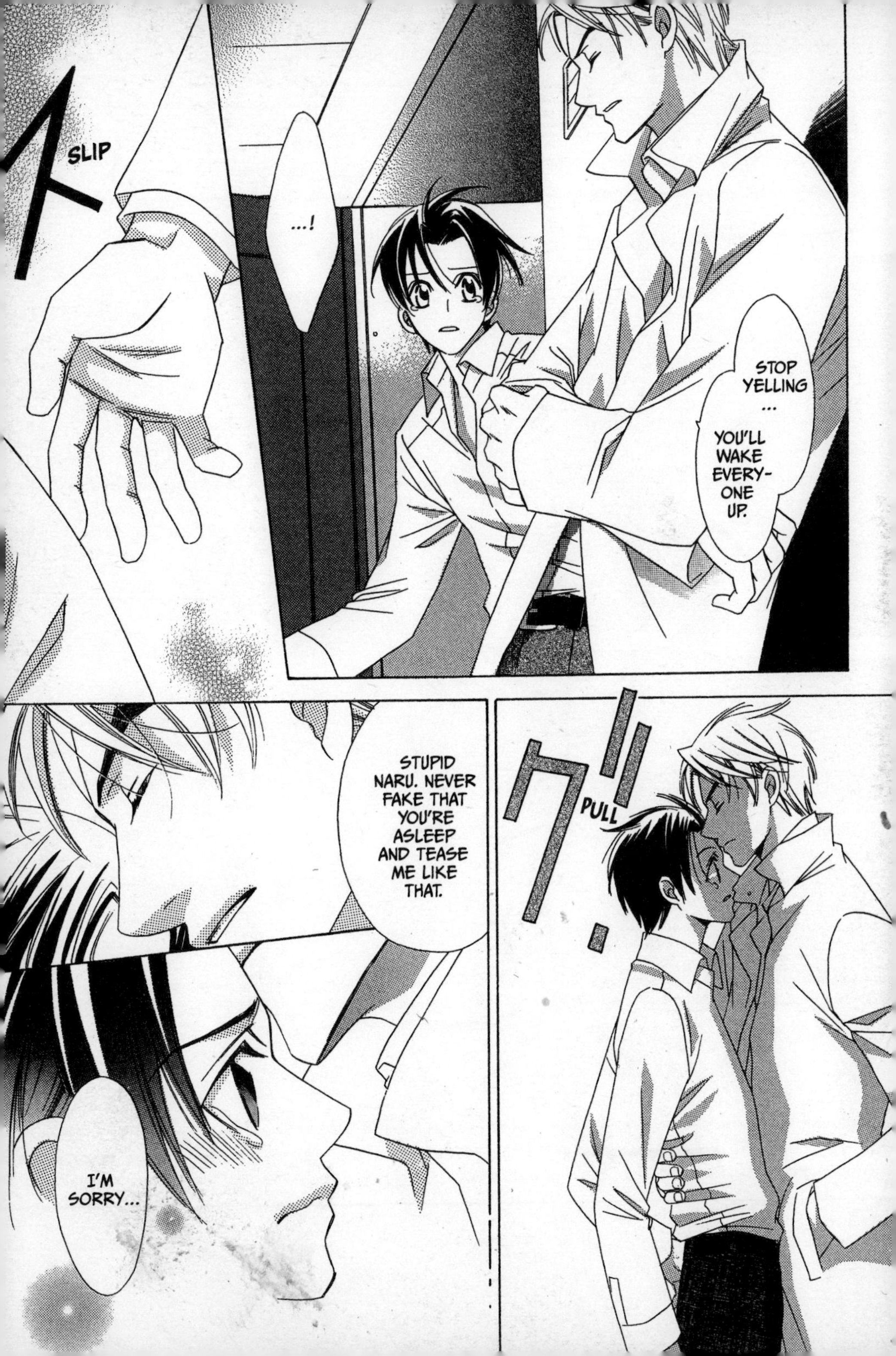
STOP YELLING ... YOU'LL WAKE EVERY-ONE UP.
...!
SLIP
PULL
STUPID NARU. NEVER FAKE THAT YOU'RE ASLEEP AND TEASE ME LIKE THAT.
I'M SORRY...

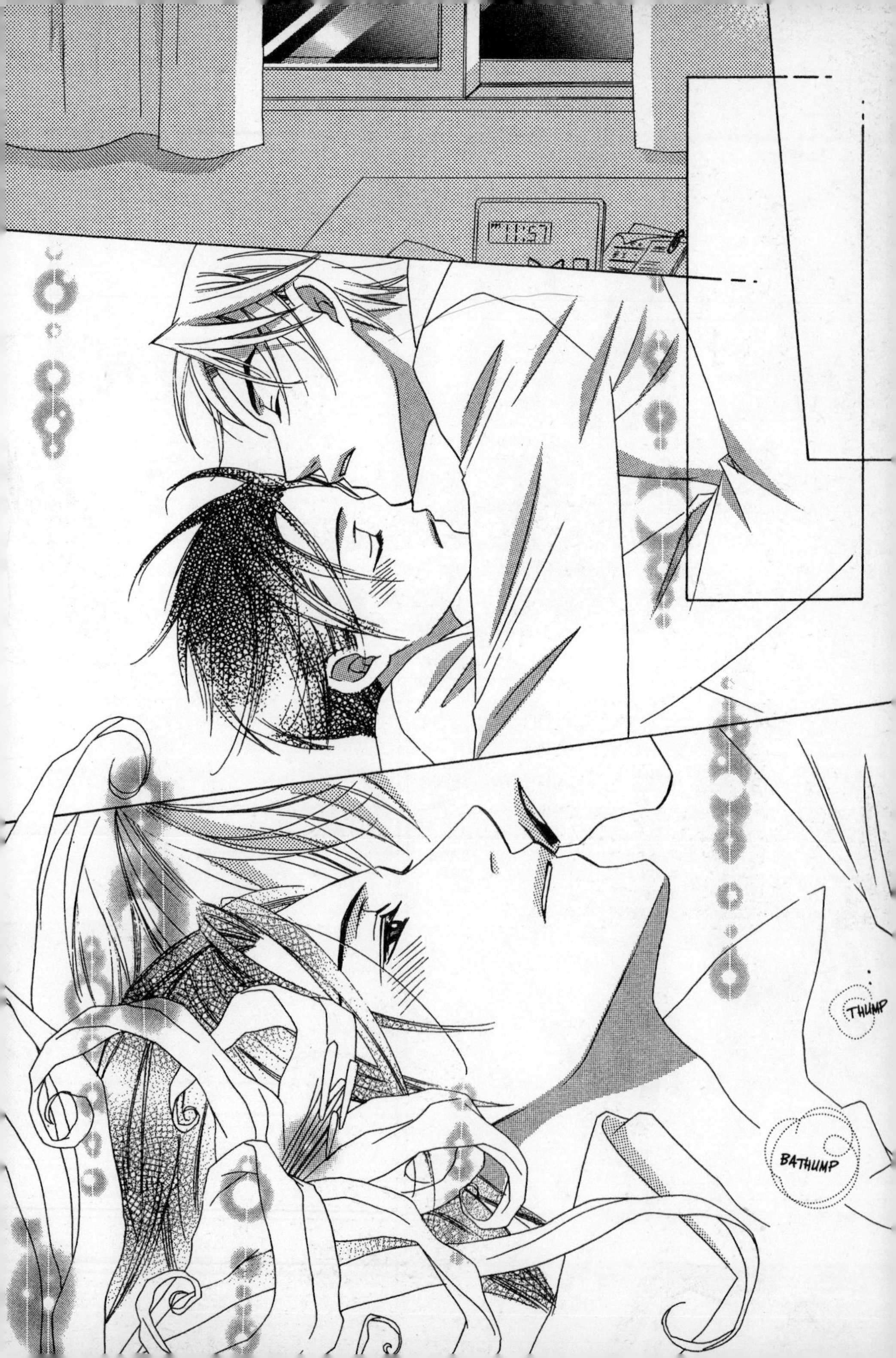
11:57
THUMP
BATHUMP

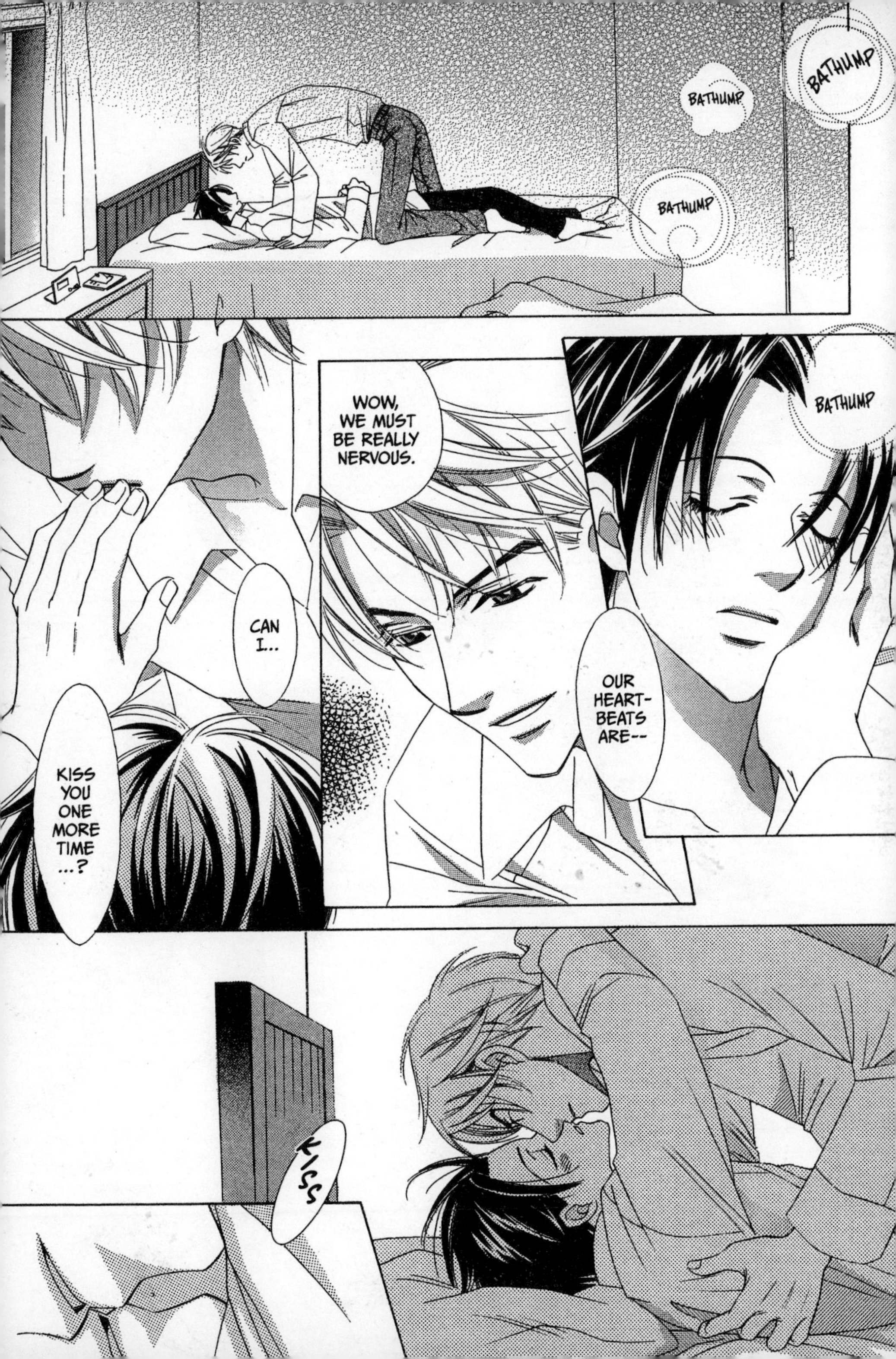
BATHUMP
BATHUMP
BATHUMP
BATHUMP
OUR HEART-BEATS ARE--
WOW, WE MUST BE REALLY NERVOUS.
CAN I...
KISS YOU ONE MORE TIME ...?
KISS

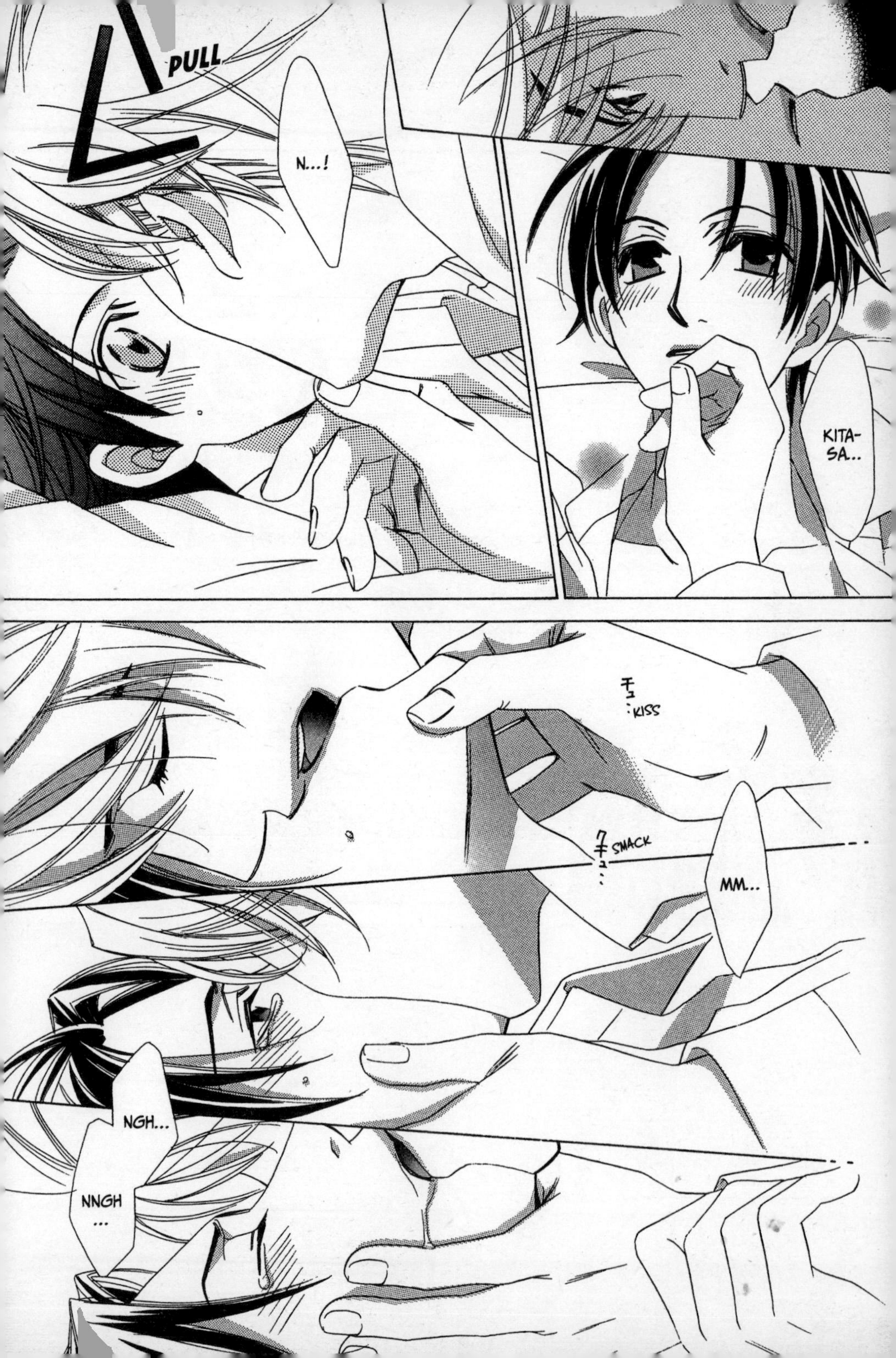
KITA-SA...
PULL
N...!
チュ :KISS
クチュ... SMACK
MM...
NGH...
NNGH ...

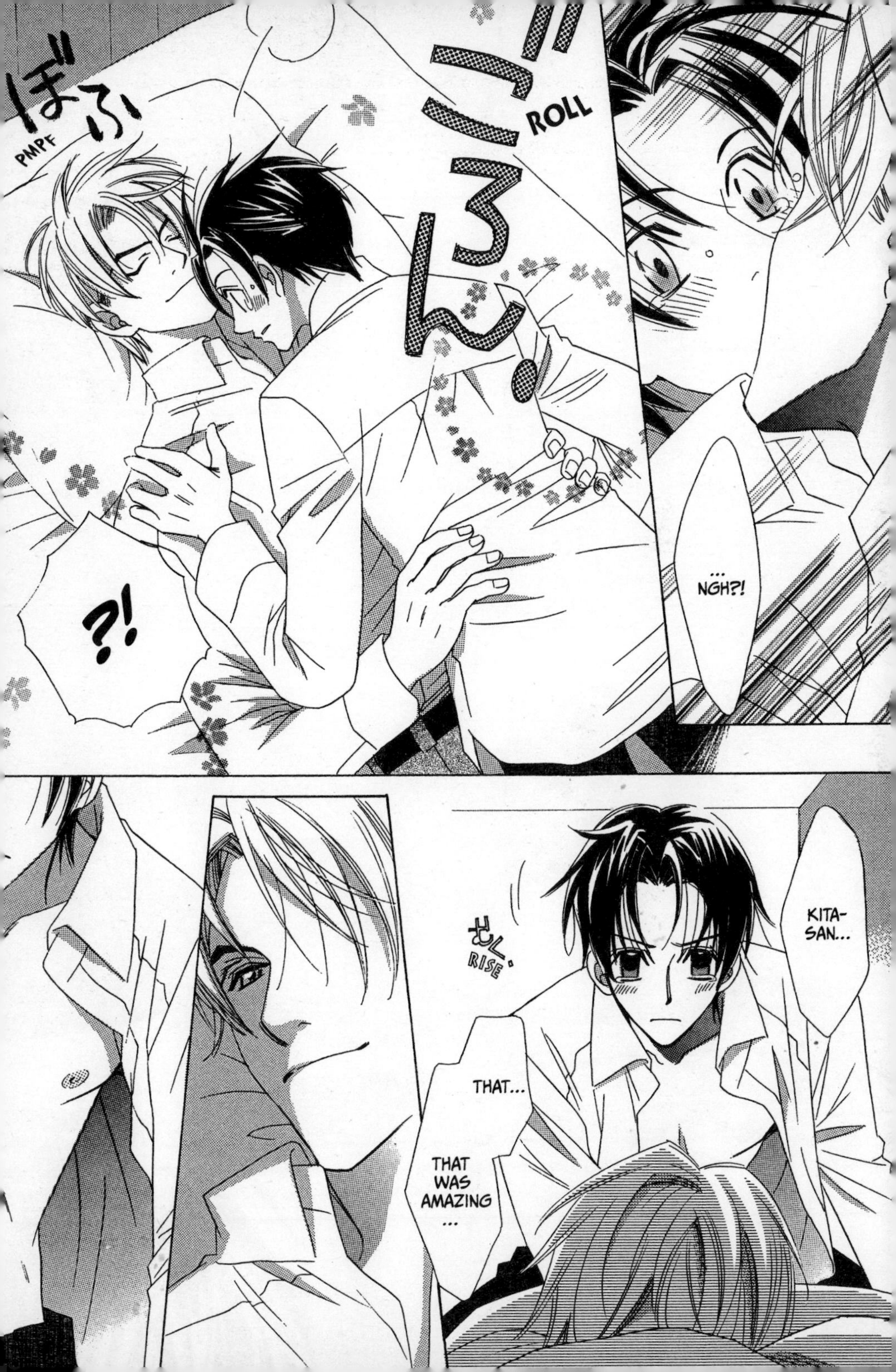

... NGH?!
ごろん
ROLL
ぼふ
PMPF
?!
KITA-SAN...
RISE
THAT...
THAT WAS AMAZING ...

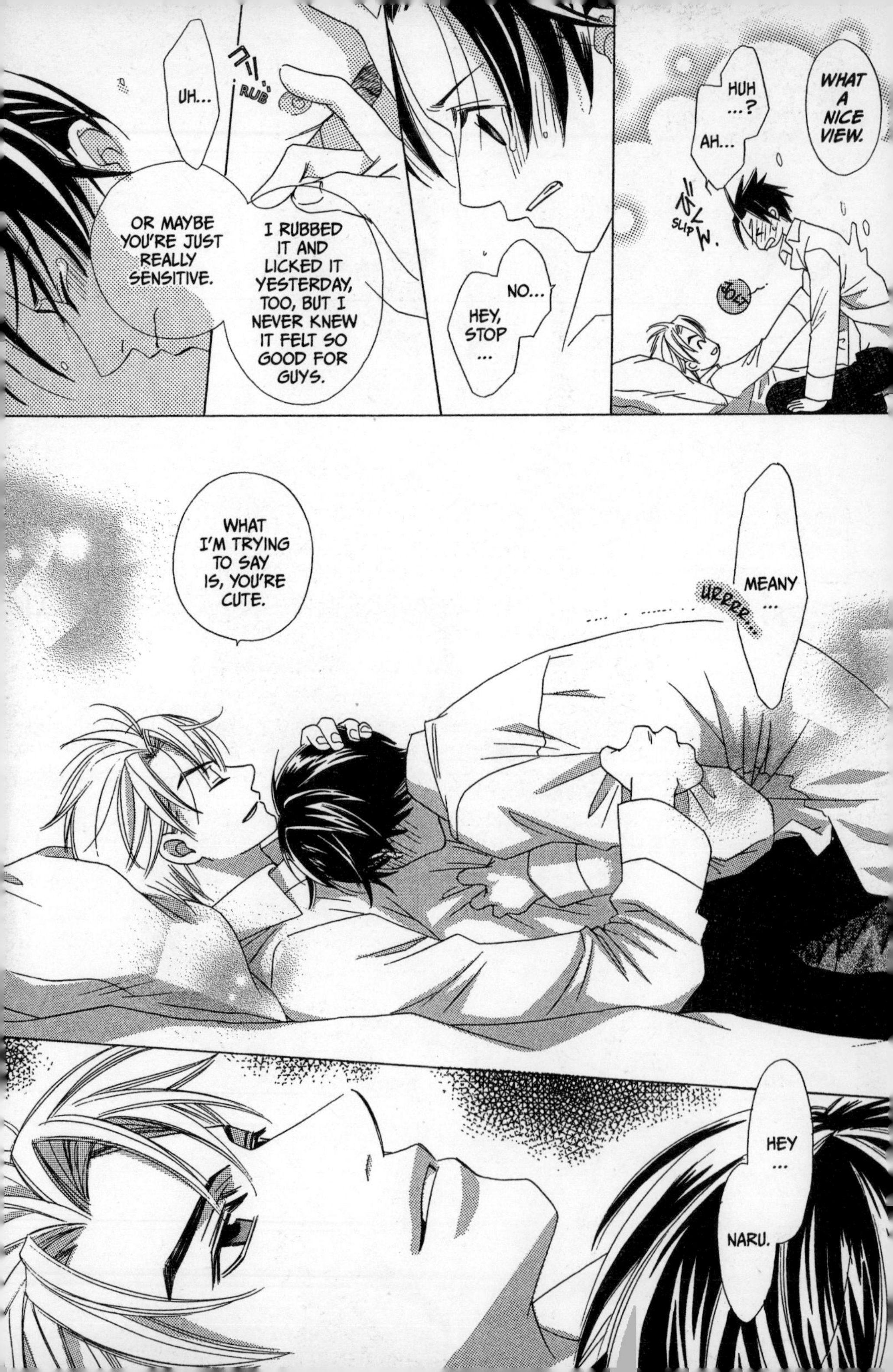
WHAT A NICE VIEW.
HUH ...? AH...
SLIP
JOLT
NO...
HEY, STOP ...
UH...
RUB
I RUBBED IT AND LICKED IT YESTERDAY, TOO, BUT I NEVER KNEW IT FELT SO GOOD FOR GUYS.
OR MAYBE YOU'RE JUST REALLY SENSITIVE.
MEANY ...
URRRR...
WHAT I'M TRYING TO SAY IS, YOU'RE CUTE.
HEY ...
NARU.

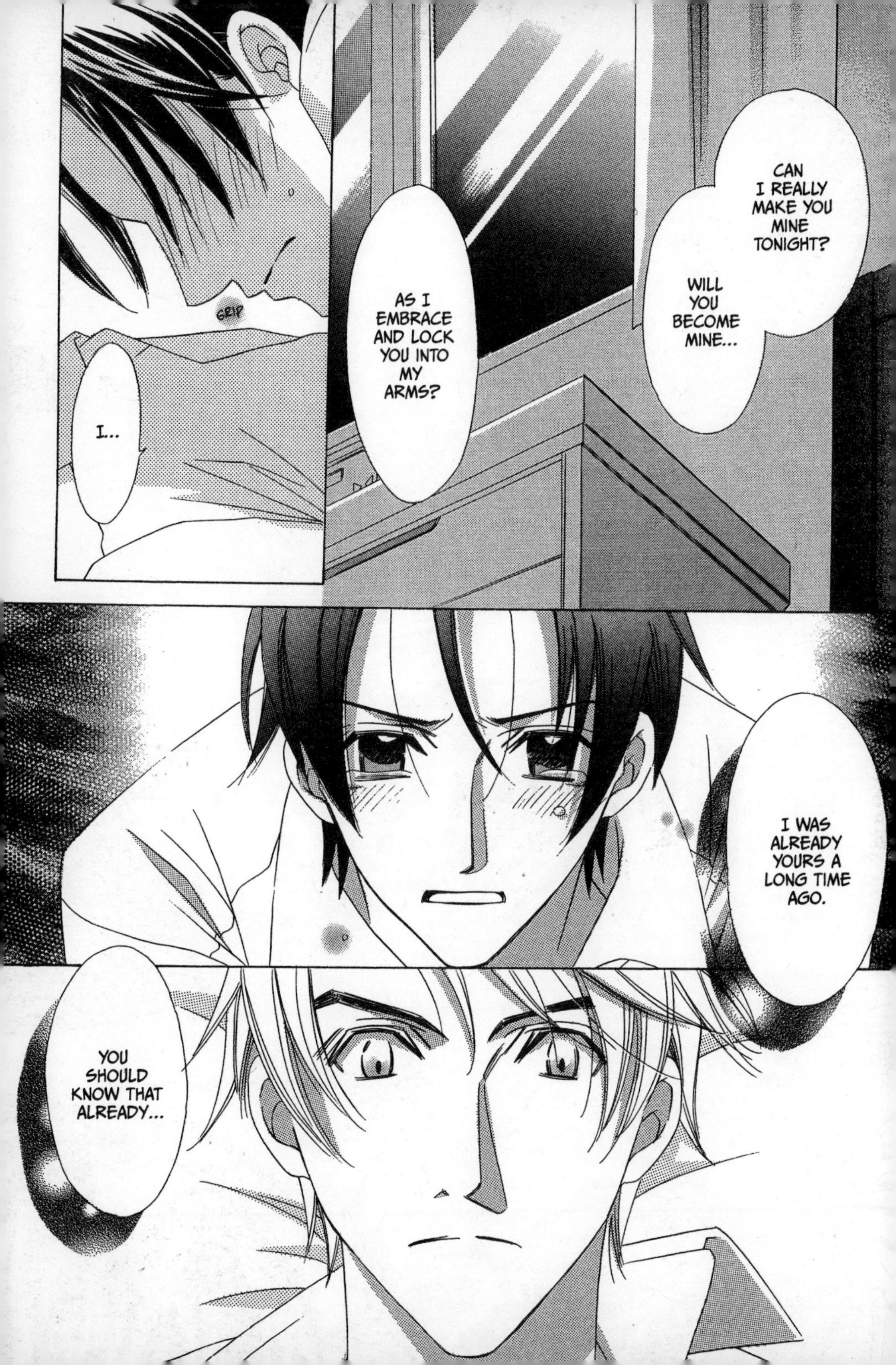
CAN I REALLY MAKE YOU MINE TONIGHT?
WILL YOU BECOME MINE...
AS I EMBRACE AND LOCK YOU INTO MY ARMS?
GRIP
I...
I WAS ALREADY YOURS A LONG TIME AGO.
YOU SHOULD KNOW THAT ALREADY...

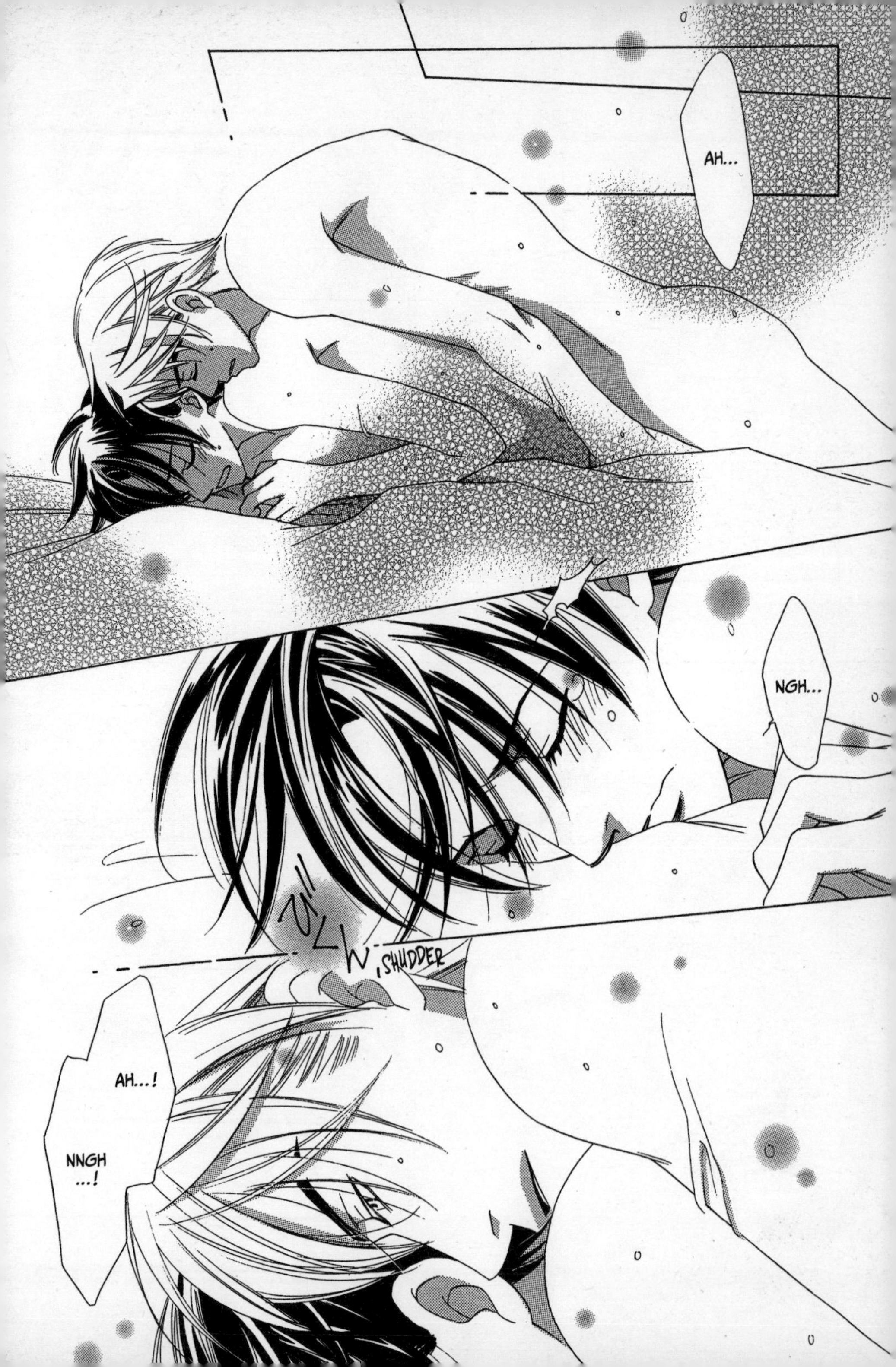
AH...
NGH...
SHUDDER
AH...!
NNGH ...!

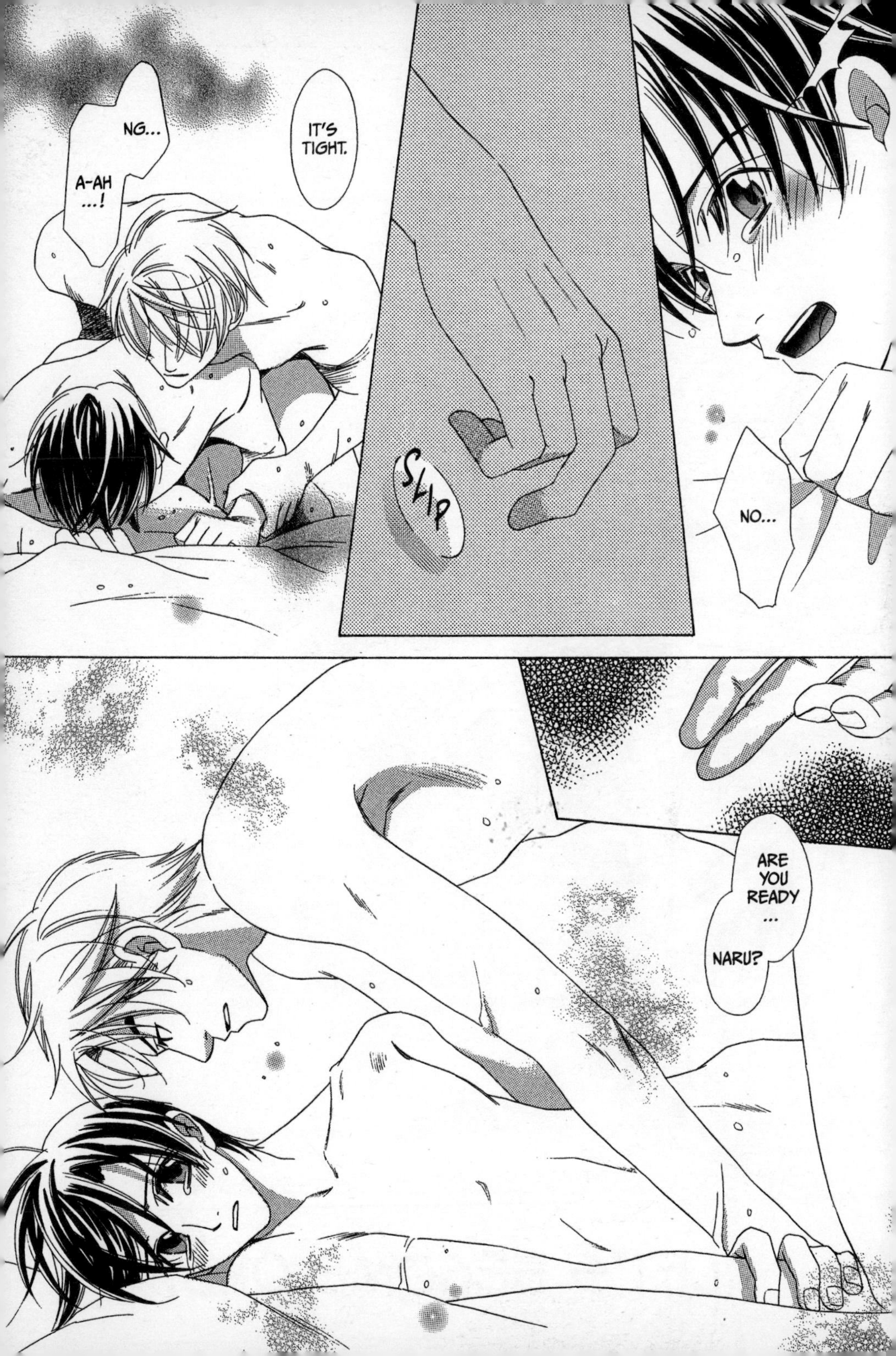
NO...
SLIP
IT'S TIGHT.
NG...
A-AH ...!
ARE YOU READY ... NARU?

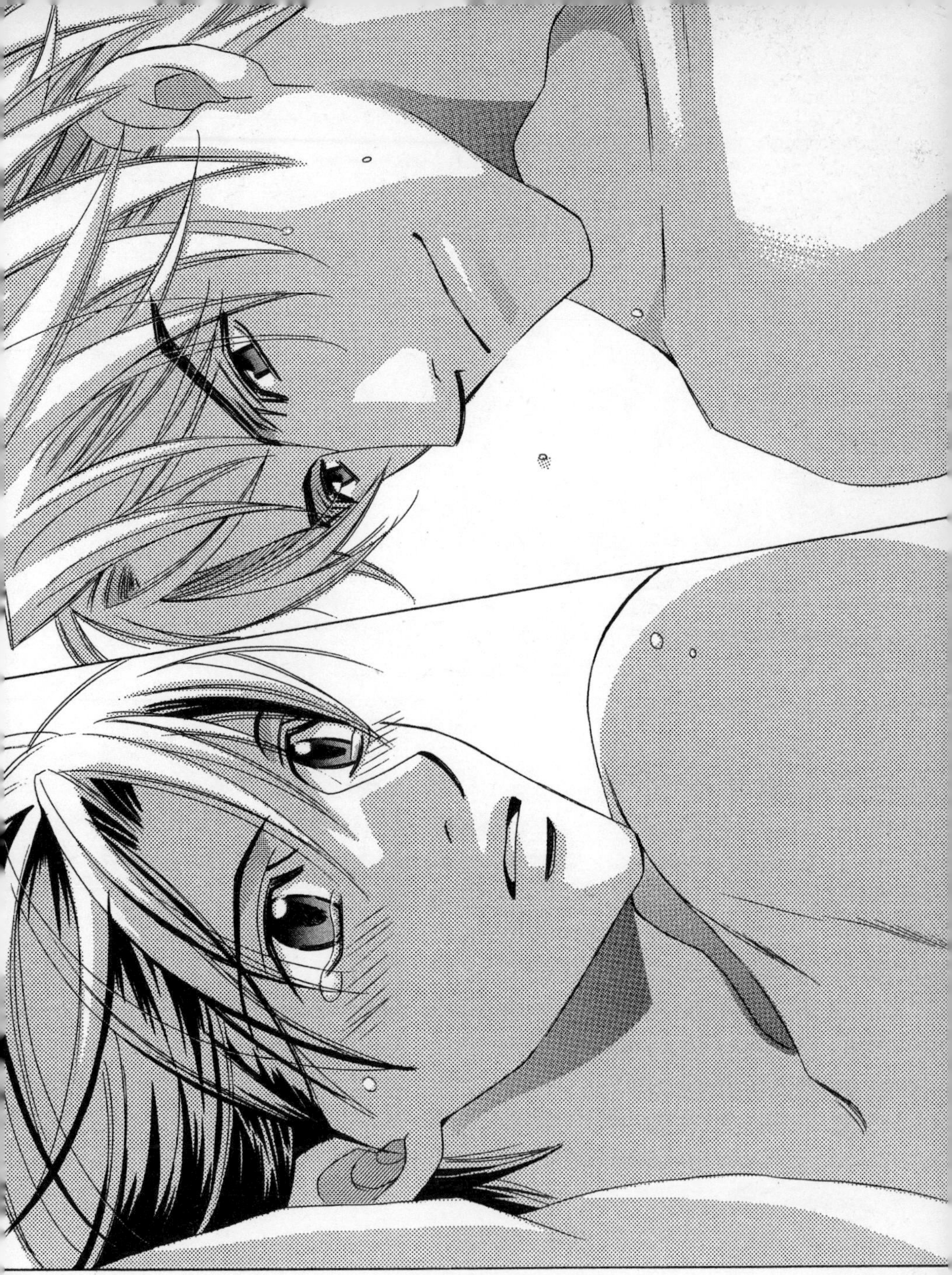

LET'S BECOME ONE.

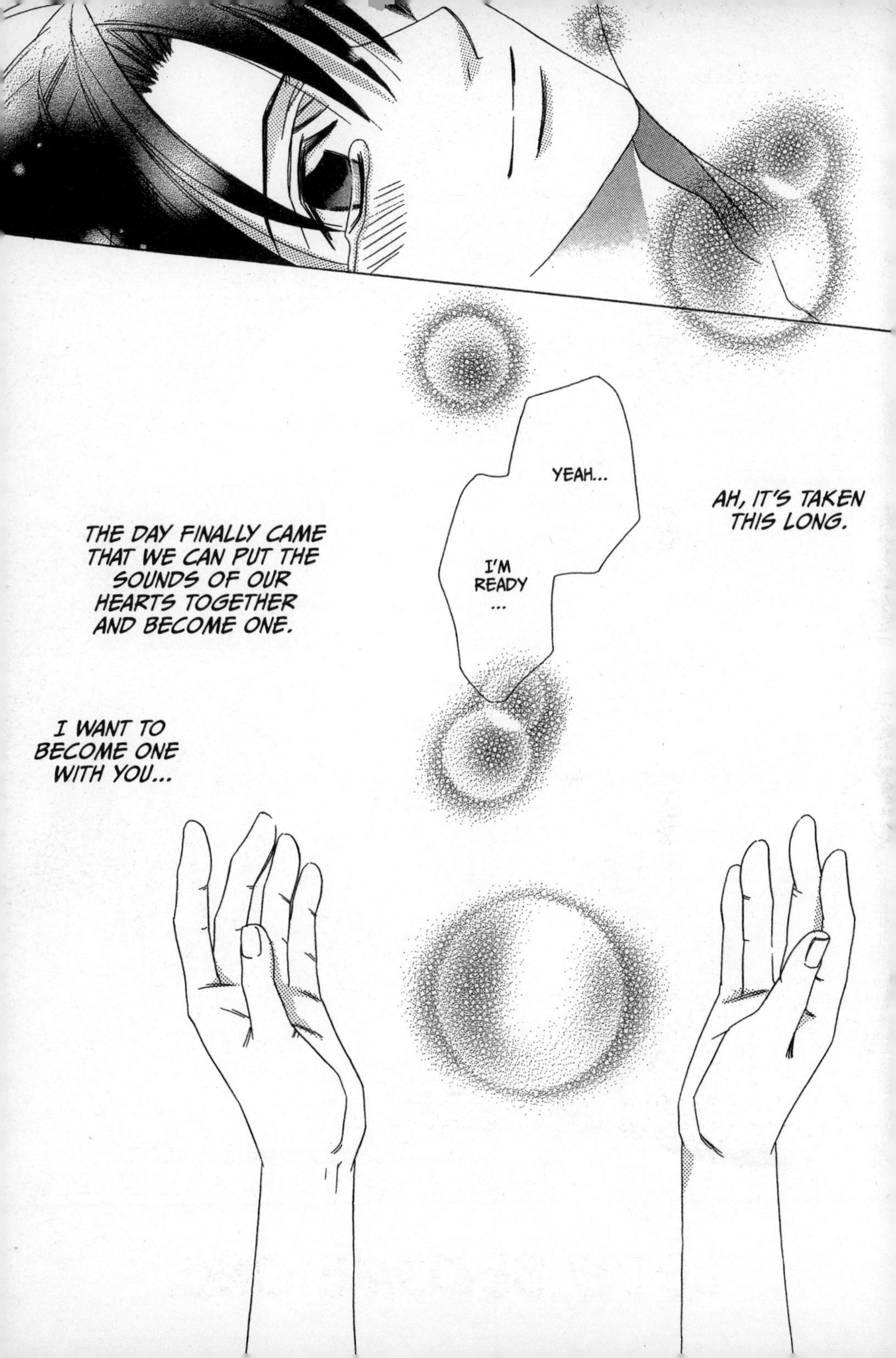
AH, IT'S TAKEN THIS LONG.
YEAH...
I'M READY ...
THE DAY FINALLY CAME THAT WE CAN PUT THE SOUNDS OF OUR HEARTS TOGETHER AND BECOME ONE.
I WANT TO BECOME ONE WITH YOU...

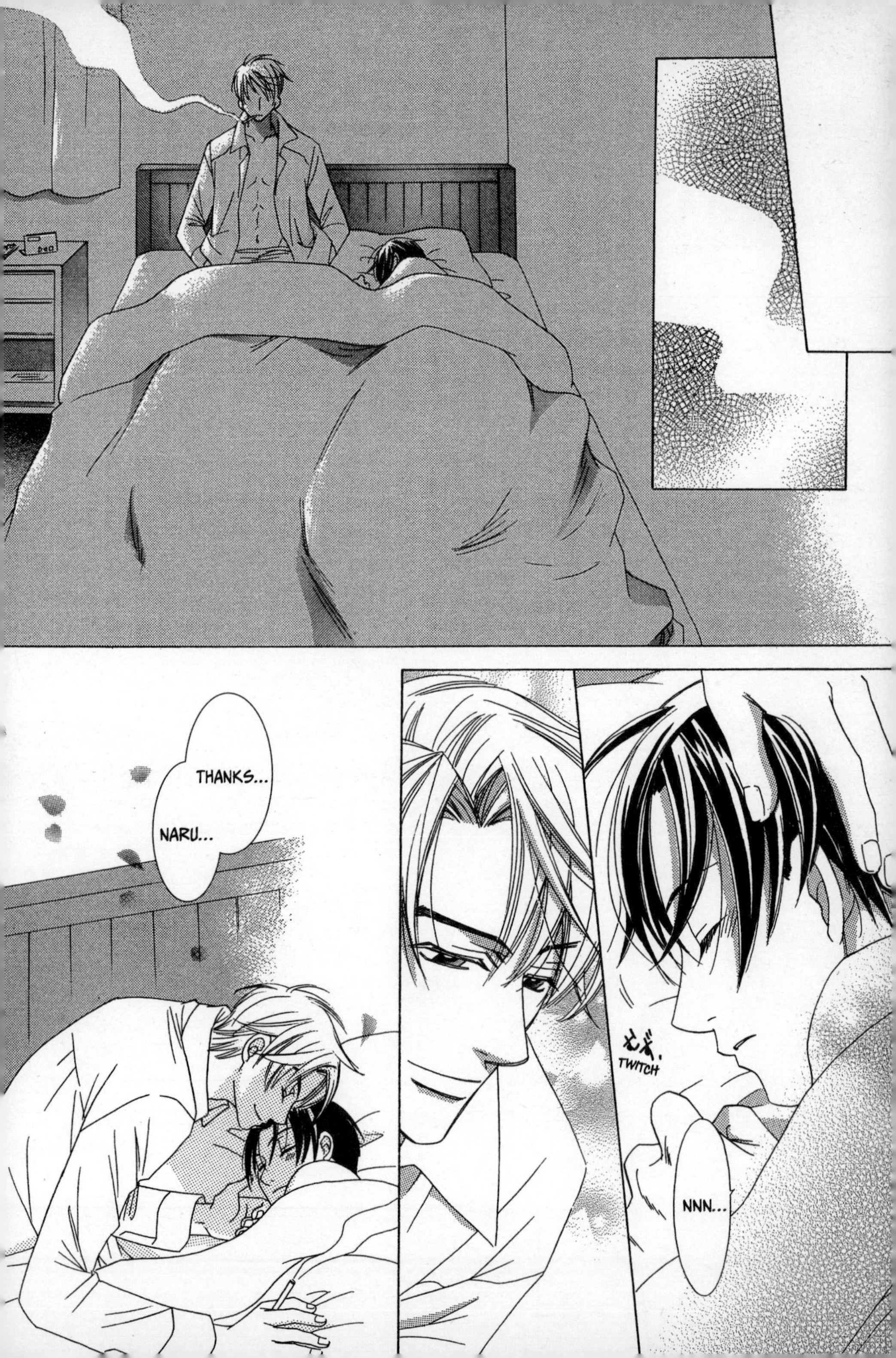
TWITCH
NNN...
THANKS...
NARU...

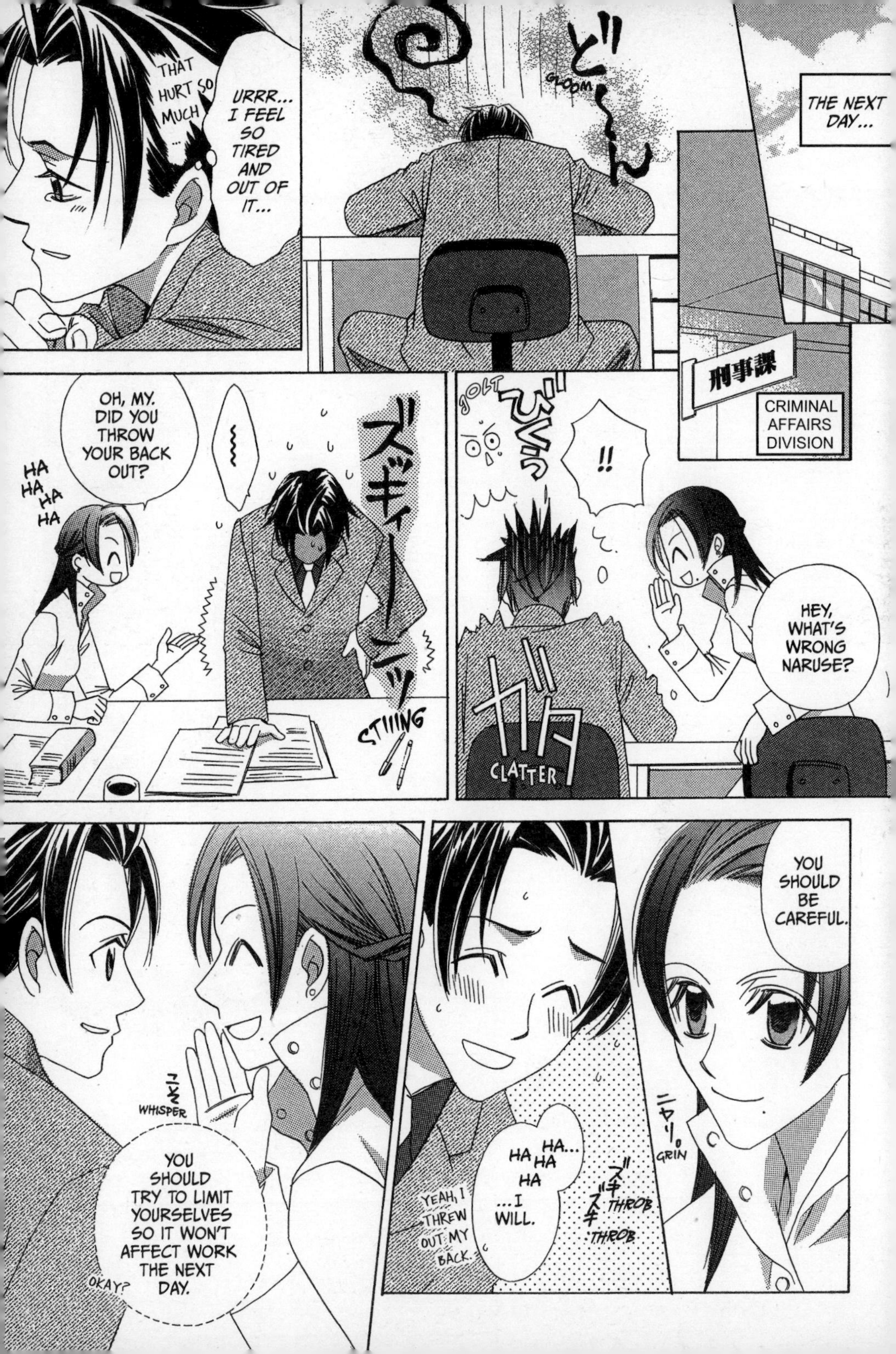
THE NEXT DAY...
刑事課
CRIMINAL AFFAIRS DIVISION
どよ～ん
GLOOM
URRR... I FEEL SO TIRED AND OUT OF IT...
THAT HURT SO MUCH...
びくっ
JOLT
!!
HEY, WHAT'S WRONG NARUSE?
ガタ
CLATTER
ズキィーンッ
STIIING
OH, MY. DID YOU THROW YOUR BACK OUT?
HA HA HA HA
YOU SHOULD BE CAREFUL.
ニヤリ
GRIN
HA... HA HA ...I WILL.
ズキズキ
THROB THROB
YEAH, I THREW OUT MY BACK.
こそ
WHISPER
YOU SHOULD TRY TO LIMIT YOURSELVES SO IT WON'T AFFECT WORK THE NEXT DAY.
OKAY?

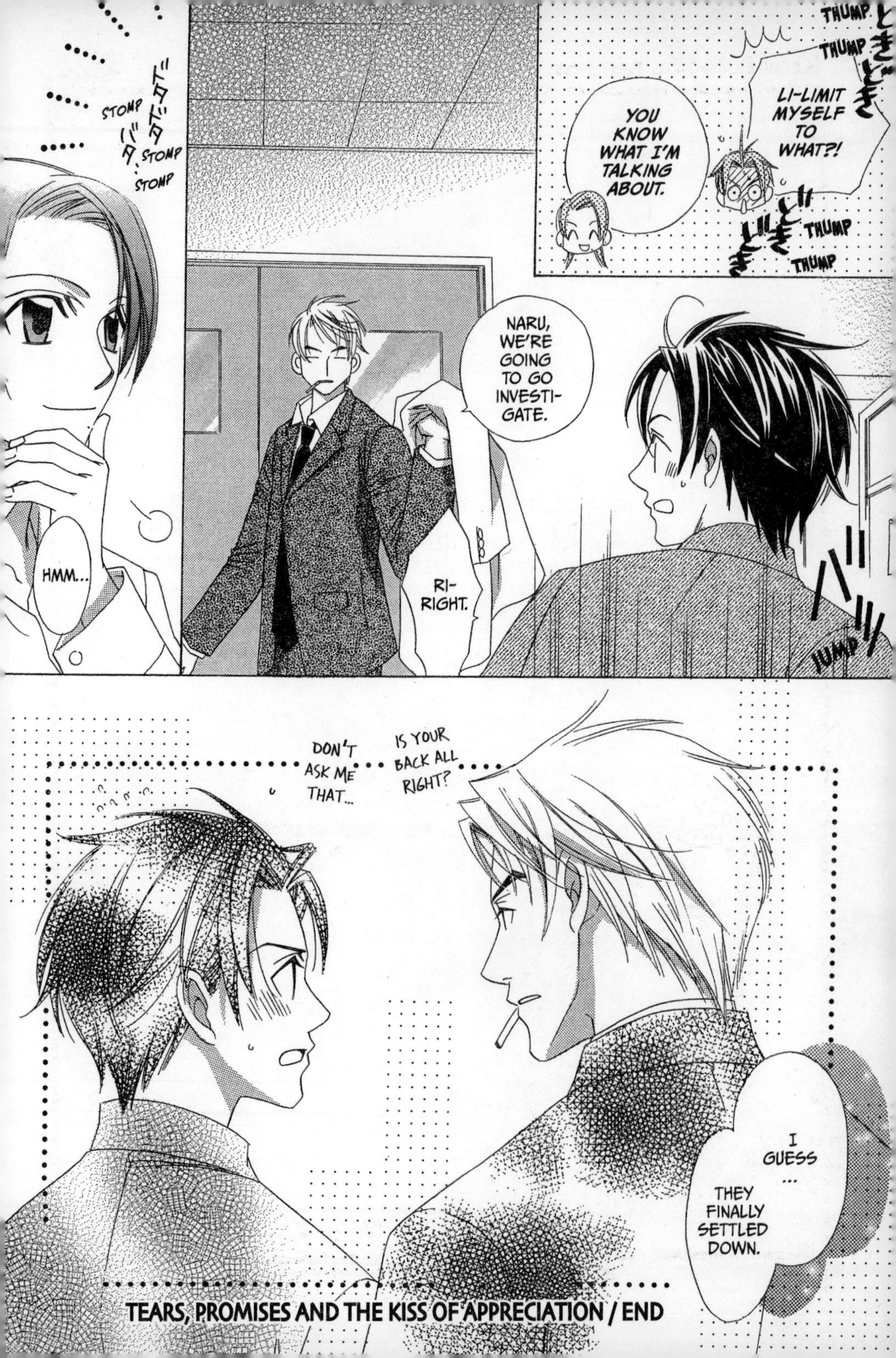
THUMP
THUMP
LI-LIMIT MYSELF TO WHAT?!
THUMP
THUMP
YOU KNOW WHAT I'M TALKING ABOUT.
JUMP
NARU, WE'RE GOING TO GO INVESTI-GATE.
RI-RIGHT.
STOMP
STOMP
STOMP
HMM...
I GUESS...
THEY FINALLY SETTLED DOWN.
IS YOUR BACK ALL RIGHT?
DON'T ASK ME THAT...

TEARS, PROMISES AND THE KISS OF APPRECIATION / END

Kita & Naru series

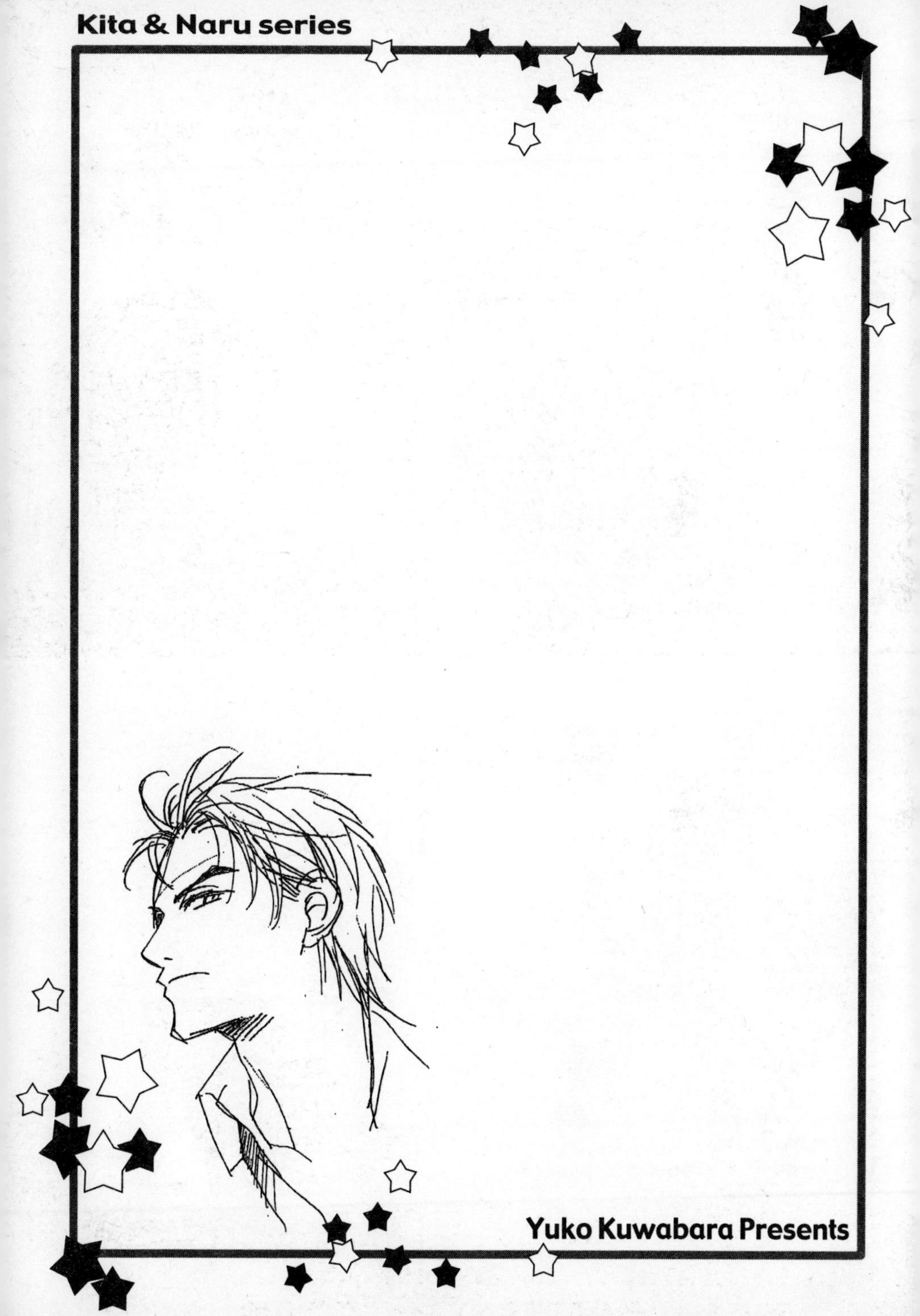

Yuko Kuwabara Presents

Kita & Naru series

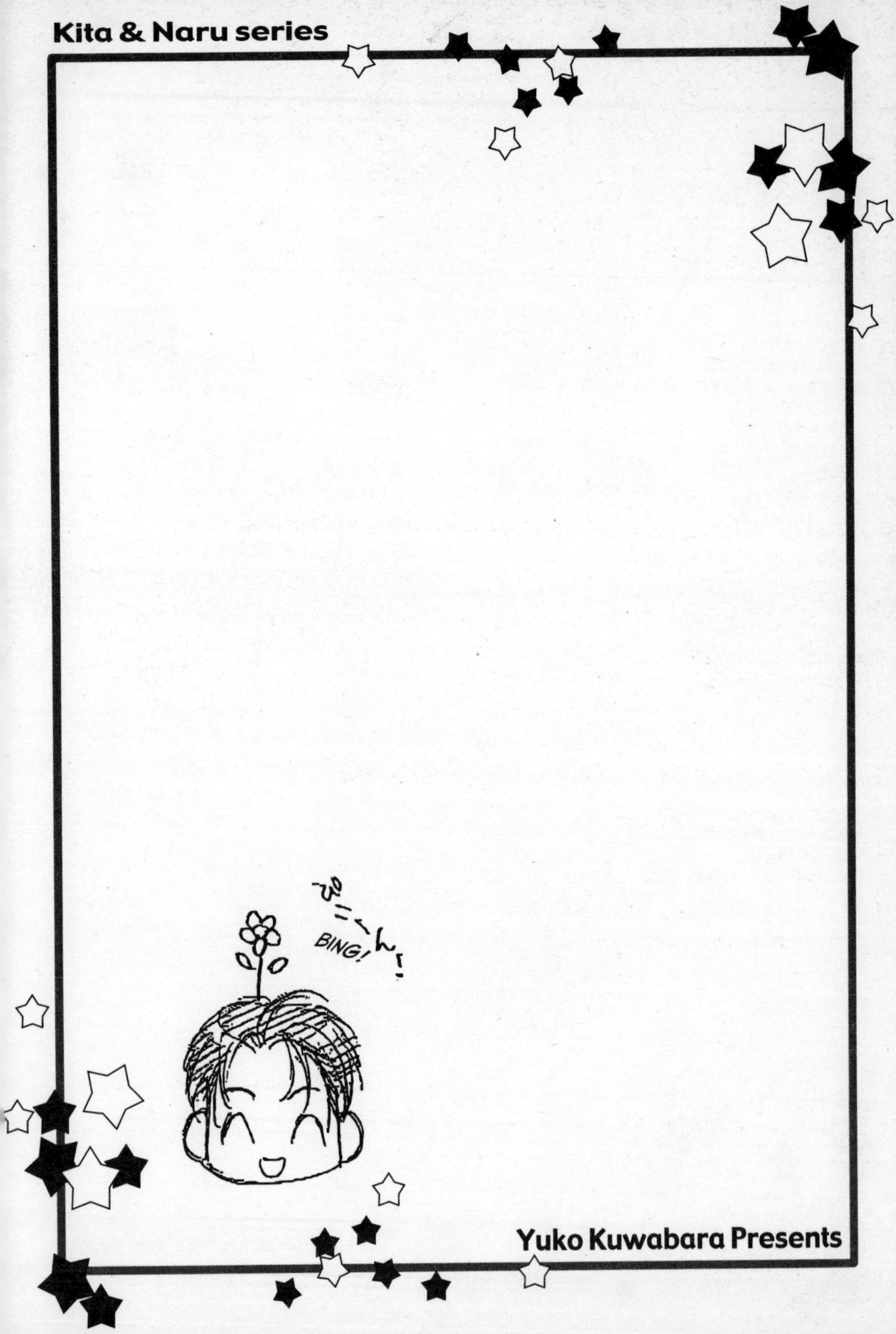
BING!

Yuko Kuwabara Presents

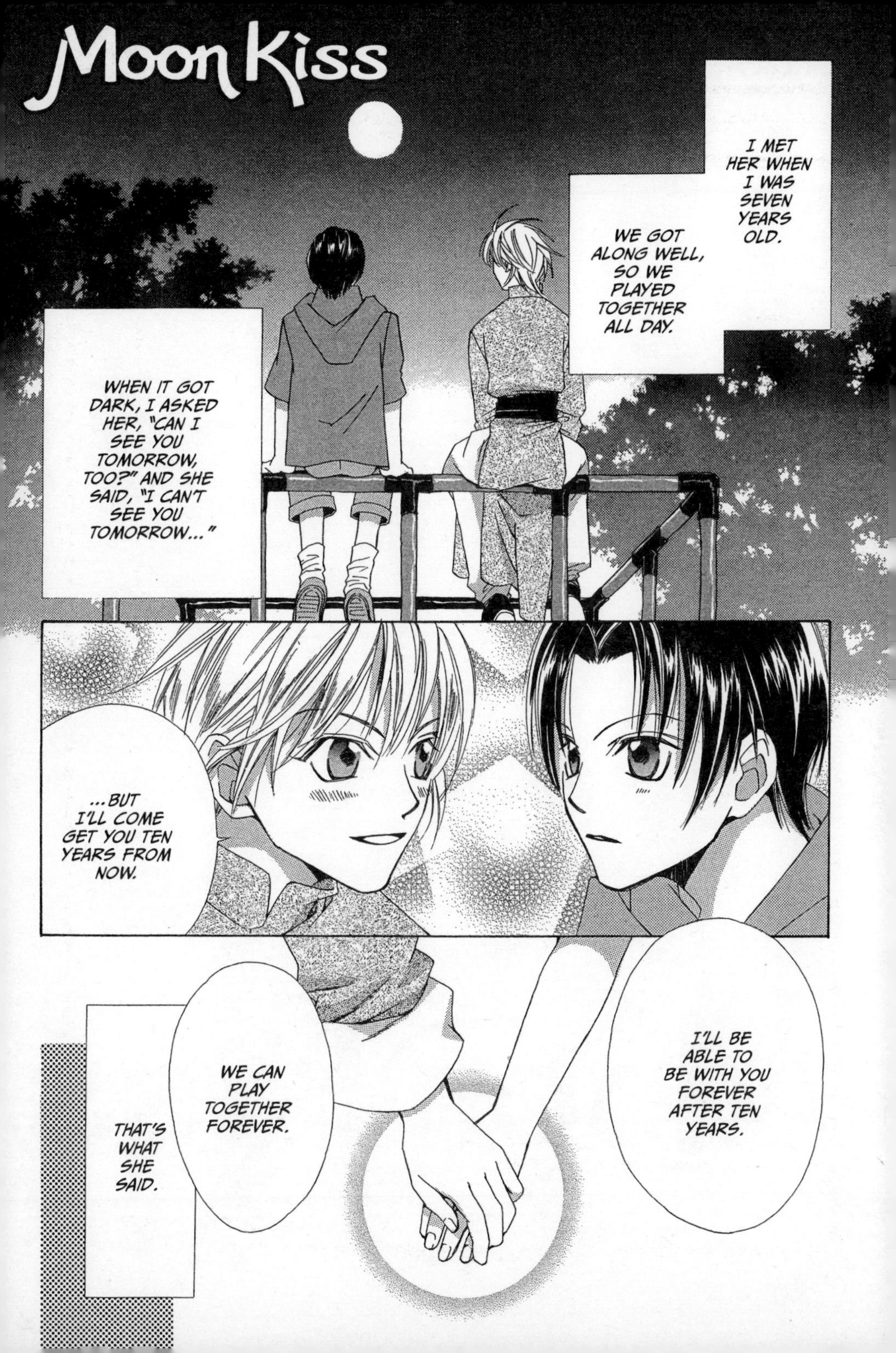
Moon Kiss
I MET HER WHEN I WAS SEVEN YEARS OLD.
WE GOT ALONG WELL, SO WE PLAYED TOGETHER ALL DAY.
WHEN IT GOT DARK, I ASKED HER, "CAN I SEE YOU TOMORROW, TOO?" AND SHE SAID, "I CAN'T SEE YOU TOMORROW..."
...BUT I'LL COME GET YOU TEN YEARS FROM NOW.
I'LL BE ABLE TO BE WITH YOU FOREVER AFTER TEN YEARS.
WE CAN PLAY TOGETHER FOREVER.
THAT'S WHAT SHE SAID.

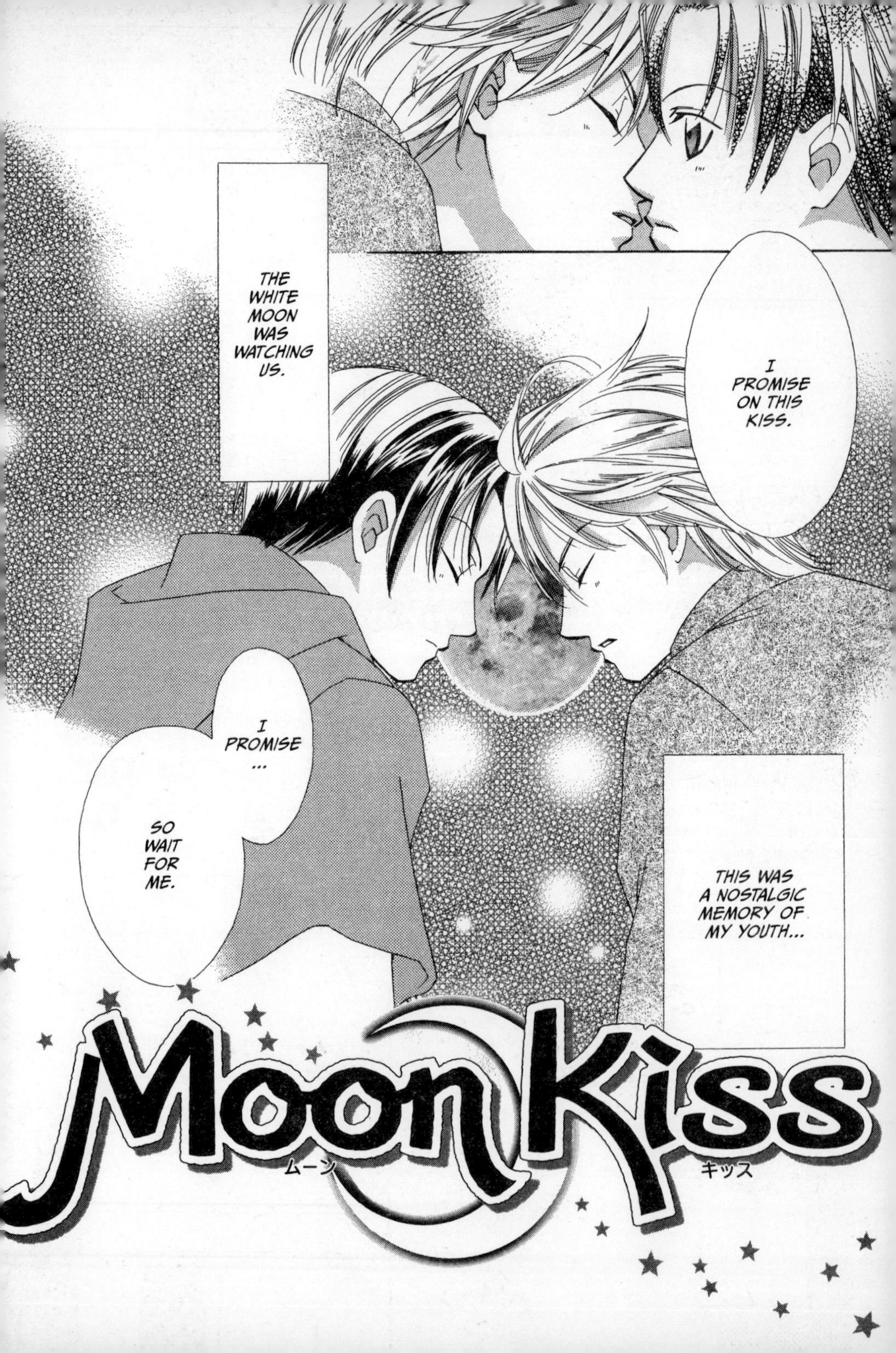
THE WHITE MOON WAS WATCHING US.
I PROMISE ON THIS KISS.
I PROMISE...
SO WAIT FOR ME.
THIS WAS A NOSTALGIC MEMORY OF MY YOUTH...
Moon Kiss
ムーン
キッス

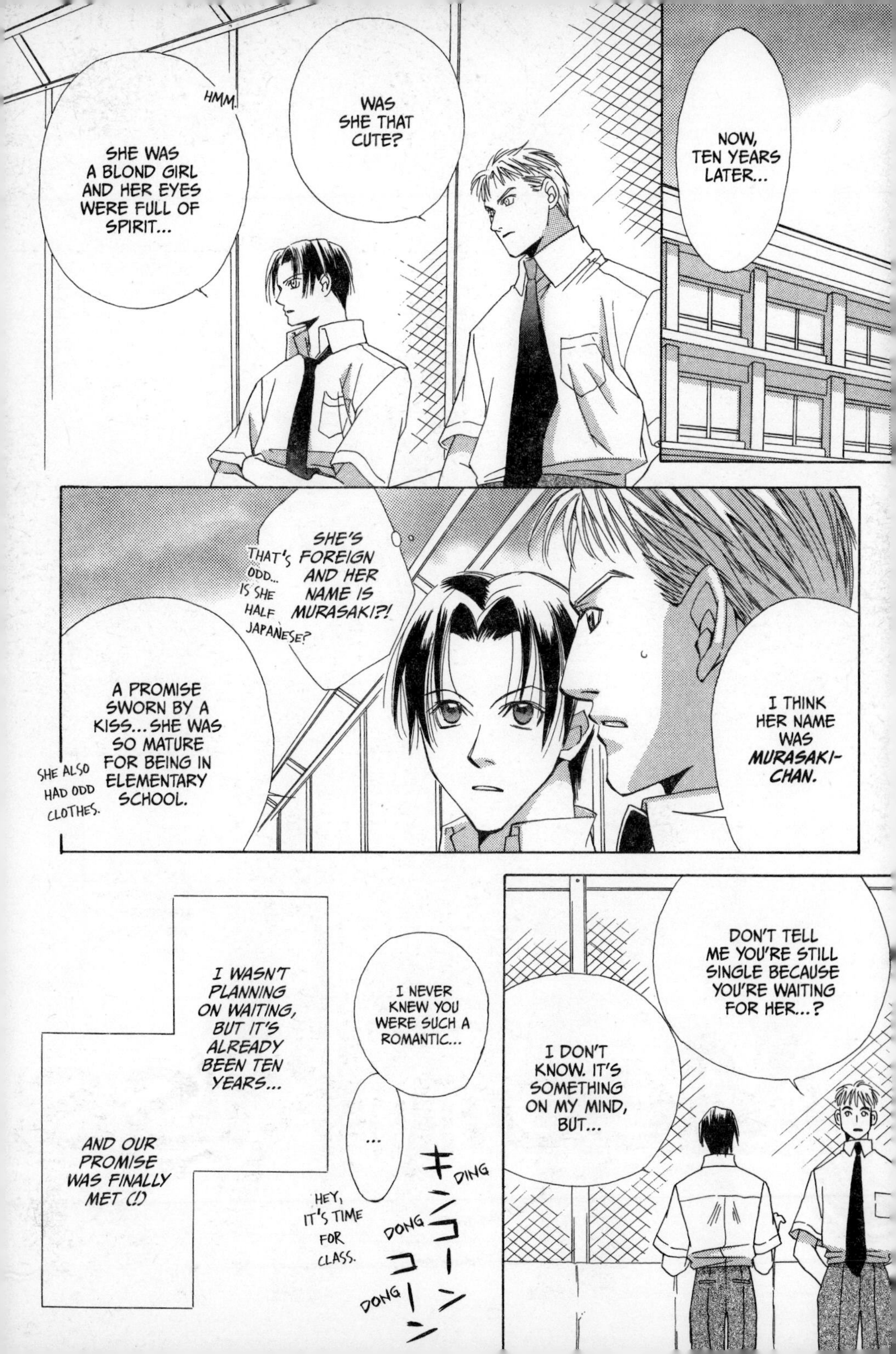
NOW, TEN YEARS LATER...
WAS SHE THAT CUTE?
HMM.
SHE WAS A BLOND GIRL AND HER EYES WERE FULL OF SPIRIT...
I THINK HER NAME WAS *MURASAKI-CHAN.*
SHE'S FOREIGN AND HER NAME IS MURASAKI?!
THAT'S ODD... IS SHE HALF JAPANESE?
A PROMISE SWORN BY A KISS... SHE WAS SO MATURE FOR BEING IN ELEMENTARY SCHOOL.
SHE ALSO HAD ODD CLOTHES.
DON'T TELL ME YOU'RE STILL SINGLE BECAUSE YOU'RE WAITING FOR HER...?
I DON'T KNOW. IT'S SOMETHING ON MY MIND, BUT...
I NEVER KNEW YOU WERE SUCH A ROMANTIC...
...
DING
DONG
DONG
HEY, IT'S TIME FOR CLASS.
I WASN'T PLANNING ON WAITING, BUT IT'S ALREADY BEEN TEN YEARS...
AND OUR PROMISE WAS FINALLY MET (!)

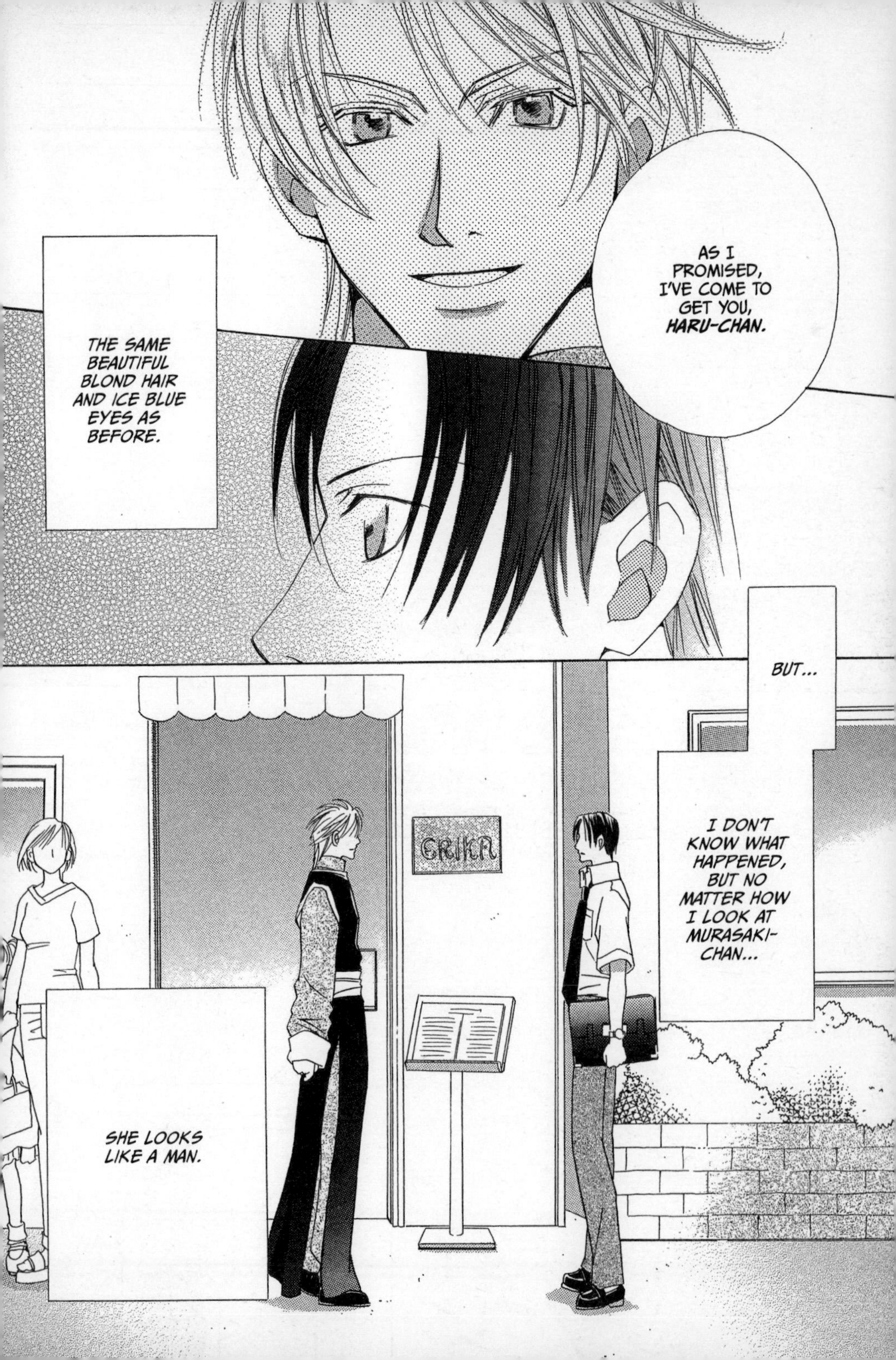
AS I PROMISED, I'VE COME TO GET YOU, HARU-CHAN.
THE SAME BEAUTIFUL BLOND HAIR AND ICE BLUE EYES AS BEFORE.
BUT...
I DON'T KNOW WHAT HAPPENED, BUT NO MATTER HOW I LOOK AT MURASAKI-CHAN...
SHE LOOKS LIKE A MAN.
ERIKA

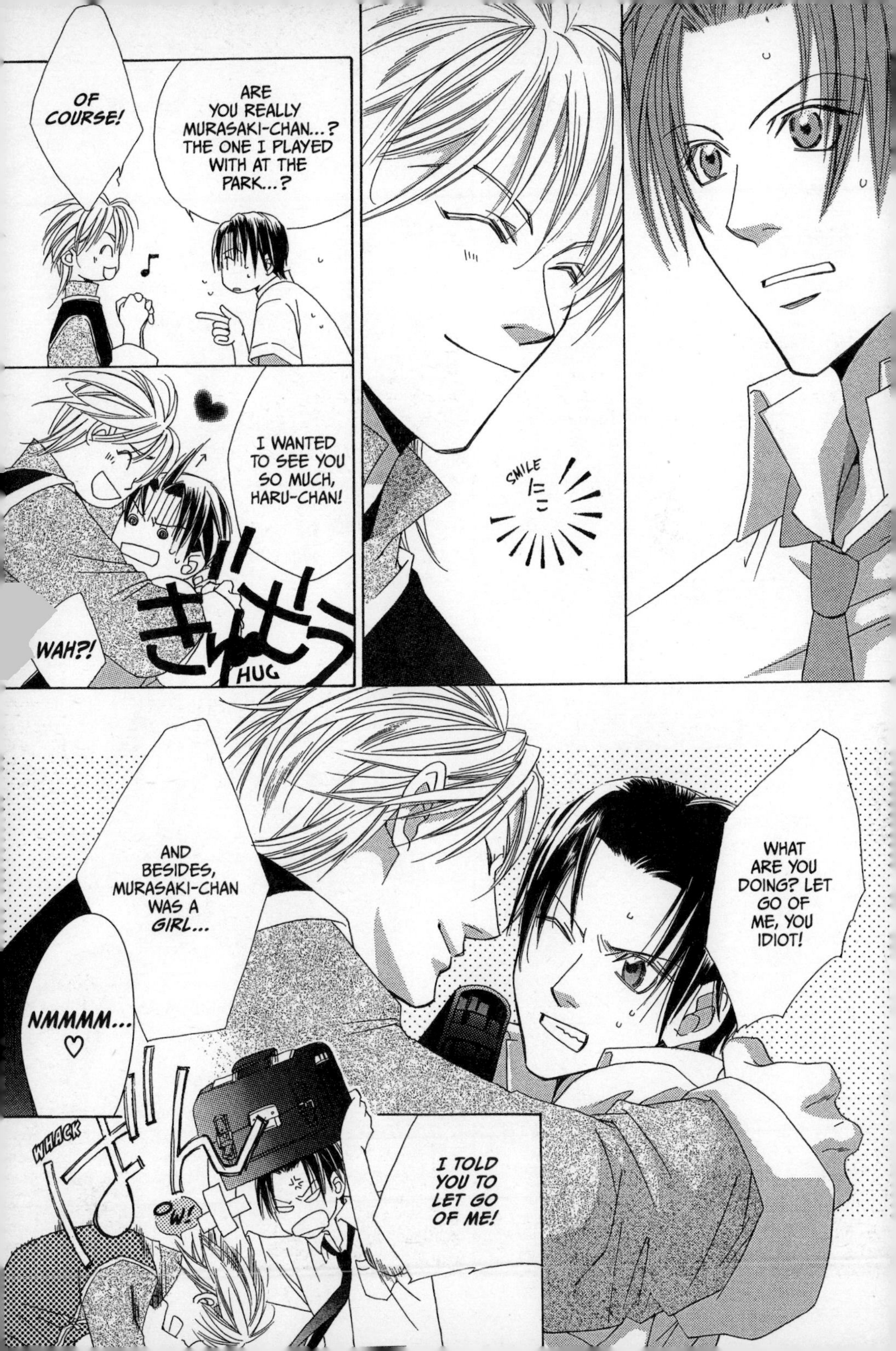
SMILE
ARE YOU REALLY MURASAKI-CHAN...? THE ONE I PLAYED WITH AT THE PARK...?
OF COURSE!
I WANTED TO SEE YOU SO MUCH, HARU-CHAN!
WAH?!
HUG
WHAT ARE YOU DOING? LET GO OF ME, YOU IDIOT!
AND BESIDES, MURASAKI-CHAN WAS A GIRL...
NMMMM... ♡
I TOLD YOU TO LET GO OF ME!
WHACK
OW!

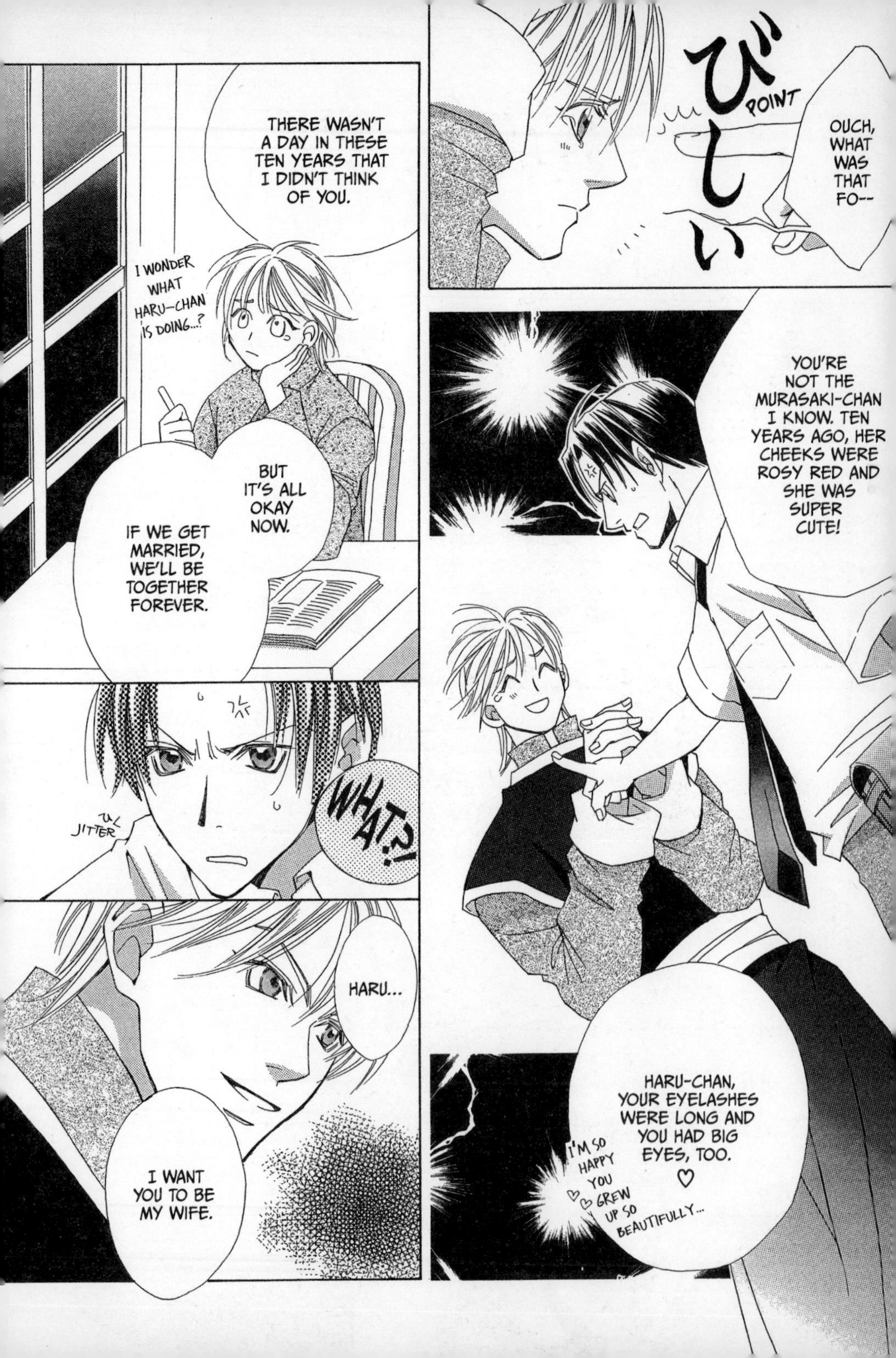

びしい
POINT
OUCH, WHAT WAS THAT FO--
YOU'RE NOT THE MURASAKI-CHAN I KNOW. TEN YEARS AGO, HER CHEEKS WERE ROSY RED AND SHE WAS SUPER CUTE!
HARU-CHAN, YOUR EYELASHES WERE LONG AND YOU HAD BIG EYES, TOO. ♡
I'M SO HAPPY YOU GREW UP SO BEAUTIFULLY...
THERE WASN'T A DAY IN THESE TEN YEARS THAT I DIDN'T THINK OF YOU.
I WONDER WHAT HARU-CHAN IS DOING...?
BUT IT'S ALL OKAY NOW.
IF WE GET MARRIED, WE'LL BE TOGETHER FOREVER.
WHAT?!
JITTER
HARU...
I WANT YOU TO BE MY WIFE.

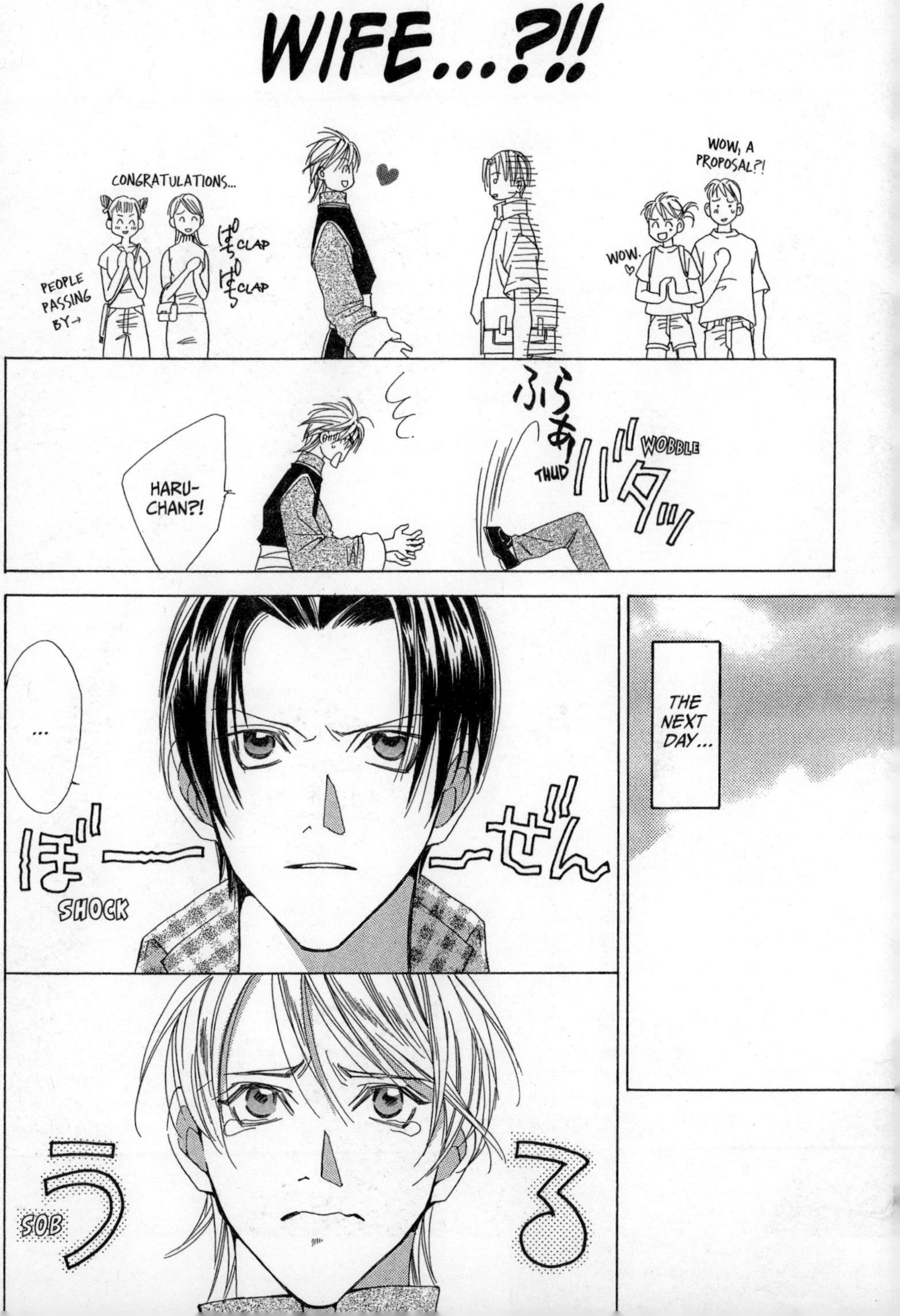
WIFE...?!!
WOW, A PROPOSAL?!
WOW.
CONGRATULATIONS...
ぱち CLAP
ぱち CLAP
PEOPLE PASSING BY→
ふらあ
WOBBLE
バタッ
THUD
HARU-CHAN?!
THE NEXT DAY...
...
ぼーーぜん
SHOCK
うる
SOB

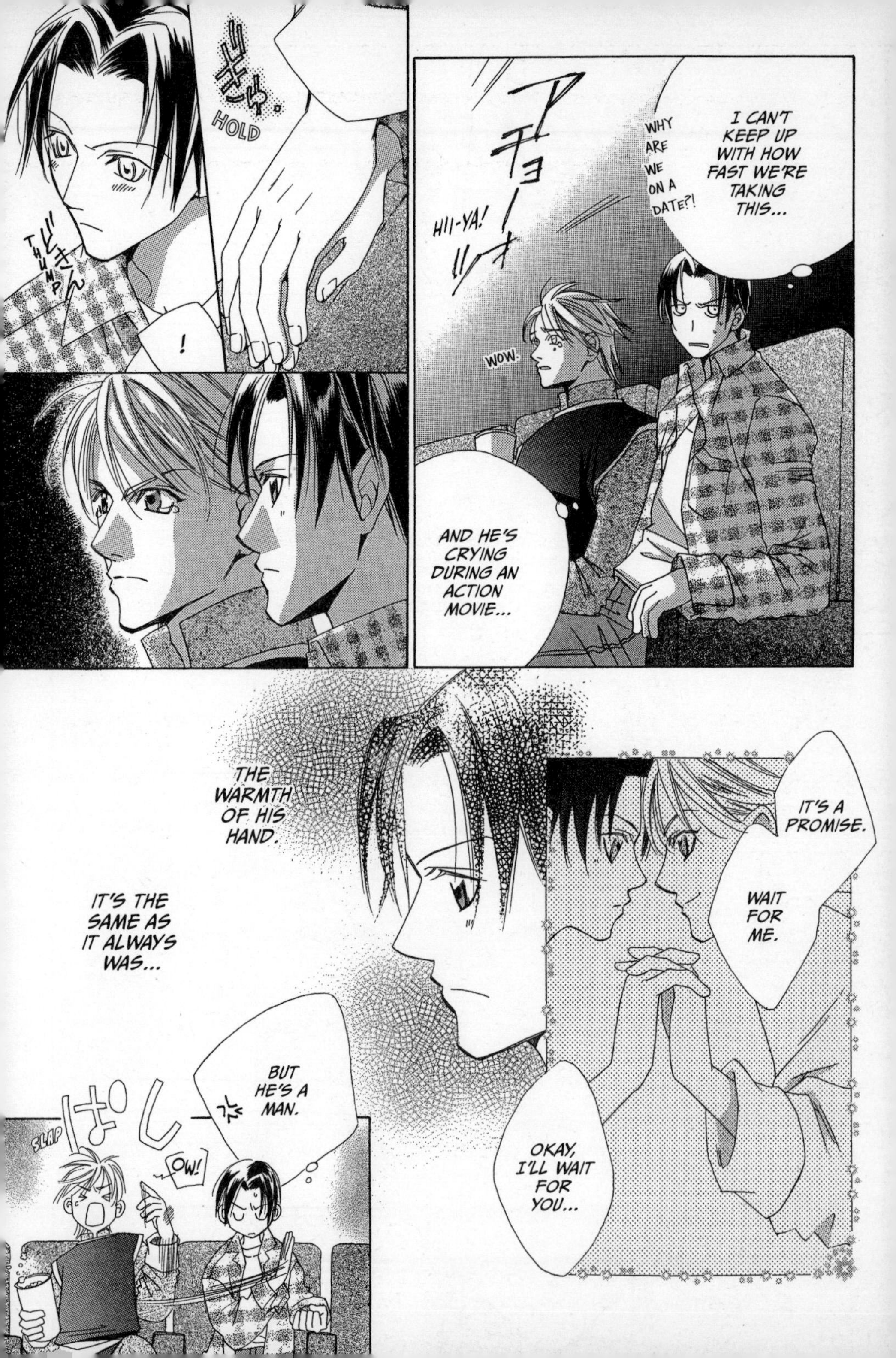

WHY ARE WE ON A DATE?!
I CAN'T KEEP UP WITH HOW FAST WE'RE TAKING THIS...
HII-YA!
WOW.
AND HE'S CRYING DURING AN ACTION MOVIE...
HOLD
THUMP
!
IT'S A PROMISE.
WAIT FOR ME.
OKAY, I'LL WAIT FOR YOU...
THE WARMTH OF HIS HAND.
IT'S THE SAME AS IT ALWAYS WAS...
BUT HE'S A MAN.
ぱし
SLAP
OW!

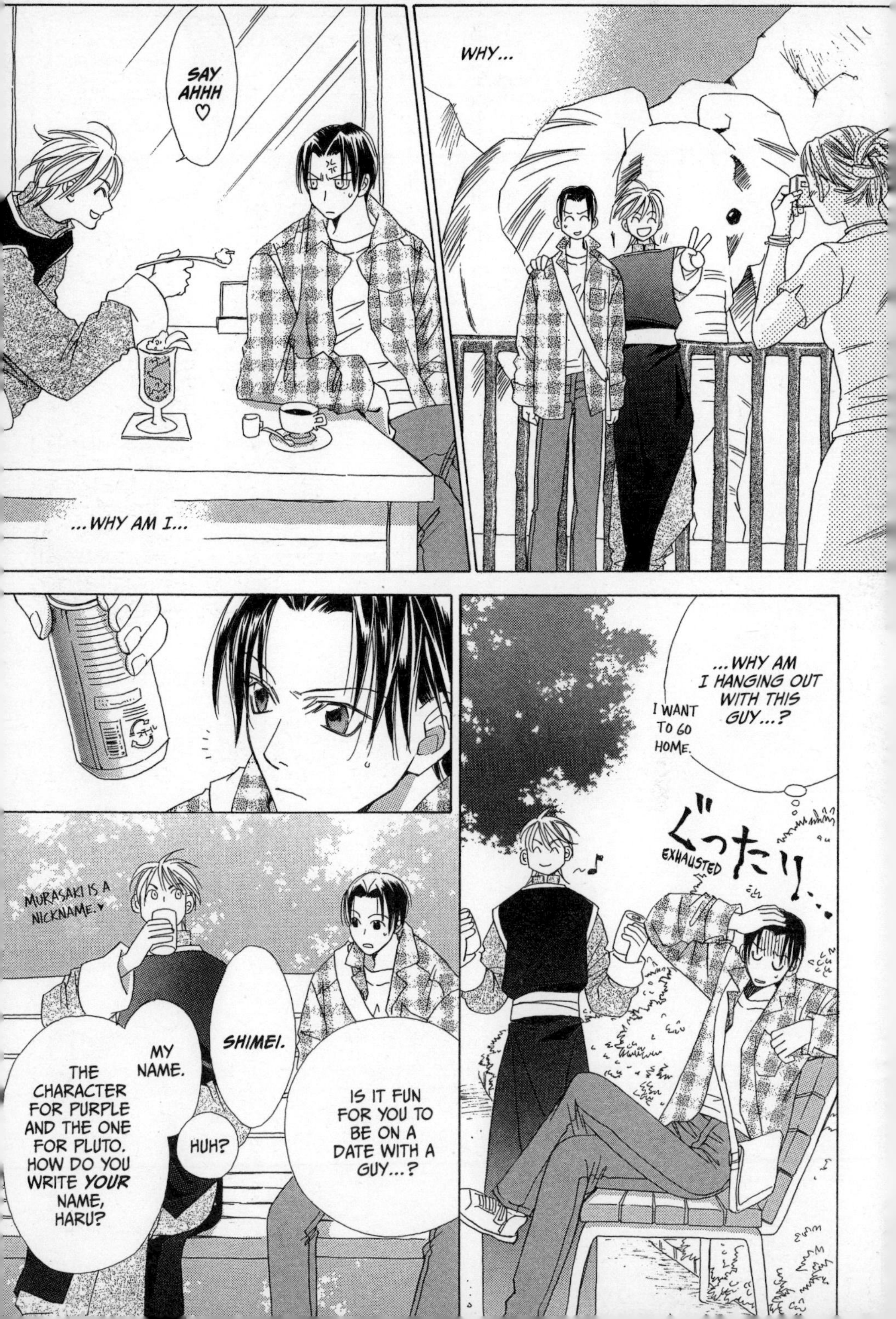
WHY...
SAY AHHH ♡
...WHY AM I...
...WHY AM I HANGING OUT WITH THIS GUY...?
I WANT TO GO HOME.
ぐったり
EXHAUSTED
IS IT FUN FOR YOU TO BE ON A DATE WITH A GUY...?
SHIMEI.
HUH?
MY NAME.
THE CHARACTER FOR PURPLE AND THE ONE FOR PLUTO. HOW DO YOU WRITE YOUR NAME, HARU?
MURASAKI IS A NICKNAME.

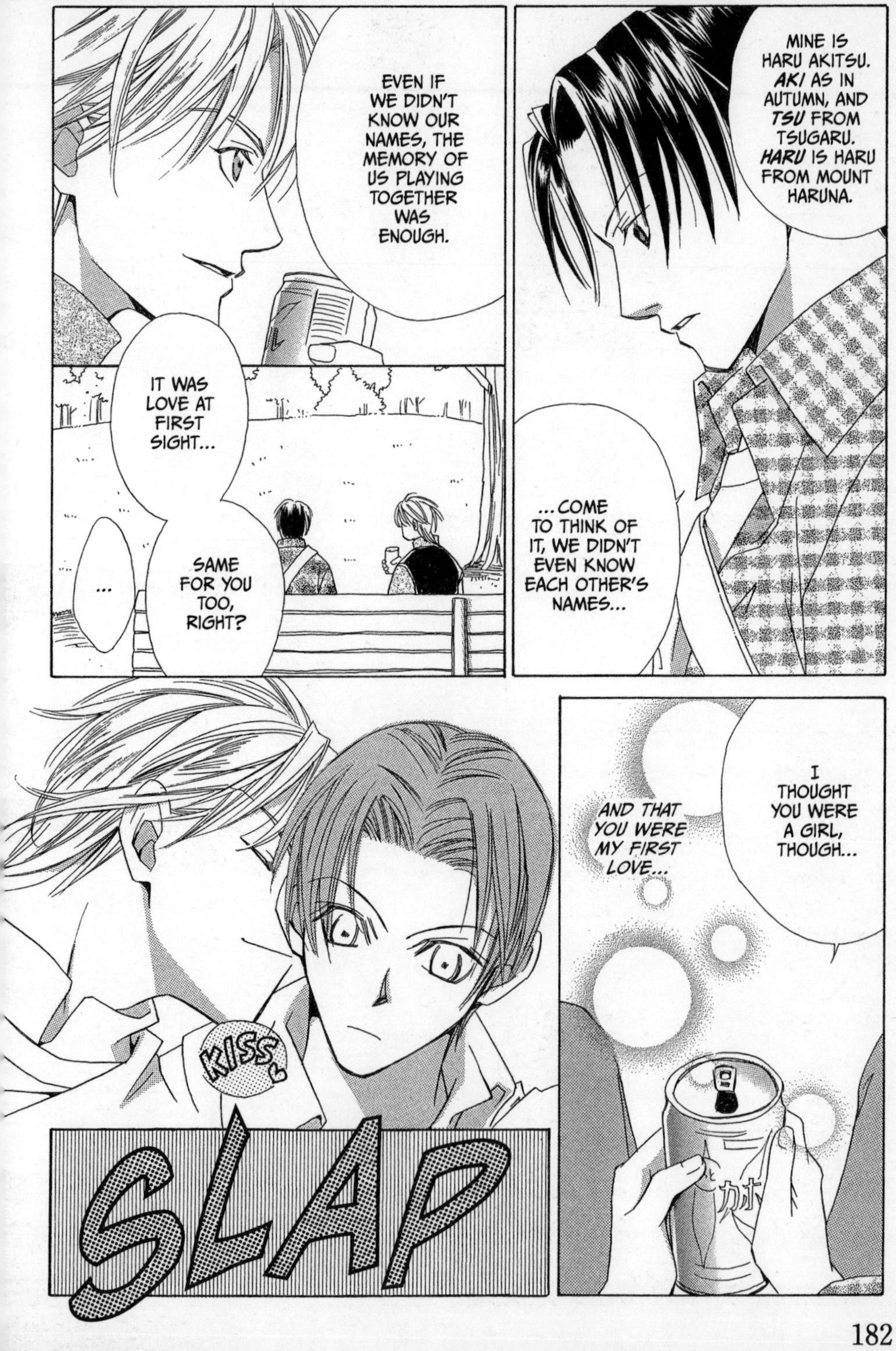
MINE IS HARU AKITSU. *AKI* AS IN AUTUMN, AND *TSU* FROM TSUGARU. *HARU* IS HARU FROM MOUNT HARUNA.
...COME TO THINK OF IT, WE DIDN'T EVEN KNOW EACH OTHER'S NAMES...
EVEN IF WE DIDN'T KNOW OUR NAMES, THE MEMORY OF US PLAYING TOGETHER WAS ENOUGH.
IT WAS LOVE AT FIRST SIGHT...
SAME FOR YOU TOO, RIGHT?
...
I THOUGHT YOU WERE A GIRL, THOUGH...
AND THAT YOU WERE MY FIRST LOVE...
KISS
SLAP

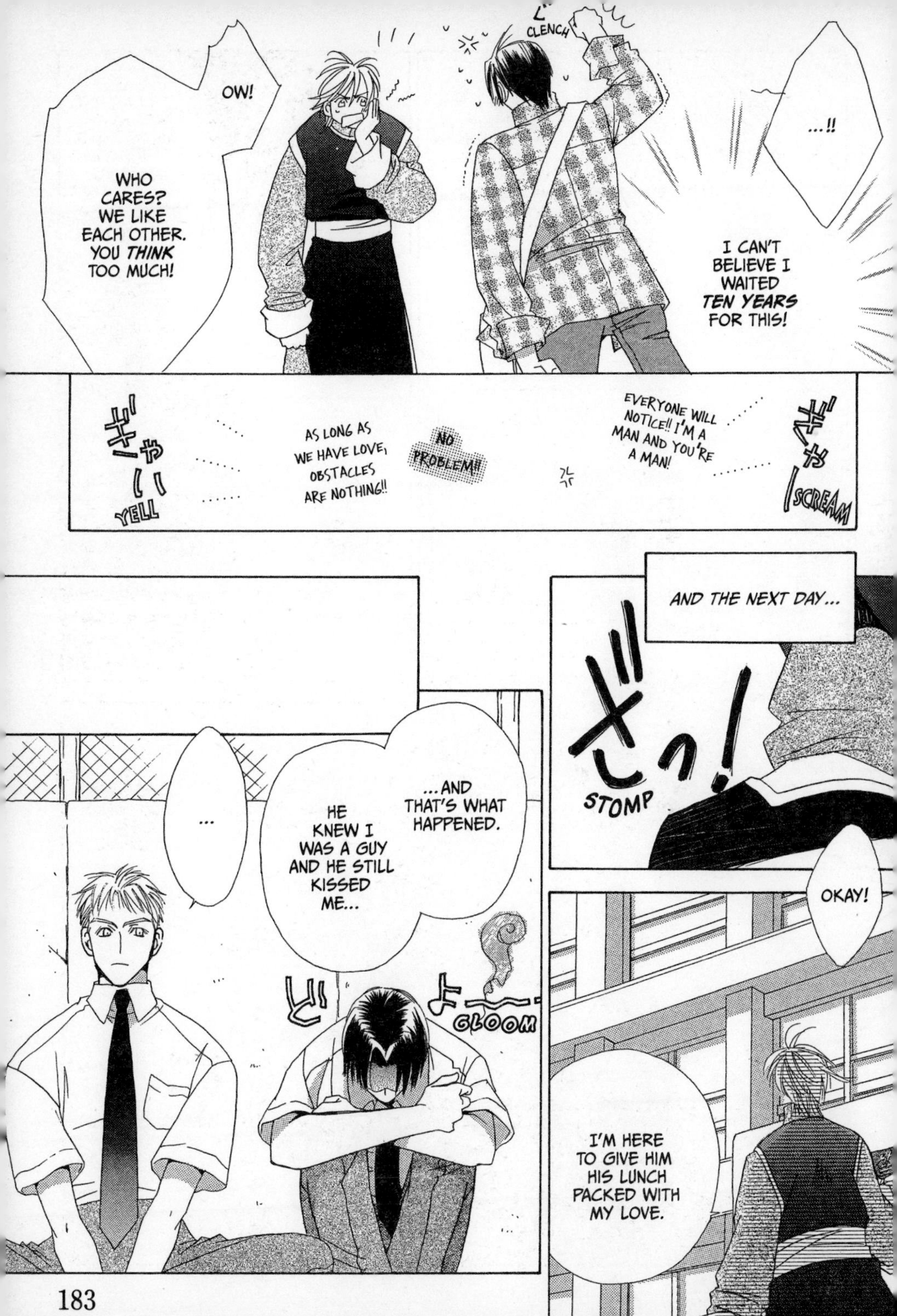
...!!
I CAN'T BELIEVE I WAITED *TEN YEARS* FOR THIS!
CLENCH
OW!
WHO CARES? WE LIKE EACH OTHER. YOU *THINK* TOO MUCH!
SCREAM
EVERYONE WILL NOTICE!! I'M A MAN AND YOU'RE A MAN!
NO PROBLEM!!
AS LONG AS WE HAVE LOVE, OBSTACLES ARE NOTHING!!
YELL
AND THE NEXT DAY...
STOMP
OKAY!
I'M HERE TO GIVE HIM HIS LUNCH PACKED WITH MY LOVE.
...AND THAT'S WHAT HAPPENED.
HE KNEW I WAS A GUY AND HE STILL KISSED ME...
...
GLOOM

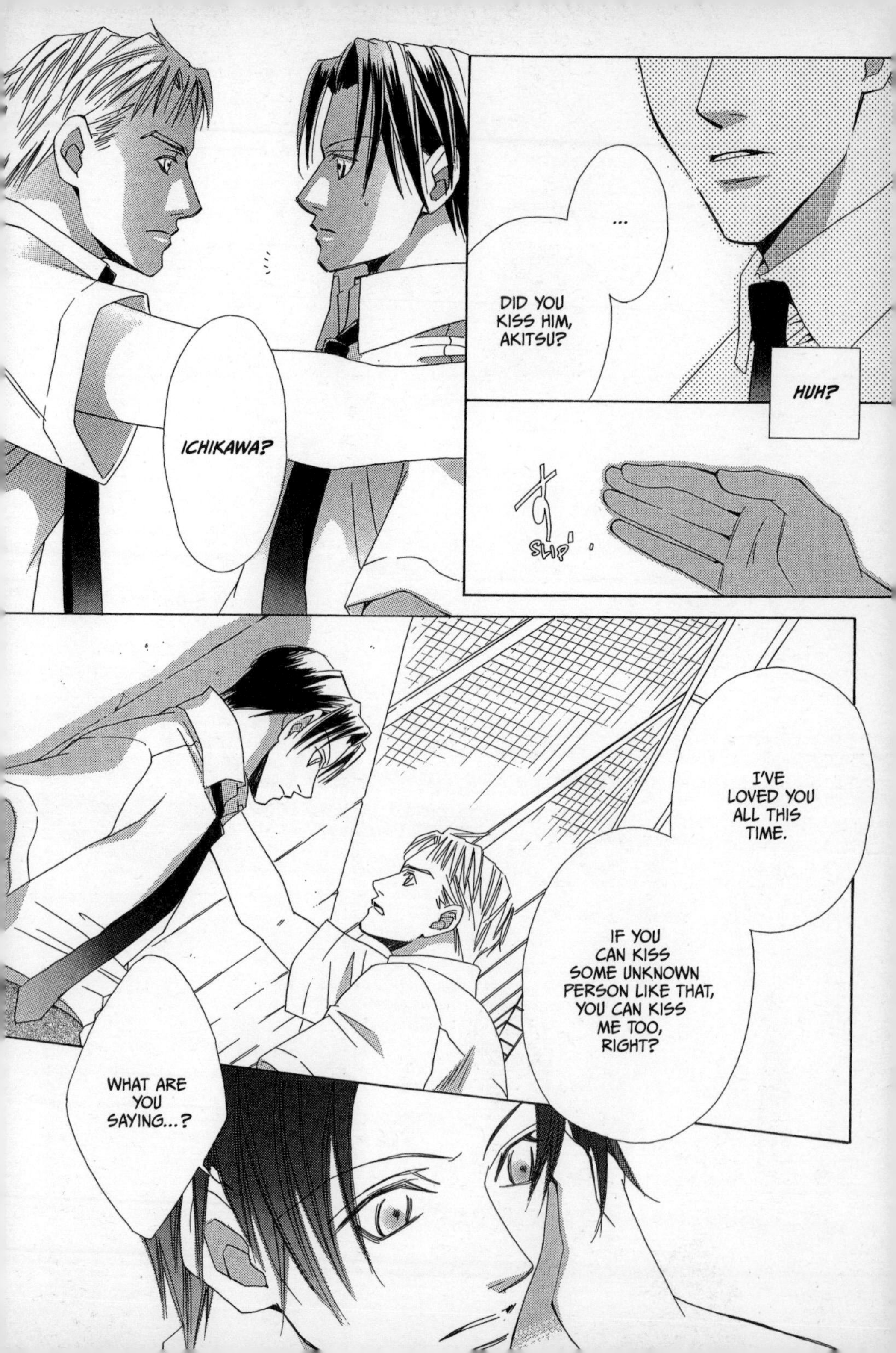
...
DID YOU KISS HIM, AKITSU?
HUH?
SLIP
ICHIKAWA?
I'VE LOVED YOU ALL THIS TIME.
IF YOU CAN KISS SOME UNKNOWN PERSON LIKE THAT, YOU CAN KISS ME TOO, RIGHT?
WHAT ARE YOU SAYING...?

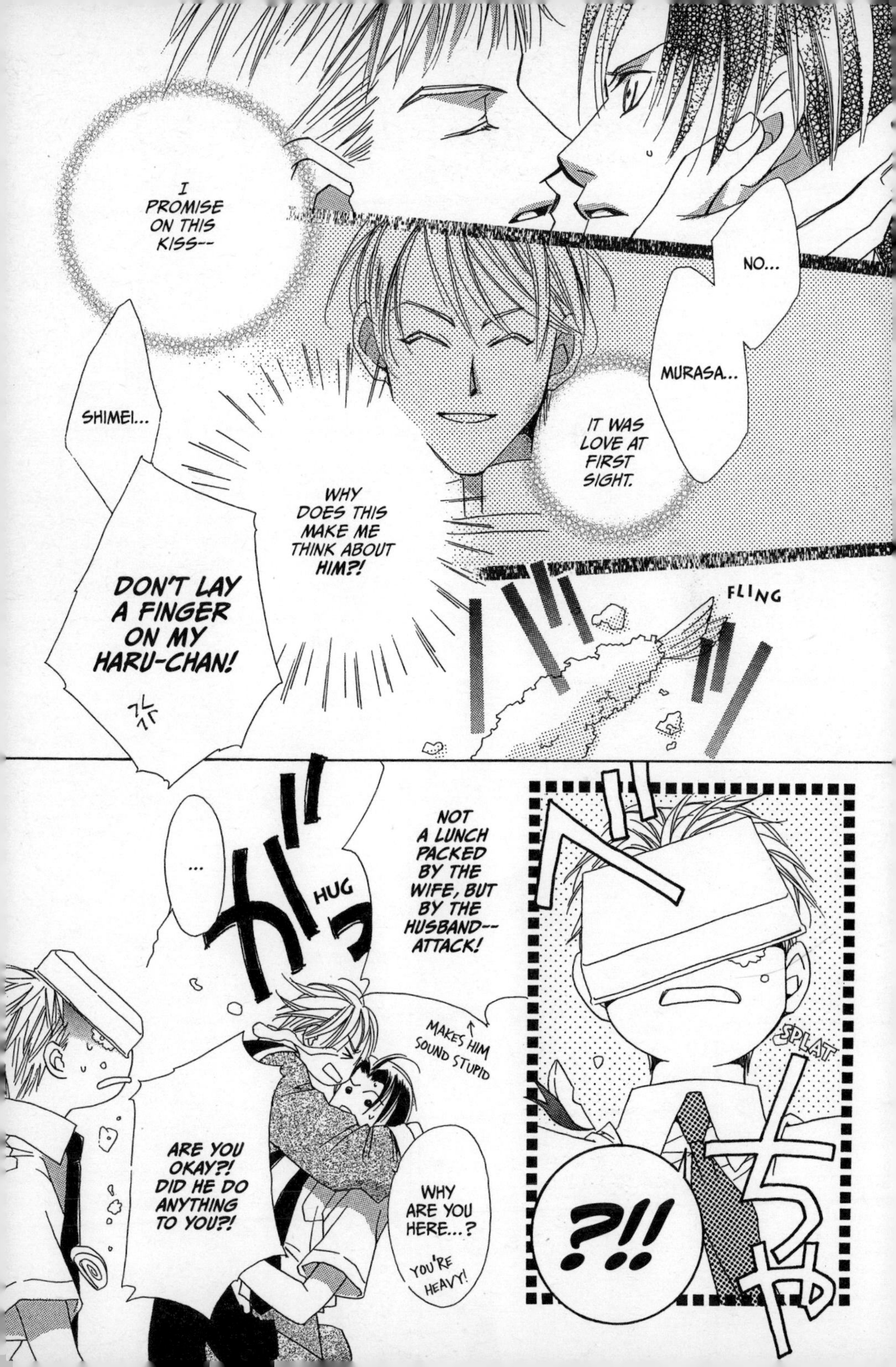
I PROMISE ON THIS KISS--
NO...
MURASA...
IT WAS LOVE AT FIRST SIGHT.
WHY DOES THIS MAKE ME THINK ABOUT HIM?!
SHIMEI...
DON'T LAY A FINGER ON MY HARU-CHAN!
FLING
SPLAT
?!!
NOT A LUNCH PACKED BY THE WIFE, BUT BY THE HUSBAND-- ATTACK!
MAKES HIM SOUND STUPID
...
HUG
WHY ARE YOU HERE...?
YOU'RE HEAVY!
ARE YOU OKAY?! DID HE DO ANYTHING TO YOU?!

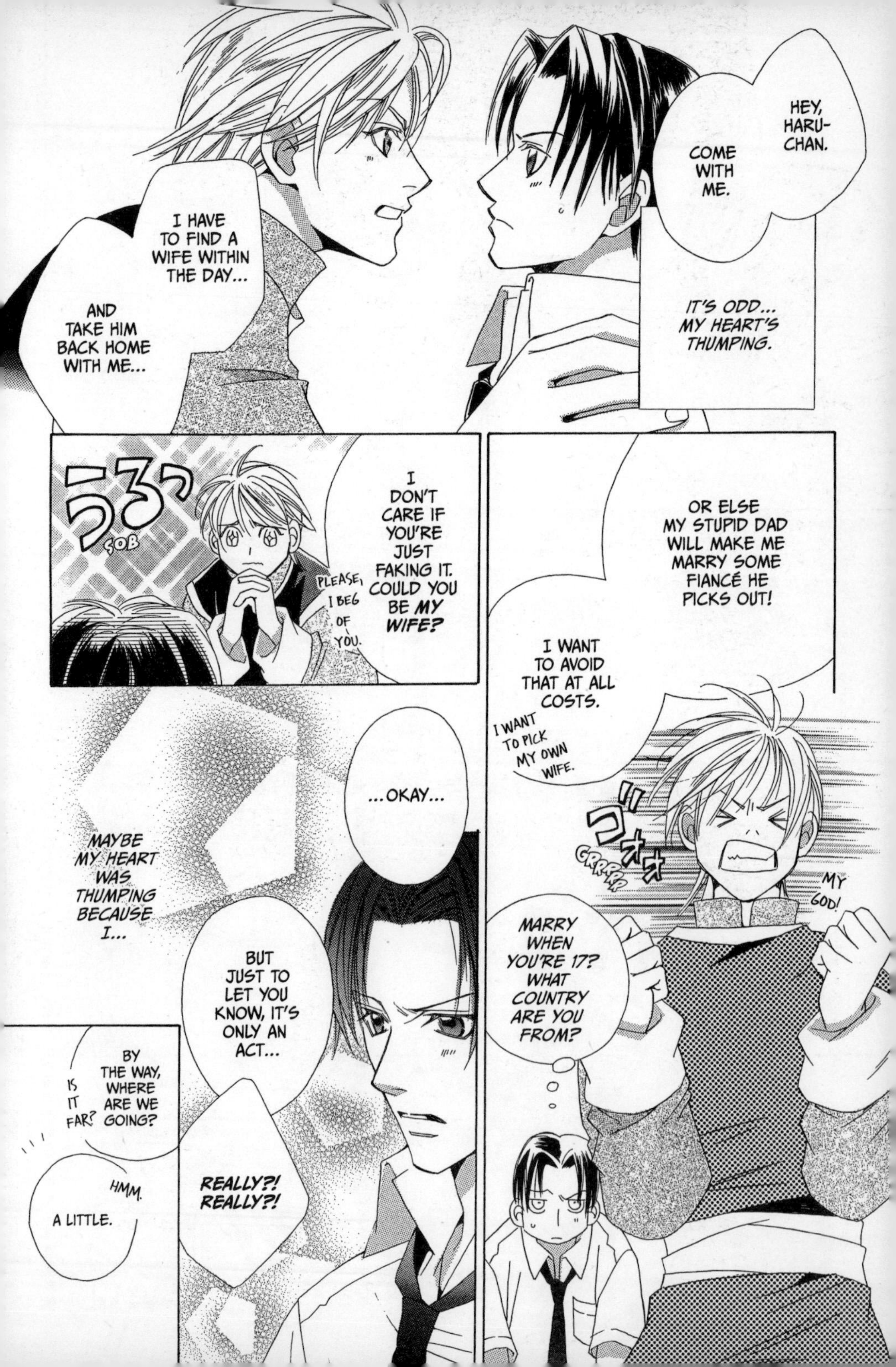
HEY, HARU-CHAN.
COME WITH ME.
IT'S ODD... MY HEART'S THUMPING.
I HAVE TO FIND A WIFE WITHIN THE DAY...
AND TAKE HIM BACK HOME WITH ME...
OR ELSE MY STUPID DAD WILL MAKE ME MARRY SOME FIANCÉ HE PICKS OUT!
I WANT TO AVOID THAT AT ALL COSTS.
I WANT TO PICK MY OWN WIFE.
ゴオオ
GRRRR
MY GOD!
MARRY WHEN YOU'RE 17? WHAT COUNTRY ARE YOU FROM?
うるっ
SOB
I DON'T CARE IF YOU'RE JUST FAKING IT. COULD YOU BE *MY WIFE?*
PLEASE, I BEG OF YOU.
...OKAY...
MAYBE MY HEART WAS THUMPING BECAUSE I...
BUT JUST TO LET YOU KNOW, IT'S ONLY AN ACT...
REALLY?! REALLY?!
BY THE WAY, WHERE ARE WE GOING?
IS IT FAR?
HMM.
A LITTLE.

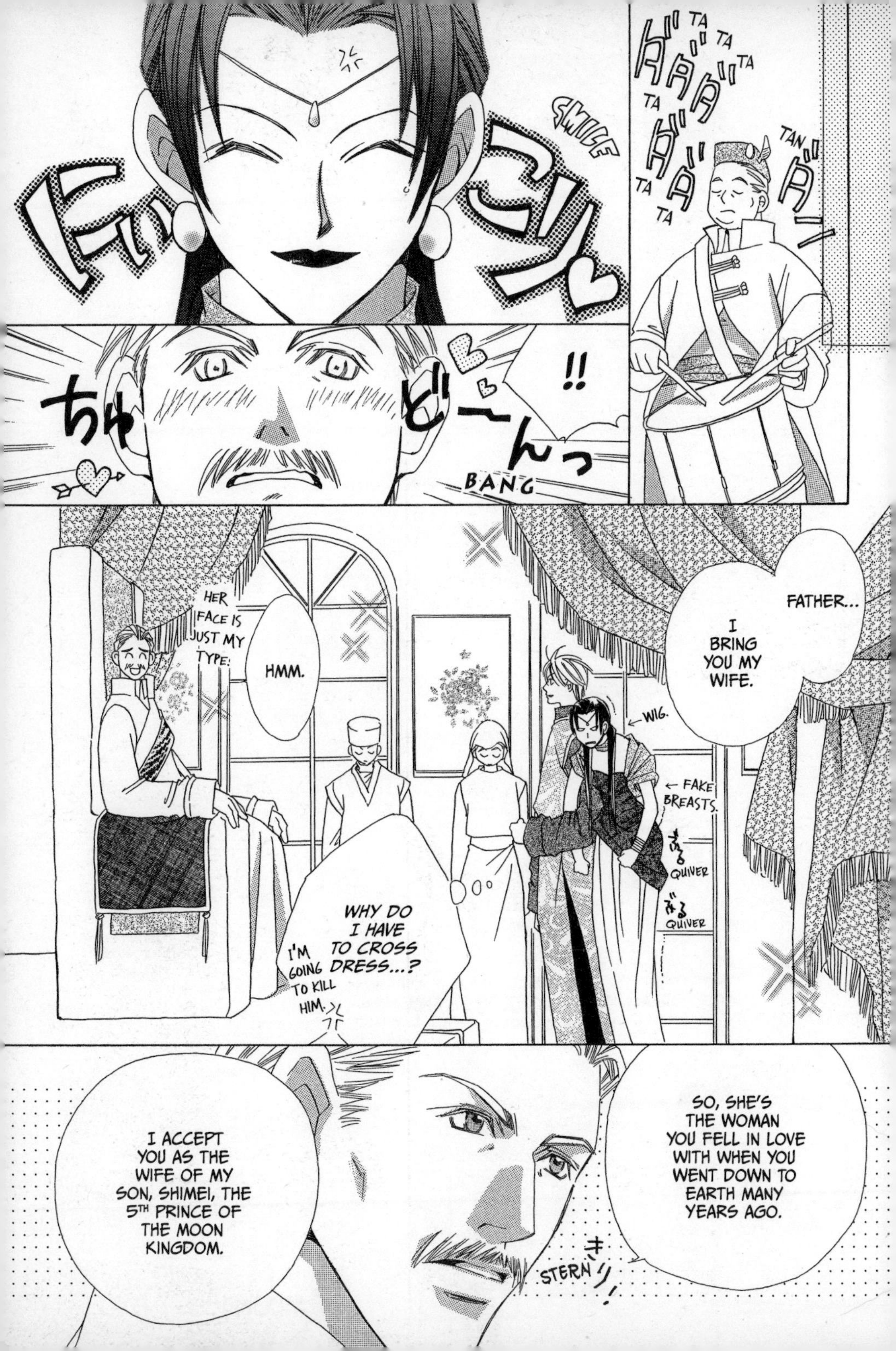
TA TA TA TA TA TA TAN
SMILE
!!
BANG
FATHER...
I BRING YOU MY WIFE.
WIG.
← FAKE BREASTS.
QUIVER
QUIVER
HMM.
HER FACE IS JUST MY TYPE!
WHY DO I HAVE TO CROSS DRESS...?
I'M GOING TO KILL HIM.
SO, SHE'S THE WOMAN YOU FELL IN LOVE WITH WHEN YOU WENT DOWN TO EARTH MANY YEARS AGO.
STERN
I ACCEPT YOU AS THE WIFE OF MY SON, SHIMEI, THE 5TH PRINCE OF THE MOON KINGDOM.

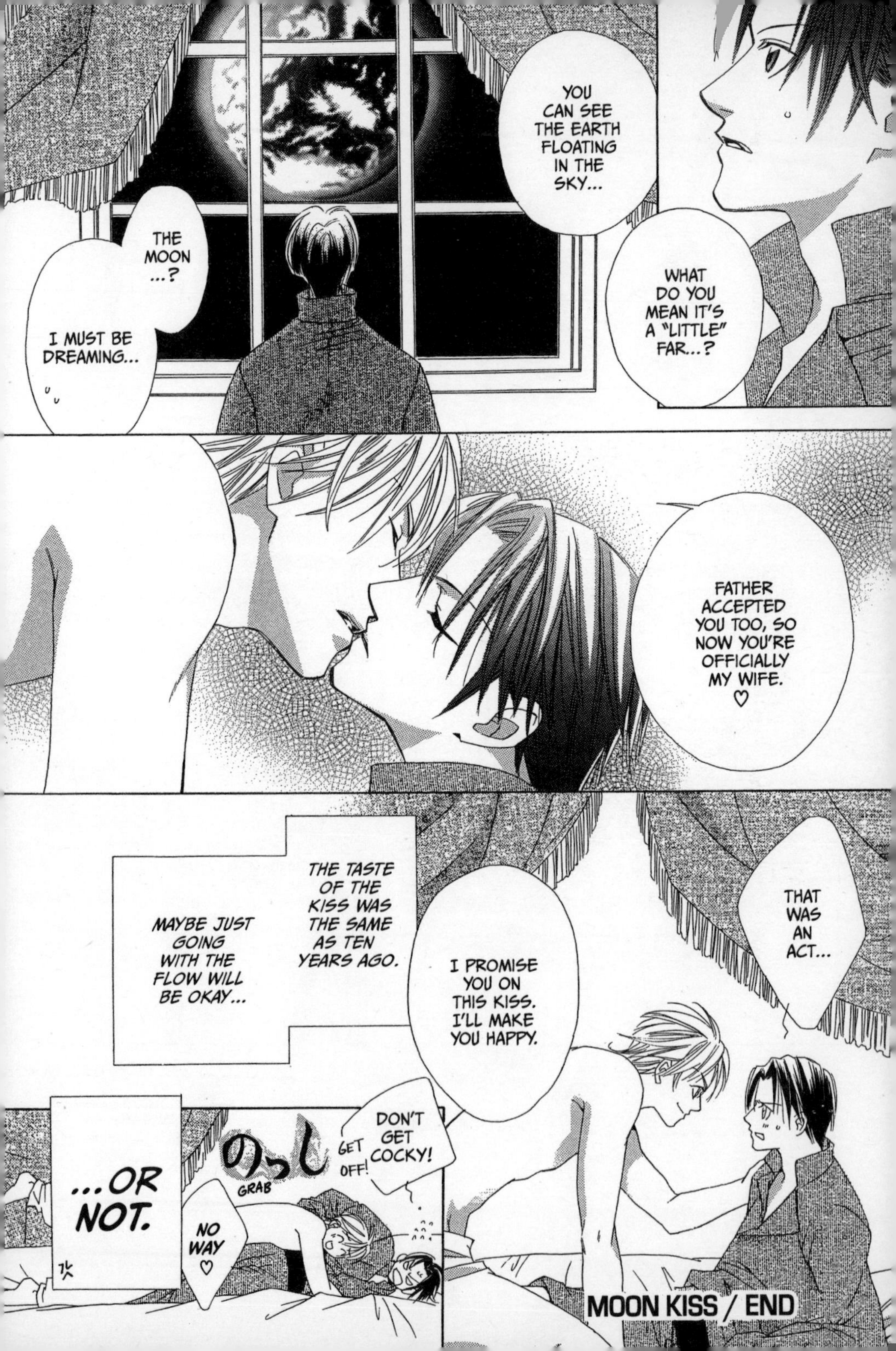
YOU CAN SEE THE EARTH FLOATING IN THE SKY...
WHAT DO YOU MEAN IT'S A "LITTLE" FAR...?
THE MOON ...?
I MUST BE DREAMING...
FATHER ACCEPTED YOU TOO, SO NOW YOU'RE OFFICIALLY MY WIFE. ♡
THAT WAS AN ACT...
I PROMISE YOU ON THIS KISS. I'LL MAKE YOU HAPPY.
THE TASTE OF THE KISS WAS THE SAME AS TEN YEARS AGO.
MAYBE JUST GOING WITH THE FLOW WILL BE OKAY...
DON'T GET COCKY!
GET OFF!
のっし
GRAB
NO WAY ♡
...OR NOT.
MOON KISS / END

□ HELLO.
I CAN'T BELIEVE IT, BUT MY BOOK IS OUT. MY FIRST BOY'S LOVE BOOK. YEAH, I'VE DONE IT NOW... IN MORE WAYS THAN ONE... EVEN IF IT IS A LITTLE SOFTCORE AND BORING...

□ ...
A HOLE... IF I HAD A HOLE TO HIDE MYSELF, I'D JUMP IN. PLEASE, LET ME IN... AND SOMEONE, BURY ME AND STEP ON IT TO SECURE IT. I'M SERIOUS. OR I'D LIKE FOR SOMEONE TO YELL THIS AT THE CENTER OF THE EARTH:

GOOOD DAAAAMN IIIIIIIIITTTTTT!!!!!

I'M EMBARRASSED, AND AT THE SAME TIME, I'M REALLY HAPPY THAT I GOT TO PUBLISH MY BOOK. BUT I'M EMBARRASSED!! I DON'T KNOW WHAT TO DO. THIS IS HOW I HONESTLY FEEL. I NEED TO CALM DOWN (MY HEAD IS SPINNING).

□ BUT PUTTING THE SCREAMS OF MY HEART ASIDE, THIS BOOK WENT OUT TO THE WORLD AND INTO YOUR HANDS. I'M VERY THANKFUL TO YOU FOR BUYING IT. I TRIED MY HARDEST (AND I TRULY MEAN MY HARDEST) ON THIS BOOK AND I LOVE IT TO PIECES. IF I WERE TO WRITE A BL BOOK AGAIN, I'D LIKE TO TRY HARDER AND GET BETTER AT IT. YEAH, I'LL BE EMBARRASSED, BUT I'LL SCREAM IN SHYNESS AND TRY IT AGAIN!!

YUKO KUWABARA
NOVEMBER 2004

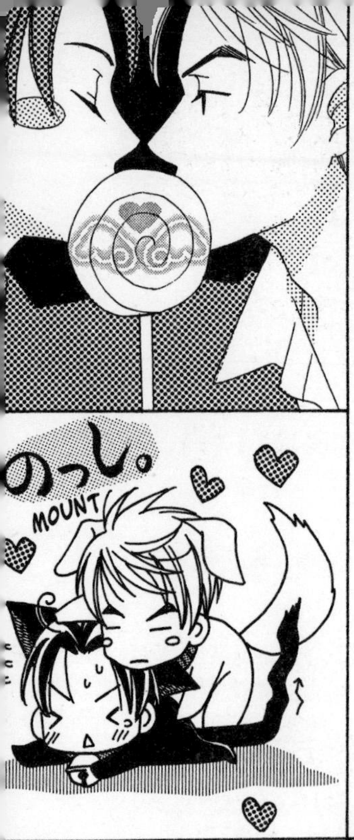
のっし。
MOUNT

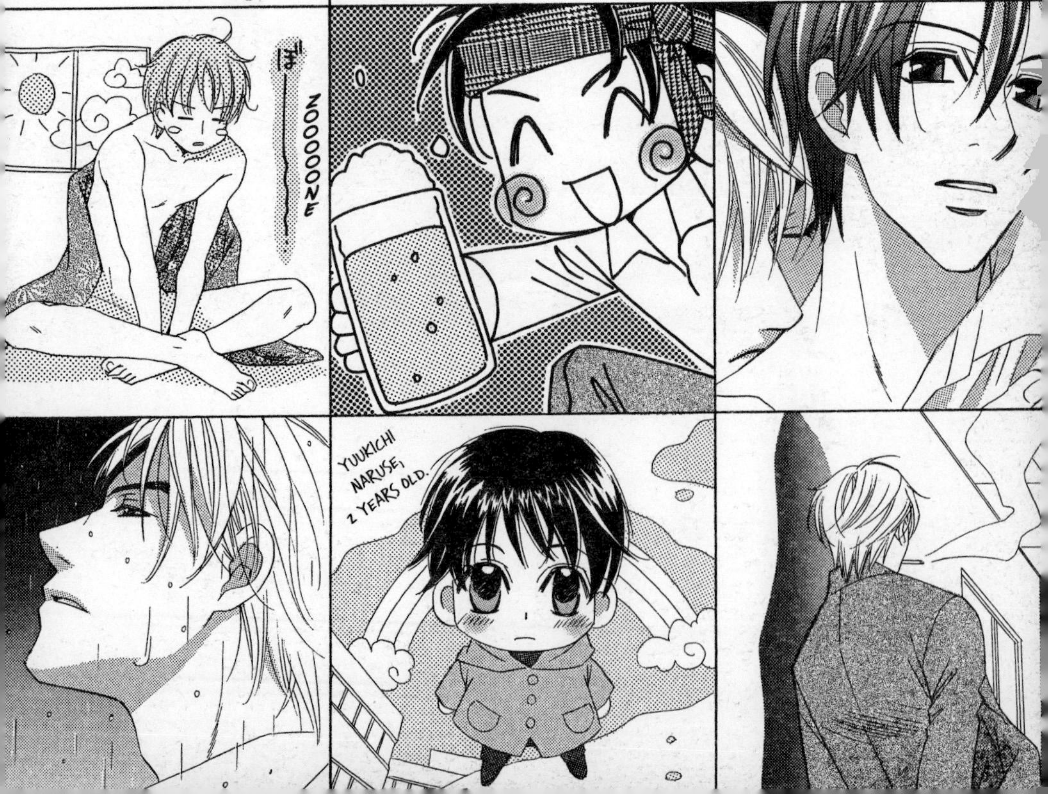
ず
ZOOOOOONE
YUUKICHI NARUSE, 2 YEARS OLD.

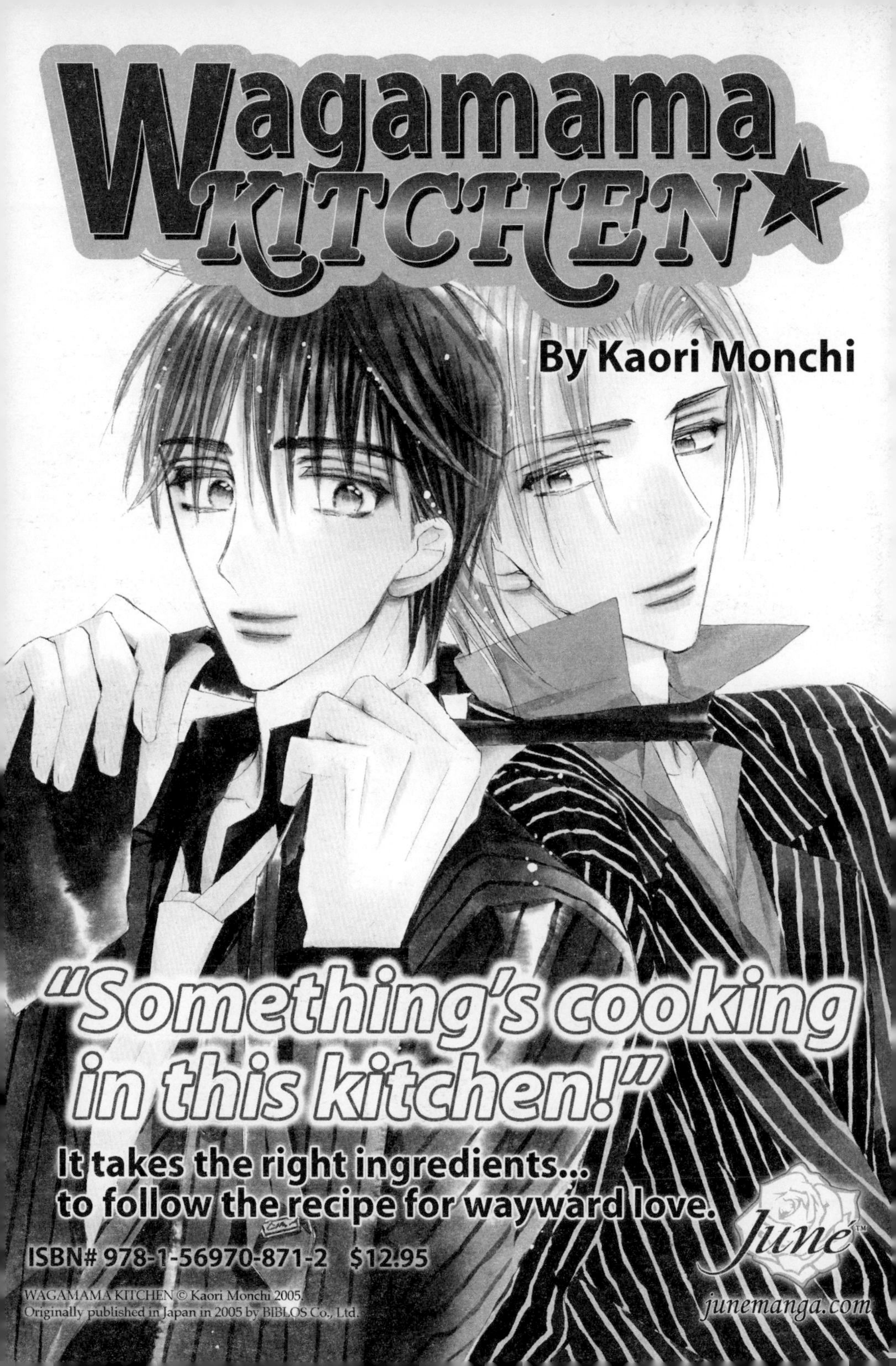
Wagamama KITCHEN★
By Kaori Monchi
"Something's cooking in this kitchen!"
It takes the right ingredients... to follow the recipe for wayward love.
ISBN# 978-1-56970-871-2 $12.95
WAGAMAMA KITCHEN © Kaori Monchi 2005.
Originally published in Japan in 2005 by BIBLOS Co., Ltd.
Juné™
junemanga.com

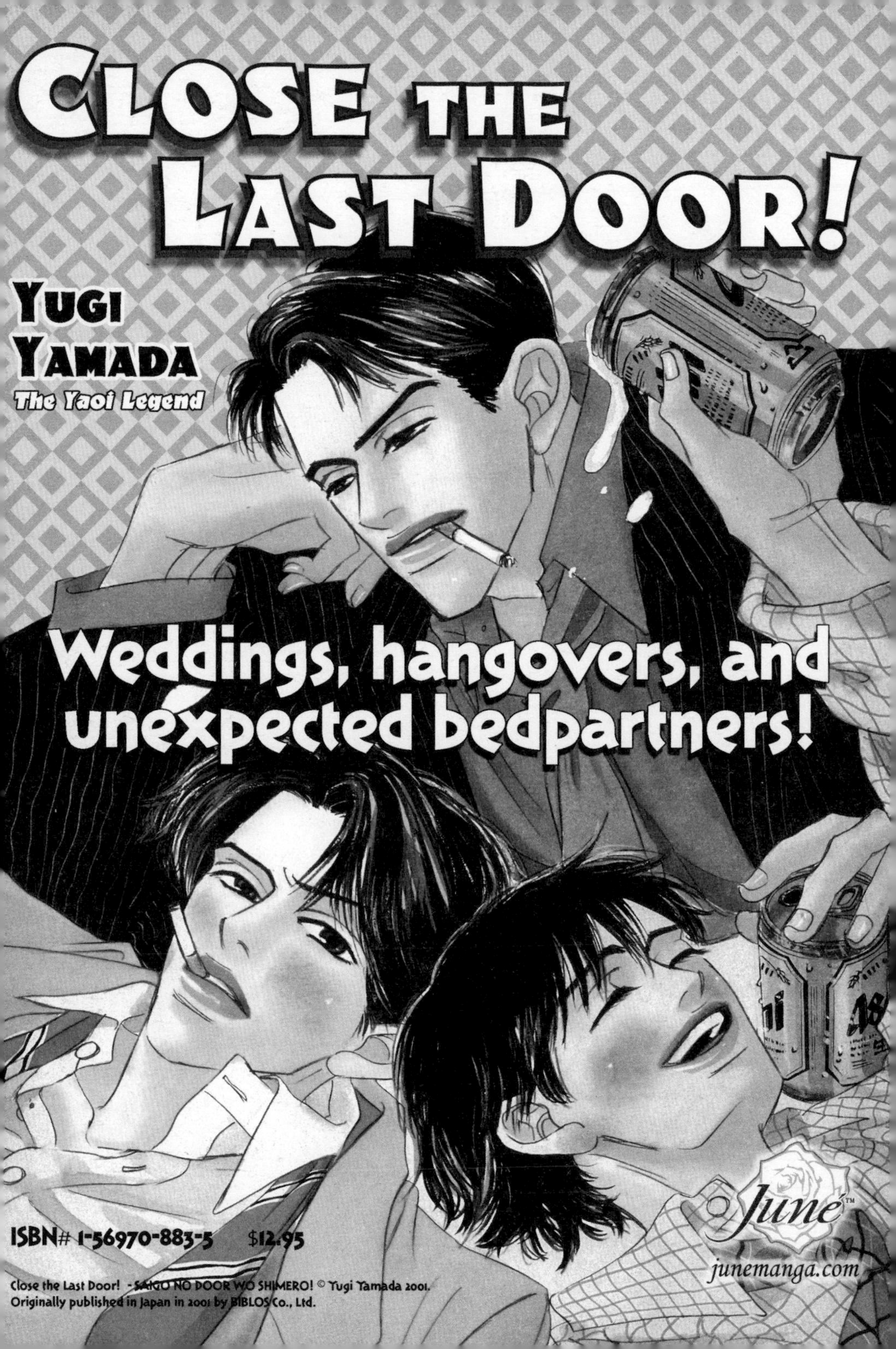

CLOSE THE LAST DOOR!
YUGI YAMADA
The Yaoi Legend
Weddings, hangovers, and unexpected bedpartners!
ISBN# 1-56970-883-5 $12.95
Close the Last Door! - SAIGO NO DOOR WO SHIMERO! © Yugi Yamada 2001.
Originally published in Japan in 2001 by BIBLOS Co., Ltd.
June™
junemanga.com

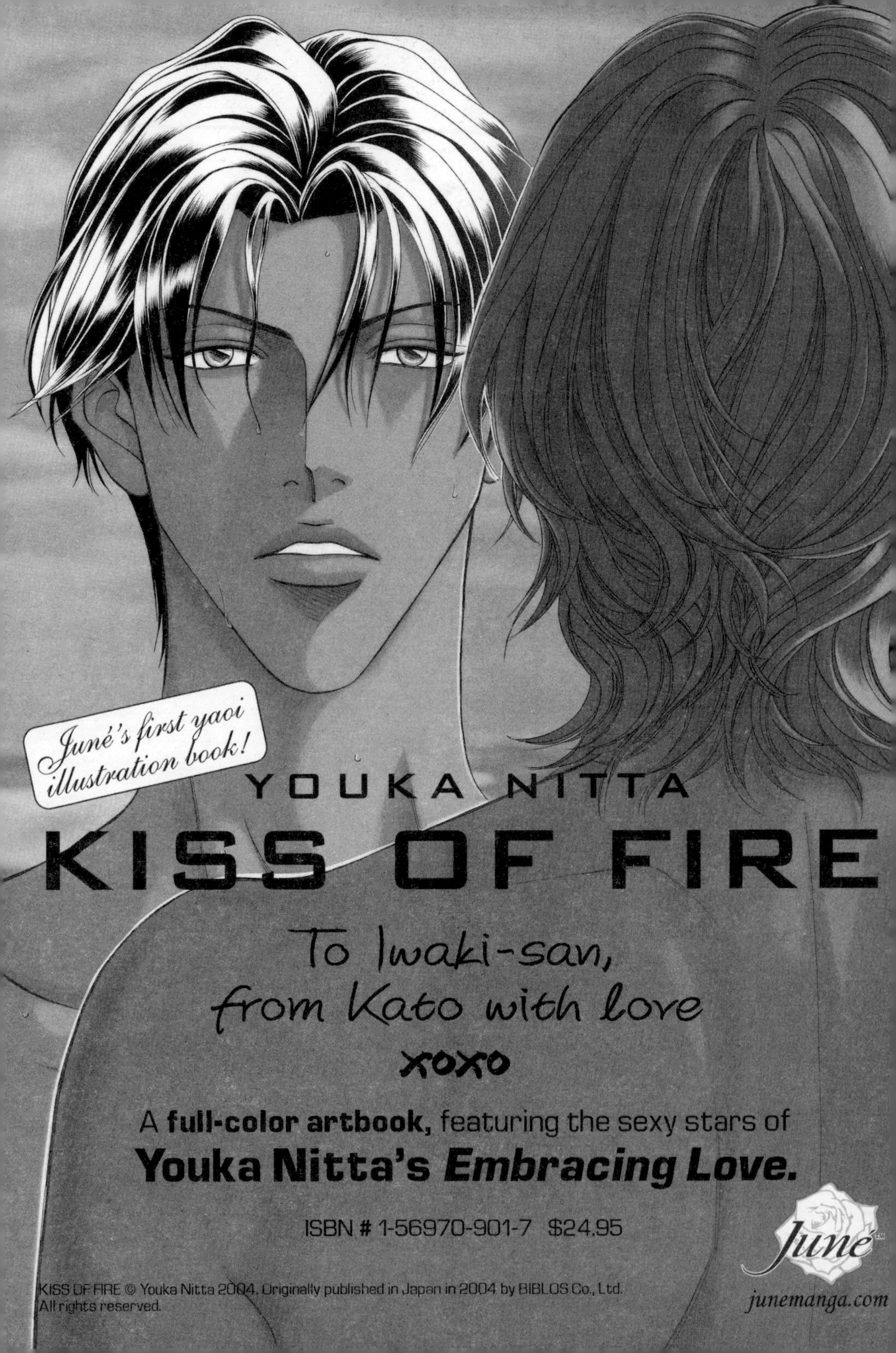
June's first yaoi illustration book!
YOUKA NITTA
KISS OF FIRE
To Iwaki-san,
from Kato with love
xoxo
A full-color artbook, featuring the sexy stars of
Youka Nitta's Embracing Love.
ISBN # 1-56970-901-7 $24.95
Juné
junemanga.com
KISS OF FIRE © Youka Nitta 2004. Originally published in Japan in 2004 by BIBLOS Co., Ltd.
All rights reserved.

PASSION

熱情

vol. 3

Shinobu Gotoh
Shoko Takaku

What's love without jealousy and passion?

Volume 3 - ISBN # 1-56970-854-1
Volume 2 - ISBN # 1-56970-977-7
Volume 1 - ISBN # 1-56970-978-5

June

junemanga.com

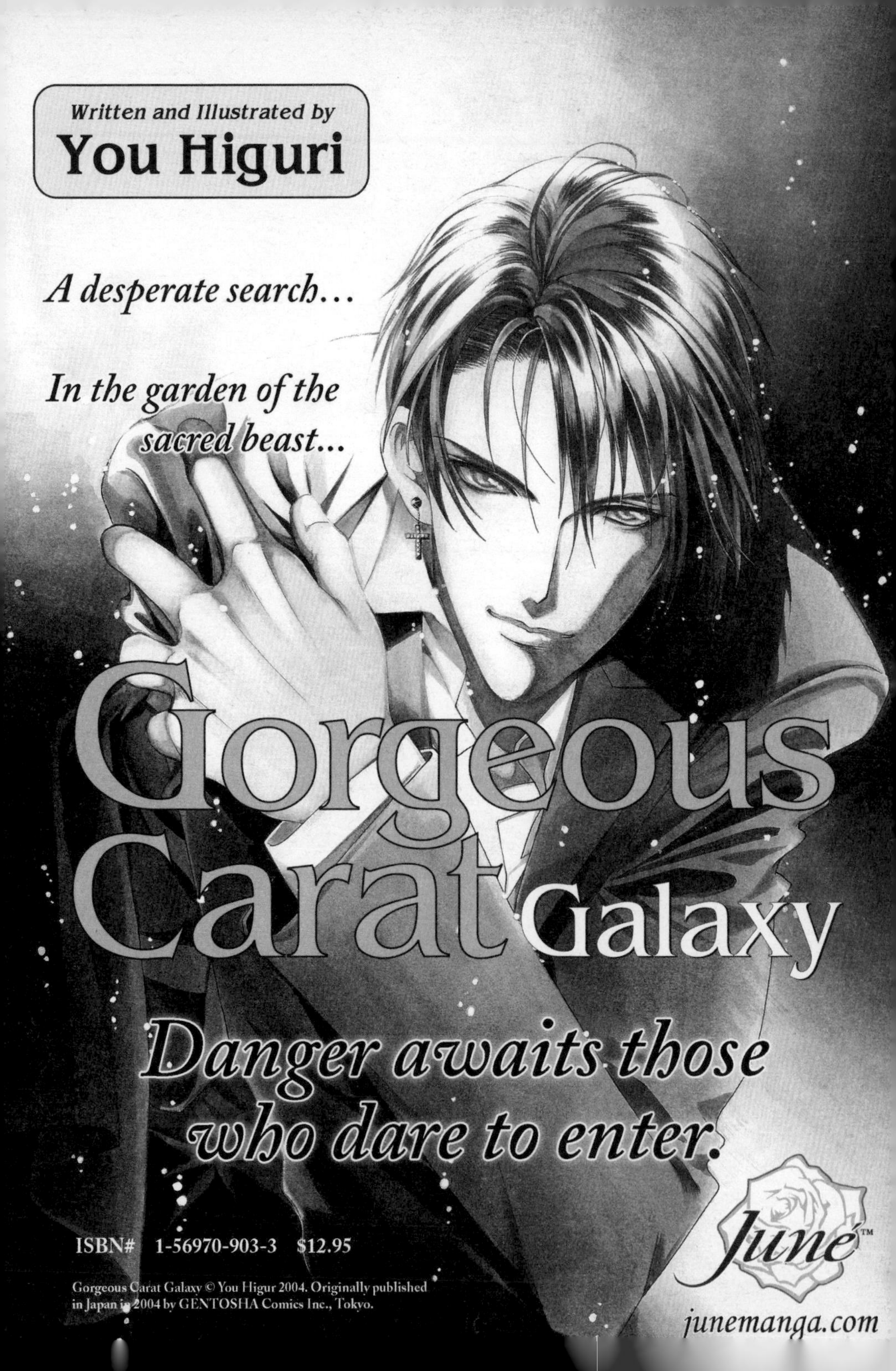
Written and Illustrated by
You Higuri
A desperate search...
In the garden of the sacred beast...
Gorgeous Carat Galaxy
Danger awaits those who dare to enter.
ISBN# 1-56970-903-3 $12.95
Gorgeous Carat Galaxy © You Higur 2004. Originally published in Japan in 2004 by GENTOSHA Comics Inc., Tokyo.
June™
junemanga.com

OUR KINGDOM

When the Prince falls for the Pauper...

The family inheritance will be the last of their concerns.

Written & Illustrated by
Naduki Koujima

Volume 1   ISBN# 1-56970-935-1 $12.95
Volume 2   ISBN# 1-56970-914-9 $12.95
Volume 3   ISBN# 1-56970-913-0 $12.95
Volume 4   ISBN# 1-56970-912-2 $12.95

june
by DMP
junemanga.com

Digital Manga Inc. presents...

POP JAPAN CULTURE
Anime and Manga
THE ULTIMATE TOUR!

POP ポップ JAPAN TRAVEL

For reservations or inquiries, please contact:
Pop Japan Travel: (310) 817-8010 Fax: (310) 817-8018
E-mail: travel@popjapantravel.com Web: www.popjapantravel.com

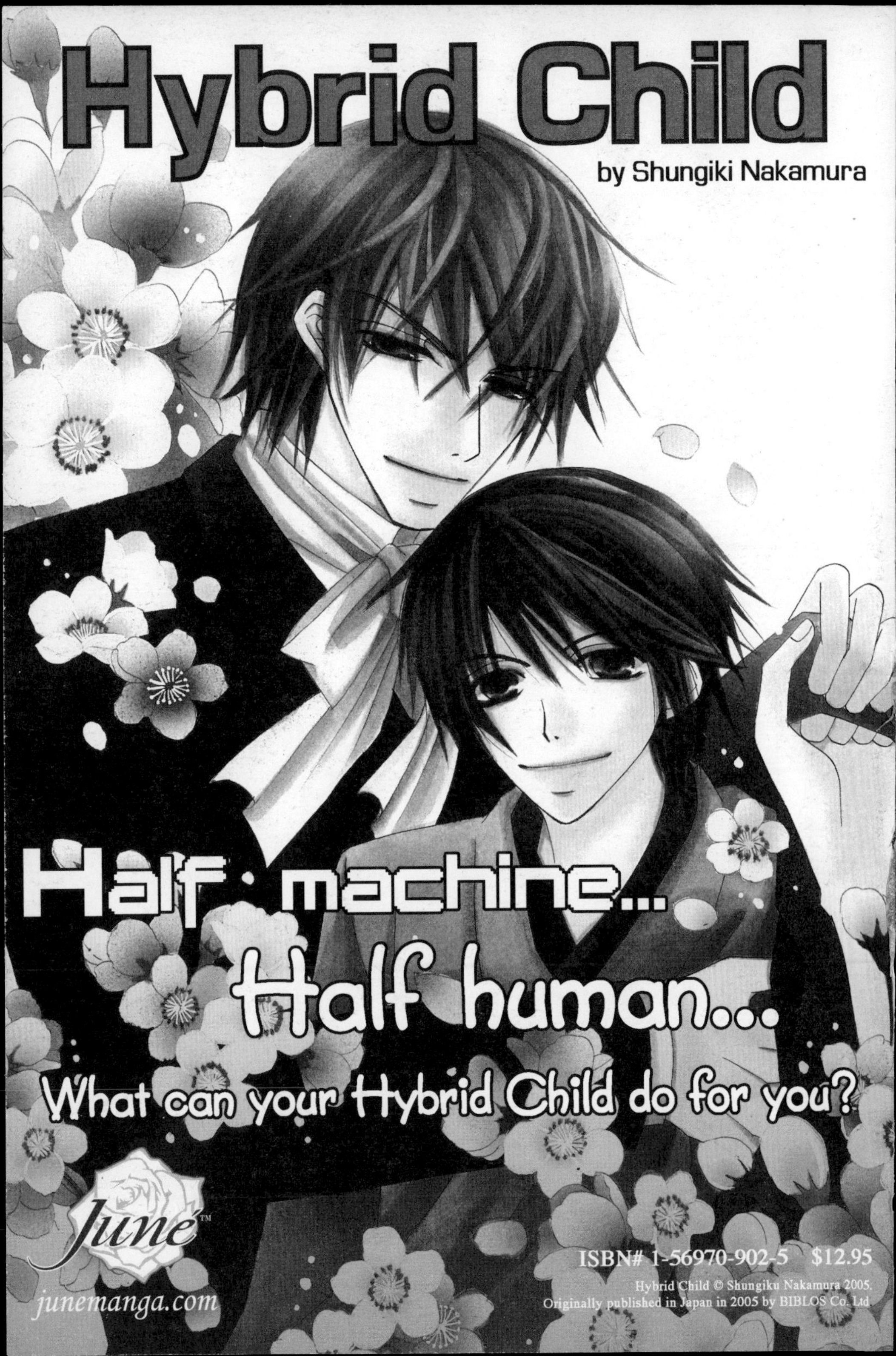
Hybrid Child
by Shungiki Nakamura
Half machine...
Half human...
What can your Hybrid Child do for you?
June™
junemanga.com
ISBN# 1-56970-902-5 $12.95
Hybrid Child © Shungiku Nakamura 2005.
Originally published in Japan in 2005 by BIBLOS Co. Ltd

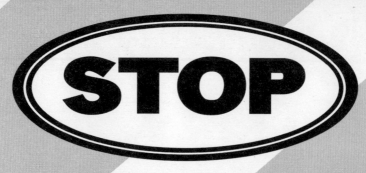

STOP

This is the back of the book! Start from the other side.

NATIVE MANGA readers read manga from _right to left_.

1
2
1
3
2
3
5
4
6
5
7
8
6

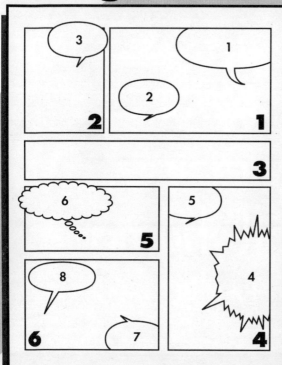

*If you run into our **Native Manga** logo on any of our books... you'll know that this manga is published in it's true original native Japanese right to left reading format, as it was intended. Turn to the other side of the book and start reading from right to left, top to bottom.*

Follow the diagram to see how its done.
Surf's Up!

NATIVE MANGA
READ RIGHT TO LEFT

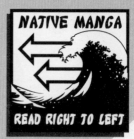